# OUT OF THE MARGIN

## Feminist Perspectives on Economics

*Edited by Edith Kuiper
and Jolande Sap*

**with Susan Feiner, Notburga Ott
and Zafiris Tzannatos**

London and New York

First published 1995
by Routledge
11 New Fetter Lane, London EC4P 4EE

Simultaneously published in the USA and Canada
by Routledge
29 West 35th Street, New York, NY 100001

© 1995 Edith Kuiper and Jolande Sap with Susan Feiner, Notburga Ott and
Zafiris Tzannatos

Selected material from *A Room of One's Own* is reproduced with permission of
Bruce Harcourt Company

Typeset in Garamond by
J&L Composition Ltd., Filey, North Yorkshire
Printed and bound in Great Britain by
T.J. Press (Padstow) Ltd, Padstow, Cornwall

*British Library Cataloguing in Publication data*
A catalogue record for this book is available from the British Library

*Library of Congress Cataloguing in Publication Data*
has been applied for

ISBN 0–415–12531–6
ISBN 0–415–12575–8 (pbk)

I had come at last, in the course of this rambling, to the shelves which hold books by the living; by women and by men; for there are almost as many books written by women now as by men. Or if that is not yet quite true, if the male is still the voluble sex, it is certainly true that women no longer write novels solely. There are Jane Harrison's books on Greek archaeology; Vernon Lee's books on aesthetics; Gertrude Bell's books on Persia. There are books on all sorts of subjects which a generation ago no woman could have touched. There are poems and plays and criticism; there are histories and biographies, books of travel and books of scholarship and research; there are even a few philosophies and books about science and economics.

(Virginia Woolf [1928] (1957) *A Room of One's Own*: 79)

# CONTENTS

CONTENTS

## Part III Interpreting economics

## Part IV Economic measurement

## Part V Empowerment of women

# CONTRIBUTORS

**Bina Agarwal** is Professor of Economics at the Institute of Economic Growth, New Delhi, India. She has published extensively on poverty and inequality, rural development, environmental issues, and technological change, especially from a political economy and gender perspective. Her books include: *A Field of One's Own: Gender and Land Rights in South Asia* (1994); *Cold Hearts and Barren Slopes: The Woodfuel Crisis in the Third World* (1986); and *Structures of Patriarchy: State, Community and Household in Modernising Asia* (ed.) (1988).

**Diane Elson** is a reader in the School of Economic Studies, University of Manchester, and director of a research program on Gender Analysis and Development Economics funded by the Swedish International Development Authority. She is editor of *Male Bias in the Development Process* (1991) and has recently published in the *Journal of International Development* and the *Review of African Political Economy.* She is also a member of the editorial boards of the journals *Feminist Economics* and *Development and Change.*

**Susan Feiner** is Visiting Professor of Women's Studies at the College of William and Mary, Williamsburg, Virginia. She is also senior research associate of the National Association for Equal Educational Opportunity (NAFEEO), Washington, DC. She is the founder and chair of the Committee for Race and Gender Balance in the Economics Curriculum. Her research has been published in the *American Economic Review, Gender and Society,* the *Journal of Economic Education* and the *Journal of Psychoanalytic Studies.* She is editor of *Race and Gender in the American Economy: Views from across the Spectrum* (1994).

**Siv S. Gustafsson** is Professor of Economics at the University of Amsterdam and teaches population economics, comparing welfare states and microeconomics of the family. Her research focusses on the effects of public policies on women's work, especially income taxation, daycare subsidies and parental leave policies. Her recent publications have appeared in the *Journal of Human Resources, Journal of Population Economics,* in an NBER volume on *Social Protection versus Flexibility* (ed. R. Blank) and in *Gendering Welfare States* (ed. D. Sainsbury) (1994).

**Barbara E. Hopkins** received her PhD in economics from the University of Maryland. She is currently Assistant Professor of Economics at Wright State University in Dayton, Ohio.

**Frances Hutchinson** works at Bradford University. She has taught economics in the UK, Zambia and Sierra Leone. She is a member of the European Association for Evolutionary Political Economy and the New Economics Foundation.

**Arjo Klamer** is Professor of Economics at the Department of History and Art Studies, Erasmus University, Rotterdam, The Netherlands. He was previously an associate professor at the Economics Department of The George Washington University, Washington, DC. He has published extensively in the fields of philosophy and methodology of economics. He is co-author (with David Colander) of *The Making of an Economist* (1990) and co-editor (with Donald McCloskey and Robert Solow) of *The Consequences of Economic Rhetoric* (1988).

**Edith Kuiper** is researcher at the Department of Economics, University of Amsterdam, and the Tinbergen Institute. She was one of the initiators of the "Out of the Margin" conference and a founding member of the Feminist Economics Network in The Netherlands.

**Lee B. Levin** is a graduate student at the University of Massachusetts, Amherst.

**Martha MacDonald** is a Professor in the Department of Economics, Saint Mary's University, Halifax, Canada. She is a Vice-President of the International Association of Feminist Economics and is on the executive board of the Canadian Women Economists Network. Her research interests are gender, restructuring and macroeconomic policy. Her publications include "Feminism and Economics: The Dismal Science?", *Studies in Political Economy* (1984) and she is co-author of *Women and the Labor Force* (1990).

**Julie A. Nelson** is an Associate Professor of Economics at the University of California, Davis, USA. Her publications on feminist theory include "Gender, Metaphor, and Economics", *Economics and Philosophy* (1992) and "Feminism and Economics", *Journal of Economic Perspectives* (1995). She co-edited the volume *Beyond Economic Man: Feminist Theory and Economics* (1993). In addition, she studies household demand behavior, and has published on this topic in journals including *The Journal of Political Economy* and *Econometrica*.

**Notburga Ott** is Assistant Professor of Economics at the Johan Wolfgang Goethe University, Frankfurt, Germany. Her research interests include new home economics, labor market, social policy, constitutional economics, public choice, decision theory, econometrics and fuzzy mathematics. She is author of *Intrafamily Bargaining and Household Decisions* (1992).

**Diane Perrons** is Senior Lecturer in Social Economics at London Guildhall University. Her current research interests and publications are concerned with equal opportunities and the monitoring of gender inequality in employment and with regional inequality and social cohesion in Europe. She is currently Visiting Lecturer at the University of Sussex and is involved in the European Science Foundation Network on Gender Inequality and the European Regions. She is author of *The Arena of Capital* (1983) and co-editor with Jenny Shaw of *Making Gender Work*.

**Solomon W. Polachek** is Professor and Chair of the Economics Department at the State University of New York at Binghampton. He is currently editor of *Research in Labor Economics*, co-editor of *Peace Economics, Peace Science and Public Policy*, and on the editorial boards of *Conflict Management and Peace Science* and the *International Studies Quarterly*. He is co-author (with W. Stanley Siebert) of *The Economics of Earnings* (1993). His work on earnings differences is widely published in learned journals, as is his work relating international affairs to country economies.

**Livia Polanyi** works at the Center for the Study of Language and Information at Stanford University and is an Associate Professor of Linguistics and Semiotics at Rice University Houston, Texas. She previously worked at the English Institute of the University of Amsterdam and as a researcher in Artificial Intelligence in Cambridge, MA. She has published extensively in many sub-fields of linguistics and in the social sciences.

**Michèle Pujol** is Associate Professor in Women's Studies at the University of Victoria, Canada. She is the author of *Feminism and Anti-feminism in Early Economic Thought* (1992). Her main fields of research are feminist approaches to economic thought, equity policies and feminist research methods.

**Esther Redmount** is Associate Professor of Economics and Business at Colorado College in Colorado Springs. During the conference she served there as the Director of Women's Studies. At present she is Assistant Chair of the Department of Economics and Business.

**Jolande Sap** is scientific staff member of the Emancipation Council, an advisory body of the Dutch government on gender aspects of policy issues. She was one of the initiators of the "Out of the Margin" conference, and is presently engaged in various follow-up activities aimed at improving the institutional infrastructure for feminist economics. Her current research focusses on the potentials of bargaining theories to analyze the relation between power, institutions and women's economic position.

**Amartya K. Sen** is Lamont University Professor and Professor of Economics and Philosophy at Harvard University. He is a past president of the American Economic Association, the Indian Economic Association, the Econometric Society and the International Economic Association. He has published extensively in the fields of social choice theory, development economics, economic methodology, economic measurement problems, and moral and political philosophy. His publications include *Collective Choice and Social Welfare* (1970), *Choice, Welfare and Measurement* (1982), and *Inequality Reexamined* (1992).

**Diana Strassmann** is founding editor of *Feminist Economics*, the official journal of the International Association for Feminist Economics, and a Vice-President of the International Association for Feminist Economics. She is currently Senior Research Fellow at the Center for Cultural Studies at Rice University. She has published a wide variety of articles in the areas of industrial organization, environmental policy, economic theory and feminist economics.

**Eileen Trzcinski** is Associate Professor at the Wayne State University, School of Social Work and College of Urban, Labor, and Metropolitan Affairs at Detroit. Her research interests center on work and family policy, international family policy, and the dynamics of self-employment. Her research has been published in journals such as *Journal of Applied Social Sciences* and *Journal of Human Resources*.

**Zafiris Tzannatos** is a labor economist in the Education and Employment Division, Population and Human Resources Department of the World Bank, Washington, DC. He is co-author (with A. Zabalza) of *Women and Equal Pay. The Effects of Legislation on Female Employment and Wages in Britain* (1985), and *Women's Employment and Pay in Latin America* (with G. Psacharopoulos) (1992).

# ACKNOWLEDGEMENTS

The Conference "Out of the Margin. Feminist Perspectives on Economic Theory" (University of Amsterdam, Amsterdam, The Netherlands, 2–5 June 1993) would never have been possible without the dedicated support of numerous people and institutions. We want to thank the members of the Preparatory Committee, the Scientific Advisory Committee and the Programme Committee for their valuable assistance in planning the conference. A special debt is owed to the members of the various study groups who worked for over a year to frame the five themes of the conference.

Many people worked tirelessly to make this conference the international success it was. We wish we had space to thank them all personally. A few who were absolutely invaluable are: Ina Brouwer, Else Rose Kuiper, Siv Gustafsson and Monika Triest.

Institutions providing essential financial support for the conference were: the Belle van Zuylen Institute, University of Amsterdam; the City of Amsterdam; Cultural Foundation of Mama Cash; the Emancipation Committee, University of Amsterdam; Faculty of Economics, University of Amsterdam; Faculty of Economics, University of Brabant; Faculty of Economics, Free University of Amsterdam; Ministry of Economic Affairs; Ministry of Education and Science; Ministry of Social Affairs; Foundation PWT; the Tinbergen Institute; and Foundation VSB.

Producing a book from a conference with over 100 papers was no simple task. We are indebted to the efforts of our co-editors: Susan Feiner, Notburga Ott and Zafiris Tzannatos. We also thank Henriette van de Kooi for her work on the preparation of this manuscript. We are grateful to the Belle van Zuylen Institute in Amsterdam for their financial support for the book. We also want to thank our colleagues of the Dutch Emancipation Council and the research group Comparative Gender and Emancipation Economics at the University of Amsterdam for their patient support of our work on this project.

Finally our enormous thanks to all our friends and family members who stood by us until late at night for weeks and months, while we worked on this book.

# INTRODUCTION

## Edith Kuiper and Jolande Sap

When you asked me to speak about women and fiction I sat down on the banks of a river and began to wonder what the words meant. They might mean simply a few remarks about Fanny Burney; a few more about Jane Austen; a tribute to the Brontës and a sketch of Haworth Parsonage under snow; some witticisms if possible about Miss Mitford; a respectful allusion to George Eliot; a reference to Mrs Gaskell and one would have done. But at second sight the words seemed not so simple. The title women and fiction might mean, and you may have meant it to mean, women and what they are like; or it might mean women and the fiction they write; or it might mean women and the fiction that is written about them; or it might mean that somehow all three are inextricably mixed together and you want me to consider them in that light. But when I began to consider the subject in this last way, which seemed the most interesting, I soon saw that it had one fatal drawback. I should never be able to come to a conclusion.

(Woolf [1928] (1957): 3)

This book grew out of a conference, which itself grew out of a dream. As economists and as feminists we had been searching for reflections of ourselves and our concerns in economic research and teaching. Never quite finding the questions or answers we hoped for, we wondered how we might discover that which economics seemed so intent upon missing. Over a coffee, in a café by a canal, we asked ourselves these questions and wondered if economics would ever expand enough to include the range of issues relating to gender. Although a considerable amount of work had been done on women's economic status, little attention had yet been paid to the role of gender in the formation of economic theory. Then inspiration: "Let's organize a seminar to explore the intersections of economics, gender, and science!" From that moment forward we started to move out of the margin.

When we began exploring the possibilities for a seminar on feminist economics we were initially surprised to discover how few economists in

1

The Netherlands or neighboring nations were interested in this project. Though several Western European countries had vital research traditions in women's studies and feminist scholarship, feminist investigations in economics were rare. Critical self-reflection was (and still is) an alien practice to most economists, and many with whom we spoke feared that a fundamental examination of the discipline from a feminist perspective would simply waste precious research time. We could not then anticipate that a simple seminar on feminist economics would grow into an international conference with over 300 participants from more than 20 nations.

Our initial efforts to develop feminist economics here in Holland coincided with encouraging developments in the United States and the international economic community. Beginning in the late 1980s a series of pathbreaking papers appeared which explored the gendered nature of economic theory[1]. These papers complemented the already impressive empirical, policy-oriented research of other feminist economists[2]. In 1990, the annual meetings of the American Economic Association for the first time included panels elaborating specifically feminist perspectives on economics (Ferber and Nelson 1993: ii). Simultaneously the National Science Foundation lent its support to work bringing this scholarship into economic education (Bartlett and Feiner 1992)[3]. In another first, major international agencies criticized traditional economic thinking on gender relations and called for further debate on the role of women in economic development[4]. In all of these areas of economics – theory, methodology, teaching, and development – feminist research was revealing the limits of conventional approaches. These events confirmed our belief that feminist economics was more than the extension of existing economic methods and theories to the status of women. But this recognition meant that we would have to expand our plans for a seminar to include all these topics, and we knew that adequate coverage of this terrain would require cooperation with feminist economists from around the world.

In January 1992 we traveled to New Orleans, Louisiana to issue a call for papers for the conference "Out of the Margin: Feminist Perspectives on Economic Theory." We explained that over the past decades economists of many schools had become increasingly aware of the deep impact of gender on the economy. Thus far, however, little attention had been paid to the impact gender might have on the practice of economics itself. The conference "Out of the Margin" would focus on the relationship of gender to economic science. We asked potential conference participants to take into account feminist developments in other disciplines as we felt that such insights could be profitably extended to economics[5]. Our announcement generated a great deal of excitement and discussion. Many shared our desire to explore the role of gender in economics.

"Gender, as the word is used by many feminists, means something quite different from biological sex. Gender is the *social meaning* given to biological differences between the sexes; it refers to cultural constructs rather than to biological givens" (Ferber and Nelson 1993: 9–10) [emphasis in the original]. To explore the extent to which gender bias has or has not influenced economics, our call for papers asked for contributions in all of the areas of economics: the history of economic ideas; the assumptions, contents and concepts which inform economic theory; the philosophy and methodology of the discipline; the tools of empirical research through which data are constructed and interpreted; and the implications of the above for policy, including, of course, policies affecting women. The response was overwhelming. We knew now that the time was ripe for a feminist rethinking of the limitations and potentials of received economic approaches.

One of the remarkable features of the papers we received was that they emerged from every perspective within economics: neoclassical, Marxian, post-Keynesian, institutional, and Austrian, as well as more recent developments like social constructivism and post-modernism. Clearly there is no one unique research agenda which captures the essence of feminist economics. This pluralism is one of the major strengths of the field. In intellectual as well as natural environments diversity is a *sine qua non* of robust good health. We share the conviction that there is no singular approach which in its universality can apprehend the totality of economic phenomena. Referring to Jacob Viner's famous statement,[6] we paraphrase: "feminist economics is what feminist economists do."

## WHAT FEMINIST ECONOMISTS DO

Contemporary feminist economics began in the 1960s with a reevaluation of received neoclassical and Marxian views on the social roles of women. Feminist economists responding to neoclassical analyses[7] of women showed how notions of men as breadwinners and women as secondary earners permeated the mainstream understanding of women's employment. They argued that this picture is far from the reality of many women whose incomes are essential to the support of their families. When women are seen as working for pin money their concentration in low-paying occupations can be seen as a result of their own choices. If, on the other hand, one recognizes the centrality of work and income in the lives of women this occupational crowding can be seen as a form of discrimination. Other feminist economists challenged the findings of the "New Home Economics" which, in the Victorian tradition, sees women as having a natural superiority in nurturing and housekeeping. On this view, the traditional division of labor within the family appears to be both efficient and mutually beneficent. If, however, one recognizes that gender roles are socially constructed, the sexual division of labor within the family no longer appears as natural, and the assumed harmony of interest between spouses can be recast in terms of inequalities of power and conflicts of interest.

3

Feminist economists responding to radical analyses took issue with the traditional Marxist view that capitalism would pave the way for women's liberation as it would destroy private property within the proletarian family, make household work redundant and draw all women into the labor market. In the domestic labor debate feminists showed the importance of both private property and the sexual division of labor in maintaining women's subordinate economic status. They argued that patriarchal households would not simply wither away because they played essential roles in the accumulation of capital, the reproduction of labor power and the class struggle. Feminists challenged the genderless notions of the proletariat, exploitation, production and reproduction, to show the dialectical relationship between gender and class. Based on a feminist reading of the sexual division of labor, they criticized the view that there was a natural congruence of economic interest between men and women in the working class[8].

Though the premises and methods of the radical and neoclassical traditions are very different, feminist economists discovered that both schools are shaped by a common neglect of the adverse conditions facing women as paid and unpaid workers. They showed that historically these schools treated the sexual division of labor in the family and society as if it were biologically given. In this, both mainstream and radical economic traditions were shaped by Victorian ideology. Questions about sexual inequalities in the labor market or the family were pushed to the margin by the conceptualization of sex roles as complementary and natural (Pujol 1992, and below; Folbre 1991).

The status of women remains an important focus of feminist economics today. However, many feminist economists go beyond this to illuminate the ways in which assumptions about gender influence virtually all aspects of economic reasoning. Feminist economists believe that uncovering the gender biases in economics is a necessary prelude to constructing an economics which can encompass the perspectives and embody the realities of both women and men. If gender biases do indeed permeate the discipline, then the positivist notion that norms do not influence economic research is called into question. Radical economists would probably be comfortable with this since they recognize that all theories are shaped by social forces. Mainstream economists, on the other hand, may find such a project antithetical to their vision of economics as a universal, value free science.

Sociologists and philosophers of science,[9] and some economists such as Klamer et al. (1988), McCloskey (1985) and Weintraub (1991) have seriously questioned the positivist world view. This research shows that the choice of questions asked as well as the analytics employed are all unavoidably the products of social construction. Despite the impressive literature revealing these weaknesses, positive notions of objectivity continue to propagate rules of "good research" in economics. In these notions, value neutrality is held up as an important condition for "real" science.

The first plenary speaker at the conference, Sandra Harding (1993), criticized this view when she argued that "something is wrong with the prevailing objectivity ideals and/or practices if so much sexist and andro-centric research in biology and the social sciences can manage to pass undetected through purportedly 'good science'." Harding asked why "empirically and theoretically more adequate feminist research can be dismissed as not objective"? (1993: 4). To answer this question she distinguished between situations in which value neutrality protects objec-tivity, and situations in which value neutrality threatens objectivity.

In the first case, the traditional canons of science pose a barrier to outside agencies (the state, the church, or corporations) which may inter-vene in science to advance vested interests. In the second case, though, value neutrality is an obstruction to objective knowledge because science has itself become part of the dominant institutional structure. When the values of dominant institutions coincide with those of scientists them-selves, the very presence of a value-laden agenda is rendered invisible. When this occurs, insistence on scientific objectivity simply functions to close off discussion and thus perpetuate the dominance of some interests over others. Ironically, then, scientists who make their value positions explicit may actually be "more objective" in their ability to recognize problems and biases which have been hidden by the dominant value structure.

Consequently the quest for objectivity does not imply value neutrality. In the words of Sandra Harding, "maximizing objectivity is about the validity of a claim; value neutrality is about commitment to it" (1993: 16). Within present-day mainstream economics, objectivity and value neutrality need to be uncoupled. Economists' claims to value neutrality do not guarantee objectivity since implicit in their practice is a set of (gender-laden) values, including freedom to choose, the importance of detachment, the omnipre-sence of scarcity and the absence of connection. These ideals seem so obvious and natural to most economists that they are not considered values. Yet they are values and so normal science as practised in economics privileges masculine ideals.

Building on these insights, Julie Nelson, in a series of paradigmatic essays (1992a, 1992b), has shown how economic science continues to be influ-enced by traditional notions of gender embedded in a series of hierarchical dualisms. In a plenary address to the conference (Nelson 1993) she analyzed the dominant tendency of western thought to characterize the world by means of dualisms like good/bad, hard/soft, rational/emotional and objective/subjective. Traditionally the poles of these oppositions are viewed as mutually exclusive, and within each opposition one pole is given a privileged position with respect to the other; objectivity, for example, is taken to be superior to subjectivity. Gender bias enters when these hierarchical dualisms are metaphorically associated with sexual difference: the superior pole of a dualism takes on masculine characteristics, and the inferior pole is associated with the feminine.

Following feminist philosophers of science, Nelson pointed out that the image of the scientist has long been associated with the masculine ideals of objectivity, separation, logical consistency and individual accomplishment. In contrast, subjectivity, connection, intuitive understanding and cooperation, characteristics with historical and social links to femininity, are usually considered irrelevant, or, worse, actually disruptive for science. The heavy emphasis on mathematical models of rational behavior within economics exemplifies this tendency to focus on masculine "virtues" to avoid feminine "vices." Nelson's analysis shows that economists' exclusive focus on masculine virtues (like competition and individuation) not only blinds them to such feminine virtues as cooperation and relatedness but also produces a very one-sided view of personhood.

To overcome these problems of masculine biases Nelson developed the "gender/value compass," which breaks the traditional link of masculinity with superiority and femininity with inferiority. In contrast to the dualism of traditional economic stereotypes, Nelson suggested a unified definition of selfhood drawing on the positive aspects of masculinity and femininity, separation and connection. She argues that the conscious and explicit inclusion of gender in economics requires "not just rational arguments and tinkering here and there, but a radical rethinking and even refeeling of the relation of gender to value" (Nelson 1993: 18).

## OUT OF THE MARGIN

The papers brought together in this book reflect the diverse interests, concerns and approaches of feminist economics. The parts of the book correspond to the five themes of the conference: Herstory of Economics; Economic Theory; Interpreting Economics; Economic Measurement; and the Empowerment of Women. Original comments on the papers close each part. Together the papers and comments highlight the depth and scope of feminist economics.

### Herstory of economics

Part I begins with Michèle Pujol's essay "Into the Margin!" She shows that strongly held traditional Victorian values played a major role in shaping the neoclassical view of women and women's issues. Neoclassical economists have, since Jevons, Edgeworth and Marshall, defined the economic position of women in terms of their status as dependents: as married or to be married, as economically dependent on a father or husband, as primarily mothers and housewives, as less productive than men and unfit as economic agents. As Pujol so forcefully argues, this has had very important consequences for both theory and policy. Her account asks us to question the extent to which pure reason motivates the economic analysis of women.

Frances Hutchinson's chapter "A Heretical View of Economic Growth and Income Distribution" discusses the Social Credit Movement associated with the British economist and politician Major Douglas. He proposed various reforms to provide all citizens with an income, which he called "the National Dividend." Women were especially strong supporters of the Douglas Social Credit Movement since they believed that a national dividend would free them from dependence on their husbands. Hutchinson presents the economic ideas upon which Douglas drew and asks why this early feminist economic movement received such a negative assessment from virtually all established quarters.

Amartya K. Sen evaluates these chapters in terms of their contribution to the analysis of the material, political and/or theoretical deprivation of women. One of the strengths of feminist economics is, according to Sen, its attention to inequalities within the household. He points to several ways in which economic theory overlooks the realities of women living both traditional and non-traditional lives. He urges feminist economists to extend attention to the multiple deprivations of race and class and argues that connecting these to gender will strengthen economic analysis.

## Economic theory

Part II begins with Solomon W. Polachek's essay "Human Capital and the Gender Earnings Gap." He presents his views on feminist economics and reviews his work on male/female wage differentials in light of feminist criticisms. For Polachek, the explanatory power of the human capital school is unsurpassed in explaining women's economic status. He argues that feminist interpretations which see these results as "blaming the victim" misunderstand the relevant causation: women's disadvantaged status is not due to market discrimination but is due instead to societal discrimination. Polachek's essay confirms the importance of a positive dialogue between mainstream and feminist economics.

Notburga Ott's "Fertility and Division of Work in the Family" demonstrates the potential of game theory for feminist economic analysis. Ott extends the rationality principle to the private sphere by modeling household decisions as a dynamic bargaining process between husbands and wives. She shows that family decision making about fertility and household work may resemble the well-known prisoner's dilemma. In contrast to traditional models which imply a trade-off between equality and efficiency, Ott's contribution shows that policies to promote gender equality may at the same time improve efficiency.

"Toward a Feminist, Post-Keynesian Theory of Investment" is the intriguing title of Lee B. Levin's essay. Levin challenges the view that rationality is the sole motivation behind economic behavior. His analysis of the epistemological underpinnings of feminist *vis-à-vis* Cartesian approaches permits the construction of a theory of investment which takes into account the social and emotional aspects of agent knowledge. This original, innovative synthesis of feminist and post-Keynesian theory succeeds in establishing some of the dynamics of capital markets which are not easily understood from within conventional approaches.

Julie A. Nelson makes the point that good economic research should reveal something new about the subjects of study. By this standard, Nelson argues, Polachek's and Ott's contributions fall short of the mark as they both rely on models with restrictive assumptions far removed from the real world. Although she finds that Levin's work does meet this standard, his subjectivist rhetoric is likely to alienate mainstream readers. The challenge for future work is to find a language which enables a fruitful dialogue between mainstream and feminist economists.

## Interpreting economics

Part III begins with Diana Strassmann and Livia Polanyi's essay "The Economist as Storyteller." The authors use the tools of literary criticism to show that mainstream economic analyses are not the impersonal, universal accounts most economists believe them to be. Instead, they illustrate the connection between these economic stories and the historical, cultural backgrounds of their producers. Going beyond the rhetorical school's position that the "market place of ideas" will accurately decide which accounts are superior, Strassman and Polanyi analyze the mechanisms which protect this marketplace from deviant and all too different stories.

In "Reading Neoclassical Economics" Susan F. Feiner uses psycho-analytic theory to interpret some of the hidden, symbolic meanings within neoclassical economics. According to Feiner, concepts like perfect markets and Say's law (supply creates its own demand) are shaped by powerful repressions stemming from infantile experiences of frustration and longing. She uses object relations theory to show how fantasies about perfect mothers coincide with economic stories about perfect markets. Feiner's work asks us to consider the relationship between psychological development, exchange and sharing.

Arjo Klamer suggests that the majority of economists will not be persuaded by this interpretation because it is based on "mere words." Although he raises several questions about the findings of these papers, he argues for the use of interpretative methods since they enrich the conversations of economists. Klamer asks us to consider the insights produced by these papers for our understanding of the formation and propagation of neoclassical theories.

## Economic measurement

In Part IV, "The Empirical Challenges of Feminist Economics" by Martha MacDonald addresses various aspects and technical problems of data gathering. She shows how the interplay of epistemology and methodology produces gender bias in data sets. She argues that questions relating to the measurement/valuation of women's unpaid work, intra-household distribution of labor, income and resources, and gendered processes in the paid labor market can not be adequately analyzed using secondary data sources. MacDonald argues that making gender a central analytical component in primary data collection methods is a major challenge for feminist economics.

In "Measuring Equality in Opportunity 2000" Diane Perrons develops an Equality Index to assess various dimensions of labor market inequality. She applies the index to changes in male/female employment conditions following a major affirmative action initiative in British industry. Perrons' analysis suggests that although women's position improved, the quality of these improvements can be questioned since they are largely caused by a deterioration of male jobs and the expansion of full-time work for women, rather than a more fundamental change in the structure of pay or traditional gender hierarchies.

In "Toward a Feminist Econometrics" Esther Redmount questions the typical use of gender categories in econometric models. She separates the social roles traditionally ascribed to women and men from biological sex to model the rational choices underlying the gendered household division of labor. In her model the division of labor is endogenous and not ascribed on *a priori* grounds to persons of a certain sex. Redmount challenges the widespread use of a simple binary construct of sex roles and asks us to develop rational choice models less distorted by masculine biases.

Siv S. Gustafsson defends economists' use of secondary data sets. In contrast to MacDonald she stresses the need to build feminist questions into multipurpose data sets. Gustafsson sees Perrons' equality index as a means to support feminist economic policies. She finds in Redmount's work an important contribution to feminist economics since it models gender as a social construct. Gustafsson asks us to consider the importance of working with existing empirical methods for feminist economics.

## Empowerment of women

Part V begins with Eileen Trzcinski's paper "The Use and Abuse of Neoclassical Theory in the Political Arena," which analyzes the role of neoclassical ideology debates on family and medical leave in the United States. Trzcinski argues that conservatives easily use textbook economics to support policies which reinforce traditional gender roles. She attributes this misuse of economics to the neglect of empirical research by policy advocates. To counter this, Trzcinski calls for more empirical research on the effects of progressive social policies.

In "Women and Children Last" Barbara E. Hopkins analyzes how women are affected by the privatization processes now taking place in the former socialist countries. The growing separation of public and private spheres, and of family and work life, shifts the responsibility for care taking on to women. Hopkins argues that when privatization is accompanied by lower pay and reductions in health services and childcare support, efficiency does not increase. The redistribution of wealth and resultant decrease in women's autonomy actually undercuts efficiency. She argues that any accurate assessment of the welfare effects of privatization must include such gender-based effects.

In "Gender, Property, and Land Rights" Bina Agarwal discusses the connection between gender inequalities and command over landed property. Her analysis highlights an important lacuna in feminist analyses and economic (development) policies which mainly focus on wage labor. Agarwal argues that land ownership and control is central to the development of rural women's economic autonomy. Recognizing the need to support politically women's claims to land she urges feminists to discuss strategies and institutional arrangements which promote women's access to land.

For Diane Elson the empowerment of women involves "changing the parameters within which individual women live their lives." She praises these papers for showing how economic arguments are often used to undercut women's rights to economic security. Elson argues that the contribution of neoclassical economics to the empowerment of women is severely limited by its focus on static equilibrium analysis. The challenge for feminist economics is to develop an economic theory which goes beyond describing the status quo to emphasize process and conceptualize the obstacles and conditions for change.

Individually and as a group these papers interrupt "business as usual" in economics. The knowledge produced by their careful attention to the interplay of gender, economics and science does not simply invert the positions of feminist and non-feminist approaches, thereby producing a new marginalization. Instead, these essays support a reconfiguration of the terrain of economics. We hope this book is more than a voice crying in the wilderness and that many will elect to come with us out of the desert.

## ACKNOWLEDGEMENT

The authors wish to thank Susan Feiner for extensive comments on an early draft of this Introduction and stimulating support in the completion of the present version.

INTRODUCTION

**NOTES**

1 For an overview of the initial works pointing to new directions for feminist economics, see, for example: Feiner, S.F. and Roberts, B.B. (1990) "Hidden by the Invisible Hand: Neoclassical Economic Theory and the Textbook Treatment of Race and Gender", *Gender & Society*, 4, 2: 159–81; Folbre, N. and Hartmann, H. (1988) "The Rhetoric of Self-Interest: Ideology and Gender in Economic Theory", in A. Klamer, D. McCloskey and R. Solow (eds) *The Consequence of Economic Rhetoric*, Cambridge: Cambridge University Press; Harrison, K. and Strassmann, D. (1989) "Gender, Rhetoric and Economic Theory", paper presented at the Southern Economic Association on Orlando, Florida, November; Kosonen, K. (1989) "The Neoclassical Approach to Economics: An Androcentric Bias?", paper presented at the congress of the International Economic Association, Athens, Greece, August; Nelson, J.A. (1992) "Gender, Metaphor, and the Definition of Economics", *Economics and Philosophy* 8, 1: 103–25; Pujol, M. (1984) "Gender and Class in Marshall's Principles of Economics", *Cambridge Journal of Economics* 8, 3; Seiz, J. (1993) "Gender and Economic Research", in N. de Marchi (ed.) *Post Popperian Methodology of Economics: Recovering Practice*: 273–319, Boston: Kluwer-Nijhoff; Woolley, F.R. (1991) "The Feminist Challenge to Neoclassical Economics", Carleton Economics Papers 91–113, Ottawa, Ontario: Carleton University (forthcoming, *Cambridge Journal of Economics*).

2 For an overview of the initial empirical work in feminist economics, see, for example: Amsden, A.H. (ed.) (1980) *The Economics of Women and Work*, Harmondsworth: Penguin; Bergmann, B. (1986) *The Economic Emergence of Women*, New York: Basic Books; Blau, F.D. and Ferber, M.A. (1986) *The Economics of Women, Men, and Work*, Englewood Cliffs, NJ: Prentice-Hall; Hartmann, H. (ed.) (1985) *Comparable Worth: New Directions for Research*, Washington DC: National Academy Press; Lloyd, C.B., Andrews, E.S. and Gilroy, C.L. (eds) (1979) *Women in the Labor Market*, New York: Columbia University Press; Lloyd, C.B. and Reskin, B. (eds) (1984) *Sex Segregation in the Workplace: Trends, Explanations, Remedies*, Washington, DC: National Academy Press.

3 The project referred to here is titled "Improving Introductory Economics Education by Integrating the Latest Scholarship on Women and Minorities." Funding for this project comes from the National Science Foundation Division of Undergraduate Education grants numbered: 915149 and 9354006.

4 Reports by the OECD – (1991) *Shaping Structural Change: The Role of Women*, Paris and the Worldbank; (1990) *World Development Report 1990*, Washington, DC – make arguments similar to those found in Elson, D. (1991) *Male Bias in the Development Process*, New York: Manchester University Press.

5 For an overview of feminist research in related disciplines, see, for example: Bordo, S. (1987) *The Flight to Objectivity. Essays on Cartesianism & Culture*, Albany, N.Y.: State University Press; Easlea, B. (1980) *Science and Sexual Oppression, Patriarchy's Confrontation with Women and Nature*, London: Weidenfeld and Nicolson; Haraway, D. (1991) *Simians, Cyborgs, and Women, The Reinvention of Nature*, New York: Chapman & Hall; Harding, S. (1986) *The Science Question in Feminism*, Ithaca, London: Cornell University Press; Harding, S. and Hintikka, M.B. (1983) *Discovering Reality, Feminist Perspectives on Epistemology, Metaphysics, Methodology and Philosophy of Science*, Dordrecht: Reidel; Keller, E.F. (1985) *Reflections on Gender and Science*, New Haven/London: Yale University Press; Lloyd, G. (1984) *The Man of Reason: 'Male' and 'Female' in Western Philosophy*, London: Methuen; Merchant, C. (1980) *The Death of Nature: Woman, Ecology and the Scientific Revolution*, San

Francisco: Harper & Row; Pateman, C. and Gross, E. (eds) (1986) *Feminist Challenges. Social and Political Theory*, Sydney, London.

6 The statement we refer to is "economics is what economists do". See Boulding, K. (1941) *Economic Analysis*: 3, New York/London: Harcourt and Brothers.

7 For an overview of some of the early feminist challenges to neoclassical economics, see, for example: Amsden, A.H. (1980) "Introduction", in A.H. Amsden (ed.) *The Economics of Women and Work*: 11–38, Harmondsworth: Penguin; Barrett, N.S. (1981) " How the Study of Women has Restructured the Discipline of Economics", in E. Langland and W. Grove (eds) *A Feminist Perspective in the Academy: The Difference it Makes*: 101–109, Chicago: University of Chicago Press; Blau, F. and Jusenius, C. (1976) "Economists' Approaches to Sex Segregation in the Labor Market: An Appraisal" in M. Blaxall and B. Reagan (eds) *Women and the Workplace*: 181–201, Chicago: University of Chicago Press; Ferber, M.A. and Birnbaum, G. (1977) "The New Home Economics: Retrospects and Prospects", *Journal of Consumer Research* 4, 4, June: 19–28; Ferber, M.A. and Teiman, M. (1981) "The Oldest, The Most Established, The Most Quantitative of the Social Sciences – and the Most Dominated by Men: The Impact of Feminism on Economics", in Dale Spender (ed.) *Men's Studies Modified*, New York: Pergamon; Sawhill, I.V. (1977) " Economic Perspectives on the Family", *Daedalus* 106, 2: 115–25 (also published in Amsden (1980)).

8 For an overview of early Marxist feminist research, see, for example: Barrett, M. (1980) *Women's Oppression Today. Problems in Marxist Feminist Analysis*, London: Verso; Beechey, V. (1987) *Unequal Work*, London: Verso; Folbre, N. (1982) "Exploitation Comes Home: A Critique of the Marxian Theory of Family Labour", *Cambridge Journal of Economics*, 6; Hartmann, H.I. (1976) "Capitalism, Patriarchy, and Job Segregation by Sex", *Signs: Journal of Women in Culture and Society* 1, 3, Spring: 137–69; Humphries, J. (1977) "Class Struggle and the Persistence of the Working-Class Family", *Cambridge Journal of Economics* 1, September: 241–58; Sargent, L. (1981) *Women and Revolution. The Unhappy Marriage of Marxism and Feminism*, London: Pluto Press.

9 See, for example: Kuhn, T.S. (1962) *The Structure of Scientific Revolutions*, Chicago: The University of Chicago Press; Bloor, D. (1976) *Science and Social Imagery*, London: Routledge & Kegan Paul; Latour, B. and Woolgar, S. (1979), *Laboratory Life: The Construction of Scientific Facts*, Princeton, NJ: Princeton University Press; Rorty, R. (1979), *Philosophy and the Mirror of Nature*, Princeton, NJ: Princeton University Press.

# REFERENCES

Bartlett, R.L. and Feiner, S.F. (1992) "Balancing the Economics Curriculum: Content, Method and Pedagogy", *American Economic Review* LXXXII, 2, May: 559–564.

Ferber, M.A. and Nelson, J.A. (eds) (1993) *Beyond Economic Man. Feminist Theory and Economics*, Chicago: University of Chicago Press.

Folbre, N. (1991) "The Unproductive Housewife: Her Evolution in Nineteenth Century Economic Thought", *Signs* 16, 3: 463–84.

Harding, S. (1993) "Feminist Philosophy of Science. The Objectivity Question", in the *Report of the Out of the Margin Conference*, Amsterdam.

Klamer, A., McCloskey, D. and Solow, R. (eds) (1988) *The Consequences of Economic Rhetoric*, Cambridge: Cambridge University Press.

McCloskey, D. (1985), *The Rhetoric of Economics*, Madison: University of Wisconsin Press.

Nelson, J.A. (1992a) "Thinking about Gender", *Hypathia* 7, 3: 138–154.

—— (1992b) "Gender, Metaphor, and the Definition of Economics", *Economics and Philosophy* 8, 1: 103–25.

—— (1993) "Feminist Economics: What Might it Look Like?", in the *Report of the Out of the Margin Conference*, Amsterdam.

Pujol, M. (1992) *Feminism and Anti-Feminism in Early Economic Thought*, Aldershot: Edward Elgar.

Weintraub, E.R. (1991) *Stabilizing Dynamics: Constructing Economic Knowledge*, Cambridge: Cambridge University Press.

Woolf, Virginia [1928] (1957) *A Room of One's Own*, Orlando: Harcourt Brace.

# Part I

# HERSTORY OF ECONOMICS

*Editor Susan F. Feiner*

The woman composer stands where the actress stood in the time of Shakespeare. Nick Greene, I thought, remembering the story I had made about Shakespeare's sister, said that a woman acting put him in mind of a dog dancing. Johnson repeated the phrase two hundred years later of women preaching. And here, I said, opening a book about music, we have the very words used again in this year of grace, 1928, of women who try to write music. "Of Mlle Germaine Tailleferre one can only repeat Dr Johnson's dictum concerning a woman preacher, transposed into terms of music. 'Sir, a woman's composing is like a dog's walking on his hind legs. It is not done well, but you are surprised to find it done at all.'" So accurately does history repeat itself.

(Woolf [1928] (1957): 58)

# 1

# INTO THE MARGIN!

*Michèle Pujol*

## INTRODUCTION

The neoclassical economic paradigm is now over one hundred years old. Since its inception in the 1890s it has grown to be the dominant paradigm in economic theory, building its hegemonic power to the exclusion of alternative approaches. I have studied and then taught economics for nearly twenty-five years now. I had come to economics, as an undergraduate student in Paris, with a lot of excitement and trepidation: that discipline was going to help me understand what was going on in the world. I soon found out that the neoclassical paradigm, while providing some seductive modeling, did not come close to answering the questions I had. But it was only much later, in graduate school, that other questions started coming up. As a woman in the field, I started realizing that my own realities were missing, that they were dismissed or trivialized when issues of women's places in the economy were brought up.

Examining the origins of the neoclassical paradigm, one can identify the Victorian ideology which is at the roots of the treatment of women within it. The founding fathers – Marshall, Pigou, Edgeworth, and Jevons – wrote as one in a voice laden with patriarchal condescension. Unfortunately this attitude towards women has remained virtually the same. Yet, simply cataloging the neoclassical record on the status of women seems increasingly fragmentary: giving voice, again, to "the big men" could not be the sole object of an exploration of the patriarchal bias of neoclassical economics. Two other imperatives emerged.

First, to give voice to women, to feminists, writing on economic matters, asserting their disagreement with the status quo, in society and within the profession; and adding to these the voices of the few male economists approaching "the woman question" with a more sympathetic and innovative outlook.

Second, to go beyond a mere history of thought project to challenge the neoclassical monolith by rooting the contemporary feminist critique in the discipline's own history. This work contributes to the development of a feminist epistemology and ontology. It poses the questions: "who is writing theory? for what purpose?" It also challenges the notion that an epistemology based on the standpoints of women and other marginalized groups[1] in the capitalist/patriarchal system could ever find a place within the neoclassical paradigm.

Such an approach challenges two of the main silencings routinely performed within modern day neoclassical economics: the erasure of women and feminists both within the paradigm and as voices of dissent, and the dismissal of methodological critics of the paradigm. I will note here that the second erasure is explicit, while the first is still implicit only. It is relevant to mention, in this respect, that my book (Pujol 1992) has been criticized so far, not so much for its feminist stance and its challenge of the erasure of women and feminists in the discipline, but for daring to criticize the neoclassical paradigm, to suggest that it is flawed. These flaws can be seen more clearly when we analyze the five elements which characterize neoclassical views of women.

1 All women are married, or if not yet, they will be. Similarly, all women have or will have children.
2 All women are (and ought to be) economically dependent on a male relative: father or husband.
3 Women are (and ought to be) housewives, their reproductive capacities specializes them for that function.
4 Women are unproductive (whether absolutely or relative to men is not always clear) in the industrial workforce.
5 Women are irrational, they are unfit as economic agents, they cannot be trusted to make the right economic decisions.

Through all these elements women are constructed as different from the norm (men). All the above characteristics together contribute to rationalizing women's exclusion from the public realm of economics: the market. These characteristics are seldom openly and clearly stated by economists. They fall within what economists call "unstated assumptions" (even though there is so little awareness of their existence). And because they are unstated, it is not entirely easy for women in the discipline to put a name on the source of our malaise. And I quote here my own inner voice:

> my voice, the "I" I am using here, a scary thing to do (there is no I in my book). I am doing it because it is necessary for us, women/feminist economists to use our own voices, to claim the right to do so. As Diana Strassmann and Livia Polanyi say, in economics:
>
>> direct voices have seldom been female voices, seldom been voices on the margin, seldom been voices not legitimated by the mainstream of power and control ... until women speak their own thoughts and experiences in their own voices and legitimate their

speech by the authority of their own histories and experiences, we will not have a truly feminist economics.

(Strassmann and Polanyi 1992: 13–14)

Let us remember, as feminist economists, that the personal is political and the political is economic. As a woman, as a feminist, as a lesbian, and as a survivor within the discipline of economics, my identity, and the experiences I have encountered in this discipline for twenty-five years inform my analysis of economic theory[2].

We turn, now, to an examination of the work of the early neoclassical economists to show how these five unstated assumptions have been used consistently[3], and contrast them with the actual situation of women and with feminist economic analyses of women's situation.

## WOMEN AS MARRIED AND DEPENDENT

The first two characterizations, that all women are married or are to be married[4], and its immediate corollary that they are the economic dependents of men, invariably inform neoclassical discussions of women's labor force behavior, and beyond that of any economic activity in which they might be engaged. This sets the stage for questioning women's presence in the labor market or for refusing to take this presence seriously. Women, being supported, have no reason to be in the labor market. The concerns they might have – particularly for higher wage levels and for access to employment – can be and have been dismissed as inconsequential. By contrast, men's presence in the labor force has never been questioned by neoclassical economists[5].

This characterization leads economists to see women as non-autonomous agents. For Pigou, the main determinant of (all?) women's labor supply is their husbands' labor income (Pigou 1960: 565–6). In modern/Beckerian neoclassical economics, women seek employment as the result of a "household decision" (Becker 1981). One can wonder if, in neoclassical economics, the decision to seek employment is an individual decision for women. Clearly such an approach allows us to avoid asking why women continue to supply their labor when: their wages are so low; such a decision might reflect an individually non-optimal use of their productive abilities; and women are not allowed by market conditions to optimize returns to their human capital investment.

Women's presence in the labor force is not seen as a contribution to economic welfare, it is instead problematized as threatening severe negative consequences for national welfare and "household utility." Edgeworth warned with alarm that large numbers of women in the workforce would bring a "depression or débâcle of industry," a "débâcle, ultimately ruinous alike to wealth and family life" (1922: 436; 1923: 493). Marshall, Jevons and

19

Pigou all expressed concern for the impact of employment on women's household duties and on infant mortality rates (Marshall 1930: 198, 685; Jevons 1904; Pigou 1960: 187).

Ironically, the solutions to these "problems" proposed by the heretofore "free market" economists relied on draconian interventions into existing labor market conditions. Marshall supported the Factory Acts (1930: 198, 751), Edgeworth argued for the maintenance of barriers to women's entry into occupations (1923: 490–4). Jevons was more severe, advocating legislating the complete exclusion of mothers of children under the age of three from factories.

In the same vein, where Pigou advocated state intervention to correct market failure in the labor market, women were explicitly exempted[6]. Marshall, Pigou and Edgeworth were all either against legislating minimum wages for women, or against minimum wages set at the same level as men's. None of them supported equal pay for equal work legislation. These economists' opposition to women's employment went hand in hand with their support for both preserving men's privileged access to employment and an enhanced male pay packet such that all men, whether married or not, could earn a "family wage" (Edgeworth 1923). Such proposals, if implemented, would have removed what they saw as the main cause for women's labor force participation: their need to earn complementary family income.

We can find direct parallels in the contemporary neoclassical treatment of women's labor force participation. Since Mincer's (1962) seminal article, the focus has been on married women's labor supply. The main question has been "why are these (married) women in the labor force?" and not the appropriate pay scale, working conditions or utilization of their human capital investments. Hence, (all) women's waged employment is constructed as problematic, their human capital investment behavior as anomalous (see Mincer 1962; Mincer and Polachek 1974, 1978; Sandell and Shapiro 1978; Mincer and Ofek 1979). Thus the New Home Economics is a rationale for (all) women's "specialization" in reproduction and housework as opposed to income-earning employment (see Becker 1973, 1976, 1981; Schultz 1974).

By implicitly generalizing from married women to all women, the existence and the needs of women who are not attached to men are denied, and the "norm" of women's economic dependence is ideologically reinforced by both contemporary (Mincer, Polachek) and early neoclassical economists (Marshall, Pigou, Edgeworth, Jevons). One has to look hard to find references to single women, or to no longer married women, let alone to lesbians – whom economists must never have heard of[7].

Yet, the actual situation of women differed substantially from the view proffered by the neoclassical economists. In nineteenth- and early twentieth-century England, a substantial proportion of women were and remained unmarried (Bodichon 1859: 28), and among those who married, full economic support by husbands was often far from the more distressing reality (Cadbury *et al.* 1906; Smith 1915; Rathbone 1917, 1924). Women, both married and unmarried, were present in the labor force in large numbers (Scott and Tilly 1978). These facts were reported and documented by feminists who often used them as a basis for their demands for the means to economic independence for women: access to jobs, education, professional employment and equal pay (Bodichon 1859; Fawcett 1892, 1916, 1918; Webb 1914, 1919)[8]. The so-called "family wage" was described by Eleanor Rathbone (1917, 1924) as an inadequate mode of support for families, and furthermore, as a completely ineffective mode of income distribution[9]. The issue of the degree to which women supported themselves and their dependents was hotly debated and the object of contradictory empirical claims[10].

Feminist writers who discussed issues of women's economic status, in the pages of the *Economic Journal* and elsewhere, provided ample documentation and analysis to contradict the assumptions and normative reasoning of neoclassical economists. Economic historians such as Georgiana Hill (1896), Edith Abbott (1910), Elizabeth Hutchins (1915), Alice Clark (1968) and Ivy Pinchbeck (1981) documented the work and economic contributions of women, from the Middle Ages to the late nineteenth century. The research team of Edward Cadbury, Cecile Matheson and George Shann published an extensive sociological study of working women in 1906. The Fabian Women's Group's survey of *Working Women and their Dependants* in 1915 (Smith 1915) was corroborated by Hogg's study published in *Economica* in 1921.

Indeed, these studies documented the ongoing productive role of women, married and not married, and their contribution to their own support, the support of their dependents and to the overall economy. In the pages of the *Economic Journal*, Ada Heather-Bigg argued that it was not women's work, but their earning of an income, which was objectionable to the opponents of women's employment. She clearly perceived that the overwork of women was of no concern to patriarchal ideologues, but their fear of women's access to economic independence was, to quote her colourful words, "the veriest scooped-out, sheet-draped turnip that ever made a village dolt take to his heels and run" (1894: 55).

Feminists writing on these issues pointed out the necessity of women's employment as a source of economic support for themselves and others, thereby challenging the "family wage" and "pin money" doctrines. They argued and empirically demonstrated that there was no such thing as universal support of women by men, that men's earnings were insufficient to support their families, and that women contributed a high proportion of subsistence needs out of their meagre earnings and hard work. Out of these observations arose serious challenges to some of the justifications for existing labor market conditions.

Feminists saw the Factory Acts as discriminatory restrictions to women's entry into the labor market. They denounced them as protecting the "monopoly" of men over some occupations (Bodichon 1857; Fawcett 1916, 1918; Webb 1914, 1919; Mill 1965, 1970; Taylor 1970) and the license of employers to exploit (Smart 1892). The "family wage" ideal was also seen as a protection of male privilege, of men's right to a job and to a pay cheque whether or not they had a family to support. Furthermore, it reinforced their power in the home (Rathbone 1917, 1924)[11]. Policy proposals to exclude women from the labor force were denounced by feminists as a means to disempower women, to thwart their efforts to organize, and as an encouragement to employers to exploit them (Smart 1892; Fawcett 1918; Webb 1919).

## WOMEN AS MOTHERS

Characterizing all women as married or to be married goes along, in the writing of the early neoclassical economists, with the third characterization of seeing them as mothers whose duty is to raise children properly and carry out related housework. Any other occupation was seen as interfering with this obligation and therefore causing major losses in economic and general welfare. Marshall maintained that (all) women's employment "tempts them to neglect their duty of building a true home, and investing their efforts in the personal capital of their children's character and abilities" and insisted on the necessity of their presence in the home (1930: 685, 721). He asserted that the "degradation of the working classes varies almost uniformly with the amount of rough work done by women" and more particularly with mothers losing their "tender and unselfish instincts" due to "the strain and stress of unfeminine work" (1930: 564).

Pigou advocated shorter workdays for women to provide them with "opportunities for better care of their homes" (1960: 463). He believed that "a woman's work has a special personal value in respect of her own children" (188) which led him to assign women to the home in his blueprint for economic welfare. Jevons asserted that "there are no duties which are more important in every respect than those which a mother is bound by with regard to her own children" (1904: 166). He also proclaimed "the right of the infant to the mother's breast" (171). Women's rights are never mentioned in such fashion[12].

Marshall, Pigou, and Jevons' advocacy of full-time domesticity for mothers was based entirely upon alarmist accounts of high infant mortality in districts where women could find industrial employment (Jevons 1904: 153; Marshall 1930: 198, 529; Pigou 1960: 187). Other factors which might have caused high infant mortality, particularly starvation level wages and the resulting unsanitary living conditions in working-class households were not investigated.

In fact, the evidence cited did not support the economists' claims regarding the negative effects of mothers' employment, but it was authoritatively dismissed anyway. Jevons, for example, attempted to explain away the case of Liverpool, which held "the place of dishonour" with the nation's highest infant mortality rate although there were no women employing industries in Liverpool! Liverpool was an "anomaly" due to its population mix (1904: 153–4). In similar fashion, Pigou invoked *ceteris paribus* reasoning in his attempts to dismiss the annoying evidence that working mothers provided a remedy to poverty and infant mortality:

> The reality of this evil [working mothers' alleged neglect] is not disproved by the low, and even negative, correlation which sometimes is found to exist between the factory work of mothers and the rate of infant mortality. For in districts where women's work of this kind prevails there is presumably – and this is the cause of women's work – great poverty. This poverty, which is injurious to children's health, is likely, other things being equal, to be greater than elsewhere in families where the mother declines factory work, and it may be that the evil of the extra poverty is greater than that of the factory work. This consideration explains the statistical facts that are known. They, therefore, militate in no way against the view that, *other things equal*, the factory work of mothers is injurious.
>
> (Pigou 1960: 187)

Reasoning like this was used effectively to depict women who cared for children as criminals. Mothers who sought employment "and go earn good wages in the mills" (Jevons 1904: 166) along with the wet and dry nurses who provided childcare for the employed mothers, were held directly responsible for the death of children. Curiously, these women were not perceived by neoclassical economists as economic agents who exercised rational decision making under the specific constraints they faced.

Furthermore, working mothers were described as acting unnaturally. Jevons compared them unfavorably to female animals: "The very beasts of the field tend and guard their whelps with instinctive affection. It is only human mothers which shut their infants up alone, or systematically neglect to give them nourishment" (1904: 166). Casting employed mothers in such a light was obviously meant to generate public outrage and gain support for restrictions of their employment.

The economists' prescriptions were outright punitive. Jevons stated: "I will go so far as to advocate the *ultimate complete exclusion of mothers of children under the age of three years from factories and workshops*" (1904: 167–8, emphasis in text). He proposed to fine the husbands and employers of the derelict mothers, as well as the nurses. Mothers were not treated as responsible

agents. Instead, they were patronized, and economists attempted to reinforce their dependency by making their husbands and employers answer for
their actions. Pigou and Marshall also advocated the prohibition of employment for mothers. But, while Marshall showed no concern for how this
might affect the income of working-class households and women's ability
to feed their children, Pigou proposed some form of state-funded "relief to
those families whom the prohibition renders necessitous" (1960: 188).

The argument about mothers' nurturing instinct (although it was found
lacking by economists) and of the special value of their reproductive work
towards their own children was used to reject all other solutions, particularly that of day nurseries which could provide adequate childcare (Jevons
1904: 164–5). While he acknowledged that factory-supervised crèches
observed in France "have produced most beneficial results," Jevons supported the idea only as a transitional measure for the period of adjustment
to the new regime of employment prohibition. As for relief, it was to be
provided only to "widows and deserted wives" to be "employed" by the
state "as nurses to their own children" (169). Hence, a sexual division of
labor which served patriarchal interests and kept women in the domestic
sphere, without access to an independent income source, was assumed as
"natural." As an element of nature, it could then become the "logical" basis
for policy prescriptions.

Whereas the proposed policy of prohibition of employment targeted
specifically the mothers of young children, the economists cast a wider
net to ensure the domestification of women in general. In particular, they
uniformly supported the Factory Acts – Jevons praised them as "one of the
noblest products of legislative skill and patience" at the end of his article on
"Married Women in Factories" (172). The status quo of below-subsistence
wages was also seen as inducing domesticity among women in general.
Marshall explicitly opposed a rise of women's wages which he claimed to be
detrimental to the performance of their domestic duties (1930: 685). More
generally, Marshall, Pigou, and Edgeworth's opposition to equal pay, to
minimum wages for women, to access to industrial training all intended to
keep women dependent and domestified.

The strange paradox is that women do not seem to want to do what is
claimed to be "natural" for them, they have to be coerced on to that path.
In the name of their "natural duties," women were kept away from making
their own decisions. Severe legislation to keep them in the home was
proposed as the panacea for the "evil" of infant mortality. Jevons evoked
idyllic images of "the wife . . . a true mother and a housekeeper; and round
many a Christmas table troops of happy, chubby children" which will
miraculously appear once the legislator speeds up what he saw as a process
of evolution whereby "the manufacturing population would become fitted
to its environment" (1904: 171–2). Meanwhile, as working-class women
were to be coerced into the dependent reproductive role, their economic

24

contribution to their family and to society as a whole was to be further denied and made invisible: their work, although seemingly essential would receive no economic return or recognition[13].

Contemporary neoclassical economists reveal an intimate commitment to nineteenth-century patriarchal ideology by their continued reliance upon the assumption that women are naturally suited for reproductive work. The New Home Economics takes this further and insists that women have a "comparative advantage" in the performance of mothering and household duties. Not only does this "scientific reasoning" reinforce the dominant sexual division of labor within the home and in society, it also bolsters the human capital school's circular explanation of women's lower wages: since women earn less than men, it is to their advantage and the advantage of their families for them to remain specialized in reproductive work. Women's assumed "comparative advantage" in nurturing is used to privilege their contribution to the human capital of others (husband, children) over maximizing returns to their own human capital (Becker 1973, 1976, 1981; Mincer and Polachek 1974; Schultz 1974).

All this fails to address the reality of women's "double workday" and the oddity of the lack of monetary return for the activities in which women have a "comparative advantage." We can see that, in spite of greater sophistication and more complex mathematical expression, very little change in either assumptions or reasoning has occurred since Marshall. Now, as then, this economic "logic" tends to justify and maintain a status quo of female dependence, domesticity and "specialization" in reproductive work.

Feminists of the first wave of the women's movement opposed the existing barriers to women's access to the labor market. They denounced the Factory Acts (Bodichon 1859; Mill 1965, 1970; Strachey 1969; Taylor 1970) as well as trade boards and trade union restrictions on women's entry and access to skills and apprenticeship (Fawcett 1892, 1916, 1918; Webb 1914, 1919). However, in the feminist economic writings I have studied, I did not find anyone directly taking on the infant mortality argument of the neoclassical economists. But, as I have already mentioned, a number of studies documented the extent of income earning support generated by working women[14].

Eleanor Rathbone, however, focussed specifically on the economic position of working-class mothers in England post World War I. She criticized the ideologies of the "family wage" and of the male breadwinner as utterly flawed representations of the income earning reality of working-class households and as an inadequate income distribution system (1917: 62). She developed a proposal for a "motherhood allowance" where mothers would receive from the state an independent income to provide for the subsistence needs of their children. Whereas she supported the position that mothers should stay home to take care of their children, she maintained that their reproductive work must receive the economic recognition of a specific income payment. She rejected the situation where mothers were the dependent victims of a patriarchal order. Her mother's allowance system proposed to provide mothers with an independent, state-funded income, to recognize their role and their work in the household and to generate economic support for children independent of the sometimes uncertain labor market earnings of men.

The economists of the time did not sanction Rathbone's proposals. As already mentioned, Pigou endorsed state allowances only in the case of widows, with the express purpose of maintaining them domesticated and dependent on the state. He did not favor schemes which would economically recognize mother's reproductive work while ensuring them access to an independent income. Edgeworth opposed motherhood allowances after applying a strict economic cost/benefit analysis to them (1922: 450–3) and was not willing to recognise that, in a wider social welfare approach, the balance might tip in their favor (1923: 494)[15].

## PRODUCTIVITY

The fourth assumption, that of women's low industrial productivity, is pervasive in the early (and late) neoclassical economists' writings. For instance, women were repetitively characterized as unskilled and "low grade workers" by Pigou (1960: 607, 723). Pigou never demonstrated this and never stopped to wonder about employers' continued demand for women's labor, particularly in specific "women's" industries[16]. The argument that women receive low wages as a result of low productivity is also reinforced by the assumption of perfect competition in the labor market. Given this assumption, women's low wages are seen as "proof" of their low productivity. Yet, the absence of a necessary correlation between women's wages and productivity is paradoxically confirmed by Pigou. He argued that women's wages should be pegged at a presumably "fair" market determined level even when their productivity should warrant a higher wage (Pigou 1960: 566–70)[17].

The views of neoclassical economists were contradicted in their days by the more realistic observations and theories of first wave feminists. Fawcett (1892, 1916) and Mill (1965) put forward a theory of non-competing groups which provided an alternative to the neoclassical unified labor market. The concept of crowding, which has today become an accepted approach to labor markets, was first developed by Bodichon (1859), Fawcett (1892, 1916), Smart (1892), Cannan (1914) and Beatrice Webb (1914, 1919). As early as 1859, Bodichon identified institutional and customary barriers to women's entry into industry. This analysis was refined by Mill (1965, 1970), Fawcett (1892, 1916) and Webb (1914, 1919). Others developed a "customary wage" approach whereby customs and tradition were greater determinants of women's wages than actual productivity (Marshall and Marshall 1881; Smart 1892). Discrimination between the sexes in the form of a dual system of women's subsistence wage and men's "family wage" was another approach proposed by Smart (1892), Rathbone (1917, 1924) and Webb (1914, 1919). William Smart's 1892 comprehensive and incisive critique of the economists' use of the law of demand and supply to justify women's low wages is just as relevant today and testifies to the ossification of the discipline[18].

It is interesting to see how the biases of the neoclassical economists were reasserted in spite of these other approaches and in spite of their own acknowledgement of less than competitive conditions in the labor market. Edgeworth listed three reasons why the labor market is not competitive: employers' power, their preference for hiring men even at a productivity disadvantage, and trade unions' interference (1922: 439). Yet he asserted "I submit as an *inference based on general impressions and ordinary experience* that, even if all restrictions on the competition between male and female workers were removed we should still find the average weekly earnings of the former to be considerably higher" (1922: 442, emphasis added). Here, against all precepts of positivist science, assertion prevails over evidence and proof.

Pigou's suggestions on the problem of non-competing markets for women workers was to keep them such. In contrast, where men receive wages below the value of their marginal product Pigou recommended state intervention to raise these wages to their efficiency level. No such solution was proposed in the case of women, as their wages were decreed "fair" if they corresponded to what women were "paid elsewhere," regardless of their actual productivity level (1960: 569–70). Pigou forgot his usual efficiency concerns and used instead the apparently solicitous argument that higher wages would deter employers from hiring women and thus harm women's position in the labor market. Reading on, we find out, however, that he was a lot more concerned with employers' access to a supply of cheap female labor than with women's employment opportunities (600–602).

The belief that women have low industrial productivity did not lead to proposals to raise productivity levels via either training or education. The neoclassical economists saw such schemes as wasteful since they believed that women should not remain in the labor force, that their dependent status removed all motivation for productivity improvement, or that women's unproductivity is irremediable (Pigou 1960: 616). In a nutshell, any proposal to improve women's wage earning capacity, whether through increased skills and training, through wages reflecting more adequately women's actual productivity, or through equal pay (and in some cases minimum wages) measures, were opposed (Edgeworth 1922, 1923; Pigou 1960, 1952; Marshall 1930: 715).

Such measures were seen as harmful to the market, to employers, and to overall economic welfare. Edgeworth believed they could cause a "débâcle of industry," or worse, men's rights to jobs and their status as breadwinners might be challenged (Edgeworth 1922, 1923). Pigou saw such measures as threatening to harm general welfare by "divert[ing] women into industrial activity away from home-making, child-rearing and child-bearing" (1952: 224–5) and as unnecessary because women do not need higher labor income, being dependents and only temporarily present in the labor market.

Once again we see direct parallels with contemporary human capital theory: the market is assumed to be both perfect and infallible in its determination of wages which truly reflect productivity; women's lower employment income is therefore attributed to their own choice in human capital investment and choice of low productivity occupations. Any legislative approach (pay equity/comparable worth, affirmative action) will only create market imperfections and jeopardize women's chances in the labor market (Killingsworth 1985).

These positions are directly opposed to feminist analysis of women's labor force situation and to feminist economic policy recommendations[19]. What is so striking is the neoclassical economists' heavy reliance on their patriarchal bias rather than on theoretically and methodologically sound approaches to support their policy recommendations. The pervasiveness of this bias raises the question of whether feminist ideas and approaches can ever gain a place within the paradigm. To date, feminist critiques of human capital theory and of the new home economics have largely been ignored.

## RATIONALITY

The four assumptions/characterizations discussed above are closely linked. They reinforce each other and contribute to a specific construction of women by the early neoclassical economists. Through their combined effects (in theory and policy) women are seen as occupying a radically different place in the capitalist economy than men, who are conversely constructed as "rational economic men."[20]

In neoclassical economics, men are autonomous, independent individuals while women are dependents who cannot stand on their own. Women are always defined as members of family units, as wives, daughters, mothers. Men make economic decisions based on their own needs and their own abilities and options, they circulate freely in the market sphere. In contrast, women have limited access to the market and even more limited access to their own utility maximizing decision-making. Even in the single example Marshall uses where women are seen to skilfully exercise such decision-making, by stretching (i.e. "maximising the allocation" of) the meagre household budget[21], (1930: 195–6) it is not their own utility which is maximized, but that of the household[22]. Where men may choose across an array of occupations, women are assigned to a single one: motherhood.

In this construction, women lack access to the conditions required to act freely and rationally in the capitalist marketplace. The complete absence of these conditions for women is mirrored in the monopoly exerted over them by men – a means through which the masculinity of *homoeconomicus* is erected. Women's condition is closest to that of the pre-capitalist serfs or slaves whose lives are determined and whose decisions are made by someone else: husband, father, guardian. Isn't this why Jevons proposes to fine husbands when women break the law[23]?

But are women's economic actions really so different? Don't they seek employment to support themselves and their families? Don't they respond to the economic incentive of starvation and poverty (their own and their children's) by seeking employment? And don't they try to make the best of the limited opportunities offered by the labor market? But, given the misogyny of neoclassical economists, we are not surprised to see women blamed for competing against each other and driving down their own wages (are men ever chastised for competing against each other?). Viewed from a feminist standpoint, it is obvious that women's behavior is rational despite the incredible restrictions they continue to face.

Women are seen as irrational, not because they act against the laws of economic rationality, but because they are not allowed to act rationally, or because they act in contravention of the roles that are prescribed as "natural" for them. Taking this further, it seems that women's access to economic rationality is perceived as a threat to the economy and to society. Marshall, Jevons, Edgeworth and Pigou share this view and it leads them to oppose systematically attempts by women to claim an equal economic status and to create for themselves the conditions for that status.

## CONCLUSION

Approaches to women in neoclassical economics have not changed much since the founding of the paradigm in the last decade of the nineteenth century. The men who wrote then and the many men and women who write from this perspective today share a common commitment to a methodology which is imbued with patriarchy, sexism and misogyny. As in the early days, women and feminists are excluded from developing or establishing alternative theoretical approaches. Our words are not heard within the "malestream" of the discipline. Can neoclassical economics be cleansed of its patriarchal bias so that it can open its eyes to the methodological flaws resulting from its ingrained sexism? With the authors of other papers in this collection, I want to suggest that the very logic, rhetoric and symbolism of the paradigm may be inseparable from the five sexist assumptions I have discussed here. Neoclassical economics has a *his*tory of stifling feminist approaches. We cannot wait for it to change. We must transcend it.

## ACKNOWLEDGEMENT

I gratefully acknowledge the support of Brook Holdack and the invaluable editorial help of Susan Feiner.

## NOTES

1 On standpoint theory, see in particular Nancy Hartsock (1983, 1991).
2 Just as your experiences and identity shape your analyses.
3 I will focus on the following early neoclassical works: A. Marshall's *Principles of Economics* (1930), S. Jevons' 1904 article "Married Women in Factories", A.C. Pigou's *Economics of Welfare* (1960) and F. Edgeworth's two articles "Equal Pay to Men and Women for Equal Work" (1922) and " Women's Wages in Relation to Economic Welfare" (1923).
4 This goes back to the origins of patriarchal thought: Elizabeth Spelman, in *Inessential Woman*, discusses how, for Aristotle, women were acknowledged only if they were wives of citizens. All other women simply did not exist (1988: 45–7).
5 Their only worry is where it is deemed insufficient: e.g. in discussions of the Poor Rates impact on the (male) supply of labor.
6 See Pigou's discussion of unfair wages (1960: 549–70).
7 Widows – with children – are the only women not dependent on a male breadwinner who have elicited some interest. Pigou specifically devises state welfare schemes to keep them away from the labor force, staying home to reproduce the next generation, and to keep them economically dependent – on the state (1960: 722–3).
8 In the Cambridge degree controversy, the argument used by Marshall to oppose women's admissions was his *belief* that most (90 per cent) female students would marry and consequently not require the economic independence provided by a degree. On the opposite side of the controversy, E.M. Sidgwick documented, in a statistical study of families from which students would be drawn, that the marriage rate would be under 50 per cent (McWilliams Tullberg 1992: 24).
9 On the "family wage", see also Land (1979–80) and Barrett and McIntosh (1980).
10 Two studies by Smith (1915) and Hogg (1921) show a high rate of self-support among women workers (85 per cent in Smith's study), and additionally they show that one in three working women fully or partially supported dependents besides themselves. By contrast, Rowntree-Seebohm and Stuart (1921) found that only 12 per cent of working women supported dependents. The latter, in spite of its dubious methodology, was used by Edgeworth to dismiss women's contribution.
11 Note that Edgeworth's reply to the feminists in 1923 does not contradict this analysis, but instead reasserts men's rights in the labor force as a rationale for unequal pay.
12 This position is by no means unique to the early neoclassical economists. We find it expressed by the feminist Mill (1965, 1970) who argued against married women's employment, and by Marx (1967) and Engels (1968) who saw the

employment of married women as harmful to the living conditions and the autonomy of the working class.

13 Both Marshall (1930: 79–80, 524) and Pigou (1960: 32–3) prescribe the outright and unjustified exclusion of women's contribution from national income accounts (see Folbre 1991; Pujol 1992).

14 Similarly today feminist studies point out how much worse poverty statistics would be without women's income contribution.

15 Interestingly, one of Edgeworth's arguments in favor of the status quo is the "seriously deleterious" effect that "relieving the average house-father from the necessity of providing necessaries for his family . . . would remove a great part of his incentive to work" (1922: 453). It becomes clear, here, that constraining women to economic dependence on their husbands provides the further economic benefit to the nation (to capital) of increasing and stabilizing the male supply of labor.

16 This contradiction was acknowledged by Edgeworth (1922: 437).

17 See Pujol (1992) for a more detailed analysis of the approaches of Marshall, Edgeworth and Pigou to the issue of women's productivity and wages.

18 With thanks to Susan Feiner for this assessment.

19 See, for instance, Hartmann (1976), Phillips and Taylor (1980), Treiman and Hartmann (1981), England (1982), Bergmann (1986), Blau and Ferber (1986), Folbre and Hartmann (1988), Waring (1988), Ferber and Nelson (1993).

20 An important element of the different construction of women and men by the neoclassical economists lies in their assigned relationship to the market. See Grapard (1993) and Hewitson (1993).

21 Curiously, this is the only instance where women are allowed access to training (in home economics).

22 Here, we can see the close connection between the early neoclassical economists and the New Home Economics.

23 For a full discussion of these dichotomies, see Folbre and Hartmann (1988), McCrate (1991) and Nelson (1992, 1993).

## REFERENCES

Abbott, E.G. (1910) *Women in Industry*, New York: Appleton.

Barrett, M. and McIntosh, M. (1980) "The 'Family Wage': Some Problems for Socialists and Feminists", *Capital and Class* 11, Summer: 51–72.

Becker, G.S. (1973) "A Theory of Marriage: Part I", *Journal of Political Economy* July–August: 813–46.

———— (1976) "Altruism, Egoism and Genetic Fitness: Economics and Sociobiology", *Journal of Economic Literature* XIV, 3, September: 817–26.

———— (1981) "Altruism in the Family and Selfishness in the Market Place", *Economica* 48: 1–15.

———— (1981) *Treatise on the Family*, Cambridge, MA: Harvard University Press.

Bergmann, B. (1986) *The Economic Emergence of Women*, New York: Basic Books.

Blau, F. and Ferber, M. (1986) *The Economics of Women, Men, and Work*, Englewood Cliffs, NJ: Prentice-Hall.

Bodichon, B.L. Smith (1857) *Women and Work*, English edn, London: Bosworth and Harrison; reprinted in C.A. Lacey (ed.) (1987) *B.L. Smith Bodichon and the Langham Place Group*, New York/London: Routledge and Kegan Paul; American edn: with introduction by C.M. Sedgwick (1859), New York: C.S. Francis & Co.

Cadbury, E., Matheson, M.C., and Shann, G. (1906) *Women's Work and Wages, A*

*Phase of Life in an Industrial City*, American edn (1907), Chicago: University of Chicago Press.

Cannan, E. (1914) *Wealth, A Brief Explanation of the Causes of Economic Welfare*, London: P.S. King & Son.

Clark, A. (1919) *The Working Life of Women in the Seventeenth Century*, London: Routledge & Sons.

Edgeworth, F.Y. (1922) "Equal Pay to Men and Women for Equal Work", *Economic Journal* XXXII, December: 431–57.

———— (1923) "Women's Wages in Relation to Economic Welfare", *Economic Journal* XXXIII, December: 487–95.

Engels, F. (1968) *The Condition of the Working Class in England*, Stanford, CA: Stanford University Press.

England, P. (1982) "The Failure of Human Capital Theory to Explain Occupational Sex Segregation", *Journal of Human Resources* 17: 358–70.

Fawcett, M. Garrett (1892) "Mr. Sidney Webb's Article on Women's Wages", *Economic Journal* II, March: 173–6.

———— (1916) "The Position of Women in Economic Life", in W.H. Dawson (ed.) *After-War Problems*, London: Allen & Unwin.

———— (1918) "Equal Pay for Equal Work", *Economic Journal* XXVIII, March: 1–6.

Ferber, M. and Nelson, J. (eds) (1993) *Beyond Economic Man: Feminist Theory and Economics*, Chicago: University of Chicago Press.

Folbre, N. (1991) "The Unproductive Housewife: Her Evolution in Nineteenth Century Economic Thought", *Signs* 16, 3, Spring: 463–84.

Folbre, N. and Hartmann, H. (1988) "The Rhetoric of Self Interest: Ideology and Gender in Economic Theory", in A. Klamer, D. McCloskey, R. Solow (eds) *Consequences of Economic Rhetoric*, Cambridge: Cambridge University Press.

Grapard, U. (1993) "How to See the Invisible Hand, or from the Benevolence of the Butcher's Wife", paper presented at the conference "Out of the Margin. Feminist Perspectives on Economic Theory", Amsterdam, June.

Hartmann, H. (1976) "Capitalism, Patriarchy, and Segregation by Sex", *Signs* 1,3, Spring: 137–69.

Hartsock, N. (1983) *Money, Sex and Power*, Boston: North Eastern University Press.

———— (1991) "The Feminist Standpoint Revisited", paper presented at the International Political Science Association, Buenos Aires.

Heather-Bigg, A. (1894) "The Wife's Contribution to Family Income", *Economic Journal* IV, March: 51–8.

Hewitson, G. (1993) "Deconstructing Robinson Crusoe", paper presented at the conference "Out of the Margin. Feminist Perspectives on Economic Theory", Amsterdam, June.

Hill, G. (1896) *Women in English Life from Medieval to Modern Times*, London: R. Bentley.

Hogg, M.H. (1921) "Dependants on Women Wage Earners", *Economica* January: 69–86.

Hutchins, E. Leigh (1915) *Women in Modern Industry*, London: G. Bell.

Jevons, S. (1904) "Married Women in Factories", in *Methods of Social Reform and Other Papers*, London: Macmillan: 151–73.

Killingsworth, M.R. (1985) "The Economics of Comparable Worth: Analytical, Empirical and Policy Questions", in H. Hartmann (ed.) *Comparable Worth: New Directions for Research*, Washington, DC: National Research Council.

Land, H. (1979–80) *The Family Wage*, Eleanor Rathbone Memorial Lecture, Liverpool University Press.

McCrate, E. (1991) "Rationality, Gender and Domination", working paper,

Women's Studies Program and Department of Economics, University of Vermont.

McWilliams Tullberg, R. (1992) "Mary Paley Marshall, 1850–1944", unpublished.

Marshall, A. (1930) *Principles of Economics*, 8th edn reprinted, London: Macmillan; (1961) Guillebaud edn, London: Macmillan.

Marshall, M. Paley and Marshall, A. (1881) *The Economics of Industry*, 2nd edn, London: Macmillan.

Marx, K. (1967) *Capital*, vol. 1, New York: International Publishers.

Mill, J.S. (1965) "Principles of Political Economy, with some of their Applications to Social Philosophy", in J.M. Robson (ed.) *Collected Works of John Stuart Mill*, II and III, Toronto: University of Toronto Press.

——— (1970) "The Subjection of Women", in A.S. Rossi (ed.) *Essays on Sex Equality*, Chicago: University of Chicago Press.

Mincer, J. (1962) "Labor Force Participation of Married Women, A Study of Labor Supply", in *Aspects of Labor Economics*, Princeton, NJ: NBER.

Mincer, J. and Ofek, H. (1979) "The Distribution of Lifetime Labor Force Participation of Married Women", *Journal of Political Economy*, February.

Mincer, J. and Polachek, S. (1974) "Family Investment in Human Capital and the Earnings of Women", *Journal of Political Economy*, March–April.

——— (1978) "Women's Earnings Reexamined", *Journal of Human Resources*, Winter.

Nelson, J. (1992) "Gender, Metaphor and the Definition of Economics", *Economics and Philosophy*.

——— (1993) "The Study of Choice or the Study of Provisioning? Gender and the Definition of Economics", in M. Ferber and J. Nelson (eds) *Beyond Economic Man*, Chicago: University of Chicago Press.

Phillips, A. and Taylor, B. (1980) "Sex and Skill: Notes Towards a Feminist Economics", *Feminist Review* 6: 79–88.

Pigou, A.C. (1960) *The Economics of Welfare*, London: Macmillan.

Pinchbeck, I. (1981) *Women Workers and the Industrial Revolution, 1750–1850*, London: Virago.

Pujol, M. (1992) *Feminism and Anti-feminism in Early Economic Thought*, Aldershot: Edward Elgar.

Rathbone, E. (1917) "The Remuneration of Women's Services", *Economic Journal* XXVII, March: 55–68.

——— (1924) *The Disinherited Family, A Plea for the Endowment of the Family*, London: Edward Arnold & Co.

Rowntree-Seebohm, B. and Stuart, F.D. (1921) *The Responsibility of Women Workers for Dependants*, London: Clarendon Press.

Sandell, S.H. and Shapiro, D. (1978) "An Exchange: The Theory of Human Capital and the Earnings of Women: A Reexamination of the Evidence", *Journal of Human Resources*, Winter.

Schultz, T.W. (ed.) (1974) *Economics of the Family, Marriage, Children and Human Capital*, Chicago: University of Chicago Press.

Scott, J. and Tilly, L. (1978) *Women, Work and the Family*, New York: Holt Rinehart & Winston.

Smart, W. (1892) "Women's Wages", Proceedings of the Philosophical Society of Glasgow XXIII, 87–105, Glasgow: J. Smith & son.

Smith, E. (1915) *Wage-earning Women and their Dependants*, on behalf of the Executive Committee of the Fabian Women's Group, London: The Fabian Society.

Spelman, E. (1988) *Inessential Woman*, Boston: Beacon Press.

Strachey, R. (1969) *The Cause*, Port Washington, New York: Kennikat Press.

Strassman, D. and Polanyi, L. (1992) "Shifting the Paradigm: Value in Feminist Economics", unpublished paper presented at the first Conference of the International Association for Feminist Economics.

Taylor, Harriet (1970) "The Enfranchisement of Women", in Alice S. Rossi (ed.) *Essays on Sex Equality*, Chicago: University of Chicago Press.

Treiman, D. and Hartmann, H. (1981) *Women, Work and Wages: Equal Pay for Jobs of Equal Value*, Washington DC.

Waring, M. (1988) *If Women Counted*, San Francisco: Harper & Row.

Webb-Potter, B. (1914) "Personal Rights and the Woman's Movement, v. Equal Remuneration for Men and Women", *The New Statesman*, 1 August: 525–7.

—— (1919) "Minority Report", War Cabinet Committee on Women in Industry, Cmd 167.

# 2

# A HERETICAL VIEW OF ECONOMIC GROWTH AND INCOME DISTRIBUTION

*Frances Hutchinson*

## INTRODUCTION

The Douglas/New Age Social Credit economics popular throughout the English-speaking world in the inter-war years is consistent with many of the tenets of both institutionalist and feminist economics. Deriving from the work of Major C.H. Douglas and A.R. Orage (the guild socialist editor of the influential journal *New Age*) Social Credit explicitly considered the needs of women in both the formal and informal economies. In the Social Credit Movement attention to the economic status of women led directly to the advocacy of policies designed to liberate women from economic dependence on men. Not surprisingly, both the economic analyses and policy prescriptions of this school were anathema to virtually all other established social movements, Conservative, Liberal, and Radical. For in the perspective of the dominant political organizations, as in science more generally, "the idea of heresy and the independence of women were inextricably linked" (Noble 1992: 46).

The most influential schools of economics in the early part of this century were masculine in approach and deaf to the policy issues advocated by first wave feminists (Pujol 1992). In orthodox economic theory, for example, the only recognized actor is "the self-centered and self-interested utility maximizer" or Rational Economic Man (Lutz and Lux 1988: 97–100). *Homoeconomicus* is reared in the Cartesian nursery and matures in ontological suspended animation divorced from his social and natural environment (Hodgson 1992). Meanwhile, radical economic theory deriving from Marx posits the "belief that exploitation constitutes an inherent element of capitalist/worker relations" (Burkitt 1984: 3). Here the legitimate actor is the worker with the right and duty to engage in paid employment in order to feed his family. Each school pays attention to social institutions and gender roles only in so far as these are related either to paid employment in the material mode of production or to the choices made by individual agents in markets.

35

But for institutionalist or evolutionary economists (Waring 1989; Waller and Jennings 1990a, 1990b; Wheelock 1990; Hodgson 1992; Ekins and Max-Neef 1992; Hodgson, Samuels and Tool 1994) as for Major C.H. Douglas, the actor is the citizen whose economic motivations are heavily influenced by roles and learned behavior deriving from non-economic influences.

> The whole of society is in one sense part of the economy, in that all of its units, individual and collective, participate in the economy. Thus households, universities, hospitals, units of government, churches etc. are in the economy. But no concrete unit is purely economic.
> (Parsons and Smelser 1956, quoted in Ekins and Max-Neef 1992: 58)

Removing the emphasis on "productive" labor as primary justification for an income by the institutionalists opens the way to a theoretical framework which can include the forms of work traditionally undertaken by women in the informal economy. As we will see, this view was central to the policies advocated by Major Douglas.

## INSTITUTIONALISM AND SOCIAL CREDIT

Many women (and men) in the inter-war years recognized that the economics of the Douglas/New Age Social Credit Movement held the potential to improve the socio-economic status of women. Douglas is frequently classed as a heretical economist (King 1988), a member of the group who "operate outside and cut across the paradigm which guides orthodox analysis" (Dutton and King 1986) and have never "held an academic appointment in economics" (Gaitskell 1933)[1]. An engineer by profession, he had no pretensions to political power or academic recognition. His writings most closely accord with the American Institutionalist School. Veblen, an early proponent of that school, is frequently quoted by Douglas. Veblen rejected the "natural rights" approach to private property, i.e. the claim that the ownership of "productive" labor or "productive" capital gave a legitimate claim to its possession and to the ensuing flow of income deriving from it.

> This natural rights theory of property makes the creative effort of an isolated, self-sufficing individual the basis of ownership vested in him. In doing so it overlooks the fact that there is no isolated, self-sufficing individual . . . . Production takes place only in society – only through the co-operation of an industrial community. This industrial community may be large or small . . . but it always comprises a group large enough to contain and transmit the traditions, tools, technical knowledge, and usages without which there can be no industrial organization and no economic relation of individuals to one another or to their environ-

36

ment. . . . There can be no production without technical knowledge; hence no accumulation and no wealth to be owned, in severalty or otherwise. And there is no technical knowledge apart from an industrial community. Since there is no individual production and no individual productivity, the natural rights preconception . . . reduces itself to absurdity, even under the logic of its own assumptions.

(Veblen, quoted in Hunt 1979: 307–8)[2]

In similar vein, although without such stylistic clarity, Douglas argued that "production is 95 per cent a matter of tools and process, which tools and process form the cultural inheritance of the community" (Douglas 1919b: 95). This "cultural heritage" encompasses the whole process of "the progress of industrial arts" (a quote from Veblen used by Douglas) and "is the legacy of countless numbers of men and women, many of whose names are forgotten and the majority of whom are dead." The "proper legatees" are "the general community, as a whole." "No one person can be said to have a monopoly share . . . by any qualification of land, labor or capital" (Douglas 1919b: 49–50)[3].

Douglas and Veblen shared the view that the citizen was the sovereign actor. The economy could and should be consciously controlled by citizens within the non-economic context of the needs and values of society as a whole. In contrast, they saw the competitive motivation behind capitalist decision-making as predatory and parasitic. Competition of itself produced nothing but merely drew upon the technological innovations which created commodities. Invention was the product of the free play of "idle curiosity" and its development and use depended upon cooperative endeavor. Both rejected the prevailing orthodoxy that greed and the necessity to earn a subsistence living were essential prerequisites for cooperation in the economy. Freed from dependence on an income arising out of predation or paid employment, the engineer, the inventor, the artist and the citizen would be no less committed to participation in communal endeavor. Routine and unpleasant tasks could be inventively transformed through technology. The endurance of employment as a necessary evil arose, in Veblen's view, from acceptance of the ruling class ideology of patriotism, militarism and imperialism and from the treadmill of emulative consumption (consumerism) (Veblen 1899).

More recently Hodgson (1988: 249) has argued that "there are material preconditions for the existence of the economic agent that are subsumed or neglected in the orthodox approach." The utilitarian analysis is based on the untenable assumption that the opportunity to "choose, act, imagine, conjecture and be entrepreneurial is available to all: there are simply individual differences in ability, situation and knowledge." In reality, the necessity to meet basic needs on a hand-to-mouth basis radically limits the choices available to socio-economic actors in general and women in particular.

Before economic actors can choose and act, they must be fed, clothed, rested and healthy. The material preconditions for the existence of the economic agent are assumed and therefore discounted as relevant influences upon choice by economic orthodoxy. Like artists and engineers–indeed, as artists and engineers–women perform services which are essential to the continuation of society but which the formal economy does not directly recognize or reward. Douglas' heretical National Dividend proposals sought to create an equal base from which all citizens could communicate their wishes to the marketplace. These proposals were highly significant for women.

## SOCIAL CREDIT AND WOMEN: THE HISTORICAL CONTEXT

The Social Credit Movement offered "every woman a birthright income–i.e. the National Dividend on the productive capacity of the community to ensure economic independence and freedom." The arguments offered in support of such liberating policies echo the demands of many contemporary feminists. Like many advocates for women today, the Social Credit movement believed that women ought not to be:

1 Tied to the home when she wishes to live her own life;
2 Treated as a drudge, or as an inferior – i.e. the 'chattel' status;
3 Driven to marry for the sake of economic security;
4 Bound to some man who ill-treats her, or is in some other way unsuitable as a person to live with;
5 Driven to wage-work slavery in competition with men in order to keep alive.

(Hargrave 1945: 52)

In another prescient policy position Social Credit offered women equal pay for equal work:

1 Because a Social Credit Government will naturally stand for fair play for all citizens without distinction;
2 Because employers will no longer need 'cheap labor'; and
3 Because each individual woman will be able to say – 'If I do this job as well as a man could do it, I shall want the same pay as a man.' And if the employer says, 'No,' she will be able to say: 'Very well, I refuse the job. After all, I can live on my National Dividend.' This places every woman in a very powerful position. (It will apply equally, of course, to badly-paid male workers.)'

(Hargrave 1945: 53)

The Social Credit Movement articulated a clear and unequivocal commitment to economic security for women to be achieved through the establishment of equal treatment of women and men in waged employment. The difference between this position and the positions of all other economists in this period is quite stark.

Throughout the inter-war years Social Credit aroused powerful negative reactions in practically all established centers of male socio/economic power – among mainstream economists, socialists, communists, trade unionists, bankers and politicians of all parties. Dobb (1922) considered "the quack remedy of Douglasism" in the *Communist Review*, and the *New Statesman* (1922) took two long pages to explain the Fabian view that "the whole 'scheme' is moonshine, a preposterous fraud." Ramsey (1922) labelled Douglas "always obscure and often absurd" but deemed it appropriate to use the then novel tool of integral calculus to support his argument. The prestigious *Economic Journal* declaimed that "the Credit Power doctrinaires, like the Marxists, remain self-satisfied: the only matters that worry them are the obtuseness of the public, the contrariness of economists, and the 'psychology' of the bankers" (Biddulph 1932).

Marxists were angered by this and by Keynes' listing of Douglas alongside Marx in *The General Theory*. According to Keynes, Douglas was "a private perhaps, but not a major in the brave army of heretics" (Keynes 1936: 371). Hawtrey (1937) titled his chapter on Douglas "The Financial Misfit." Orage neatly summarized Labour opposition to Social Credit in the 1920s. The Webbs were, he said, "touched to their puritanic quick . . . [They would never] countenance a proposal to give every citizen a birthright income of an annual share of the communal production. [This would] make future social reforms unnecessary; and where would the Fabians be then, poor things?". In turn, G.B. Shaw "with his workhouse scheme of a universal dividend in return for a universal industrial service," was "silently contemptuous of Douglas" (Orage 1926: 404).

Had the Douglas/New Age texts lacked substance, not only the widespread support[4] but more particularly the frequency, length and vehemence of attacks would suggest an epidemic of irrationality. Evidence indicates the texts were closely perused by leading proponents of orthodoxy. Before launching into his "overkill" dismissal of Douglas, Ramsey cited "Mr. W.A. Orton, late of Christ's College" who "regards the Douglas-Orage analysis as the most searching critique of the existing order which has appeared" (Ramsey 1922). Hawtrey took Keynes to task for failing to acknowledge his debt to Douglas in his analysis of company sinking funds as a potential source of deflation, and claimed his own theory of depreciation as originating from Douglas (King 1988: 151). Meade has suggested Douglas led Keynes to his theory of demand management[5], and his own work on consumer credits (Meade 1936) and "Agathotopia" ("a good place to live in") (Meade 1989) is strongly reminiscent of the Douglas/New Age texts.

By the early 1930s Social Credit groups had sprung up throughout the UK. A review of advertisements in *The New Age* and *Social Credit* in 1934

39

and 1935 reveals that groups existed in Birmingham, Cardiff, Belfast, Manchester, London, Aberdeen, Oxford, Dublin and Glasgow. Even small towns like Keighley possessed their own Social Credit presses. Popular interest and support was so extensive that Gaitskell and Durbin established their reputations as socialist economists and became household names by touring the UK refuting the heresy (Durbin 1985)[6]. Despite the active opposition of virtually all powerful interests, however, Social Credit flourished. Douglas was invited to tour Canada, the United States, Australia, New Zealand and South Africa, giving rise to Social Credit movements in each country, to the establishment of political parties and to the formation of a Social Credit Government in Alberta in 1935 (Macpherson 1953; Irving 1959; Finlay 1972; Finkel 1989). Edith Douglas, an engineer in her own right, accompanied her husband and took an active role in meetings of established women's groups (Douglas 1937: 57; Irving 1959: 80). In the 1935 UK general election Social Credit candidates stood in Birmingham, Bradford and Leeds, achieving an average 9 per cent of the vote (*The New Age* (1935) 21 Nov 1935).

Evidence of women's enthusiasm for and active participation in the Social Credit Movement in the UK emerges from readers' letters to its major publications, *The New Age* and *Social Credit*, and from tantalizingly obscure advertisements for meetings: "Women actively interested in social problems and the abolition of poverty should read the Women's Section of Prosperity," says a notice in the 11 October 1934 issue of *The New Age*. Women's sections were formed in Central London, Shoreditch, Battersea, Deptford, Stockton-on-Tees and Rochdale, with nuclei of members in Coventry, Sheffield, Leeds, Edmonton, Preston and Blackburn (*Social Credit* and *The New Age* 1934–5).

Specific indications of women's active involvement are presented in the Canadian *Calgary Herald* (1934). Promotion of Social Credit in Alberta was centered on Aberhart's Bible Institute. The "conversion" to Social Credit of a number of women "leaders" caused "invitations for lectures on the new economics to pour into the Institute from women's groups in every corner of the city (Edmonton)" (Irving 1959: 68). "On January 17 a mass meeting of 700 women in the Institute voted unanimously to wire a resolution to the United Farm Women of Alberta, then in convention in Edmonton, to give its support to an investigation by the Alberta government of the Douglas System" (quoted by Irving from the *Calgary Herald*).

The principal speaker on this occasion, Mrs W.E. Callbeck, "claimed that since manual labor is being replaced by mechanization, work can no longer be the medium by which purchasing power may be distributed" (Irving 1959: 69). At the same meeting "Mrs W.W. Rogers outlined her work as women's organizer, and Aberhart (the charismatic leader of the movement in Canada) spoke briefly." Irving notes an announcement "typical of scores of others" inviting "women who are interested in economics" to a discussion of "the Douglas System of social credit." "Members of the economics groups of the University Women's Club, the Business and Professional Women's Club, and the women school teachers of this city are especially invited to attend." A series of classes was organized by Rogers, while women speakers promoted Social Credit at evening meetings in outlying towns and villages (Irving 1959: 70, 244–8).

By the outbreak of World War II, however, Social Credit had failed to secure a foothold in the enduring structures of the socio/political economy. The "informal financial-political club," representing forces which have "the same world view, aspire to similar goals and take concerted steps to attain them" (George 1988: 2) operated against the implementation of Social Credit legislation in Alberta (Douglas 1937). The enthusiasm and dedication of able campaigners was spent. The Social Credit Movement which had proved a substantial threat to class-socialism (Durbin 1985) and to the career prospects of (male) Labor politicians later faced the not entirely unfounded accusation of being a movement of the far right[7].

Women who studied the economics of the Social Credit Movement and campaigned for it in the inter-war years had accurately assessed its potential for improving the socio-economic status of women. Helen Corke rejected competition and "the economic philosophies of the Age of Scarcity" in which the weakest (predominantly women) were pushed to the wall in the rush for economic growth measurable in financial terms (Corke 1934). Although not a self-identified feminist, she offered a history of the evolution of the financial machinery which showed its connection to the continued economic subordination of women. Corke advocated a National Dividend for all "payable periodically and in equal shares to every citizen without respect to age, sex or other source of income, as his or her inalienable right," as well as increased leisure (Corke 1934). This was in close accord with Storm Jameson's eloquent plea for income security and for the conversion of economic activity from dictator to a tool in the formulation of social policy (Jameson 1935). If only for its innovative framing of these issues Social Credit remains a productive subject for contemporary feminist economic analysis.

## THE DOUGLAS ANALYSIS AND ECONOMIC DEMOCRACY

Douglas argued that the technological legacy of an advanced country offered the potential to meet the needs of all, women and men. Flaws in the financial system resulted in resources lying idle, even the destruction of products, while needs went unmet.

> Real (as opposed to economic) demand is the proper objective of pro-
> duction . . . there must first be a production of necessaries sufficient to

meet universal requirements; and, secondly, an economic system must be devised to ensure their practically automatic and universal distribution.

(Douglas 1919b: 90–2).

When these targets have been achieved, "manufacture of articles having a more limited range of usefulness" could follow if desired. "If finance cannot meet this simple proposition then finance fails, and will have to be replaced" (Douglas 1919b: 90–2). Throughout his writings Douglas questioned the legitimacy of the power of finance to determine the structure and distribution of production.

Douglas also challenged the work ethic, i.e. the necessity to engage in paid employment primarily for the purpose of securing an income (1919b: 49–51). Wage drudgery was not ennobling. The artificial stimulation of wants through advertising, the production of "a new model by a manufacturer . . . with the object . . . of rendering the old model obsolete before it is worn out," and the mountain of clerical work necessary to maintain the financial system, in the name of producing employment from which incomes could be derived, represented (even when Douglas wrote, at the end of World War I) "a stupendous waste of effort" (Douglas 1920).

As things stood in the early decades of the twentieth century, the technical means existed to "adapt the world's natural resources to the highest requirements of humanity" using "a very small fraction of the (labour) hours available" (Douglas 1919b: 65). Improvements in technological processes offered the option of increased leisure as an alternative to the quest for a constant growth in production[8]. However, such an option could not become available under the existing system of financing production and distribution. Furthermore, under this system, labor-saving technology looked increasingly capable of depriving citizens of incomes by throwing them out of work.

The only winners under such circumstances were those who appropriated profit through their control of financial credit. According to Douglas and others in the Social Credit Movement the root of the problem lay in the fact that:

the existing economic system distributes goods and services through the same agency which induces goods and services, i.e. payment for work in progress . . . if production stops, distribution stops, and, as a consequence, a clear incentive exists to produce useless or superfluous articles in order that useful commodities already existing may be distributed.

(Douglas 1919b: 85)

Control of production and distribution, Douglas argued, was currently exercised by the financial system. Decisions about future production and the distribution of current output amongst citizens depended upon a complex interplay of financial mechanisms focussing upon short term outcomes. None of these mechanisms were divinely ordained, and all reflected the central motivating power of competitive greed (Douglas 1919b: 82).

Central planning by the state was not the answer. Anticipating Galbraith (1967) Douglas predicted that a combination of finance, technology and the "will to power" would inevitably create massive organizations ("pyramids of power") to direct from the top downwards the planning necessary to maintain production in this form. Whether the technostructure was in private hands or directly state controlled was irrelevant; the preferences of the citizen-consumer could be respected only through decentralization of the finance and production of each industry on a regional basis (Douglas 1919a, 1920: appendix).

## SOCIAL CREDIT

Douglas' complex remedies and his convoluted writing style led to the confusion of the terms "Social Credit" by which the movement became known and "National Dividend" which constituted the activists' main demand. "Social Credit," a complicated set of propositions, encompassed the mechanism of the Just Price (not the medieval version) through which those aspects of pricing relating to purely financial costs (as opposed to real costs of production) were eliminated. The concept of the Just Price was that it was price sufficient to allow consumer demand, rather than the requirements of creating (future) financial profits, to regulate production. Based upon the ratio of changing patterns of demand to future supply capacity, the Just Price would also remove the element of financial speculation[9].

Exploration of the relationship between finance and material production is central to the Douglas texts. The initiation of production is controlled by credit issue[10]. According to Douglas, the faith or "credit" which provides the motive power for the economy can be divided into two categories: "financial credit" and "real credit." "'Financial credit' is simply an estimate of the capacity to pay money." It is the driving force behind the creation of loan credit, and is generated by the banking system (Douglas 1922: 52–3). Douglas observed that bank loans constitute newly created money, not "old" money which has been saved (Canadian House of Commons, Canada 1923). Purchasing power is created on financial criteria. Producers of goods can borrow money if they are also potential producers of money. Hence under orthodoxy, financial viability determines choices even though needs go unmet while resources lie idle.

"Real credit" in contrast "is a measure of the effective reserve of energy belonging to the community. The banking system has been allowed to

43

become the administrator of this credit and its financial derivatives with the result that the creative energy of mankind has been subjected to fetters which have no relation whatever to the real demands of existence" (Douglas 1919b: 118).

Douglas argued that potential wealth in society (i.e. real credit) is communal in origin and should therefore belong to the entire community. Under orthodoxy financial credit is administered by the banking system "primarily for the purpose of private profit, whereas it is most definitely communal property" (Douglas 1919b: 118) or "social credit." Hence orthodox finance directs attention to short-run profitability and severs the connection between social needs and social production.

The capitalist financial system facilitates production and distribution of goods only incidentally, as an adjunct to its primary *raison d'être*, to secure a title to a share of those goods and services (the "real credit" of the community) through the agency of interest payments. Credit issued in the present period enables a producer to prepare for future production by purchasing goods and services. The producer must sell goods in the future period at a sufficiently high price to cover not only the original credit issued but also the interest payments on the debt. Since the credit issued to the producer has already been spent (on goods produced in a preceding period), fresh credit must now be issued to this producer (or some other producer in order that the new goods can be purchased on the market. If interest payments are to be met, a greater volume of credit must be issued at an increasing rate. The recurring cycles of debt creation and repayment with interest require a constant growth in the overall economy if it is to function effectively[11].

In view of the trade cycle problems of the inter-war years, Douglas was assumed to be proposing solutions to those problems. This was not the case. *Economic Democracy*, published in 1919, before the post-war depression set in, contains all the analysis which later appealed to social creditors. Economic growth requires a constant expansion not only of production but more particularly of consumption, where "consumption" is defined as "purchase on the market with the use of money." Eating of food grown in an allotment meets a basic need, but is not "consumption." To sustain growth, capitalist finance looks with particular favor on three types of enterprise:

1 Production of goods which need to be continually replaced due to planned obsolescence or changes in fashion stimulated by advertising and salesmanship, most notably armaments and motor cars.
2 Deliberately wasteful production, including disposable packaging and throw-away clothing.
3 The creation of new "wants" and artificial scarcities, including convenience foods, travel, and the patenting of human, plant and animal life forms.

(Douglas 1918, 1919b; Mishan 1967; Shiva 1993)

Shortages of money do not necessarily imply any shortage of resources, whether land, labor or capital. For Douglas the relevant question was not "Where is the money to come from?," it was rather "What is money?[12]".

## FROM NATIONAL DEBT THROUGH NATIONAL ASSET TO NATIONAL DIVIDEND

Douglas observed that at the outset of World War I the money with which to fight did not exist[13]. The government faced two options:

1 To create the paper money necessary to purchase ammunition and supplies, and to meet the soldiers' wages.
2 To create money on paper via the existing financial system based on the creation of "credit."

The government selected the latter option. Therefore, through a complicated series of paper transactions, "loans" were secured from individuals and institutions to finance the war. These "loans" did not represent any consumption foregone. Nevertheless, by the end of the war the National Debt had risen from about £660m in August 1914 to about £7,700m in December 1919 (Douglas 1924: 135). This loan, which held a claim to interest at 4–6 per cent from the public purse, "simply represents communal credit transferred to private account" (Douglas 1919b: 119–24).

The phenomenon was significant on two counts. First, it established the principle of payment of an unearned income from the state, unrelated to work record or to any other tangible contribution to the formal economy. This principle had already been established by the payment of Old Age Pensions from 1908, being "in effect nothing other than a system of National or Communal Dividends, in that the right to receive an Old Age Pension is based on membership of the Community alone, and not on work done or services rendered" (Hattersley 1922: 103). Second, the unearned income from the National Debt was drawn against the future production of society as a whole. It followed that there could be no logical objection to the principle of paying a National Dividend to all citizens regardless of age, sex or employment status on the basis of the "real" or "social" credit built up in the past and arising from the common cultural heritage.

Such payments would involve the conversion of the National Debt to a National Asset. The state should lend rather than borrow, and use the interest earned on its loans to pay the National Dividend (House of Commons, Canada 1923; Douglas 1919b: 119–33). Meade's "Topsy-Turvy Nationalisation" is based on precisely the same premise (Meade 1989)[14].

## CONCLUSIONS AND CURRENT CONSIDERATIONS

Women social creditors of the inter-war years are the forgotten pioneers of a concept of economic citizenship which has a positive role for both women and men. The social credit concept of an income distribution system based purely on the common cultural inheritance offers women equality with men in determining the terms of their consent for participation in the public and private spheres of economic activity (Pateman 1989: 9). Indeed, the flaws in the contemporary quest for gender equality through an economic citizenship (Lister 1989) based entirely on ability to earn a wage (Pateman 1988) were anticipated by the Social Credit Movement. As O'Duffy (1932) and Munson (1934) demonstrated, equal rights access to waged employment by no means guarantees that employment will be made available. In many ways the "civil right" (Twine 1992) to an income for all citizens encompassed by the National Dividend proposals of the inter-war years was more soundly based than the elusive "civil opportunity" (Twine 1992) to earn an equal wage (with its accompanying pension and insurance coverage). Equality of opportunity in earning power between men and women would seem to require a revolution in economic theory and practice of far more radical proportions than those proposed by social creditors.

A basic or "Citizen's" Income based purely on the redistribution of the incomes of those in work (Parker 1989, 1993) would also require a seachange in political attitudes, however cogently arguments in favor were presented. While a partial income from a National Dividend might be supported by a partial income from transfer payments as Meade (1989) suggests, a Citizen's Income of subsistence proportions based wholly on tax transfer would require a prohibitive income tax rate of 70 per cent (Parker 1989). A Douglas National Dividend is not divisive: it does not involve a transfer of wealth from one section of the community (e.g. those in business or employment) to another section (e.g. those who are classed as "idle"). Labor is not penalized by high rates of taxation, neither is the payment of a National Dividend dependent upon the artificial generation of wasteful consumption in the name of wealth creation and economic growth[15]. On the contrary, a National Dividend based upon social credit would provide the foundations for a conflict-free economy (Smith 1962) characterized by gender equality and environmental sustainability.

The "deconstruction of employment status" and "the conversion of waged work into an activity which is genuinely optional for everyone" (Purdy 1988: 219–29) would have a number of salutary effects on the economy. One might well be a diminution in the number of women forced into low status, low-paid work under poor employment conditions. At the very least women's role in supporting the economic system through unpaid and low-paid work would be made explicit. A renegotiation of the domestic division of labor becomes more, not less, likely with minimal income security for each member of the household. The proposal also possesses the potential to alleviate poverty within families, which occurs when well-paid fathers/husbands refuse to share their incomes with children/wives (Bannerman and Wilson 1987). Once male claims to be occupied in securing a "family" wage hold no further justification, women's role in the creation and recreation of what Hirsch has termed the "pre-market social ethos" (Hirsch 1976), upon which the very existence of the market economy depends, will become apparent.

Money is a man-made commodity. Hence the question "where is the money to come from?" becomes redundant and policy formation must encompass the engineering of financial structures designed to prioritize social need and minimize economic conflict. Feminist approaches to economic theory and policy will be enhanced through closer scrutiny of the communal regulation of finance and the payment of a National Dividend. The range of effects of such heretical policies upon the national and international socio-economic environments should keep economists, feminists and others, fully employed for the foreseeable future.

## NOTES

1 See, especially, King (1988) on heretics: they "ask embarrassing questions, investigate problems which are not generally accepted as legitimate, and provide answers which rely on unusual concepts, unfamiliar reasoning and inadmissable evidence" (Dutton and King 1986).

2 As Veblen's writing "cannot be recaptured by paraphrasing" (Hunt 1979: 300) I use extensive quotes throughout.

3 Page numbers refer to most recent editions as these are more generally available (see references).

4 Apart from the Canadian phenomenon, documentation of popular support for Social Credit is sparse. Evidence is emerging of dynamic movements in Australia and New Zealand (Pullen and Smith 1991) and the US (Generoso 1981).

5 In conversation with the author.

6 Between them, Gaitskell and Durbin wrote extensively in refutation of Social Credit, including Gaitskell (1933) and Durbin (1933a, 1933b).

7 Although Douglas was an outspoken opponent of fascism, Social Credit's opposition to usury was attractive to anti-semitic elements (Finlay 1972: 176–9). Further, Ezra Pound was a well-known proponent of Social Credit and his wartime association with Italian fascism colored perceptions of the movement.

8 Social creditors used the term "leisure" to mean time for cultural, artistic, inventive and socially responsible activities, as distinct from mere idleness and relaxation from enforced "productive" labor.

9 Douglas drew attention to the discrepancy between economic theory and practice. In theory consumer preferences operated through the mechanisms of demand and price to determine supply. In reality demand was regulated through advertising and artificially generated scarcity.

10 That is, production is debt driven. For a history of money creation mechanisms see Niggle (1990).

11 This aspect of the Douglas texts was drawn upon by Foster and Catchings (1925). See also Mehta (1983) for a more detailed exploration of this section of Douglas economics.

12 Douglas focussed attention on the financial foundations of the industrial system. As Galbraith (1975: 29) more recently noted, "The process by which banks create money is so simple the mind is repelled. Where something so important is involved, a deeper mystery seems only decent". As both observers realized, a bank loan creates a (new) deposit (and hence new spending power) without diminishing any existing deposit.

13 Hostilities commenced, foolishly in Douglas' view. The Major was no war-monger and his outspoken opposition to militarism lost him the support of a large section of the male community.

14 Meade had read Douglas as a young man in the early 1920s, before embarking upon his distinguished career as an orthodox economist (conversation with the author).

15 For an exploration of alternative indicators of economic progress see Ekins (1986) Chapter 6. Environmentally and socially destructive activities are con-ventionally registered as an increase in GNP.

# REFERENCES

Bannerman, J. and Wilson, G. (eds) *Give and Take in Families: Studies in Resource Distribution*, London: Allen and Unwin.

Biddulph, G. (1932) "The Monopoly of Credit Review", *The Economic Journal* XLII, June: 268–70.

Burkitt, B. (1984) *Radical Political Economy*, London: Harvester.

Corke, H. (1934) *A Short Course in Economic History*, London: Stanley Nott.

Dobb, M.H. (1922) "Does the World Need More Money?", *Communist Review*: 29–41.

Douglas, C.H. (1918) "Delusions of Super-Production", *English Review*: 428–32.

—————— (1919a) "The Pyramid of Power", *English Review* 28: 49–58, 100–107.

—————— (1919b) *Economic Democracy*, Sudbury: Bloomfield (1974 edn).

—————— (1920) *Credit-Power and Democracy*, London: Cecil Palmer.

—————— (1922) *The Control and Distribution of Production*, London: Stanley Nott (1934 edn).

—————— (1924) *Social Credit*, Vancouver: Institute of Economic Democracy (1979 edn).

—————— (1937) *The Alberta Experiment: An Interim Survey*, London: Eyre and Spottis-woode.

Durbin, E.F.M. (1933a) *Purchasing Power and Trade Depression*, London: Chapman Hall.

—————— (1933b) *Socialist Credit Policy*, London: New Fabian Research Bureau.

—————— (1985) *New Jerusalems: The Labour Party and the Economics of Democratic Socialism*, London: Routledge and Kegan Paul.

Dutton, H.I. and King, J.E. (1986) "A Private Perhaps but not a Major", *History of Political Economy* 18, 2: 259–79.

*The Ecologist* (1992) "Whose Common Future", 22.4, July–August (special issue).

Ekins, P. (ed.) (1986) *The Living Economy*, London and New York: Routledge and Kegan Paul.

Ekins, P. and Max-Neef, M. (eds) (1992) *Real Life Economics: Understanding Wealth Creation*, London: Routledge.

Finkel, A. (1989) *The Social Credit Movement in Alberta Toronto*, Toronto: University of Toronto Press.

Finlay, J.L. (1972) *Social Credit: The English Origins*, Montreal and London: McGill Queens University Press.

Foster, W.F. and Catchings, W. (1925) *Money*, Boston: Houghton Mifflin.

Gaitskell, H.T.N. (1933) "Four Monetary Heretics", in G.D.H. Cole (ed.) *What Everybody Wants to Know About Money*, London: Gollancz.

Galbraith, J.K. (1967) *The New Industrial Estate*, London: Penguin.

—— (1975) *Money: Whence It Came and Where It Went*, London: Penguin.

Generoso, J. (1981) "Social Credit 1918–1945: with special reference to the American contributors", mimeo.

George, S. (1988) *A Fate Worse Than Debt*, London: Penguin.

Hargrave, J. (1945) *Social Credit Clearly Explained*, London: SCP.

Hattersley, C.M. (1922) *The Community's Credit*, London: Credit Power Press.

Hawtrey, R.G. (1937) *Capital and Employment*, London: Longman. (The chapter on Douglas was omitted from the 1952 edition.)

Hirsch, F. (1976) *Social Limits to Growth*, Cambridge, MA: Harvard University Press.

Hodgson, G.M. (1988) *Economics and Institutions*, London: Polity Press.

—— (1992) "Rationality and the Influence of Institutions", in P. Ekins and M. Max-Neef (eds) *Real Life Economics*, London: Routledge.

Hodgson, G.M., Samuels, W.J. and Tool, M.R. (eds) (1994) *Elgar Companion to Institutional and Evolutionary Economics*, Aldershot: Edward Elgar.

House of Commons, Canada (1923) *Proceedings of Select Standing Committee on Banking and Commerce*, Ottawa.

Hunt, E.K. (1979) *History of Economic Thought: A Critical Perspective*, New York: Wadsworth.

Irving, J.A. (1959) *The Social Credit Movement in Alberta*, Toronto: Toronto University Press.

Jameson, S. (1935) *The Soul of Man in the Age of Leisure*, London: Stanley Nott.

Keynes, J.M. (1936) *The General Theory of Employment, Interest and Money*, London: Macmillan.

King, J.E. (1988) *Economic Exiles*, London: Macmillan.

Lister, R. (1989) *The Female Citizen*, Liverpool: Liverpool University Press.

Lutz, M.A. and Lux, K. (1988) *Humanistic Economics*, New York: Bootstrap Press.

Macpherson, C.B. (1953) *Democracy in Alberta*, Toronto: Toronto University Press.

Meade, J.E. (1936) *An Introduction to Economic Analysis and Policy*, Toronto: Toronto University Press.

—— (1989) "Agathotopia: The Economics of Partnership", *Hume Paper* 16, Aberdeen: Aberdeen University Press.

Mehta, G. (1983) "The Douglas Theory: A New Interpretation", *Indian Journal of Economics* 64: 121–9.

Mishan, E.J. (1967) *The Costs of Economic Growth*, London: Staple.

Munson, G.B. (1933) "The Douglasites", *Commonweal* 18, 13 October: 551–3.

—— (1934) "Social Credit: The Economics of Tomorrow", *Independent Woman* (USA) June: 161, 182.

*New Statesman* (1922) "Editorial", 18 February: 552–4.

Niggle, C.J. (1990) "The Evolution of Money, Financial Institutions and Monetary Economics", *Journal of Economic Issues* XXIV, 2: 443–50.

Noble, D. (1992) *A World Without Women: A History of the Christian Clerical Culture of Western Science*, Oxford: Oxford University Press.

O'Duffy, E. (1932) "Life and Money", London and New York: Putnam.

Orage, A.R. (1926) "An Editor's Progress. Part 2", *Commonweal* 17 February, 3: 402–4.

Parker, H. (1989) *Instead of the Dole: An Enquiry into Integration of the Tax and Benefit Systems*, London: Routledge.

—————— (ed.) (1993) *Citizen's Income and Women*, London: Citizens Income.

Parson, T. and Smelser, N. (1956) *Economy and Society: A Study in the Integration of Economic and Social Theory*, London: Routledge and Kegan Paul.

Pateman, C. (1988) "The Patriarchal Welfare State", in A. Gutman (ed.) *Democracy and the Welfare State*, Princeton, NJ: Princeton University Press.

—————— (1989) *The Disorder of Women*, Cambridge: Polity Press.

Pujol, M.A. (1992) *Feminism and Anti-feminism in Early Economic Thought*, Aldershot: Edward Elgar.

Pullen, J.M. and Smith, G.O. (1991) "Major Douglas and the Banks", paper presented to History of Economic Thought Society, Australia, Monash University.

Purdy, D. (1988) *Social Power and the Labour Market*, London: Macmillan.

Ramsey, F.P. (1922) "The Douglas Proposals", *Cambridge Magazine* 11: 74–6.

Shiva, V. (1993) *Monocultures of the Mind*, London: Zed Books.

Smith, H. (1962) *The Economics of Socialism Reconsidered*, Oxford: Oxford University Press.

Twine, F. (1992) "Citizenship: Opportunities, Rights and Routes to Welfare in Old Age", *Journal of Social Policy* 21, 2: 165–75.

Veblen, T. (1899) *Theory of the Leisure Class*, New York: Macmillan.

Waller, W. and Jennings, A. (1990a) "On the Possibility of a Feminist Economics: The Convergence of Institutional and Feminist Methodology", *Journal of Economic Issues* XXIV, 2, June: 611–22.

—————— (1990b) "Constructions of Social Hierarchy: The Family, Gender and Power", *Journal of Economic Issues* XXIV, 2: 623–31.

Waring, M. (1989) *If Women Counted: A New Feminist Economics*, London: Macmillan.

Wheelock, J. (1990) *Husbands at Home*, London: Routledge.

# 3

# VARIETIES OF DEPRIVATION

## Comments on chapters by Pujol and Hutchinson

### *Amartya K. Sen*

The remarkable development of feminist economics in recent years is informed by the recognition of inequities, suffered by women, of three quite different types:

1 *material deprivation*, deep-seated and far-reaching gender inequalities, which affect the economic lives of women, in the real world;
2 *political disempowerment*, the *de facto* (and often *de jure*) derogation of women's authority in public and private decision-making processes which reinforces material deprivation;
3 *theoretical degradation*, the neglect or distortion of women's position and contribution in the world of theory – including economic theory.

These three issues are distinct but interrelated. Women's opportunities to influence the ideas and interpretations that claim to characterize and assess the real world have been restricted by the limitations of women's power and decisional authority in that world. On the other side, the tolerance and survival of material inequalities are aided by distortions in theory, which tend to obscure the nature and extent of that deprivation as well as its causation. Indeed, even our comprehension and awareness of material deprivation is inevitably linked with the theoretical framework employed to understand and interpret the world.

These relationships are important to bear in mind in discussing contributions to pure theory, as these chapters clearly are, presented at the first international conference dedicated to "feminist perspectives on economic theory." These contributions to economic theory must be seen in the light of the nature and variations in inequality in the world in which women and men live.

## SOCIAL CREDIT AND GENDER-NEUTRAL FREEDOM

Frances Hutchinson's (1994) analysis begins by separating "institutionalist" economics from mainstream "orthodox economic theory" and from "radical economic theory deriving from Marx." She concentrates on the

51

specific institutional approach pioneered by Major Douglas (1918, 1920), which in turn relates to earlier works by Veblen (1899). The "social credit" approach to economics is indeed an important example of nonconformist radicalism, and Hutchinson presents a broadly sympathetic account of this movement and its relevance for feminist economics today.

The deprivation with which Hutchinson is especially concerned relates to the misery and subservience of women – as well as of underprivileged men – resulting from having to decide on important matters of living in the absence of the freedom to turn down unjust, unacceptable proposals. In the social credit approach the need for the life-shaping decisions of women and men to be based on freedom, and not just forced by inescapable necessity, was emphasized. The Social Credit Movement advocated a "national dividend" which would come to all by virtue of citizenship, rather than the work/wage contract or the private ownership of finance or capital.

Hargrave (1945), a great exponent of the social credit approach, explained how potential employees would be able to reject exploitative or unjust arrangements because of the security of the national dividend. (As Hutchinson quotes Hargrave, faced with an unfair proposal, the job seeker could respond: "Very well, I refuse the job. After all, I can live on my National Dividend.") The implications of social credit arrangements for the freedom of women are explored by Hutchinson. It eliminates, for example, the necessity to marry for the sake of economic security, to be driven to "wage-work slavery" in very unfavorable terms because of the sheer necessity of survival, and so on. She also compares the different versions of these claims (including mixed systems exemplified by James Meade's 1989 proposal for "Agathotopia"), and outlines the advantages of an approach of this kind in securing economic justice – for both women and men.

Frances Hutchinson is particularly critical of the financial control of the world of production and distribution of real commodities, and concentrates on lifting, as it were, "the veil of money." She shares the view that "the capitalist financial system facilitates production and distribution only incidentally." However, on these matters she does not develop her arguments in any detail, and it is hard to assess her fairly comprehensive skepticism of any productive role of finance in the modern capitalist economy.

Hutchinson's analysis of real production disputes the view that claims to shares of the national product should relate to contributions to production. Instead citizenship is seen as the correct basis of claims to income. Claims of labor power are also undermined by Douglas' argument that "production is 95 per cent a matter of tools and processes." The claims of the private owners of means of production are similarly dismissed by Douglas' proposition that "tools and process form the cultural inheritance of the community." Such an inheritance legitimizes the claims of citizens since the productive resources do not really belong either to the nominal owners (capital is the "inheritance of the community"), or to the workers (whose entitlements relate to their citizenship, not to their work).

The system of ethical economics that Hutchinson explores, following the social credit tradition, has many attractive features. The question that remains largely unaddressed is, of course, the old one of incentives. This issue is so often discussed that it is easy to understand Hutchinson's reluctance to go into it. But the ethical system that underlies the social credit approach can be viable only if the incentive compatibility of these arrangements is adequately established. "Very well, then, I too won't work and will live on the National Dividend," is an option open to all. But if it came from everyone, the National Dividend must inescapably dwindle (even with the productive promise of the communal inheritance of tools and processes).

To make headway in pursuing the attractive arrangements in the Douglas-Hutchinson line we need a serious exploration of the psychology of work – in particular whether and to what extent people can be expected to work even with a guaranteed National Dividend. This is, of course, a classic issue which Marx (1875) addressed in the *Critique of Gotha Programme* where he came to the pessimistic conclusion that there was little hope of this until a different cultural ethos emerged in a much later – and greatly more prosperous – "higher stage of communism." Although Hutchinson does not discuss this literature, Maurice Dobb's critique of the realism of the social credit approach as well as the criticisms of Bernard Shaw and the Webbs are speedily dismissed. But no matter what we think of the extant literature on incentives – whether coming from traditional or radical quarters – economists need to address the issues of motivation, inducement, and the related problems of the psychology of work and investment.

## WOMEN IN TRADITIONAL ECONOMIC THOUGHT

Michèle Pujol's essay follows her forceful book, *Feminism and Anti-feminism in Early Economic Thought* (1992) and is specifically concerned with early neoclassical economics, though she also makes many interesting remarks on authors who cannot really be classified as neoclassical economists (including David Ricardo, John Stuart Mill, and Karl Marx). Pujol notes the tendency towards "the erasure of women and feminists" within the neoclassical paradigm, and more explicitly, the dismissal of methodological critiques of that paradigm from "voices of dissent." She presents arguments against each of these tendencies.

Pujol points out that the presence of women in the world is often not noticed by economic theorists. For example, David Ricardo gave every evidence of believing "that only one gender populates the planet." But, Pujol argues, even in so far as women are accommodated within these formulations, the characterization of women, especially in neoclassical economics, takes an oddly reductionist and heavily stereotyped form. She identifies misdescriptions of women's roles by acknowledged stalwarts of the neoclassical tradition; Jevons, Marshall, Edgeworth, Pigou, and others. Pujol uses their own words to indicate prejudices of these great authors against women. She also cites authors (mostly women – including Barbara Leigh Smith Bodichon, Millicent Garrett Fawcett, Beatrice Potter Webb, and others) who have argued against these views and their supposed policy implications. There is much of interest and importance in all this, and the reader may well be inspired to go on to read her book (Pujol 1992).

## VARIETIES OF DEPRIVATION

As an academic in a man's world, Pujol recollects receiving "daily confirmation of one's incongruous presence from one's (male) colleagues," and she goes on to invoke Jill McCalla Vicker's (1982) pithy term "ontological exile" as an experience she has had over a quarter of a century. She also makes clear that she speaks "as a woman, as a feminist, as a lesbian, and as a survivor within the discipline of economics." Pujol's experiences as well as her commitments help her to throw light on the standard characterization of women in neoclassical economics – indeed in other economic traditions as well.

Women suffer from many different deprivations, and there is room for distinct types of feminist analyses with diverse concentrations. It is no criticism of Pujol's work that her focus is very firmly on iniquities which have had a big impact on her own life and on problems she has had the opportunity to observe at close quarters. The merits of Pujol's work are clear enough, but different types of deprivations may call for a more pluralist approach.

There are issues of inequality and injustice even for those women who happen to fulfil the characteristics of the stereotype that Pujol rejects– rightly–as universal generalizations. While some women are not married, many are. Numerous women across the world are economically dependent, without any significant choice in this respect. Many have no option but to lead the life of housewives and to concentrate on rearing children and looking after others. Just as it is important to reject the false claim that these stereotyped characteristics apply to *all* women (a task that Michèle Pujol performs with much efficiency), it is also necessary to study the causal influences that operate on the lives of those women whose predicament actually includes those features.

There are criticisms to be made of received economic theories from the perspective of these deprivations as well, for the failure of the theoretical formulations to explore adequately the nature, genesis, antecedents and mutability of these features. These explorations would call for a different focus from Pujol's (for example, concentrating much more on inequalities in intra-family distributions of benefits and chores, and related issues of gender inequality). Feminist thought can be useful in analyzing deprivations of different kinds, and in establishing the diverse inadequacies of traditional theory (including *inter alia* the lack of interest in identifying and explaining these substantive inequalities)[1].

The specialized focus of Pujol's concentration is well illustrated by her evident belief that "at most only 48 per cent of the population" is male. Unless she is referring specifically to Europe and North America, this is factually not the case. (It must, however, be emphasized that this fact does not affect, in any substantial way, Pujol's critical argument that the alleged "laws of economics" would have "a major flaw" if they were to apply only to males; it is not material for that argument whether males constitute 48 per cent or 51 per cent of the world population.) The issue is of interest because the fact of "missing women" points to the underlying excess mortality of women *vis-à-vis* men in many parts of the world, despite medical reasons to expect exactly the opposite. Here too traditional economic theory may fail to note, explain or assess the corresponding substantial deprivation of women. But the failure of neoclassical economics in this respect is very different from the transgressions on which Pujol concentrates. The challenge, in this particular case, is to construct an adequate theory of inequalities *within* the household that applies even to the division of food, medical care and other vital resources on which the battle for competing entitlements may be intense in poor societies.

Given the medical evidence in favor of higher survival rates of women when symmetric care is received by females and males (even females fetuses seem to be less prone to miscarriage than their male counterparts), an extremely grave problem of female deprivation is implicit in the cold statistics that for every 100 men in the world, there are only about 98 women (in contrast with the much higher ratio of women in Europe and North America, on which Pujol's generalization is based). China and India currently have ratios around 0.93 or 0.94, and in some countries the female–male ratio is as low as 0.91. The economic and social causation that leads to unnaturally higher mortality of women in many societies can be – and has been – analyzed (leading to estimates of "missing women" ranging from 60 million to more than 100 million), and they suggest the urgent need for political action and policy initiatives[2]. This is just one illustration of the variety of problems that feminist economics can fruitfully address, and it indicates the need for a plurality of approaches in the reconstruction of economic theory.

## GENDER INEQUALITY AND OTHER DEPRIVATIONS

Aside from the variety of forms that gender inequalities can take, there is a need to consider the relationship between gender iniquities and other forms of disparities and injustices. This is important for various reasons, including the tremendous privation that is forced on people who fall in the intersection of different categories of deprivation. For example, women of unprivileged classes have a very much worse predicament in many societies compared with both (a) women from other classes, and (b) men from the unprivileged classes[3]. Also, causal analyses of different types of deprivations have many interlinkages – for example, the contingent use of similar ideologies to justify the prevalent inequalities, of gender as well as class.

There are similar issues of interrelation between gender iniquities and those related to race. For example, even though newspaper discussions in dealing with excess mortality of African Americans tend to concentrate on the greater incidence of death from violence of young black men, there is evidence that in the settled age group of 35 to 54 years, the excess mortality of black women in America compared with white women is much greater than that of black men *vis-à-vis* white men (in fact, for black men the mortality rate is 1.8 times higher than for whites, whereas for black women it is nearly three times larger)[4].

Similarly, the casualties of severe economic reforms in east Europe and the former Soviet Union, without much benefit of a "social security" net, have created specially unfavorable predicaments for women in these regions, even compared with the general destitution that has affected men as well[5]. These deprivations can be understood by combining gender-related analysis with investigations of other causes and sources of economic distress.

There are also occasions when the different categories of inequality can be in some tension with each other. A good illustration concerns the debates surrounding the complex issue of "family wages." In the context of gender relations, the very idea of a "family wage" – sought by male workers – may appear to be iniquitous and arbitrary, as it clearly does to Pujol, who goes on to note that "the feminists point out the necessity of women's employment as a source of economic support for themselves and others, thereby challenging the 'family wage' and 'pin money' doctrines." Indeed, women obviously have as much legitimacy in seeking jobs and incomes as men have, so that the burden of earning a "family wage" need not be seen as a specially male obligation. But despite that fundamental point, in the long historical battle for raising exploitatively low remunerations in ill-paid industrial work, the insistence of labor movements on an adequate "family wage" has often acted as an important and positive force (in the contingent circumstances in which the ratio of males to females in industrial employment was very high, and the actual opportunities of female employment very limited). In seeking more gender justice today, we must not overlook the historic battles against iniquities of other – very different – kinds[6]. More generally, the important concern about gender inequalities has to be integrated with similar attention to other types of inequalities which coexist.

## CONCLUDING REMARKS

To conclude, deprivations can take many different forms. Some relate to gender, while others flow from class, race and other characteristics of women and men. Even deprivations related to gender can be of many distinct types. Critiques of traditional economic theory, including those of "theoretical degradation" of women, must ultimately take adequate note of the varieties of deprivation. This is not an argument for slackening the force of the critique of particular deprivations presented from specific angles, and there are excellent reasons to be grateful for what Michèle Pujol and Frances Hutchinson have done in their papers. But the value of these critiques can be fully appreciated only by placing them in a broader context.

The deprivation with which Frances Hutchinson's paper is concerned relates specifically to the absence of freedom to make the basic choices of life without being forced to do so by economic necessity. She concentrates on ways of devising a distributional system that would give people – women and men – more freedom of this type. In this context, she points to the relevance of the ideas of the social credit school, initiated by Major C.H. Douglas. The freedom involved includes making decisions about jobs and work, and about marriage and social life. Even those – like this commentator – who would like to hear more on how the incentive problems will be dealt with in the proposed system must acknowledge the importance of the issues to which Hutchinson draws our attention. In a just social order, freedom based on substantial security must have a very important role, and the challenging task is to examine the relative merits of different proposals in this direction, including those initiated by Douglas.

Michèle Pujol's strong analysis of the limitations of neoclassical economics seen from a specific feminist perspective is both illuminating and important. This is a substantial contribution, but it does not eliminate the need to consider (a) other feminist perspectives reflecting women's deprivations of dissimilar kinds (sometimes very different from the deprivations on which Pujol's analysis concentrates); (b) deprivations other than gender-based ones (related to class, race and other variables), which would have to be considered along with problems of iniquities related to gender. They too call for reconstruction of economic theory, and these different tasks need to be integrated. It is an important and challenging program.

## ACKNOWLEDGEMENT

The author is grateful to Susan Feiner for her helpful comments and suggestions.

## NOTES

1 In the 1994 meeting of the American Economic Association there were several sessions on these and related problems. In American Economics Association (1994), see particularly the papers in the sessions on "Alternative Perspectives of Distribution within Marriage" (Julie Nelson, Shelly Lundberg and Robert Pollak, Vivianna Zelizer); "Can Feminist Thought Improve Economics?" (Myra Strober, Robert Pollak, Diana Strassmann); "Economic Issues for Work and Family" (Theresa Devine, Elaine Sorensen and Sandra Clark, Joni Hersch and Leslie Stratton); "The Economic Status of African-American Women" (Bernard Anderson, Julianne Malveaux, Charles Betsey, and Lynn Burbridge); "The Economic Support of Child-Raising" (Barbara Bergmann, Irwin Garfinkel, and Nancy Folbre).
2 On these issues, see Sen (1992) and the literature cited there. See also Klasen (1994).
3 For some illustrations and their relevance, see Dréze and Sen (1989).
4 On this see Otten et al. (1990) and Sen (1993).
5 See, for example, Aslanbeigui, Pressman and Summerfield (1994).
6 On related issues, see Humphries (1977).

## REFERENCES

American Economic Association (1994) "Papers and Proceedings of the Hundred and Sixth Annual Meeting", *American Economic Review* 84, May.
Aslanbeigui, N., Pressman, S. and Summerfield, G. (1994) *Women in the Age of Economic Transformation*, London: Routledge.
Douglas, Major C.H. (1918) *Economic Democracy*, London: Bloomfield (1974).
―――― (1920) *Credit-Power and Democracy*, London: Cecil Palmer.
Drèze, J. and Sen, A.K. (1989) *Hunger and Public Action*, Oxford: Clarendon Press.
Hargrave, J. (1945) *Social Credit Clearly Explained*, London: SCP.
Humphries, J. (1977) "Class Struggle and the Persistence of the Working-class Family", *Cambridge Journal of Economics* 1.
Hutchinson, F. (1994) "A Heretical View of Economic Growth and Income Distribution", paper presented at the international conference "Out of the Margin. Feminist Perspectives on Economic Theory", Amsterdam, June 1993.
Klasen, S. (1994) "'Missing Women' Reconsidered", *World Development*, forthcoming.
Marx, K. (1875) *Critique of the Gotha Programme* (English translation), New York: International Publishers (1938).
Meade, J.E. (1989) *Agatothopia: The Economics of Partnership*, Aberdeen: Aberdeen University Press.
Otten, Jr., Mac W., Teutsch, S.M., Williamson, D.F. and Marks, J.S. (1990) "The Effect of Known Risk Factors on the Excess Mortality of Black Adults in the United States", *Journal of the American Medical Association*, 9 February: 263.
Pujol, M. (1992) *Feminism and Anti-feminism in Early Economic Thought*, Aldershot: Edward Elgar.
―――― (1994) "Feminism, Anti-feminism and Early Neoclassical Economics", paper presented at the international conference "Out of the Margin. Feminist Perspectives on Economic Theory", Amsterdam, June 1993.
Sen, A.K. (1992) "Missing Women", *British Medical Journal*, March: 304.
―――― (1993) "The Economics of Life and Death", *Scientific American*, May: 268.
Veblen, T. (1899) *The Theory of the Leisure Class*, London: Macmillan.
Vickers, J.M. (1982) "Memoirs of an Ontological Exile", in A. Miles and G.Finn (eds), *Feminism in Canada: From Pressure to Politics*, Montreal: Black Rose Books.

# Part II

# ECONOMIC THEORY

*Editor Jolande Sap*

But these contributions to the dangerous and fascinating subject of the psychology of the other sex – it is one, I hope, that you will investigate when you have five hundred a year of your own – were interrupted by the necessity of paying the bill. It came to five shillings and ninepence. I gave the waiter a ten-shilling note and he went to bring me change. There was another ten-shilling note in my purse; I noticed it, because it is a fact that still takes my breath away – the power of my purse to breed ten-shilling notes automatically. I open it and there they are. Society gives me chicken and coffee, bed and lodging, in return for a certain number of pieces of paper which were left me by an aunt, for no other reason than that I share her name.

(Woolf [1928] (1957): 36, 37)

# 4

# HUMAN CAPITAL AND THE GENDER EARNINGS GAP

## A response to feminist critiques

*Solomon W. Polachek*

## INTRODUCTION

Throughout history numerous books and articles have been written on women's economic roles. Whether they deal with women at work, women in the household, women as volunteers, or women in other economic roles, the writings on women appear to parallel women's activities of their particular historical period. With the onset of the industrial revolution in the mid-1850s and the ensuing growth in female labor force participation, more writings appeared pertaining to women at work in the for-pay sector.

It is hard to tell when economists began to consider feminist issues. Perhaps it started in earnest with classical economist John Stuart Mill's *The Subjugation of Women* (1870), or perhaps, as Pujol (1992) indicates, with Barbara Leigh Smith Bodichon's *Women and Work* (1857). Earlier volumes such as Catherine Beecher's *A Treatise on Domestic Economy* (1841), Asenath Nicholson's *The Intellectual Housekeeper* (1835), Frances Byerley Parkes's *Domestic Duties* (1829), publisher G. Smith's *The Oeconomy of Female Life* (1751), or Gervase Markhams's *The English Housewife* (1631) deal with household management as an occupation, but it is not clear that these are feminist since they do not appear to view women as the victims of exploitation, even though they deal with important women's issues of the time.

Whenever economists began recognizing feminist concerns, the late 1980s and early 1990s witnessed a clear resurgence of interest in economics from a feminist perspective. The main point of feminist economics is that economics infrequently deals with women's issues, and when it does, it does so incorrectly because inherent "male" biases are deeply ingrained in economic practitioners, at this time mostly men. Some feminist economists are rather harsh in their criticisms of modern mainstream economics, others are milder, merely seeking to apply current economic principles to topics particularly of interest to women.

One topic with a long economic history concerns male and female roles

61

in the economy. As was indicated above, early literature on women appears to deal with women in household roles. Later literature (beginning with Bodichon 1857) looks at women as workers in the labor market. More modern literature integrates women's labor market and family activities (Mincer 1962), while the most recent works (beginning with Mancer and Brown 1980 and McElroy and Horney 1981) embed these home and market decisions into a game theoretic framework. In addition, a long literature from Charlotte Perkins Stetson (1898) through Gary Becker's *Treatise on the Family* (1981) and beyond analyzes the social evolution of the male-female economic relation.

Much of my own research concentrates on one gnawing aspect of the labor market: Why do women earn less than men?[1] In this research, I apply the human capital model to explain how lower lifetime labor force participation (in the paying market) causes women to invest less in market-oriented human capital, thereby preventing women from obtaining the better jobs, while at the same time lowering their market wages. This work has come under heavy criticism by feminist scholars.

Since male-female wage differentials have public policy implications, getting the logic straight has more than pedagogical benefits. At issue is which societal institutions are responsible for this wage disparity. Are they the global international corporations, country governments, or simply societal structures embedded within our culture? Indeed if one knew where within the economy discrimination lies, one would be able to formulate appropriate policies to eradicate such disparities. For example, if firms blatantly discriminate in hiring, promotion and pay practices, then equal opportunity laws (possibly including quotas) might be warranted. On the other hand, if the wage gap emerges because of differences in human capital brought on by differences in lifetime labor supply (either because of tax laws unsympathetic to women, or societal forces giving rise to divisions of labor in the home), then policies making it cheaper for women to work for pay, such as making daycare more readily available or eradicating marriage taxes, might be in order. As I shall show, a careful look at the data strongly indicates that labor supply differences dominate and that the human capital model provides the most cogent explanation.

The purpose of this chapter is to review my research in light of feminist criticisms. I divide the chapter into four parts. First in part one (pages 63–4), to ground these criticisms within the feminist framework, I present my understanding of the principle ideas of feminist economics, and show that much of feminist economics is consistent with aspects of the scientific method. In part two (pages 64–9), to deal with feminist critiques of my work on gender differences, I review the feminist models of the late 1960s (and early 1970s) when I began my research. I show how in reality I employed a scientific method similar to feminists. I did then what feminists do now: I found fault with both the theoretical and empirical implications of the then prevailing feminist models, only I came up with an alternative model by adopting the life cycle human capital paradigm to analyze investments from what I thought would be a woman's perspective. The model is consistent with the data and explains phenomena feminists consider. Despite this, feminists have criticized the approach – so I devote part three (pages 69–74) to illustrating the model's power in explaining the facts, and to addressing feminist critiques of this human capital approach. Finally, in part four (pages 74–5) I look at policy implications, addressing how human capital is the empowering mechanism to emancipate women.

## FEMINIST THEORY

Doing justice to women in the economic system is the main underlying theme espoused by feminist economists. Sounds simple and indeed consistent with present-day economic mores which deal with gender, race, poverty, taxation, and earnings redistribution in gender neutral terms. But feminists argue that androcentric mainstream economics[2] fails on many counts: from the subject matter defining the topics economists study, to the language and rhetoric describing the issues, to the methodology regarding whether statistically oriented econometrics or more laid-back story telling is appropriate, and even to the very philosophical underpinnings questioning whether agents are really rational or "imaginatively rational" instead (Nelson 1993: 33). Indeed the feminist critique is far reaching. Yet not all feminists agree on the issues. In describing feminist views on the equal pay for men and women debate taking place in the early 1900s (see, for example, Webb 1914; Rathbone 1917; Fawcett 1918) Pujol (1992: 9) argues that there is "not a single coherent feminist position." The same appears to be true today. For example, see Jennifer Roback's (1986) *A Matter of Choice: A Critique of Comparable Worth by a Skeptical Feminist*.

At issue is how to incorporate gender in order to do justice to women in the economy. Some feminists advocate ridding economics of rationality and efficiency, the currently prevailing paradigms. The most radical feminists seek either to demolish or throw out economics and start anew, while the more moderate seek to modify some standard economics assumptions so that economics can be more attuned to women, and hence become more realistic, accurate and bias free. In contrast, other feminists advocate using the current methodology to study topics germane to women: childcare, women in the labor market, women's role in the family, gender wage disparities, women's productivity in non-market activities, and many other topics.

Is the feminist approach any different from other research methodologies? I claim not. Science always progresses by finding fault with the status quo. Questioning the status quo can be done empirically by finding idiosyncratic anomalous results such as a new virus in medicine, a black hole in astronomy, a quirk in physics; or an unexplained wage differential such as a large gender gap for married men and married women yet a relatively small one for singles in the economy. By the same token, finding fault with the status quo can be done logically by questioning the validity of the very axioms and assumptions upon which a science is based: that not all quadratic equations could be factored led to the quadratic formula; that not all integrals could be solved analytically led to numerical integration; or that the elasticity of substitution restrictions in the Cobb-Douglas production function led to the CES, CPES, CRESH, VES, and other flexible forms. Indeed virtually every group of economists critical of neoclassical economics derided the emphasis on logic, rigor, quantification, abstraction, precision and objectivity, just as do the feminists (see e.g. Nelson 1992). Yet I find it strange that feminists apparently fail to cite their predecessors: the radicals, the institutionalists, the post-Keynesians, and others[3]. What possibly makes feminism unique is that it takes a woman's perspective and concentrates predominantly on issues dealing with gender. But clearly mainstream economists such as Jacob Mincer, Gary Becker, and others concentrate on gender issues as well.

## GENDER IN THE MARKETPLACE

### Refuting feminist occupational theories of the 1960s

My own excursion into studying women's issues began as a graduate student in the late 1960s. At the time the US had just gone through two decades of excruciatingly difficult political turmoil with the civil rights movement. Since there was little work on women's wages, I thought I could fill a void. The "new" home economics had still not been developed, but its beginnings were there, known then as the "Morningside Heights" model. Based on what I had learned from the US Civil Rights Movement, market discrimination must be rampant, or why else would women be so disadvantaged in the marketplace?

The prevailing model of demographic group wage differentials was that of occupational segregation popularized by Barbara Bergmann. Her (1971) original work related to blacks; her article on women (Bergmann 1974) was still not in print. The model made eminent sense, as it was based on accurately depicted facts: (a) women earned less than men; (b) women were occupationally segregated in what appeared to be less well paid occupations. Indeed these observations were consistent with dual labor market theory, a popular paradigm prevalent at the time. The occupational segregation model simply related both these facts: women earned less because women were segregated into low-paying jobs. Barbara Bergmann's (1974) innovation was to illustrate how blatant employer discrimination in hiring practices could cause both occupational segregation, and at the same time be responsible for the observed wage gap. Simply put, Bergmann's approach applied the concept of a neoclassical multi-market equilibrium. If firms discriminate by refusing to hire women in the so-called "good" jobs, then the supply of these women would shift to the "poor" low-paying jobs, thereby causing wage disparities among equally productive workers.

At the time, no one used data to test the validity of this theory[4]. Thus my first task was to devise an index measuring the explanatory power of occupational segregation. To do this, I asked: How much would the wage gap change if women were assigned a male occupational distribution? (I also asked how much the wage gap would change if males were assigned a female occupational distribution.) The results (reported in Chiswick *et al.* 1975 and repeated with different data in Treiman and Hartmann 1981) were in stark contrast to my expectations: at most only 35 per cent of the aggregate male-female wage differential could be explained. Indeed most experiments yield an explanatory power of less than 10 per cent. Other research using regression analysis found an even smaller explanatory power[5]. In summary, I did then (back in the early 1970s) what feminists do today: I questioned the prevailing model (but within a statistical framework) and found that the prevailing literature had significantly less explanatory power than expected. I must admit that the results puzzled me for well over a year, as it seemed that the Bergmann model appeared logical in every detail. In retrospect, I now realize that supply forces were completely neglected.

## Demographics and the gender wage gap: a supply side approach

For me the big breakthrough in trying to understand the male-female wage differential came about more or less by accident. Rather than follow the procedure usually used to estimate discrimination (i.e. to estimate a gender categorical dummy variable coefficient in a standard earnings function), I interacted gender with marital status. This yielded one gender discrimination measure for marrieds and another for singles (Polachek 1975b). The results were startling: what was a 35 per cent gap diminished to about 18 per cent for single-never-married males and females, but increased dramatically to over 60 per cent for married-once-spouse-present males and females. Further, children exacerbated the gap. Each extra child less than 12 years old widened female-male pay disparity by 10 per cent. In addition, large spacing intervals between children widened wage disparity further. Even now, Blau and Kahn (1992) show that these differences hold, and are not unique to the US. These same marital status effects are exhibited across various countries in Table 4.1. Using data for Germany, the UK, the US, Austria, Switzerland, Sweden, Norway and Australia, Blau and Kahn found single women to earn 90 to 101 cents on the dollar, yet married women

*Table 4.1* Female/male earnings ratios by marital status corrected for hours

| Country (earnings measure) | Married workers | Single nonmarried workers |
|---|---|---|
| Germany (monthly) | 0.57 | 1.03 |
| UK (annual) | 0.60 | 0.95 |
| USA (annual) | 0.59 | 0.96 |
| Austria (monthly) | 0.66 | 0.97 |
| Switzerland (monthly) | 0.58 | 0.94 |
| Sweden (annual) | 0.72 | 0.94 |
| Norway (annual) | 0.72 | 0.92 |
| Australia (annual) | 0.69 | 0.91 |

*Source*: Blau and Kahn 1992: 534

earn about 65 cents on the dollar. In short, marital status, marriage duration, children and child spacing affect female and male wages.

The evidence is clear: were corporate hiring and promotion discrimination responsible for gender wage disparities as advocated by feminist occupational segregation models, then corporate discrimination would have to explain why single women have approximate wage parity with single men, while married women do not. Were corporate hiring and promotion discrimination responsible for gender wage disparity, then corporate discrimination would have to be responsible for children widening the wage gap. Corporations also would have to be responsible for large child spacing intervals exacerbating the gap. No doubt, as invasive as is the current corporation, it is not obvious that these demographic variables form the basis for hiring, pay and promotion policies. Indeed, were one really to understand gender-pay differentials, one would need a theory to explain these demographic patterns of pay disparity. Clearly, demand-driven market discrimination of the type advocated by the 1960s feminists did not fit the bill. For this reason I tried a human capital supply side approach.

## The human capital approach

The human capital model argues that earnings are directly related to human capital stock acquired by investing in oneself. These investments take the form of education, health, on-the-job training, job search, geographic mobility, and other activities that enhance market earnings. How much one invests depends on costs and benefits. Costs consist of direct expenditures as well as foregone earnings. Benefits accrue over one's whole lifetime through enhanced wages, and are crucially dependent upon expected lifetime labor force participation. Those who expect to work long hours, and those who foresee the greatest number of years of work have the highest expected returns. This is why young workers with a lifetime of work ahead invest more and have steeper age-earnings profiles than older workers. It is also why the young exhibit more geographic mobility, and why the young have higher job turnover (Hartog 1992; Polachek and Siebert 1993). In addition, it is a potential reason why women have lower and flatter age-earnings profiles than men (Polachek 1975a).

For the US the biggest change in the labor market this last century has been the rapid rise of married female participation rates (Mincer 1962). Despite this, women's labor force participation still lags behind men's. It is well known that lifetime labor force participation varies by gender, marital status, and number of children as well as child birth spacing intervals. Married-spouse-present men have the highest labor force participation; married-spouse-present women have the lowest; single men and single women participate at rates in between. Lower lifetime labor force participation implies lower gains from human capital investment, and less lifetime investment. In turn, lower investment levels imply lower and flatter age-earnings profiles[6].

The human capital hypothesis was initially tested by fitting a segmented earnings function that incorporates intermittent labor force participation especially exhibited by married women with children (Mincer and Polachek 1974). Although there is some debate about magnitudes (see Sandell and Shapiro 1978; Mincer and Polachek 1978), these analyses consistently show earnings potential to depreciate (or atrophy) $\frac{1}{2}$ percent to $4\frac{1}{2}$ percent for each year out of the labor force, independent of one's gender (Kim and Polachek 1994). Indeed atrophy rates vary according to consistent patterns. The more educated who have higher amounts of human capital exhibit the largest depreciation rates, as do those in more technical and managerial type occupations.

More importantly, differing atrophy rates have implications concerning occupational segregation. One can minimize losses associated with intermittent labor market behavior by choosing to work in an occupation that minimizes the costs of labor market intermittency. Despite criticisms by

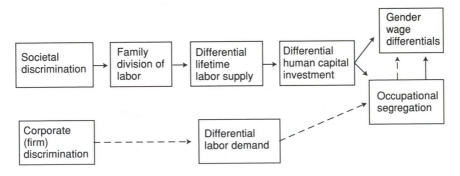

*Figure 4.1* The human capital approach contrasted with the theory of occupational segregation

feminist sociologist Paula England (1982) which have already been addressed in the literature (Polachek 1984, 1985 and 1987), I argue that one aspect of this decision to minimize the costs of intermittent labor force participation entails choosing lower atrophy occupations. But clearly other job attributes such as hours flexibility and working conditions are also important (Polachek 1981). If this is the case, then at least some occupational segregation can be explained using a supply side approach. In short, supply side factors explain both occupational segregation and gender wage differences. These aspects of the human capital model are pictured in the top right half of Figure 4.1. (The role of societal discrimination also pictured in Figure 4.1 will be discussed later, page 71.)

## The empirical power of the human capital approach

Dropping out of the labor market explains up to 93 percent of the gender wage gap. Let me illustrate: the typical intermittent worker's earnings profile can be depicted as OABF (Figure 4.2)[7]. OA reflects earnings growth during the initial work segment ($e_1$). During time out of the labor force (H), earnings power typically declines. Finally upon re-entering the labor market

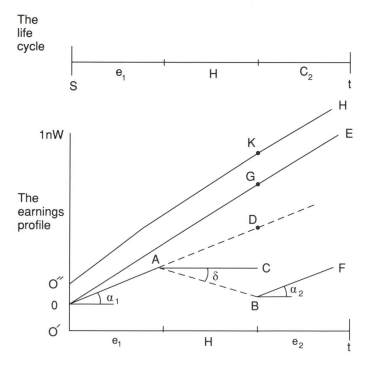

*Figure 4.2* Labor force intermittency and its effect on earnings
*Source*: Polachek and Siebert (1993: 161)

68

(period $e_2$), earnings again rise. The typical continuous worker has profile O"H. This implies a wage gap of BK.

To estimate discrimination it is often asked what the intermittent worker would earn were there no intermittency? Most studies project the initial earnings function to point D. As such earnings are enhanced by the components: BC and CD. BC represents the depreciation of earnings and CD represents the loss in earnings potential attributable to lost seniority. The problem, however, is that BD understates the amount by which earnings would rise. Were one to have zero home time, one would have greater lifetime work expectations, a higher marginal gain from investment, and hence a higher rate of investment even before one drops out of the labor force at point A. This usually manifests itself by selecting[8] jobs entailing greater on-the-job investment potential, such as management trainee type positions. Alternatively one can select a job requiring a specific market-oriented curriculum such as medicine or law (Paglin and Rufolo, 1990). Thus were one not to drop out of the labor force the earnings profile initially would rise at a steeper rate (to reflect greater training) and at the same time be higher to reflect more market oriented education. DG and GK represent these biases in the original estimate.

One set of studies tries to account for these biases by adjusting for the lower rates of human capital acquisition caused by expected labor market intermittency (see Polachek 1975a; Goldin and Polachek 1987; Kao *et al.* 1994). These results, summarized in Table 4.2, analyze gender wage differences for Taiwan and the US. For the US between 30 percent and 48 percent of the gap is explained by schooling and experience (age minus education minus six) while between 63 percent and 93 percent of the gap is explained by expected lifetime labor force participation[9]. For married men and women in Taiwan in 1989, there is a NT$9,760 wage differential. Adjusting for schooling and experience (measured as age minus education minus six) explains only 24 percent of the gap. However, adjusting for lifetime labor force expectation explains 84 percent of the gap.

# FEMINIST CRITIQUES OF THE HUMAN CAPITAL MODEL

The human capital model explains upwards of 90 per cent of the male-female wage gap, a far greater explanatory power than any other model (recall that occupational segregation explained at best 35 per cent). Yet of all explanations for male-female differences the human capital model appears to be the most subject to feminist criticism. I am not sure why, but suspect three main reasons and shall deal with each in turn:

1 that feminists interpret the human capital model as blaming women for their own plight;

*Table 4.2* Gender wage differentials: the explanatory power of the human capital model

| | United States Married men and married women | | | |
| --- | --- | --- | --- | --- |
| | *1960* | | *1980* | |
| | *Wage gap $* | *Explanatory power (%)* | *Wage gap $* | *Explanatory power (%)* |
| Raw earnings differentials | 4,740 | | 11,059 | |
| Wage gap: adjusted for schooling and experience | 3,032 | 36 | 7,741 | 30 |
| Wage gap: adjusted for anticipated intermittent labor force participation | 324 | 93 | 1,717 | 84 |

| | Single men and single women | | | |
| --- | --- | --- | --- | --- |
| | *1960* | | *1980* | |
| | *Wage gap $* | *Explanatory power (%)* | *Wage gap $* | *Explanatory power (%)* |
| Raw earnings differentials | 1,300 | | 4,141 | |
| Wage gap: adjusted for schooling and experience | 671 | 48 | 2,424 | 41 |
| Wage gap: adjusted for anticipated intermittent labor force participation | 486 | 63 | 1,378 | 67 |

| | Taiwan Married men and married women | | | |
| --- | --- | --- | --- | --- |
| | *1987* | | *1989* | |
| | *Wage gap NT$* | *Explanatory power (%)* | *Wage gap NT$* | *Explanatory power (%)* |
| Raw earnings differentials | 7,539 | | 9,760 | |
| Wage gap: adjusted for schooling and experience | 5,776 | 23 | 7,437 | 24 |
| Wage gap: adjusted for anticipated intermittent labor force participation | 1,917 | 75 | 1,549 | 84 |

*Sources:* Polachek 1975a; Goldin and Polachek 1987; Kao *et al.* 1994

2 that feminists claim that demand side discrimination is not considered;
3 that empirical predictions concerning narrowing of the male-female pay gap are not upheld by the data.

## Societal discrimination and division of labor in the home

Many misinterpret the supply side human capital approach. It is true that I claim that had women invested in more market oriented human capital, they would have achieved higher levels of economic success. However, I do not claim that it is women's own fault for investing less, as feminists argue (e.g. Bergmann 1986: 81). Investment must be motivated by economic returns. Being shackled with home responsibilities, either by one's own choice or for some other external reason, does not bode well for providing sufficient economic incentives for women to invest at levels comparable to men. Whereas I have not researched why there is a division of labor in the home which causes this gendered dichotomy, I do note societal and governmental forces at work.

From the societal perspective women are invariably younger, and at least in the past less educated, than their husbands, thereby causing a male comparative advantage towards specialization in labor market activities (Polachek 1975b). Some very promising and innovative work on allocation within the family and hence on the division of labor adopts a game theoretic approach (Mancer and Brown 1980; McElroy and Horney 1981). Indeed work in this area is beginning to blossom (see McElroy 1990; Dassgupta 1993; Ott 1993). In addition, this game theory approach is being used to explain other market areas in which bargaining may put women at an economic disadvantage (Sap 1993).

From the perspective of government forces, women have consistently been subjected to marriage taxes, restrictive work rules, and the unavailability of daycare. Even in 1994 Daniel Feenberg and Harvey Rosen (1994) find that 52 per cent of American couples will pay an average of $1,244 in marriage taxes, and that some couples may pay marriage taxes in excess of $10,000.

As such I have consistently emphasized societal as opposed to market discrimination (Polachek 1984). Figure 4.1 (top half) illustrates the link between societal discrimination, family division of labor in the home, human capital investment, occupational segregation and wages. This should be contrasted with the bottom half which illustrates Bergmann's occupational segregation theory.

## Causality

One cannot help but note the direction of causality implied in Figure 4.1. I argue that societal discrimination causes a division of labor in the home, which in turn causes differential human capital investments, manifested by women being in less prestigious, lower-paying jobs. Critics rightfully argue that causality may be the reverse: lower women's wages (perhaps caused by market discrimination) decrease women's incentives to invest thereby causing lower women's labor force participation which results in a division of labor in the home.

Back in 1973, Jacob Mincer and I knew that causality would be an issue with which researchers would have to deal. Indeed our 1974 paper addresses this question (Mincer and Polachek 1974). Basically, there are two ways to test for causality. One can use cross-sectional simultaneous equations estimation, or one can use time-series Granger causality tests. Frankly, I have reservations about both. In cross-sectional analysis the necessary identification restrictions are often ad hoc. In time-series analysis, it is not clear there is causality just because one event follows another. Nevertheless, the Mincer and Polachek paper (1974) explicitly used a cross-sectional instrumental variables technique. We found that our original depreciation parameters hold when one assumes that the time out of the labor force is motivated by economic considerations. Later work applies panel data techniques which follows individuals over time (Mincer and Polachek 1978; Mincer and Ofek 1982). It establishes "that real wages at reentry are, indeed, lower than at the point of labor force withdrawal, and the decline in wages is greater, the longer the interruption" (Mincer and Ofek 1982: 3). Finally my latest work combines panel estimation techniques with cross-sectional methods (Kim and Polachek 1994). The results are unambiguous. The unexplained male-female wage gap declines from 40 per cent to 20 per cent when one uses panel data. When further adjusting for simultaneity using cross-sectional approaches, this 20 percent panel data estimate of the gender earnings gap falls and approaches zero per cent. These results hold for two separate subsamples of the University of Michigan Panel Study of Income Dynamics data.

Landes (1977), Lazear and Rosen (1990), and Kuhn (1993), as well as others show that it is efficient for firms to discriminate (a form of statistical discrimination) in hiring and pay practices if they expect intermittent labor force participation, even for women who themselves expect never to drop out. Despite the rationale they provide for such corporate behavior, my empirical work finds stronger support for supply differences. While I do not deny the possibility of demand forces, I believe strongly that neglecting supply forces in devising policies to combat gender inequality runs the risk of putting women at a strong future economic disadvantage. I believe many feminists have come around to realize the importance of supply side considerations (see e.g. Blau and Kahn 1993). More on these policy issues later.

## Time trends in the male-female wage gap

Given the rapid increases in female labor force participation, the human capital model predicts that women's earnings should be rising secularly. From 1960 to 1980 the male-female wage gap barely changed at all. Women in 1960 earned 59 cents on the dollar, yet in 1980 women barely earned 63 cents on the dollar. Clearly, if the human capital model were to be accurate, one should see wage convergence rather than a stable male-female wage gap. Indeed many believe that the 40 per cent wage gap exists over all recorded history[10].

As it turns out, the decades from 1960 to 1980 are an anomaly. In October 1992 an article appeared in the *New York Times* with the headline "Women's Progress Stalled? Just Not So," based on work by Claudia Goldin, June O'Neill and myself, as well as Francine Blau and Marianne Ferber (Nasar 1992), indicating the overall convergence in the wage gap between 1890 and 1990. Clearly, from this article, one sees that the time period 1960 to 1980 is atypical. Female relative wages were rising before 1950 and since 1980. Indeed my own recent research (Figure 4.3) indicates the differing rates of male-female pay convergence between the 1970s and the 1980s. The 1970 to 1980 wage gap narrowed very slowly, while from 1980 on the wage gap narrowed more quickly at about 1.7 per cent per year.

In a sense this more rapid wage convergence of the 1980s compared to the 1970s is strange because female labor force participation rose dramatically in the 1970s, yet the rise in female labor force participation tapered off in the 1980s. This 1980s wage convergence trend is equally startling for advocates of strong Equal Employment Opportunity policies, since in the

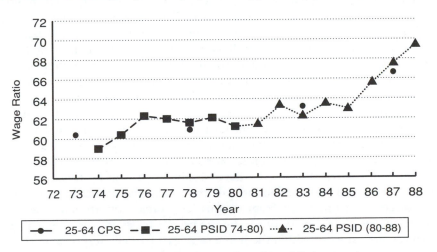

*Figure 4.3* Female-male wage ratios: white full-time workers
*Source:* Polachek (1990)

1970s enforcement of anti-discrimination laws increased twenty-fold, while in the 1980s affirmative action activities actually fell. Yet women's wages rose relative to men's in the 1980s but hardly appreciated in the 1970s.

My recent research indicates that these exceedingly paradoxical trends are consistent with the human capital model (Polachek 1990). The rapidly rising female labor force participation of the 1960s and the 1970s actually brought down female wages because new inexperienced workers earned less than older more senior workers, thereby making female wage growth appear less rapid. The decline played itself out in the 1980s as the relative growth in female labor market entrants diminished, and as the proportion of women's years actually worked increased. If one were to adjust appropriately for labor market joiners and labor market leavers, the male-female wage convergence is actually the same in both decades. Indeed the findings by Blau and Kahn (1993) indicate that current research understates male-female wage convergence in the 1970s and 1980s, as well. Using statistical techniques that account for changes in the earnings structure, they find that women's progress is far greater than previously thought. Thus skepticism concerning the human capital model is clearly unwarranted.

## GOVERNMENT POLICY AND THE EMPOWERMENT OF WOMEN

Some have argued that I claim that demand side discrimination does not exist. This is as far from the truth as imaginable. Yes, there is a tendency for long-run competitive forces to drive out any business enterprises engaging in discrimination. However, not all economic sectors are competitive. Enterprises such as government, public institutions, and regulated monopolies do not compete in the marketplace. They need not minimize costs, nor maximize profits. As such, these entities are indeed capable of discriminating. In fact, past studies have illustrated this point for regulated monopolies (see e.g. Alchian and Kessel 1962)[11]. Since non-competitive forces are the prime cause of unequal opportunity, promoting economic competition is the greatest weapon in preventing discrimination.

Government policies have not concentrated on opportunity, but instead on outcome measures. Outcome measures are defined as the level of economic success observed for various demographic groups. It has been alleged that an unequal economic outcome among women is prima facie evidence for discrimination to have resulted. Obviously, based on the model of wage determination just presented, unequal economic outcomes in society need not result from unequal economic opportunities, though some studies clearly imply this to be the case[12]. It has just been illustrated that division of labor within the home is at least partially responsible. Thus even the most stringent anti-discrimination legislation cannot eradicate sex differences, if differences in human capital investment incentives remain.

74

Whereas it is not up to the state to legislate how many children families should have or whether the husband or wife must take responsibility in raising children, it is the state that helps set up the costs for these decisions. High marginal tax rates on wives' earnings decrease their labor market incentives. Unavailability of low-cost daycare centers do the same. Indeed government tax policies, especially marriage taxes, have exacerbated family division of labor which has been responsible for the empowerment of women and the resulting gender wage differences. I refer to the empowerment of women by governmental and other societal forces that diminish women's incentives to participate fully in the labor market as societal discrimination. I argue that societal discrimination far exceeds what some term to be market discrimination, and that this societal discrimination is the type of discrimination that has to be eliminated. I argue that investing in human capital is the empowering mechanism to emancipate women.

## ACKNOWLEDGEMENTS

I wish to thank the following: Edith Kuiper and Jolande Sap for extensive comments and encouragement in helping me gain a stronger understanding of and appreciation for feminist economics; and Sara Ann Reiter and Nancy Wulwick for much discussion and help in obtaining bibliographical references.

## NOTES

1 Not at issue here is whether men or women should work, or whether women's (or men's) non-market activities in the home or elsewhere are appropriately valued. See Marilyn Waring (1988) for a description of these issues.
2 Pejoratively referred to as "malestream" by Pujol (1992: 200). It is hard to rationalize how *ad hominem* criticism leads to scientific discourse. I suspect personifying the "enemy" psyches one up just as ball players get psyched up by singing team chants.
3 I thank Nancy Wulwick for pointing this out to me.
4 The Becker book (1957) introduced some skepticism because in the long run competition should drive out discrimination.
5 For example, Hallerstein and Neumark (1993: 18), one of the latest papers containing a test of occupational segregation, find that "the coefficient on percent female in the occupation is positive" (not negative as would be expected) "and insignificant." Johnson and Solon (1986) get explanatory power of about 3 per cent. The explanatory power inferred from England (1982) is less than 5 per cent, and that of Fuchs (1971) is between 0 per cent and 6 per cent.
6 In addition for the US, gender labor force participation differences are smaller for non-whites than whites, implying a smaller predicted gender wage difference for blacks than whites, which incidentally is observed in the data. Other implications include initially flatter earnings profiles for those intending to be more intermittent in the labor force (Sandell and Shapiro 1980), and a tendency towards steeper earnings profiles when, after a long hiatus,

intermittent workers permanently re-enter the labor market (Mincer and Ofek 1982).

7 This diagram and explanation appear in Polachek and Siebert (1993: 161).

8 Critics espousing the demand side such as Landes (1977), Goldin (1986) and Kuhn (1993) rightfully argue that women might not be "free to choose" their job. In anticipating high job turnover among women job incumbents, firms might fear making a commitment to pay for firm specific training. As such, they may shy away from employing women in "good" jobs (Landes), or they may require more stringent standards among women incumbents (Lazear and Rosen 1990; Kuhn 1993). Indeed this might be why surveys indicate that women in better jobs claim to have faced greater discrimination levels. It is also the basis of statistical discrimination theories beginning with Phelps (1972) which argue that because of the high costs of identifying those with the greatest work expectations, firms stereotype all women as "non-workers." Later I present evidence against these demand side approaches.

9 The US computations were done before release of the 1990 US Census, and as yet the procedures were not replicated for these newer data.

10 Perhaps Victor Fuchs was the first to point to Leviticus containing the first known estimate of male–female discrimination (Chapter 27, verses 2–5): "Speak unto the children of Israel and say unto them: When a man shall clearly utter a vow in person unto the Lord, according to thy evaluation, then thy evaluation shall be for the male from 20 years old even unto 60 years old, even thy evaluation shall be 50 sheckels of silver, after the sheckel of the sanctuary. And if the speaker be a female, then the evaluation shall be 30 sheckels. And if it be some five years old even unto twenty years old, then thy evaluation shall be for the male 20 sheckels, and for the female 10 sheckels. And if it be from a month old even unto five years old, then thy evaluation shall be for the male 5 sheckels in silver, and for the female thy evaluation shall be 3 sheckels in silver."

11 Also see Cymrot (1985) on how elimination of Major League Baseball's reserve clause decreased discrimination against non-whites.

12 Studies assessing the effects of government policies find mixed results. For example Blau and Ferber (1986) state that "a review of the trends in the male–female pay gap . . . gave no indication of a notable increase in women's economic status . . . that might be attributable to the effects of government's anti-discrimination effort." For the UK, Zabalza and Tzannatos (1985) explain about 15 per cent wage convergence through the enactment of the Sex Discrimination Act.

# REFERENCES

Alchian, A. and Kessel, R. (1962) "Competition, Monopoly, and the Pursuit of Pecuniary Gain", in Universities National Bureau of Economic Research, *Aspects of Labor Economics*: 157–75, Princeton, NJ: Princeton University Press.

Becker, G. (1957) *The Economics of Discrimination*, Chicago: University of Chicago Press.

—— (1981) *Treatise on the Family*, Cambridge, MA: Harvard University Press.

Beecher, C. (1970) *A Treatise on Domestic Economy*, New York: Source Book Press [c1841].

Bergmann, B. (1971) "The Effect of White Incomes on Discrimination in Employment", *Journal of Political Economy* 79, March–April: 294–313.

———— (1974) "Occupational Segregation, Wages and Profits When Employers Discriminate by Race or Sex", *Eastern Economic Review,* April–July: 103–10.

———— (1986) *The Economic Emergence of Women,* New York: Basic Books.

Blau, F. and Ferber, M. (1986) *The Economics of Women, Men, and Work,* Englewood Cliffs, NJ: Prentice-Hall.

———— (1991) "Career Plans and Expectations of Young Women and Men: The Earnings Gap and Labor Force Participation", *Journal of Human Resources* 26, 4, Fall: 581–607.

Blau, F. and Kahn, L. (1992) "The Gender Earnings Gap: Learning From International Comparisons", *American Economic Review* 82, 2, May: 533–8.

———— (1993) "The Impact of Wage Structure on Trends in U.S. Gender Wage Differentials: 1975–87", paper presented at Labor Economics Workshop, Cornell University.

Bodichon, B.L. Smith (1857) *Women and Work,* New York: C.M. Francis.

Chiswick, B., Facklar, J., O'Neill, J. and Polachek, S. (1975) "The Effect of Occupation on Race and Sex Differences in Hourly Earnings", *Review of Public Data Use* 3, 2, April: 2–9.

Cymrot, D. (1985) "Does Competition Lessen Discrimination? Some Evidence", *Journal of Human Resources* 20, 4, Fall: 605–12.

Dassgupta, V. (1993) "The Determinants of Dowry in India", paper presented at the conference "Out of the Margin. Feminist Perspectives on Economic Theory", Amsterdam.

England, P. (1982) "The Failure of Human Capital to Explain Occupational Segregation", *Journal of Human Resources* 17, Spring: 358–70.

Fawcett, M.G. (1918) "Equal Pay for Equal Work", *Economic Journal* 28, March: 1–6.

Feenberg, D. and Rosen, H. (1994) "Recent Developments in Marriage Tax", National Bureau of Economic Research Working Paper No. 4705.

Ferber, M. and Nelson, J. (1993) *Beyond Economic Man, Feminist Theory and Economics,* Chicago: University of Chicago Press.

Fuchs, V. (1971) "Differences in Hourly Earnings between Men and Women", *Monthly Labor Review* 94, 5, May: 9–15.

Goldin, C. (1986) "Monitoring Costs and Occupational Segregation by Sex: A Historical Analysis", *Journal of Labor Economics* 4, 1: 1–26.

Goldin, C. and Polachek, S. (1987) "Residual Differences by Sex: Perspectives in the Gender Gap in Earnings", *American Economic Review* 77, May: 143–51.

Hallerstein, J. and Neumark, D. (1993) "Sex, Wages, and Productivity: An Empirical Analysis of Israeli Firm Level Data", The Maurice Falk Institute for Economics Research, Discussion Paper No. 9301, January.

Hartog, J. (1992) *Capabilities, Allocation, and Earnings,* Boston: Kluwer Academic Press.

Johnson, G. and Solon, G. (1986) "Estimation of the Direct Effects of Comparable Worth", *American Economic Review* 76, December: 1117–25.

Kao, C., Polachek, S. and Wunnava, P. (1994) "Male-Female Wage Differentials in Taiwan: A Human Capital Approach", *Economic Development and Cultural Change* 42, 2, January: 351–74.

Kim, M.K. and Polachek, S. (1994) "Panel Estimates of Male-Female Earnings Functions", *Journal of Human Resources* 29, 2, Spring: 406–28.

Kuhn, P. (1993) "Demographic Groups and Personnel Policy", *Labour Economics* 1, 1: 49–70.

Landes, E. (1977) "Sex Differences in Wages and Employment: A Test of the Specific Capital Hypothesis", *Economic Inquiry* 15, 4, October: 523–38.

Lazear, E. and Rosen, S. (1990) "Male-Female Wage Differentials in Job Ladders", *Journal of Labor Economics* Part 2, 8, January: S106–23.

McElroy, M. (1990) "The Empirical Content of Nash-Bargained Household Behavior", *Journal of Human Resources* 25, Fall: 559–83.

McElroy, M. and Horney, M. (1981) "Nash-Bargained Household Decisions: Towards a Generalized Model", *International Economic Review* 22: 333–49.

Mancer, M. and Brown, M. (1980) "Marriage and Household Decision Making: A Bargaining Analysis", *International Economic Review* 21: 31–44.

Markham G. (1631) *The English Housewife*, London: Nicholas Okes for J. Harison.

Mill, J.S. (1870) *The Subjugation of Women*, New York: D. Appleton.

Mincer, J. (1962) "Labor Force Participation and Married Women", in Universities National Bureau of Economic Research, *Aspects of Labor Economics*: 63–97, Princeton, NJ: Princeton University Press.

Mincer, J. and Ofek, H. (1982) "Interrupted Work Careers: Depreciation and Restoration of Human Capital", *Journal of Human Resources* 17, Winter: 3–24.

Mincer, J. and Polachek, S. (1974) "Family Investments in Human Capital: Earnings of Women", *Journal of Political Economy* 82: S76–108.

—— (1978) "Women's Earnings Reexamined", *Journal of Human Resources* 13, 1, Winter: 118–34.

Nasar, S. (1992) "Women's Progress Stalled? Just Not So", *New York Times*, 18 October, Section 3: 1.

Nelson, J. (1992) "Gender, Metaphor, and the Definition of Economics", *Economics and Philosophy* 8: 1, 103–25.

—— (1993) "The Study of Choice or the Study of Provisioning? Gender and the Definition of Economics", in M. Ferber and J. Nelson (eds) *Beyond Economic Man: Feminist Theory and Economics*, Chicago: University of Chicago Press.

Nicholson, A. (1835) *The Intellectual Housekeeper*, Boston: Russell, Odiorne and Co.

Ott, N. (1993) "Intrafamily Bargaining and the Division of Work: A Game Theoretic Model of Household Decisions", paper presented at the conference "Out of the Margin. Feminist Perspectives on Economic Theory", Amsterdam.

O'Neill, J. (1985) "The Trend in the Male-Female Wage Gap in the United States", *Journal of Labor Economics* 3, 1, January: S91–116.

O'Neill, J. and Polachek, S. (1993) "Why the Gender Gap in Wages Narrowed in the 1980s", *Journal of Labor Economics* 11, 1: 205–28.

Paglin, M. and Rufolo, A. (1990) "Heterogeneous Human Capital, Occupational Choice and Male-Female Earnings Differences", *Journal of Labor Economics* 8: 123–44.

Parkes, F. Byerley (1829) *Domestic Duties*, New York: J. & J. Harper.

Phelps, E. (1972) "A Statistical Theory of Racism and Sexism", *American Economic Review* 62, 4, September: 659–61.

Polachek, S. (1975a) "Differences in Expected Post-School Investment as a Determinant of Market Wage Differentials", *International Economic Review* 16, June: 205–29.

—— (1975b) "Potential Biases in Measuring Male-Female Discrimination", *Journal of Human Resources* 10, 2, Spring: 205–29.

—— (1981) "Occupational Self-Selection: A Human Capital Approach to Sex Differences in Occupational Structure", *Review of Economics and Statistics* 63: 60–9.

—— (1984) "Women in the Economy: Perspectives on Gender Inequality", in *Comparable Worth: Issues for the 80's*: 34–53, Washington, DC: US Civil Rights Commission.

—— (1985) "Occupational Segregation: A Defense of Human Capital Predictions", *Journal of Human Resources* 20, 3, Summer: 437–40, 444.

—— (1987) "Occupational Segregation and the Gender Gap", *Population Research and Policy Review.* 47–67.

—— (1990) "Trends in the Male–Female Wage Gap: The 1980s Compared to the 1970s", paper presented at the American Economics Association Meetings, Washington, DC, December.

Polachek, S. and Siebert, W.S. (1993) *The Economics of Earnings*, Cambridge: Cambridge University Press.

Pujol, M.A. (1992) *Feminism and Anti-Feminism in Early Economic Thought*, Aldershot: Edward Elgar.

Rathbone, E. (1917) "The Remuneration of Women's Services", *Economic Journal* 27, March: 55–68.

Roback, J. (1986) *A Matter of Choice: A Critique of Comparable Worth by a Skeptical Feminist*, New York: Priority Press.

Sandell, S. and Shapiro, D. (1978) "An Exchange: The Theory of Human Capital and the Earnings of Women", *Journal of Human Resources* 13, 1, Winter: 103–17.

—— (1980) "Work Expectations, Human Capital Accumulation, and the Wages of Young Women", *Journal of Human Resources* 15, 3, Summer: 335–53.

Sap, J. (1993) "Bargaining Power and Wages: A Game Theoretic Model of Gender Differences in Union Wage Bargaining", *Labour Economics*, 1, 1: 25–47.

Smith, G. (1751) *The Oeconomy of Female Life*, London: G. Smith.

Stetson, C. Perkins (1898) *Women and Economics, A Study of the Economic Relation between Men and Women as a Factor in Social Evolution*, Boston: Small, Maynard & Company.

Treiman, D. and Hartmann, H. (1981) *Women, Work and Wages: Equal Pay for Jobs of Equal Value*, Washington, DC: National Academy Press.

Waring, M. (1988) *If Women Counted: A New Feminist Economics*, San Francisco: Harper and Row.

Webb, B. Potter (1914) "Personal Rights and the Women's Movement v. Equal Remuneration for Men and Women", *The New Statesman* August: 525–7.

Zabalza, A. and Tzannatos, Z. (1985) *Women and Equal Pay*, Cambridge: Cambridge University Press.

# 5

# FERTILITY AND DIVISION OF WORK IN THE FAMILY

## A game theoretic model of household decisions

*Notburga Ott*

## INTRODUCTION

Household decisions concerning consumption, labor force participation or fertility are the topics of the "new home economics." Usually, the household is considered to be a decision unit, and models are used that are based on the maximization of a household utility function. This approach ignores the internal structure of families and assumes an intra-family consent. This is a very restrictive assumption. Increasing divorce rates show the importance of conflicts in the family. Both the formation of partnerships and their separation are based on individual decisions of the participants. Since family decisions always contain the possibility of conflict, we must assume that in an existing family the decisions are also based on individual interests and reflect the results of internal negotiations. For this reason game theoretic bargaining models may be an appropriate analytical approach.

A formalization of household decisions in form of a bargaining game was first attempted by Manser and Brown (1979) and McElroy and Horney (1981). They analyzed labor supply using a static bargaining model with a Nash solution. Their work provided the starting-point for the development of a dynamic bargaining model of family decisions with respect to household production and the accumulation of human capital. Such a model is presented in this chapter. First, the theoretical model is described and compared to the traditional approach. Then the implications for labor supply and fertility are discussed. Finally, some estimates are presented that demonstrate the empirical relevance of bargaining models.

## FAMILY DECISIONS AS A BARGAINING PROBLEM

According to Becker (1973), a necessary condition for marriage is that both individuals can expect a higher utility from living together than from living in a single-person household. For this to happen, it is necessary that the joint household produces a larger welfare than the separate households.

Following the argument of the new home economics the household is regarded as the production place of basic commodities and the family is modeled as a community of individuals who can gain extra profits by pooling resources, by the division of labor and intra-family exchange. Applying the transaction cost approach, usually three types of family transactions that generate a surplus when compared with separate single-person households are considered (see Ben-Porath 1980; Pollak 1985):

- As a production company, the family members can use comparative advantages by specializing in market work and work at home in conjunction with intra-family trade.
- As a consumer cooperative, the family allows joint use of indivisible goods and provides declining costs by economies of scale.
- As an insurance coalition, the family produces security by an exchange of mutual promises for aid.

The realization of these potential gains requires long-term contracts within the family. Because the willingness to agree to such contracts depends on individual welfare, the distribution of the total household production affects the behavior of family members. Assuming individuals who are free in their decisions, the internal distribution results from negotiations between the members. Consequently, none of the bargainers would agree to an outcome that is lower than his payoff if the agreement is not reached. So the solution depends on the members' best alternatives outside the family.

Such situations can be analyzed with game theoretic bargaining models[1]. Assuming family members are able to communicate and to make binding contracts, a cooperative game seems an appropriate approach. It offers solutions which are Pareto optimal, satisfy the above conditions, and provide an internal distribution depending on the outside options. The solution of an axiomatic cooperative game characterizes the properties of the bargaining outcome without modeling the negotiation process itself. The interest of this chapter is concentrated on the reaction of the bargaining outcome to changes in the environment. Therefore, if the axiomatic solution represents a good approximation of the negotiation result, it is not necessary to model the bargaining process explicitly. In the following, the cooperative Nash solution is used, because out of the multitude of cooperative solution concepts[2] the Nash solution is the one that can be interpreted as a result of an explicit bargaining process (Zeuthen 1930)[3].

Consider a household in which two persons jointly decide on the allocation of their resources. Let x denote a vector of goods produced in the household, $U^i(x)$ the individual utility functions of the male (i = m) and the female (i = f) partner and $D^i$ the utility outcome in the case of disagreement. Given the family income Y and the vector of prices p, the Nash solution is characterized as follows:

$$\max_{x} N = [U^m(x) - D^m]*[U^f(x) - D^f] \qquad (1)$$

$$\text{s. t. } x'p = Y$$
$$U^m(x) > D^m$$
$$U^f(x) > D^f$$

In Figure 5.1 the axes represent the individual utility level of the spouses. The aggregate of all feasible utility pairs generate the payoff space with the utility possibility frontier F, which is the locus of all Pareto optimal points corresponding to given prices and incomes. If gains of marriage exist, the pair of outcomes in the case of disagreement $(D^m, D^f)$, called the conflict or threat point, lies inside the utility frontier. Because none of the partners would accept an outcome lower than his conflict payoff $D^i$, the negotiation set is the upper right boundary between the points A and B. Geometrically the Nash solution is the tangential point C of the utility frontier F and the hyperbola $(U^m-D^m)*(U^f-D^f) = $ const. farthest away from conflict point $(D^m, D^f)$.

Hence, the conflict point plays a dual role in the bargaining game. It determines the conflict outcomes, and therefore, according to the rules of the game, the distribution within the household.

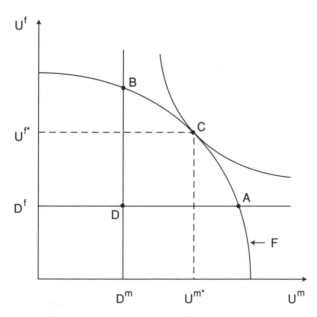

*Figure 5.1* The bargaining game: Nash solution
*Source:* Ott (1992: 35)

## COMPARISON WITH TRADITIONAL MODELS

In comparison to traditional household models, the bargaining model differs only in regard to the objective function; the budget and time restrictions are identical in both models. If the goods of the husband and the wife are separate arguments in the household utility function

$$U = U(x^m, x^f),$$

then the Nash function of the bargaining model

$$N = [U^m(x) - D^m]* [U^f(x) - D^f]$$

is formally a specific function in this function class. Up to this point, it seems unnecessary to give up the more general household utility function, because only a very specific type of intra-family distribution is determined through the solution of a bargaining game. However, there are advantages of modeling household decisions as a bargaining game: the derivation of a "household utility function" is not left to a black box, but is founded on the assumptions of rational negotiation.

It can be shown that the bargaining model leads to the same first order conditions as the traditional model if the conflict outcomes ($D^m$ and $D^f$) are fixed and exogenous[4]. Then the bargaining model brings about no additional findings for questions concerning resource allocation. The real advantages, however, of the bargaining model become apparent when the assumption of a fixed conflict point is relaxed.

Let us assume that for both spouses the best alternative outside the family is to live alone as a one-person household. This is a rather conservative assumption, that represents the minimal threat potential. At the time of negotiation living alone is in general the only alternative that can be chosen with certainty and therefore it is often the only credible threat. Then the conflict outcome results from the usual maximization problem in the single-person household and can be written as an indirect utility function:

$$D^i(p, Y^i) = \max_x U^i(x) \qquad (2)$$

s. t. $x'p = Y^i$

where $Y^i$ is the income of person i living alone

Because the so defined conflict outcomes depend on income and prices, the conflict point will change with changes of these factors. In particular, it depends on the household decisions themselves.

In order to analyze the effects of exogenous changes in prices or income, the usual instruments of comparative statics can be applied. If one assumes a hypothetical "household utility function" for comparisons with traditional approaches, then the hyperbolas $(U^m-D^m)*(U^f-D^f) = const.$ can be treated as "indifference curves of the household." The product of the individual gains remains constant on this curve. If this product is interpreted as "household utility," then the "household" regards the different points on the hyperbola as being equivalent: what one spouse loses in utility is compensated by the utility gain of the other spouse.

Figure 5.2 shows the effect of a change in prices in favor of person f. The initial point is A on the utility frontier I. The movement from A to B represents the *compensated substitution effect* (along the "indifference curve"), and from B to C the *income effect* (shift of the utility frontier to a different utility level). Up to this point, the results coincide with those of the traditional approaches.

In addition to this, there is a third effect in the bargaining model (the movement from C to D). Given the definition (2), a change in prices influences the conflict outcome too. This implies a shift in the system of "indifference curves," which can be interpreted as a "change in preferences" of the household. The commodities of husband and wife are weighted differently before and after a change in conflict outcomes because the bargaining positions of the spouses have changed[5]. This is a fundamental difference in comparison with traditional approaches, where changes in preferences can be treated only as exogenous. In the bargaining model, however, systematic changes in the preferences of a household can be analyzed, which arise solely because of a change in the external alternatives of the spouses, whereas the individual preferences remain constant.

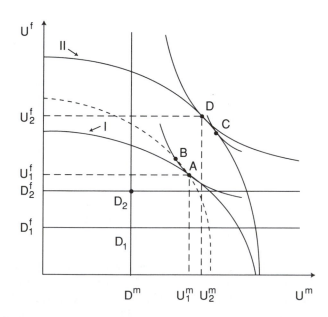

*Figure 5.2* Price change: income, substitution and bargaining effect

84

# DYNAMIC APPROACH

As has been demonstrated up to now, changes in prices and wages that also influence the external alternatives lead to a change in the allocation of household resources that is different from the results of the traditional model. Now, as we know from human capital theory, changes in wages are not only caused by exogenous factors, but also depend on investments in human capital. In particular, *on the job training* is such an investment in human capital that results in higher wages. Thus, employment does not only bring about actual income, it also increases the stock of human capital and therefore earning capacity in the future. Conversely, during non-employment human capital is depreciated as market skills are forgotten or become obsolete.

In such a setting, intra-family specialization results in a different human capital accumulation for the spouses. Specialization in market work increases the individual earning power that can be utilized independent of the household composition. Specialization in work at home, on the other hand, implies a renouncement of human capital accumulation and consequently a loss in earning power. Certainly, additional skills in household production are acquired, but utilization of these skills is limited to the household. To a large part, the goods produced in the household can be used only within the household because there is no external market for these goods or another quality of the goods is required in the market. Therefore, the returns on investments in household-specific human capital depend on the size of the household. In the case of conflict, the exchange market is withdrawn for the person specialized in work at home, and the additional skills in household production do not compensate the losses in income.

Thus, intra-family specialization affects the external alternatives of the spouses and consequently their bargaining power within the family will change. If the family contracts are not binding for a whole lifetime and renegotiations are expected to occur later on, rational individuals will take these dependencies into account when making their decisions. Because working in the market or at home will influence the future bargaining power in different ways, labor supply will be a strategic variable in the process of negotiation. This means time allocation in the household is not only chosen with the goal of attaining a maximum household production but also with regard to the future bargaining positions of the spouses.

Such a negotiation situation can be described by a dynamic model with subgame consistency as proposed by Selten and Güth (1982). For the present problem a two-period model is used. I assume that in each period a cooperative bargaining solution is reached, but that both the negotiation set and the conflict outcomes in period two depend on the solution in period one. Then the spouses bargain in period one not only about the

85

distribution of current household production but also with regard to the expected outcomes in period two. Given rational expectations, the individuals will expect a cooperative solution in period two depending on the conflict point of period two. This assumption satisfies the condition of subgame perfectness.

If we assume individual utility functions that are intertemporally additive and use an explicit household production function Z, the model is formally described as follows:

$$\max_{L^{i1},H^{i1},M^{i1}} N = (U^{m1} + U^{m2} - D^m)* (U^{f1} + U^{f2} - D^f) \qquad (3a)$$

$$\max_{L^{i2},H^{i2},M^{i2}} N_2 = (U^{m2} - D^{m2})* (U^{f2} - D^{f2}) \qquad (3b)$$

subject to

household production in each period:

$$C^{mt} + C^{ft} = Z(a^{mt} H^{mt} + a^{ft} H^{ft}, X^t) \quad t = 1, 2 \qquad (3c)$$

budget constraint in each period:

$$X^t = Y(w^{mt} M^{mt} + w^{ft} M^{ft} + I^{mt} + I^{ft}) \, t = 1, 2 \qquad (3d)$$

time constraints in each period:

$$T = M^{it} + H^{it} + L^{it} \qquad t = 1, 2 \quad i = m, f \,(3e)$$

non-negativity constraints:

$$C^{mt} > 0, \, C^{ft} > 0, \, L^{mt} > 0, \, L^{ft} > 0 \qquad t = 1, 2 \qquad (3f)$$
$$H^{mt} \geq 0, \, H^{ft} \geq 0, \, M^{mt} \geq 0, \, M^{ft} \geq 0$$

accumulation of human capital:

$$w^{i2} = f(w^{i1}, M^{i1}) \qquad\qquad i = m, f \qquad (3g)$$
$$a^{i2} = f(a^{i1}, H^{i1})$$

conflict outcome in period 2:

$$D^{i2} (w^{i2}, a^{i2}, I^{i2}) \qquad\qquad i = m, f \qquad (3h)$$

is the solution of the utility maximization in a single-person household

$$\max_{L^{i2},H^{i2},M^{i2}} U^i(C^{i2}, L^{i2})$$

$$\text{s. t. } C^{i2} = Z(a^{i1} H^{i2}, Y(w^{i1} M^{i2} + I^{i2}))$$
$$T = M^{i2} + H^{i2} + L^{i2}$$

where
$$U^{it} = U^i (C^{it}, L^{it})$$
$$D^i \text{ conflict payoff for person i in period 1 (i.e. total}$$
outcome if a conflict results in period 1)

$C^{it}$     consumption of person i in period t
$M^{it}$     hours of market work of person i in period t
$H^{it}$     hours of work at home of person i in period t
$L^{it}$     leisure of person i in period t
T     24 (total number of hours in a day)
Z     household production function
$a^{it}$     individual specific parameter of efficiency in
        household production
X     market goods
Y     net income function
$I^{it}$     non-wage income of person i in period t
$w^{it}$     wage of person i in period t
optimal allocation in the alternative situation is denoted by
italic letters

The objects of negotiation in each period are the time allocation in the household and the distribution of consumption. The dependency between the periods results from the accumulation of human capital. Solving this maximization problem leads to the following conditions for the allocation of time:

$$\Psi_M^i + Z_Y Y_M w^{i1} = Z_H a^{i1} + \Psi_H^i \tag{4}$$

where

$$\Psi_M^i = \frac{1}{U_C^{i1}} \frac{dU^{i2}}{dM^{i1}} + \frac{1}{U_C^{j1}} \frac{dU^{j2}}{dM^{i1}}, \quad \Psi_H^i = \frac{1}{U_C^{i1}} \frac{dU^{i2}}{dH^{i1}} + \frac{1}{U_C^{j1}} \frac{dU^{j2}}{dH^{i1}}$$

$$Z_Y = \frac{\partial Z}{\partial Y}, \quad Z_H = \frac{\partial Z}{\partial H}, \quad H = a^m H^m + a^f H^f$$

$$Y_M = \frac{\partial Y}{\partial M}, \quad M = w^m M^m + w^f M^f$$

$$U_C^{i1} = \frac{\partial U^{i1}}{\partial C^{i1}}, \quad U_L^{i1} = \frac{\partial U^{i1}}{\partial L^{i1}}$$

The right side of equation (4) represents the "marginal output" of work at home of individual i and the left side that of market work. These marginal outputs include the marginal product in period one and a term $\Psi_M^i$ (or $\Psi_H^i$) that stands for the weighted sum of marginal utilities of both spouses in period two. The individual specializes completely in one activity if its marginal output is larger than that of the other activity. If equation (4) holds as an equality then the person allocates time in both the market and the household sector.

This condition is customarily used for determining the reservation wage. In traditional models the reservation wage is calculated from

$$Z_H a^{i1} = Z_Y Y_M w^{i1} + \Phi \tag{5}$$

where $\Phi$ represents the changes in productivity for period two if a comparable dynamic model is used. The transformation of equation (4) in analogy to the Slutsky decomposition leads to the condition of the bargaining model[6]

$$Z_H a^{i1} = Z_Y Y_M w^{i1} + \Phi_B + \Phi_W + \Phi_S \tag{6}$$

Here $\Phi_S$ and $\Phi_W$ represent the income and the substitution effects that can be interpreted together as a counterpart to $\Phi$. The remaining term $\Phi_B$ represents the bargaining effect that is positive for the spouse whose bargaining power decreases. Remembering the discussion above, this is true for the spouse with the lower participation in market work. For this person we have an additional positive term on the right hand side, which implies that given the assumptions of the bargaining model the reservation wage is lower than it is in traditional models. This results in a higher labor force participation rate.

Further differences in comparison with traditional models appear in the conclusions for intra-family division of work. Usually static models are used to discuss these differences. From a traditional model it can be derived that no more than one member in the household will participate in both market and household activities in the optimum, whereas all other members would specialize totally in one activity (see e.g. Becker 1981: ch. 2). The counterpart for equation (4) in a traditional static model is

$$Z_H a^{i1} = Z_Y Y_M w^{i1} \tag{7}$$

If wages and household skills differ between the spouses ($w^i > w^j$ and $a^i < a^j$) then equality can hold only for one spouse. This is no longer true in the dynamic bargaining model. The $\Psi_M^i$ and $\Psi_H^i$ depend on the accumulation of human capital and on the bargaining positions. Assuming accumulation functions with decreasing growth rates, with a stronger decrease of the slopes for wage rates, the $\Psi^i = \Psi_M^i - \Psi_H^i$ are monotonically decreasing functions and therefore are different for the spouses. Then in the optimum, equation (4) may hold as an equality for both spouses and specialization is not the optimal time allocation for all cases. In principle, this result is a consequence of the dynamic approach. If human capital accumulation is considered explicitly in a model with a joint household utility function, full specialization is not the only possible result, especially if the household technology may change over the family life cycle. But, the bargaining effect makes specialization more unlikely because the differences in the $\Psi^i$ for the spouses depend mainly on differences in the bargaining power. This leads also to a highly non-linear function $\Psi^i$.

## FERTILITY AS A PRISONER'S DILEMMA

The main difference in comparison to traditional models is that in the dynamic bargaining model a solution may result that is not Pareto efficient. If the long-term contracts are not enforceable in period two, the optimal behavior does not guarantee a maximum welfare production in the household.

The basic assumption in the traditional model is that all family members are interested in maximizing household production because all family members participate in the additional production. Therefore, it is assumed *a priori* that all possible gains in the family will be realized and the optimal allocation of household resources is always Pareto efficient. In the bargaining model, however, the same decision parameter determines both the total welfare production and the distribution of this welfare between the family members. Therefore, situations are possible in which an increase in household production is combined with an intrafamily redistribution that leads to a lower outcome for one member. This person would object to such a decision and possible welfare gains would not be realized.

This can be seen from equation (6). The term for the bargaining effect $\Phi_B$ may result in a time allocation that does not maximize the household production. But, this effect becomes more apparent in discrete choices for instance on a restricted labor market. Such a situation is very similar to the well-known prisoner's dilemma.

Especially, the decision about fertility may be such a situation. We will assume that a child increases the utility of both spouses. Also we assume that the decision for a child would result in a net welfare gain for the family, which means that the gains in the total welfare of the family are larger than the costs (the direct expenditures for the child and the opportunity cost of childcaring due to foregone income). Then, the traditional model would predict a positive decision for a child. Changes in conflict outcomes resulting from a birth are not considered.

This is done in the bargaining model. Let us consider a situation where the wish for a child can be realized only by a disruption in the working life of one spouse, which is in most cases the wife. Stopping to work affects her bargaining power because her income capacity and as a consequence her conflict outcome decrease. Then a situation like a prisoner's dilemma may result. This can be illustrated graphically.

In Figure 5.3 point A represents the status quo, which means the situation without a child. The increase of welfare due to having a child implies an outward shift of the utility frontier and an area exists where both

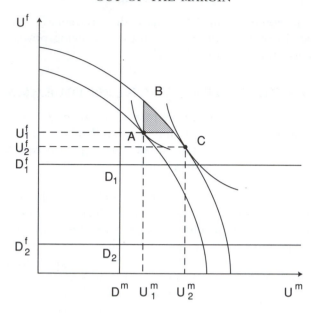

*Figure 5.3* Fertility: a prisoner's dilemma

spouses can gain in comparison to the status quo (the hatched area in Figure 5.3). Point B denotes the solution with an unchanged distribution. But, the disruption in the working life of individual f results in a shift of the conflict point (from $D_1$ to $D_2$). The solution resulting from a new negotiation is denoted by C. If the change in the bargaining position is large, the new outcome for person f ($U_2^f$) may be lower than her status quo outcome ($U_1^f$). Then she would not agree to the decision for the child.

To reach a Pareto efficient solution (point B), a contract about the future distribution is necessary. The spouses are free in period one to fix the future distribution and to agree that they will not renegotiate in period two. If this contract is binding, the change in the external alternatives is irrelevant and the distribution for the two periods depends only on the bargaining power in period one[7]. In this case the model can be written as a one step bargaining model with different production possibilities for the two periods, but a fixed and exogenous given bargaining power. Then the model is equivalent to a traditional dynamic model because "household preferences" will not change.

On the other hand, if the contract is not enforceable, the asymmetric structure of the contract works as an incentive for the spouse with the improving relative bargaining position to break the contract at a later point in time. Whereas the woman stopping market work makes her contribution immediately (i.e. in period one) and the loss in her earning capacity is irreversible, the husband is to contribute later in period two when the additional welfare benefits have already been obtained and the conflict point has changed. If he breaks the contract here and asks for renegotiation, he can gain additional benefits. If there are no external sanctions to enforce the contract, then the risk of a break-up is relatively large. By anticipating this risk, rational individuals will not agree to such a contract and possible welfare gains will not be realized.

## EMPIRICAL EVIDENCE

The bargaining approach seems more appropriate than the traditional approach in analyzing female labor supply and demographic change. But, up to now, empirical research based on bargaining models is scarce. Nevertheless, the results given in those few existing empirical papers[8] indicate the relevance of the bargaining model. I shall now present two empirical models based on German data.

The hypothesis that the bargaining power in the family depends on individual resources is analyzed with data from the housewife survey of the "Institut für Wirtschafts- und Sozialforschung" (see Pross 1975). Among other things, the women in the sample were asked to give their subjective estimates of the balance of power within their marriages[9]. Table 5.1 shows the parameter estimates of an ordered probit model in which the probability of a specific choice depends functionally on different characteristics. A positive coefficient shows a more powerful position of the wife.

The estimation results confirm the expected dependencies. Women with a higher education (high school) have a more powerful position in a

*Table 5.1* Balance of power within marriages, ordered probit model for housewives

| dependent variable: more powerful partner in marriage | (1) husband (2) both about equal (3) wife | |
| --- | --- | --- |
| | *b* | *t-value* |
| Constant 1 | −0.585 | −5.861 |
| Constant 2 | 1.101 | 10.680 |
| Own house | −0.169 | −2.294 |
| Children have left home | 0.280 | 1.646 |
| Higher education of wife | 0.419 | 1.956 |
| Own income of wife | 0.162 | 1.975 |
| Husband's income* | −0.127 | −2.464 |
| −2* log-lik= 2011.6107 | *Cases:* | 1101 |

* based on the middle of income brackets
*Source*: Ott 1992: 181

marriage than other women. The same is true if the woman has her own income. This is non-wage income or income from temporary employment because only housewives had been selected in the sample. Although the size of the income is unknown, the mere existence of an own income leads to a more powerful position for the wife. Conversely, the husband is more powerful the higher his income is.

The two remaining variables "own house" and "children have left home" can also be interpreted as indicators for the wife's possibilities to increase her bargaining power. On the one hand, managing the household of one's own house often requires more time primarily because there are more rooms and a garden. This reduces the possibilities for housewives to increase their bargaining power through other activities. On the other hand, as the children grow up and leave the parental household, the necessity to stay at home is removed, which increases the scope for other activities.

These empirical findings show that individual resources are relevant for intra-family decision-making. This implies that at least in some families no contracts concerning intra-family distributions exist. In this case a disruption of the working life and the specialization in home work implies a significant risk for individual well-being. Therefore, family formation and especially fertility should depend on the distribution of individual resources in the family.

Some insights into the relationship can be obtained from a model of birth control by young couples. Birth control has been chosen as the dependent variable since it requires a conscious decision whereas observed fertility also depends on other factors. Based on the dynamic bargaining approach the couple's optimal choice between the two alternatives "decision for an (additional) child" and "decision against a child" will be that alternative which maximizes the Nash product. Formulating the system (3) as a discrete choice problem with an additional argument for children in the utility functions, the estimation function results (see Appendix):

$$N(K + 1) - n(K) = \alpha\gamma\frac{Y^i}{Y} - \frac{\alpha\Theta}{n} + \frac{\partial h}{\partial K} + f(g_1, g_2, dK) + \epsilon \qquad (8)$$

$$= x'\beta + \epsilon$$

where
| | | |
|---|---|---|
| $N(K)$ | | Nash gain |
| $Y = Y^i + Y^j$ | | income of the household |
| $Y^i = w^i m^i$ | | income of person i |
| $n$ | | number of persons in the household |
| $h(K)$ | | utility from the children |
| $K$ | | number of children |

The data used are the first wave (1984) of the panel study *Generatives Verhalten in Nordrhein-Westfalen* of the Institut für Bevölkerungsforschung

Table 5.2 Birth control probit model for couples

| | coeff | t-value | coeff | t-value |
|---|---|---|---|---|
| Constant | −0.07 | −0.338 | −0.02 | −0.102 |
| Urban area | 0.20 | 2.006 | 0.18 | 1.728 |
| Duration of marriage | −0.03 | −1.870 | −0.04 | −2.343 |
| Children in household | | | | |
|   1 child | 0.78 | 3.941 | 0.76 | 3.856 |
|   2 children | 1.35 | 5.611 | 1.36 | 5.566 |
|   3 or more children | 0.98 | 3.071 | 1.01 | 3.101 |
| Opportunity costs | | | | |
|   couples without children < 3 | 1.24 | 2.590 | 1.21 | 2.416 |
|   couples with children < 3 | −0.19 | −0.391 | −0.23 | −0.443 |
| Employed women | | | | |
|   occupational opportunities | | | 0.29 | 1.876 |
|   (ratio of wages − 1)$^2$ | | | −0.70 | −1.393 |
| Non-employed women | | | | |
|   hypothetical wage, if youngest | | | 0.10 | 2.328 |
|     child > 5 | | | | |
| *Number of cases:* 790 | log-lik | −424.84 | log-lik | −418.71 |

*Source:* Ott 1992: 189

und Sozialpolitik, Bielefeld (see Kaufmann and Strohmeier 1987). Table 5.2 contains the estimated parameters of a probit model, which give the influences of different characteristics on the probability of practicing birth control.

Independent variables of the model are the duration of marriage, a dummy variable for urban regions, the number of children and indicator variables for the opportunity costs of childcaring. The dummy variables for the number of children control the size of the household on the one hand and measure the marginal utility of an additional child on the other hand. This corresponds to the term ($\frac{\alpha\Theta}{n} - \frac{\partial h}{\partial K}$) in equation (8). The relative loss in household income if the spouse with the lower income would leave employment is chosen as an indicator for the opportunity costs of childcaring (term $\frac{Y^i}{Y}$). This variable has the value zero if one spouse is not employed, and it is included separately for couples with and couples without children. The opportunity costs should be lower for couples with children who both work, because these couples already have found an arrangement for childcaring that usually can be extended to an additional child.

A second model version contains additional variables representing the bargaining power of the spouses (term $f(g_1, g_2)$). This is motivated by the hypothesis that a prisoner's dilemma will mainly arise in situations with a symmetrical status quo position and a relatively large expected decrease in bargaining power. The symmetry indicator for working women is the squared ratio of the spouses' wages minus one $(\frac{w_i}{w_j} - 1)^2$. In this indicator the smaller wage rate is used as the numerator. The indicator is zero for couples with equal wages, and the value increases with growing asymmetry. Occupational opportunities of the wife are chosen as indicators for potential losses in the bargaining power. For a non-working woman an additional child would reduce the possibilities to increase her bargaining power by returning to the labor market, especially if her children are older and her potential wage is high. Therefore, a hypothetical wage was imputed for wives with children over six years as an indicator for their potential increase in bargaining power.

The probability for practicing birth control is larger for couples living in urban areas and decreases with the duration of the marriage. If the couple already has children, the probability for using birth control increases and reaches a maximum at two children. This can be interpreted as decreasing marginal utility resulting from an additional child. That the probability decreases if the couple has three or more children eventually can be explained by a faster decrease of the marginal costs as compared to the decreasing marginal utility.

The indicators for the opportunity costs show the expected effects. Couples without children are more likely to practice birth control if the potential loss in household income becomes larger. For couples with children no such effect is observed. Because they already have childcare arrangements, it is probable that having an additional child will not require a disruption of working and consequently the opportunity costs are lower.

The variables measuring the bargaining power also have the expected effect. The probability for practicing birth control is larger for working women with occupational opportunities and a symmetrical status quo situation, and it is larger for non-working women with a high potential wage rate. Nevertheless, these variables cannot be interpreted unambiguously as a bargaining effect. Both the opportunity costs and the probability for a prisoner's dilemma depend on the same causal factors, the income or the income capacity of the spouses. In spite of using different functional forms the effects cannot be exactly separated because of problems of multicollinearity.

## POLICY IMPLICATIONS

Modeling household decisions as a bargaining game or by maximizing a joint household utility function leads to different predictions about family behavior. Especially the results for labor supply and fertility behavior differ between the two approaches. The empirical estimates indicate that the behavior predicted by the bargaining model seems to be empirically relevant. This means that the traditional approach neglects important aspects of family behavior.

From the traditional approach a policy is deduced which supports traditional gender roles, because maximal specialization within the household is derived as optimal behavior. The bargaining model, however, shows the importance of a symmetric intra-family bargaining situation. Whether this leads to other policy recommendations depends on the possibilities of substituting home work and marked goods.

In this regard we have observed some changes in the past. Economic development has reduced the family gains in an essential way. Market substitutes have been provided for many traditional household goods. Due to this trend and the increase in female wages, household production has become more and more inefficient and, in turn, gains from intra-family specialization have decreased. Family gains have been further reduced by external insurance markets and the social security system. Also the gains from the joint use of household public goods have lost in importance due to the increased welfare level. At the same time, the losses in relative bargaining power resulting from a disruption of employment have increased. Due to increased income and a large supply of market substitutes for household goods, household production is efficient in the single-person household only to a very restricted extent. Thus, being employed provides a large conflict payoff, while interrupting employment reduces it. This means that intra-family specialization leads to a great change in the bargaining positions resulting from both the high bargaining power of the spouse specialized in market work and the large loss in the bargaining power of the other. Therefore, today a traditional intra-family contract appears to be more asymmetrical than it was in the past.

In these circumstances, policy measures should not support the very risky behavior of traditional gender roles, but should reduce asymmetries in the bargaining position of the spouses, either by changing the conflict payoffs or by preventing asymmetrical accumulation of human capital or both. Changing the conflict payoffs means a redistribution of all returns and losses of accumulated and foregone human capital which are accrued after the divorce by alimony regulations or a singular lump-sum payment in the case of divorce[10]. Preventing asymmetrical accumulation of human capital requires substitutes for household production in such a way that periods of full specialization in household production by one of the spouses can be avoided or shortened to a harmless extent. Important for this are childcare services that allow women to combine raising a family with a professional career, but also possibilities to shorten working hours for both parents. Such an environment would empower families to choose more symmetrical arrangements and therefore to reach their optimum solution.

## APPENDIX

Because no data on time spent in the household are available in the data set we start with a simple two-period model without household production:

$$\max_{C^{i2}, K} N = (U^{m1} + U^{m2} - D^m) * (U^{f1} + U^{f2} - D^f) \tag{A1}$$

$$\max_{C^{i1}, K} N = (U^{m2} - D^{m2}) * (U^{f2} - D^{f2})$$

s. t.     $C^{mt} + C^{ft} = Y_t$     $t = 1, 2$

where $U^{it} = U^i(C^{it}, K)$     $i = m, f$

K: number of children

The couple's optimal choice between the two alternatives "decision for an (additional) child" and "decision against a child" is the alternative which maximizes the Nash product. The total differential of the Nash function is used as an approximation for the difference of both alternative Nash values. It can be written as a function of changes in income, the marginal utilities of a child and the bargaining weights in both periods (see Ott 1992):

$$dN = \lambda_1 dY_1 + \lambda_2 dY_2 \tag{A2}$$

$$+ s_1^m (U_K^{f1} + g_1 U_K^{m1}) dK + s_2^m (U_K^{f2} + g_1 U_K^{m2}) dK$$

$$+ (s_1^m - s_2^m)(dU^{f2} + g_1 dU^{m2}) + s_1^m (dU^{m2} - U_K^{m2} dK)(g_2 - g_1)$$

$$= \lambda_1 dY_1 + \lambda_2 dY_2$$

$$+ h(K)dK$$

$$+ f(g_1, g_2, dK)$$

where $U_K^{it} = \dfrac{\partial U^{it}}{\partial K}$, $\quad s_1^i = U^{i1} + U^{i2} - D^{i2}$, $\quad s_2^i = U^{i2} - D^{i2}$

and $g_t = \dfrac{s_t^f}{s_t^m}$ is a measure of the bargaining weight

In the traditional model

$$\max_{C^1, C^2, K} U(C, K) + U^1 + U^2 \tag{A3}$$

s. t. $C^t = Y_t$     $t = 1, 2$

the total differential results as follows:

$$dU = dU^1 + dU^2 \tag{A4}$$

$$= \lambda_1 dY_1 + \lambda_2 dY_2 + \frac{\partial U^1}{\partial K} dK + \frac{\partial U^2}{\partial K} dK$$

Comparing this equation with the total differential of the bargaining model, the terms in the first and the second line in (A2) can be interpreted as the effect on the household level which can also be described by the household utility function U. Then from (A2) and (A4) the following results

$$dN \approx dU + f(g_1, g_2, dK) \tag{A5}$$

which decomposes the Nash differential into one part resulting from a traditional approach and one resulting from the bargaining effect. Using a specific household utility function

$$U = \alpha \ln\left(\frac{Y}{n^\Theta}\right) + h(K) \tag{A6}$$

with
| | | |
|---|---|---|
| | $Y = Y^i + Y^j$ | income of the household |
| | $Y^i = w^i m^i$ | income of person i |
| | $n$ | number of persons in the household |
| | $h(K)$ | utility from the children |
| | $K$ | number of children |
| | $\alpha, \Theta$ | weighting factors |

the total differential results:

$$dU = \frac{\alpha}{Y} dY - \frac{\alpha \Theta}{n} dn + \frac{\partial h}{\partial K} dK \tag{A7}$$

The decision for a child implies

$$\Delta n = \Delta K = 1 \tag{A8}$$

$$\Delta Y = \Delta Y^i = \gamma Y^i \tag{A9}$$

with     i:    index of the spouse with lower income

γ:    share of person i's income which is lost by reducing market work.

Then using equation (A5) the difference between the Nash gains of the two alternatives is approximated by

$$dN \approx \alpha \gamma \frac{Y^i}{Y} - \frac{\alpha \Theta}{n} + \frac{\partial h}{\partial K} + f(g_1, g_2, dK) \tag{A10}$$

Introducing an error term ε, the following specification is obtained:

$$N(K+1) - N(K) = \alpha\gamma \; \frac{Y^i}{Y} - \frac{\alpha\Theta}{n} + \frac{\partial h}{\partial K} + f(g_1, g_2, dK)$$

$$+\epsilon = x'\beta + \epsilon \qquad\qquad (A11)$$

Since the couple will decide for a child if the condition $N(K+1) > N(K)$ is satisfied, the probability for this results as

$$\text{prob}\{K + 1\} = \text{prob}\{N(K+1) > N(K)\} = \text{prob}\{\varepsilon > -x'\beta\} \quad (A12)$$

which can be estimated by a probit model if a normal distribution error $\varepsilon$ is assumed.

## NOTES

1  For an overview see e.g. Harsanyi (1977).
2  For an overview see, for example, Shubik (1984: 179ff.).
3  As Krelle (1976: 629ff.) shows the Nash solution is an asymptotic solution also for other explicit negotiation models. Binmore *et al.* (1986) describe other dynamic non-cooperative games for which the cooperative Nash solution represents a good approximation of their equilibrium points.
4  See McElroy and Horney (1981) and Ott (1992) for this result.
5  The effects of changes in prices or wages in the bargaining model are formally identical to those of changes in preferences in a traditional model (see for details Ott 1992). The fundamental matrix equation

$$\left[\frac{dx_k}{dp_1}\right] = K - bq' + \frac{1}{\lambda}KUD_p$$

represents the change in demand that results from changes in prices or wages that can be decomposed in analogy to the traditional Slutsky decomposition. The term $K-bq'$ is the effect if the conflict point remains unchanged, and it corresponds to the results of the traditional model with constant preferences. Here $bq'$ represents the income effect and $K$ the matrix of compensated substitution effects. The remaining expression is due to the changes in conflict outcomes and can be interpreted as the *bargaining effect*. In traditional models a corresponding term is obtained if exogenous changes in preferences are introduced. With these findings the traditional model turns out to be the more specific one, because constant preferences are assumed, whereas in the bargaining model systematic changes in preferences depending on changes in the outside options are considered.
6  For the formal derivation see Ott (1992).
7  Formally this means that in the system (3) the condition (3h) is replaced by a fixed distribution:

$$\frac{U^m - D^m}{U^f - D^f} = \frac{U^{m2} - D^{m2}}{U^{f2} - U^{f2}} \qquad\qquad (3h')$$

8 For an overview see Ott (1992).
9 The question was: "Who is in fact the more powerful partner in your marriage: your husband, yourself, or do you think, you are about equal?"
10 From the Coasean point of view these regulations can be interpreted as joint property rights of both spouses on all human capital accumulated during the marriage. Then alimony regulations would guarantee a participation on after-marriage returns, whereas a lump-sum payment can be interpreted as a selling of the property rights to the partner with the increased human capital stock.

# REFERENCES

Becker, G.S. (1973) "A Theory of Marriage: Part I", *Journal of Political Economy* 81: 813–46.
——— (1981) *A Treatise on the Family*, Cambridge: Harvard University Press.
Ben-Porath, Y. (1980) "The F-Connection: Families, Friends and Firms and the Organization of Exchange", *Population and Development Review* 6: 1–30.
Binmore, K., Rubinstein, A. and Wolinsky, A. (1986) "The Nash Bargaining Solution in Economic Modelling", *Rand Journal of Economics* 17: 176–88.
Harsanyi, J.C. (1977) *Rational Behavior and Bargaining Equilibrium in Games and Social Situations*, Cambridge: Cambridge University Press.
Kaufmann, F.X. and Strohmeier, K.P. (1987) *Partnerbeziehungen und Familienentwicklung in Nordrhein-Westfalen. Generatives Verhalten im sozialen und regionalen Kontext, Abschlußbericht über das Forschungsprojekt "Generatives Verhalten in Nordrhein-Westfalen"*, Schriftenreihe des Ministerpräsidenten des Landes Nordrhein-Westfalen, Heft 50, Düsseldorf.
Krelle, W. (1976) *Preistheorie, Teil I und II*, 2. Auflage, Tübingen: J.B.C. Mohr.
McElroy, M.B. and Horney, M.J. (1981) "Nash-Bargained Household Decisions: Towards a Generalization of the Theory of Demand", *International Economic Review* 22, 2: 333–49.
Manser, M. and Brown, M. (1979) "Bargaining Analysis of Household Decisions", in C.B. Lloyd, E.S. Andrews and C.L. Golroy (eds) *Women in the Labor Market*, New York: Columbia Press.
Ott, N. (1992) *Intrafamily Bargaining and Household Decisions*, New York: Springer.
Pollak, R.A. (1985) "A Transaction Cost Approach to Families and Households", *Journal of Economic Literature* XXIII: 581–608.
Pross, H. (1975) *Die Wirklichkeit der Hausfrau*, Reinbeck: Rowohlt.
Selten, R. and Güth, W. (1982) "Game Theoretical Analysis of Wage Bargaining in a Simple Business Cycle Model", *Journal of Mathematical Economics* 10: 177–95.
Shubik, M. (1984) *Game Theory in the Social Sciences. Concept and Solutions*, Cambridge, MA: MIT Press.
Zeuthen, F. (1930) *Problems of Monopoly and Economic Welfare*, London: Routledge.

# 6

# TOWARD A FEMINIST, POST-KEYNESIAN THEORY OF INVESTMENT

## A consideration of the socially and emotionally constituted nature of agent knowledge

*Lee B. Levin*

## INTRODUCTION

Economic discourse has become increasingly open to discussions of epistemology in recent years. This is not to say, however, that there is not widespread skepticism toward those in the profession who seem to use the e-word a bit too frequently. "After all," one may think, "I'm not interested in issues of epistemology; I just want to do economics." Those economists who are interested in epistemology have a strong incentive, therefore, to show how it is an indispensable aspect of the process of "doing economics" and how epistemology exerts a profound influence upon the substance of economic analysis. It is toward such ends that this essay has been written[1].

We can take as our starting-point the following two premises:

1 Epistemology is of great concern to economics.
2 Feminists have made important contributions to epistemology which economists would do well to consider.

Let us begin by addressing ourselves to the first of these propositions. Of what consequence is epistemology to economics?

Questions concerning the nature and status of knowledge enter into economics because, as it is generally practiced, economics concerns itself with the manner in which agents make decisions based upon their understanding of the economic situation confronting them. Epistemology, therefore, lies at the very heart of economic analysis since interpretation, thought, and knowledge form the basis upon which economic decision-makers are deemed to make their choices, and choice is the *sine qua non* of most economics[2]. As G.L.S. Shackle writes: "Economics is about thoughts.

It is therefore a branch or application of epistemics, the theory of thoughts (1972: viii)."

There are, however, numerous understandings of understanding; that is, there are a number of approaches to epistemology. It is the contention here that underlying most economic thought (whether of left, right, or center) is a Cartesian, or modern, epistemology, according to which the thinking subject is considered to be an autonomous, unified, and coherent being who, through reasoned contemplation, possesses access to objective, nonsocially mediated knowledge. Many feminist theorists, however, both within and without economics, have contributed an alternative epistemological perspective which is sharply critical of Cartesian notions of subjectivity and knowledge. This brings us to the second of our two initial propositions.

There are two salient characteristics concerning the epistemological orientation of these feminist theorists which are relevant here. First is the idea that both the subject that produces knowledge and knowledge itself are socially constituted. Second is the notion that perception and understanding are strongly influenced by emotion. Emotion, that is, plays an important role in the creation of knowledge.

This essay will endeavor to show that it is possible to conceive of an economics which is based upon feminist notions of knowledge, an economics which takes the thought processes upon which agents base their decisions to be both socially and emotionally constituted. It is the contention here that post-Keynesian theory proves especially amenable to this feminist epistemological approach. We will, then, raise the possibility of, and take some steps towards outlining the general contours of, a feminist, post-Keynesian theory of investment.

Before moving on, it is important that I acknowledge that feminist theory represents an extremely diverse set of ideas and perspectives, and that, even within the area of epistemology, feminism offers a multitude of divergent approaches. I put forward this point to make clear that the feminist theory presented here represents only one strand of thought among many which comprise the entire body of feminist thought. When mention is made here of "feminist theory," what is being referred to specifically is post-structuralist and post-modernist feminist theory and, to a great degree, the work of the feminist standpoint theorists[3].

## CARTESIAN EPISTEMOLOGY

It was noted above that the distinguishing feature of a Cartesian, or modernist, approach to knowledge is its placement of objective, transcendent truth within the grasp of the thinking subject. Underlying this epistemological orientation is the notion that the contemplative individual is able to mirror the world objectively by producing knowledge which is unmediated by her social situatedness or passion.

101

Different conceptions of understanding are often premised upon alternative notions of subjectivity – alternative notions, that is, of the specific nature and status of the thinking, acting individual. Whereas the feminist view of knowledge elaborated here is often associated with a conception of subjectivity as inherently social and unstable, the traditional, Cartesian approach sees the subject as unified, sovereign, and constant. The feminist post-structuralist Chris Weedon writes:

> The assumption that it is possible to ascertain objective, true facts and to be a neutral observer . . . relies on an autonomous and coherent observing and recording subject, rather than a subject who is herself socially constructed.
>
> [Weedon 1987: 130–1]

The autonomous, coherent subject is able to gain access to transcendent, objective knowledge since there can be said to exist within her some presocial, immutable aspect which is immune from the sullying influence of social relations and is therefore able pristinely to mirror nature without distortion. From this perspective, the supposed epistemological autonomy of the Cartesian subject acts as the guarantor of unprejudiced, non socially mediated knowledge.

On the notion within modernist thought of the corruptive influence of passion upon understanding, Alison Jaggar writes, "Within the western philosophical tradition, emotions usually have been considered as potentially or actually subversive of knowledge," (1989: 145). With Descartes, as Genevieve Lloyd points out (1991: 171), came a sharpening of the distinction between mind and body. The capacity to reason was equated with the mind, and all those bodily aspects which lay outside and in opposition to it – such as passion, emotion, and desire – were seen to have an impeding and debasing influence upon the ability to exercise reason. Flax (1983) provides an analysis of how the capacity of reason to overcome and control passion represents an abiding theme within much of Western philosophy.

We turn now to a discussion of some of neoclassical theory's modernist aspects.

## THE MODERNISM OF NEOCLASSICAL ECONOMICS

The epistemological presuppositions which underlie an economic theory can be thought to impact upon that theory in two ways: first, in the status accorded to the knowledge produced by the economic theorist; and, second, in terms of the sort of knowledge which the agents within the theory are deemed to possess. There is a striking parallel within neoclassical theory between these two levels of knowledge and the manner in which they are conceived. That is, both the decision-making agent within neoclassical theory and the neoclassical theorist herself are deemed to possess

102

access to knowledge which is, in some sense, objective or transcendent. The parallel that exists between the respective knowledges of neoclassical agent and theorist is not altogether surprising since a theorist is likely to conceive of the epistemological status of the agents within her theory in a manner which is informed by the way she views her own subjectivity and knowledge.

We can, then, cite the existence of both a modernism of neoclassical theory, and a modernism within neoclassical theory[4]. The modernism of neoclassical economics is the privileging by neoclassical theorists of the knowledge which they create, the conferring upon this knowledge of an objective, value-free status. The neoclassical theorist, for example, will generally make a distinction between normative and positive economics, the latter representing an unbiased, objective economic knowledge which is open to the economist who practices the proper methodology[5].

What is of interest to us, though, is not the epistemological status of the economic theorist, but that of the agent within theory. Let us, therefore, devote some time to an examination of the modernism within neoclassical theory – that is, the bestowing of a privileged status upon the knowledge produced by the agents within neoclassical economics. Our focus will be upon the epistemic processes of those agents whose decisions impact the course and magnitude of investment. For that reason, we take a brief foray into neoclassical capital theory[6].

## Agent knowledge in neoclassical capital theory

Though many would dispute the idea that neoclassical capital theory assumes the existence of objective knowledge on the part of its agents, the case is made here that the knowledge of agents within this area of neoclassical thought is, at least in some sense, objective and determinate.

We begin by directing our attention to what might be considered the fundamental proposition of neoclassical capital theory: i.e. that "the firm, acting rationally, will tend to push investment to the point where the marginal yield on physical assets is equal to the market rate of interest" (Modigliani and Miller 1958: 261); in other words, the firm engaging in capital formation will undertake investment until the marginal product of real capital is equal to the marginal cost of financial capital. The idea which we put forward here is that both of these variables – the expected rate of return on real capital assets and the marginal cost of financial capital – involve, in neoclassical theory, assumptions of privileged knowledge on the part of economic agents.

Firms' expectations regarding the rate of return on capital assets are generally conceived in stochastic terms; that is, in analyzing firms' knowledge of the future, the probability calculus is typically brought to bear. In neoclassical capital theory, as in most economic theory, decision-making in the face of uncertainty is generally represented as a choice between probability distributions. What can we say about the knowledge which these probability distributions are taken to represent?

Probabilistic knowledge is conceived of in one of two ways by economists: either in objective or subjective terms. The objective approach to probability is generally associated with the Rational Expectations Hypothesis. From this perspective, the knowledges of agents – as revealed in the probability distributions representing that knowledge – are, on average, identical to each other and, on average, correspond to the "true" stochastic outcomes generated by the objective world. Describing the Rational Expectations Hypothesis, Muth writes:

> the expectations of firms (or, more generally, the subjective probability distribution of outcomes) tend to be distributed, for the same information set, about the prediction of the theory (or the "objective" probability distributions of outcomes).
>
> [Muth 1961: 316]

Clearly, this understanding of probabilistic knowledge is in line with Cartesian notions of knowledge as objective and transcendent.

In the case of a subjectivist approach to probabilistic knowledge, the probability distributions representing agent expectations are thought not necessarily to correspond in a one-to-one fashion with the objective world, or to each other[7]. However, even though neoclassical theorists typically claim to be operating under a subjectivist approach, the manner in which agent knowledge is generally represented by neoclassical theorists seems to indicate that agent expectations are implicitly presumed to have some objective basis.

For neoclassical theorists, the distinction between subjective and objective conceptions of probabilistic knowledge, as James Crotty writes, "constitutes a distinction without a difference" (1994: 107). Neoclassical theory assumes that agents act under the presumption that their probabilistic knowledge is, in fact, true. Clearly, it would not be rational for an agent to believe that their probabilistic expectations represent true knowledge unless the economy behaves as an "ergodic" event-generating mechanism since only an ergodic event-generating process enables one to make stochastically "true" predictions about future outcomes[8]. However, if the economy were presumed to behave in such a manner, there would be no reason to expect that agents' subjective probabilities would not correspond to the objective probabilities which actually describe future outcomes; that is, the distinction between subjective and objective expectations would collapse. We can conclude, then, that firms' expectations regarding the rate of return on capital assets, conceived of by neoclassical economists in subjective probabilistic terms, can actually be thought to constitute objective, transcendent knowledge[9].

What about the second half of neoclassical theory's fundamental proposition – that is, the cost of capital? Within neoclassical theory, the cost of capital to the firm is determined by the capital asset pricing model (CAPM), which offers the conclusion that the firm's cost of financial capital is equal to a risk-free rate of interest plus a risk premium. This conclusion is given by the equilibrium condition associated with the CAPM:

$$E(R_j) = R_F + \beta_j \, [E(R_M) - R_F]$$

Here, $E(R_j)$ is the expected rate of return on securities issued by the $j$th firm, $E(R_M)$ equals the expected rate of return on the risky market portfolio, $R_F$ is the risk-free rate of interest, and $\beta_j$ is the so-called "beta coefficient," which measures the market risk associated with the securities issued by the $j$th firm. Note that the independent variables $\beta_j$ and $E(R_M)$ are calculated from the first and second moments of the probability distributions which describe the future rate of return on the assets which comprise the financial market. What we wish to emphasize here is that it is generally assumed that these probability distributions are known to all agents, who are deemed to possess "homogeneous," or identical, expectations within the confines of this model (Sharpe 1964: 433), which certainly seems to comport with an objectivist notion of knowledge.

We can conclude, therefore, before moving on to a discussion of feminist criticism of Cartesian epistemology, that neoclassical capital theory – in its assumptions regarding both the expected rate of return on physical capital and the cost to the firm of financial capital – conceives of agent knowledge in thoroughly Cartesian, objectivist terms.

## FEMINIST CRITICISM OF CARTESIAN EPISTEMOLOGY

The most salient aspect of the feminist thought discussed here is its skepticism concerning the possibility of objective, nonsocially mediated knowledge and its contention that knowledge is both socially constituted and mediated by human passion.

### Subjectivity and knowledge as socially constituted

It was mentioned earlier that varying conceptions of knowledge are often premised upon varying notions of subjectivity. Whereas Cartesian thought grounds its appeal to objective knowledge in a view of the subject as autonomous, unified, and stable, the feminist theory deployed herein views subjectivity as unstable, fragmented, and socially mediated. It therefore offers a profoundly different conception of the status of knowledge. Like the subject that creates it, knowledge, from this perspective, is characterized by an inherent sociality and contingency which cast doubt upon any possibility of a one-to-one correspondence to the objective world.

The concept of gender represents a critical component of the critique feminists offer of the autonomous, unified subject. Gender, from this perspective, represents a social construct which is taken on and "performed" by individuals, so that rather than being an expression of a preformed, autonomous self, gender in fact constitutes the self as a subject. As Butler writes: "There exists no gender identity behind expressions of gender; that identity is performatively constituted by the very 'expressions' that are said to be its results" (1990: 25).

Behind the actions and thoughts of the thinking, acting subject, there is no autonomous presocial self; there is, as Butler indicates, "no performer prior to the performed" (1991: 24). Rather, the individual is formed as a subject by the social web into which she enters. Not only are individuals constituted as subjects by the social relations associated with gender, but they are constituted by myriad other social factors as well, such as class, race, and sexual orientation. Along these lines, Sandra Harding writes: "the subject/agent of feminist knowledge is multiple and contradictory, not unitary and 'coherent'" (1991: 180–1).

Similarly, Tamsin Lorraine concludes that: "There is nothing stable about us. We are an intersection of forces that are forever in the process of becoming" (1990: 12). From this perspective, then, there exists no transcendent self that can view the world from a non-social, Archimedean vantage point in order to produce objective, non-discursive truth. The subject is "always already" gendered – as well as raced, and classed. Lacking a presocial, interior essence, such a complexly constituted, socially situated subject has access only to knowledge that is discursively mediated.

It should be noted that feminist theory's criticism of objectivist, Cartesian epistemology shares important similarities to other strains of social thought which seek to subvert modernist conceptions of knowledge and subjectivity – primarily, postmodernism and various strains of Marxism. The affinities between post-modernist and feminist thought, for example, have been widely acknowledged. As Fraser and Nicholson observe, both feminism and post-modernism "have called into question the dominant philosophical project of seeking objectivity in the guise of a 'God's eye view' which transcends any situation or perspective" (1990: 26). Providing a description of the post-modernist perspective, Best and Kellner write:

postmodern theory provides a critique of representation and the modern belief that theory mirrors reality, taking instead 'perspectivist' and 'relativist' positions that theories at best provide partial perspectives on their objects, and that all cognitive representations of the world are historically and linguistically mediated. . . . In addition, postmodern theory abandons the rational and unified subject postulated by much modern theory in favor of a socially and linguistically decentred and fragmented subject.

(Best and Kellner 1991: 4–5)

Althusser – whose work has constituted the methodological and epistemo-logical inspiration for many contemporary Marxists – provides a critique of modernist conceptions of knowledge and subjectivity which is similarly oriented[10].

One further idea that might be mentioned before taking up the issue of the emotionally constituted nature of knowledge is the proposition raised by a number of feminists that the very concept of a Cartesian subject – the concept of an extradiscursive, transcendent, and autonomous self – repre-sents an inherently "masculine" notion of subjectivity. The Cartesian subject, that is, exhibits those traits – such as separateness, detachment, sovereignty, and independence – that are culturally linked with masculinity (and therefore privileged). Criticism of the masculine, "separative" self has constituted an important component of feminist analysis of standard economic theory[11].

## Passion as a constituent of knowledge

Cartesian philosophy, as many feminists have noted, is associated with the privileging of mind over body and reason over passion. A number of feminists critical of such a view have put forward two important points regarding this philosophical orientation. The first is that this privileging can be understood as representing a repression of the feminine since body, passion, and emotion have typically been associated with "femaleness." As Flax has expressed, "Reason is seen as triumph over the senses, of the male over the female" (1983: 269). The second point is that such pairings as mind/body and reason/passion might better be thought of as mutually constitutive relationships rather than oppositional dualities.

This second premise has been taken up by Alison Jaggar, for whom emotion represents an inherent, ever-present component of perception, understanding, and knowledge. She writes:

> rather than repressing emotion in epistemology it is necessary to rethink the relation between knowledge and emotion and construct conceptual models that demonstrate the mutually constitutive rather than oppositional relation between reason and emotion.
>
> (Jaggar 1989: 157)

Associated with this view is the idea that all interpretation and knowledge is value laden and, what is more, values are intimately linked to the emotions. In fact, as Jaggar explains, values and emotions presuppose each other (Jaggar 1989: 154). Since, therefore, knowledge is not value free, it cannot be emotion free.

We can now proceed to an investigation of the possibility of constructing a post-Keynesian approach to investment which is based upon the feminist

107

conception of knowledge as both a socially and emotionally mediated construct.

## TOWARD A SYNTHESIS OF FEMINIST EPISTEMOLOGY AND POST-KEYNESIAN INVESTMENT THEORY

Earlier we distinguished between the epistemological status of the economic theorist and that of the agent within economic theory. There is a growing literature in the discipline which seeks to analyze and interrogate the socially constituted, discursive, and "rhetorical" nature of the knowledge produced by economists[12]. Our task, however, is to apply this anti-objectivist approach to human understanding to the agents within economic theory and to investigate the possibility of constructing an economics – specifically geared toward an analysis of investment – which understands the knowledge of agents to be constituted by social and emotional influences.

What would such an economics look like? This paper proposes that it might look something like certain versions of post-Keynesian theory, particularly those which place especially great emphasis upon uncertainty and which are sometimes referred to as "fundamentalist" post-Keynesianism. Post-Keynesian fundamentalists, such as, for example, G.L.S. Shackle, advance a notion of agent knowledge which, at moments, bears striking similarities to the feminist epistemology which we have discussed here.

Our task now is to investigate these similarities and, in the process, to consider some of the ways in which the social and emotional aspects of agent knowledge impact upon the decision-making processes associated with investment. This task will be facilitated by bringing to bear certain ideas from the areas of sociology and social psychology.

### Investment and the socially constituted nature of agent knowledge

Post-Keynesian theory begins to appear congruent with feminist epistemology when we consider two fundamental aspects of this economic approach: first, its espousal of radical subjectivism, and, second, its notion of the primacy of convention in impacting agent expectations.

From the perspective of radical subjectivists – be they post-Keynesian or Austrian – agent knowledge is both radically uncertain and inherently subjective[13]. Radical subjectivism, that is, breaks the determinate link (associated with Cartesian thought) between the objective world and the knowledge which we possess of that world. Expressing this anti-objectivist approach to agent knowledge, the Austrian theorist Ludwig M. Lachmann writes:

The absence of a uniform relationship between a set of observable events which might be described as a *situation* on the one hand, and expectations on the other hand, is thus seen to be the crux of the whole matter. . . . This experience, before being transformed into expectations, has, so to speak, to pass through a "filter" in the human mind, and the undefinable character of this process makes the outcome of it unpredictable.

(Lachmann 1943: 14)

Along the same lines, Shackle writes: "At the root of my theme lies the supposition that thought can be an uncaused cause" (1988: 6); that is, there exists no necessary one-to-one correspondence between our internal thought processes and the external world, so that our knowledge is not strictly determined by objective reality. It is for this reason that he elsewhere describes agent knowledge as being characterized by an "objective baselessness" (Shackle 1972: 199).

Rather than constituting the determinate effect of an objective world, agent knowledge (especially knowledge of the future) is for many post-Keynesians considered to be the indeterminate and unstable product of convention. Convention, of course, is an irreducibly social phenomenon. Post-Keynesian theorists, therefore, present a vision of knowledge as socially constituted which is not unlike that put forward by feminists. When the post-Keynesian Douglas Vickers writes critically of "the neoclassical omniscient economic man, an autonomous creature who is untouched epistemically by the forces that swirl around him" (1992: 462), his argument closely resembles the feminist critique of autonomous subjectivity and epistemological sovereignty associated with modernist thought.

One possible objection to this interpretation is that post-Keynesian theory presents a much more limited notion of subjective, socially generated knowledge than is indicated here. That is, post-Keynesian theorists (one might say) only apply the concepts of radical subjectivism, uncertainty, and conventionally mediated understanding to agent knowledge of the future. Agent knowledge of past and present, and the knowledge of the post-Keynesian theorist herself, are not subject to uncertainty and social mediation. Amariglio (1990) makes this very argument. While his position is, in fact, borne out by much of the post-Keynesian literature, there are a number of noteworthy exceptions. Shackle, for example, at various moments in his writing indicates that no knowledge, whether of past, present or future (including the knowledge created by economic theorists), can ever provide an objective mirroring of the world. In describing the impossibility of objectively constructing theory, Shackle writes: "Theory, let us boldly say, is not right or wrong but less or more powerful in affording 'a good state of mind' to men confronted with an unfathomable universe" (1972: 355).

Let us now pose the following question: What can we say about the course of investment expenditure (and the economy in general) when it is assumed that the knowledge upon which decisions are based is socially and conventionally mediated? Post-Keynesian theory indicates that one might expect there to arise periods of relative, provisional stability interrupted by bouts of extreme instability – a dynamic which Shackle terms "Keynesian Kaleidics." In the face of uncertainty, convention confers a veneer of order upon economic relations and helps to keep chaos temporarily at abeyance. Because conventional knowledge, however, is characterized by an objective baselessness, such periods of tranquillity can only be transitory and ephemeral. It is for this reason that Shackle refers to such moments as haunted equilibria (1974: 77). Agent expectation, writes Keynes, "being based on so flimsy a foundation . . . is subject to sudden and violent changes" (1937: 214–15). The functional relationships which determine the course of investment, therefore, are given to bouts of fitful instability; so that the money demand curve, for instance (which determines the rate of interest), "must be looked upon as a thread floating in a gusty wind" (Shackle 1967: 217).

The idea presented here, then, is that although one would expect a certain amount of instability within a system where subjectivity and knowledge are socially constituted, one might also expect there to arise a measure of provisional stability as an effect of convention. As Rogers notes: "Seen from this perspective the message of the so-called fundamentalist Keynesians is not that the world is inevitably chaotic but that the stability that we do enjoy has a rather fragile basis" (1989: 269).

We will direct our focus now to some of the ways in which the subjective, conventionally mediated character of knowledge can be thought to affect the decisions of those participating in capital markets.

Minsky has provided extensive analysis of the conventional nature of what constitutes an appropriate liability structure for a firm, as well as how changing conventions in this area help to generate business cycles through their impact on investment expenditure (1975, 1986). Increases in conventionally acceptable degrees of leverage during economic upswings, for example, help to fuel investment booms that lead eventually to investment busts.

We can enrich our discussion of the impact of socially mediated knowledge on investment by importing into post-Keynesian theory some ideas from sociology which emphasize the inherently social nature of agent thought and which offer interesting insights into the process of capital formation.

One such idea concerns the role of rumor in structuring individuals' knowledge and behavior. As Turner writes, "rumor should be treated as a collective decision-making process in which norms emerge to coordinate the action of individual members" (1964: 403). The idea of rumor as a guide to action seems to apply well, for example, to behavior within securities markets. Rumor, a socially generated form of knowledge, serves to condition agent choice in securities markets since agents here (as elsewhere) face extreme uncertainty and lack the knowledge necessary to make decisions which are *ex ante* optimal and because the speculative motive plays an especially important role in financial market activity, so that participants have a particularly strong incentive to act on new information immediately, before it spreads further[14]. The need to act on new information as quickly as possible results in a situation where the onset of a rumor can cause an immediate rise or fall in stock price which becomes self-sustaining as the rumor moves outward in concentric circles from the market "insiders" to the "outsiders."

Another idea from sociology which has implications for the dynamics of financial markets (and therefore of investment expenditure) is "social comparison theory." According to this theoretical approach, individuals have a need to evaluate continually their beliefs, and, as Michael Klausner indicates, "if 'objective' physical criteria are not relevant or available for the purpose of determining the 'correctness' of individuals' beliefs and behaviors, people compare their decisions with those of others" (1984: 75). This process clearly imparts a conventional character to the thoughts of individuals acting within social situations.

Developing this point further, Leon Festinger writes: "An opinion, a belief, an attitude is 'correct,' 'valid,' and 'proper' to the extent that it is anchored in a group of people with similar beliefs, opinions, and attitudes" (1950: 272–3). One way that individuals engage in social comparison processes, therefore, is to gauge their beliefs against "like others" – individuals, that is, whom an agent finds similar to herself. As an example, investment fund managers assiduously gauge their beliefs and actions against each other. Consistent with the notion of Keynesian Kaleidics, this practice can help confer stability upon financial markets, but can also lead to precipitous instability owing to the great volume of assets controlled by many fund managers. For example, if one or a few funds begin selling a particular stock (or group of stocks) in large quantities, this can lead to voluminous dumping of the assets involved as the other funds join in the selling. This, of course, can cause a collapse in asset prices and a drastic increase in the cost of capital to firms.

A final sociological concept that can serve to highlight the impact of socially constituted knowledge upon capital markets is the important role played by fad and fashion in determining what constitutes appropriate and proper behavior. Investment "fads" clearly influence the behavior of investors in both real and financial assets. On the propensity of investors to direct their funds toward assets that are considered "hot," Blotnick explains: "Investor behavior is similar in many ways to consumer behavior generally. When people go into a bookstore, they usually buy best sellers. . . . And when they buy stocks, they prefer to stick with the current favorites" (1979: 116).

Adler (1981), for example, documents a succession of stock market fads that arose in the decades following World War II. In terms of fads governing investment in real assets, the commercial real estate "craze" of the 1980s might be thought to constitute an example. The acceleration of commercial real estate construction in Texas and New England during this period, even as vacancy rates were reaching record levels, seems to accord well with Turner and Killian's description of fads and crazes: "the behavior, or the excessive indulgence in it, appears ridiculous, dangerous, or immoral to persons who are not caught up in the collective obsession" (1972: 129).

## Investment and emotion[15]

The Keynesian concept of uncertainty is linked not only to the primacy of convention in determining agent knowledge but is connected, as well, to the importance of emotion in structuring the epistemic processes of agents. In short, because of the abiding epistemological dilemma which faces economic agents (that is, the unmitigated uncertainty which characterizes the nature of things), the knowledge of agents is inherently social and it is inalterably impacted by emotion.

This epistemological dilemma subjects the post-Keynesian agent to a certain level of emotional anguish. A further concept from sociology – cognitive dissonance – might serve to illuminate this idea[16]. A person experiences cognitive dissonance when she holds cognitions (knowledges or beliefs) that "do not fit together" (Festinger 1957: 13). The necessity of action in the face of uncertainty, therefore, is clearly going to be associated with the experiencing of cognitive dissonance since the cognition that one must act is incongruent with the cognition that one lacks the information necessary to determine the "correct" (*ex ante* optimum) course of action. This cognitive dissonance can be thought of as a sort of "epistemological angst," or emotional agitation, that exerts a determinate influence upon an individual's perception, thought, and action.

An important proposition of cognitive dissonance theory is that the desire to reduce cognitive dissonance (and to seek self-consistency) constitutes an important behavioral motivation. One can reduce cognitive dissonance either by adding an additional cognition (a cognition which attenuates the conflict between the original cognitions), or one can seek to change a cognition. Keynes seems to indicate that individuals generally take the latter course by pretending not to be ignorant. As individuals who must operate in the face of uncertainty, we manage to "save our faces as rational, economic men," by adopting various "pretty, polite techniques," which help us to overlook the "awkward fact" that "we simply do not know" (Keynes 1937: 214–15). Among these techniques is the falling back upon convention in forming our expectations of the future. Keynes writes:

> Knowing that our own individual judgment is worthless, we endeavor
> to fall back on the judgment of the rest of the world which is perhaps
> better informed. That is, we endeavor to conform with the behavior of
> the majority or the average.
>
> (Keynes 1937: 214)

Here we see a relation in post-Keynesian thought between the notion of
socially constituted knowledge and the influence of emotion on the thought
processes of the individual.

Keynes is at times quite explicit in his espousal of the idea that sentiment
plays a fundamental role in determining agent choice. He contends that
when individuals lack access to the knowledge necessary to make rational
decisions, the primary spur to action is one's emotion. As he indicates: "a
large proportion of our positive activities depend on spontaneous optimism
rather than on a mathematical expectation, whether moral or hedonistic or
economic" (Keynes 1964: 161). Elucidating this point further, Keynes
writes:

> We are merely reminding ourselves that human decisions affecting the
> future, whether personal or political or economic, cannot depend on
> strict mathematical expectation, since the basis for making such calcu-
> lations does not exist; and that it is our innate urge to activity which
> makes the wheels go round, our rational selves choosing between the
> alternatives as best we are able, calculating where we can, but often
> falling back for our motive on whim or sentiment or chance.
>
> (Keynes 1964: 162–3)

Our understanding of the role of sentiment in prompting agent action can
be further developed by borrowing another conceptual tool from sociology: contagion theory. "The basic assumption of contagion theory," writes
Klausner (1984: 60), "is that increased degrees of suggestibility, emotion-
ality and emotional diffusion lead members of a mass to behave in similar
ways." Associated with this idea is the notion that people become increasingly vulnerable to suggestion when under emotional stress, and in such a
state they exhibit an increasing propensity to engage in panic- or craze-type
crowd behavior.

Contagion theory seems to characterize aptly the dynamics of financial
panics and crazes, in which people become possessed of intensifying
feelings of fear and pessimism (in the case of a panic), and hope and
optimism (in the case of a financial craze). In "normal," or relatively
tranquil, times people are unlikely to succumb to such emotions since
the illusion of stability allows individuals to minimize the cognitive dissonance associated with undertaking action in the face of uncertainty; that
is, they are more easily able to persuade themselves that the economy
behaves in a predictable and ordered manner. However, in "abnormal"

times, when convention and stability break down, one's ability to keep cognitive dissonance at a minimal level is impaired as agents can no longer suppress their knowledge of the insufficiency of knowledge. At such moments, people become especially susceptible to emotionally charged, self-amplifying buying or selling frenzies. In other words, their thoughts concerning the future course of asset prices and appropriate investment strategies are profoundly shaped by passion. Keynes seems to espouse a position along the lines of contagion theory when he writes:

> In abnormal times in particular, when the hypothesis of an indefinite continuance of the existing state of affairs is less plausible than usual even though there are no express grounds to anticipate a definite change, the market will be subject to waves of optimistic and pessimistic sentiment, which are unreasoning and yet in a sense legitimate where no solid basis exists for a reasonable calculation.
>
> (Keynes 1964: 154)

One final idea concerning the role of emotion in constituting people's thought processes relates to Keynes's conception of money demand. The primary source of liquidity preference for Keynes is the emotional anguish associated with uncertainty. Developing this point, Keynes poses the following question: "Why should anyone outside a lunatic asylum wish to use money as a store of wealth?" (1937: 216). Why, that is, should people hold their wealth in the form of an asset which offers minimal or no yield when they might invest their purchasing power in income earning assets such as bonds? His answer is that the existence of unmediated uncertainty makes us reluctant to give up liquidity. The emotional turmoil associated with our awareness of the "objective baselessness" of the knowledge upon which we base our decisions causes an emotional anguish that can only be assuaged through the comfort which liquidity offers. "The possession of actual money lulls our disquietude," Keynes writes, "and the premium which we require to make us part with money is the measure of the degree of our disquietude." The interest rate acts as a gauge, that is, of our emotional state. It indicates the degree to which agents have succumbed to the fear of commitment to the illiquidity associated with physical capital and long-term financial assets. By holding money we can avoid altogether the cognitive dissonance caused by taking action in the face of uncertainty since the flight to liquidity constitutes, in a sense, a withdrawal from action and a retreat into economic inaction.

## CONCLUSION

This chapter has sought to raise the possibility of constructing a theory of investment which takes as its basis a feminist approach to epistemology – an approach to investment theory, that is, which conceives of agent knowledge, thought, and perception as socially and emotionally constituted. The argument was advanced that post-Keynesian economics constitutes an appropriate starting-point for such a theory since its anti-objectivist notion of knowledge shares some compelling affinities with feminist epistemology. In emphasizing and expanding on those aspects of post-Keynesian theory which exhibit commonalities with feminist epistemology and discussing some of their implications for dynamics within capital markets, the general contours of a feminist, post-Keynesian theory of investment were established.

We finish with two final thoughts as to why one might wish to undertake a synthesis of post-Keynesian investment theory and feminist epistemology. First of all, let me raise the idea that feminist and other similar epistemologies represent a compelling and powerful challenge to standard economic theory on many levels. The more widely such ideas are deployed within economic thought, the more likely they are to transform the discipline. One way to work towards this goal is to incorporate feminist and related notions of knowledge and understanding into economic theory in as many different ways as possible. The affinities between post-Keynesian theory and feminist epistemology that I have elaborated here make post-Keynesianism just one of many fruitful points of entry for anti-objectivist epistemological approaches into economic theory – some of which have already been taken and some of which have yet to be breached.

However, feminist and related theories of knowledge are not the only party to gain from this undertaking. Mainstream theorists have decried for years what they see as the lack of an adequate theoretical foundation – that is, a microfoundation – for the ideas of Keynes. This has led to efforts among many economists, such as the so-called New Keynesians, to ground Keynesian concepts in firmly microfounded reasoning. I would suggest, however, that instead of conceding methodological ground to the micro-foundationalists – who espouse a Cartesian notion of subjectivity and a modernist understanding of knowledge – one could move in the opposite direction. That is, one could conceivably establish for Keynes's ideas a theoretical foundation based upon the notion that subjectivity and knowledge are socially constituted. This chapter contends that feminist epistemology can validly represent such a theoretical foundation.

## ACKNOWLEDGEMENTS

I would like to thank Julie Graham, the economics department of the University of Massachusetts at Amherst, and Susan Feiner for making it possible for me to attend the "Out of the Margin" conference and Barbara and Gerald Levin for providing the beautiful and serene location at which this essay was written. I would also like to extend my gratitude, for

115

intellectual. guidance and inspiration, to Carol Levin, Jack Amariglio, and once again, Susan Feiner.

## NOTES

1 It should be pointed out that many of the arguments made in this essay appeared earlier in Levin *et al.* (1993).

2 This is not to say, of course, that the choice-theoretic approach is the only valid economic methodology. It is this approach, however, to which this paper will address itself, and, in fact, it is an approach which this paper shall seek to critique and transform.

3 Exemplary and authoritative guides to post-structuralist feminism and feminist standpoint theory are, respectively, Weedon (1987) and Harding (1991).

4 This terminology is analogous to Resnick and Wolff's distinction between essentialism *of* theory and essentialism *in* theory (Resnick and Wolff 1987).

5 See, for example, Friedman (1951).

6 One characteristic of the modernism within neoclassical theory which we will not develop here is the way in which the agents within neoclassical theory are conceived to have mastered desire and passion through the application of reason to objective circumstances. The process of rational optimization of utility can therefore be conceived as the Cartesian triumph of reason over passion.

7 See Lawson (1988: 41).

8 In explanation of the term ergodic, Davidson writes as follows: "By definition, an ergodic stochastic process simply means that averages calculated from past observations cannot be persistently different from the time average of future outcomes" (Davidson 1991: 132).

9 Another way in which subjective approaches to probability can be thought to place objective knowledge within the grasp of the decision-making agent is indicated by a number of post-Keynesian theorists. Loasby, for example, in making this point notes that, although the agent may lack knowledge of the true probabilities associated with various possible outcomes, "he must still possess a complete list of outcomes" (Loasby 1976: 8).

10 Althusser's epistemological position is elaborated by Amariglio, who describes how Althusser adopts an epistemology which views the creation of knowledge as a "process without a subject" (1987: 188).

11 Examples of such criticism are England (1989, 1993), Hartsock (1983), Nelson (1992), and Strassman (1993a, 1993b).

12 McCloskey (1985) represents an "ovular" work in this area.

13 Burczak's (1994) analysis of the post-modern aspects of Hayek's subjectivism demonstrates persuasively that there are to be found in the Austrian theoretical tradition, as well as the Keynesian school, theorists who have embraced an epistemology which acknowledges the discursively, or socially, constituted nature of knowledge.

14 For an early sociological study of the impact of rumor on the behavior of stock market prices, see Rose (1951).

15 Here, perhaps, the feminist aspects of this essay become particularly clear. Whereas other discourses besides feminism, as noted above, affirm the socially constituted nature of human understanding, feminism tends, more than these alternative discourses, to emphasize as constituents of knowledge and action factors such as emotion, passion, and desire, factors which are often associated

with "the feminine" and – consistent with a patriarchal bias – are therefore taken to be corruptive (rather than constitutive) of knowledge.

16 The concept of cognitive dissonance had been employed previously by economists writing from within the post-Keynesian tradition. Crotty (1990) and Starmer (1993) are examples.

# REFERENCES

Adler, P. (1981) *Momentum: A Theory of Social Action*, Beverly Hills, CA: Sage Publications.

Amariglio, J. (1987) "Marxism Against Economic Science: Althusser's Legacy", in P. Zarembka (ed.) *Research in Political Economy*: 159–94, Greenwich, CT: JAI Press.

———— (1990) "Economics as a Postmodern Discourse", in W.J. Samuels (ed.) *Economics as Discourse: An Analysis of the Language of Economists*: 15–46, Boston: Kluwer Academic Publishers.

Best, S. and Kellner, D. (1991) *Postmodern Theory*, New York: The Guilford Press.

Blotnick, S. (1979) "Stocks Are Like Books", *Forbes* 28 May: 116–17.

Burczak, T.A. (1994) "The Postmodern Moments of F.A. Hayek's Economics", *Economics and Philosophy* 10, April: 31–58.

Butler, J. (1990) *Gender Trouble: Feminism and the Subversion of Identity*, London: Routledge, Chapman & Hall, Inc.

———— (1991) "Imitation and Gender Insubordination", in D. Fuss (ed.) *Inside/Out: Lesbian Theories, Gay Theories*: 13–31, New York: Routledge.

Crotty, J. (1990) "Keynes on True Uncertainty, Conventional Decision-making and the Instability of the Capitalist Growth Process", unpublished manuscript.

———— (1994) "Are Keynesian Uncertainty and Macrotheory Compatible? Conventional Decision Making, Institutional Structures, and Conditional Stability in Keynesian Macromodels", in G. Dymski and R. Pollin (eds) *New Perspectives in Monetary Macroeconomics: Explorations in the Tradition of Hyman P. Minsky*: 105–39, Ann Arbor: University of Michigan Press.

Davidson, P. (1991) "Is Probability Theory Relevant for Uncertainty? A Post-Keynesian Perspective", *Journal of Economic Perspectives* 5, Winter: 129–43.

England, P. (1989) "A Feminist Critique of Rational-Choice Theories: Implications for Sociology", *The American Sociologist*, Spring: 14–28.

———— (1993) "The Separative Self: Androcentric Bias in Neoclassical Assumptions", in M.A. Ferber and J.A. Nelson (eds) *Beyond Economic Man: Feminist Theory and Economics*: 37–53, Chicago: University of Chicago Press.

Festinger, L. (1950) "Informal Social Communication", *Psychological Review* 57: 271–82.

———— (1957) *A Theory of Cognitive Dissonance*, Stanford, CA: Stanford University Press.

Flax, J. (1983) "Political Philosophy and the Patriarchal Unconscious: A Psychoanalytic Perspective on Epistemology and Metaphysics", in S. Harding and M.B. Hintikka (eds) *Discovering Reality: Feminist Perspectives on Epistemology, Metaphysics, Methodology, and Philosophy of Science*: 245–81, Boston: D. Reidel Publishing Company.

Fraser, N. and Nicholson, L.J. (1990) "Social Criticism without Philosophy: An Encounter between Feminism and Postmodernism", in L.J. Nicholson (ed.) *Feminism/Postmodernism*: 19–38, New York: Routledge.

Friedman, M. (1953) "The Methodology of Positive Economics", in *Essays in Positive Economics*: 2–43, Chicago: University of Chicago Press.

Harding, S. (1991) *Whose Science? Whose Knowledge?*, Ithaca, NY: Cornell University Press.

Hartsock, N. (1983) *Money, Sex, and Power: Toward a Feminist Historical Materialism*, Boston: Northeastern University Press.

Jaggar, A.M. (1989) "Love and Knowledge: Emotion in Feminist Epistemology", in A.M. Jaggar and S. Bordo (eds) *Gender/Body/Knowledge: Feminist Reconstructions of Being and Knowing*: 145–71, New Brunswick, NJ: Rutgers University Press.

Keynes, J.M. (1937) "The General Theory of Employment", *Quarterly Journal of Economics* 51, February: 209–23.

———— (1964) *The General Theory of Employment, Interest, and Money*, San Diego, CA: Harcourt Brace Jovanovich.

Klausner, M. (1984) "Sociological Theory and the Behavior of Financial Markets", in P.A. Adler and P. Adler (eds) *The Social Dynamics of Financial Markets*: 57–81. Greenwich, CT: JAI Press.

Lachmann, L.M. (1943) "The Role of Expectations in Economics as a Social Science" *Economica* 10: 12–23.

Lawson, T. (1988) "Probability and Uncertainty in Economic Analysis", *Journal of Post-Keynesian Economics* 11: 38–65.

Levin, L., Amariglio, J. and Graham, J. (1993) "Toward a Postmodern, Feminist Reconstruction of the Economic Subject", paper presented at the annual ASSA meetings, Anaheim, California.

Lloyd, G. (1991) "Reason as Attainment", in S. Gunew (ed.) *A Reader in Feminist Knowledge*, 166–80, New York: Routledge.

Loasby, B.J. (1976) *Choice, Complexity and Ignorance: An Enquiry into Economic Theory and the Practice of Decision-Making*, Cambridge: Cambridge University Press.

Lorraine, T.E. (1990) *Gender Identity and the Production of Meaning*, San Francisco, CA: Westview Press.

McCloskey, D. (1985) *The Rhetoric of Economics*, Madison: University of Wisconsin Press.

Minsky, H.P. (1975) *John Maynard Keynes*, New York: Columbia University Press.

———— (1986) *Stabilizing an Unstable Economy*, New Haven, CT: Yale University Press.

Modigliani, F. and Miller, M.H. (1958) "The Cost of Capital, Corporation Finance, and the Theory of Investment", *American Economic Review* 48, 3: 261–97.

Muth, J.F. (1961) "Rational Expectations and the Theory of Price Movements", *Econometrica* 29, July: 315–35.

Nelson, J. (1992) "Gender, Metaphor, and the Definition of Economics", *Economics and Philosophy* 8: 103–25.

Resnick, S. and Wolff, R. (1987) *Knowledge and Class: A Marxian Critique of Political Economy*, Chicago: University of Chicago Press.

Rogers, C. (1989) *Money, Interest and Capital: A Study in the Foundations of Monetary Theory*, Cambridge: Cambridge University Press.

Rose, A.M. (1951) "Rumor in the Stock Market", *Public Opinion Quarterly* 15: 461–86.

Shackle, G.L.S. (1967) *The Years of High Theory*, Cambridge: Cambridge University Press.

———— (1972) *Epistemics & Economics: A Critique of Economic Doctrines*, Cambridge: Cambridge University Press.

———— (1974) *Keynesian Kaleidics*, Edinburgh: Edinburgh University Press.

———— (1988) *Business, Time, and Thought: Selected Papers of G.L.S. Shackle*, New York: Macmillan.

Sharpe, W.F. (1964) "Capital Asset Prices: A Theory of Market Equilibrium Under Conditions of Risk", *The Journal of Finance* 19, 3: 425–42.

118

Starmer, C. (1993) "The Psychology of Uncertainty in Economic Theory: A Critical Appraisal and a Fresh Approach", *Review of Political Economy* 5, 2: 181–96.

Strassman, D. (1993a) "Not a Free Market: The Rhetoric of Disciplinary Authority in Economics", in M.A. Ferber and J.A. Nelson (eds) *Beyond Economic Man: Feminist Theory and Economics*: 54–68, Chicago: University of Chicago Press.

—— (1993b) "The Stories of Economics and the Power of the Storyteller", *History of Political Economy* 25, 1: 145–63.

Turner, R.H. (1964) "Collective Behavior", in R.E.L. Farris (ed.) *Handbook of Modern Sociology*: 382–425, Chicago: Rand McNally & Company.

Turner, R.H. and Killian, L.M. (1972) *Collective Behavior*, Englewood Cliffs, NJ: Prentice-Hall, Inc.

Vickers, D. (1992) "The Investment Function: Five Propositions in Response to Professor Gordon", *Journal of Post-Keynesian Economics* 14, Summer: 445–64.

Weedon, C. (1987) *Feminist Practice & Poststructuralist Theory*, New York: Basil Blackwell.

# 7

# ECONOMIC THEORY AND FEMINIST THEORY

## Comments on chapters by Polachek, Ott, and Levin

### *Julie A. Nelson*

The contributions by Solomon W. Polachek, Notburga Ott, and Lee B. Levin offer a rich context for discussing the contributions of feminist theory to economic theory. As regrettably few mainstream economists consider women and families to be interesting subjects of study, and fewer still realize that a feminist critique of standard economics even exists, each of these essays breaks in some way from standard practice. Each, however, takes a different path. To determine effectively the vigor of feminist economics, it is important to see how far these approaches can take us.

Considering the general lack of attention to women and feminism in economics in general, Polachek's work is unusual and commendable. I hope, however, that publication of this book represents a growing strength and acceptance of feminist economics, such that we no longer need to be satisfied with attention *per se*, but can begin to concern ourselves with the quality of the analysis as well. By this standard, Polachek's contribution falls short of the mark.

In presenting his understanding of feminism, Polachek repeatedly asserts that feminist economics is economics about "women's issues"[1]. While feminists of course argue for including women in the realm of concern, the feminist methodological critique is much more far-ranging. The way in which feminist scholarship leads to a re-evaluation of models and techniques, irrespective of subject, has been well discussed in the introduction to this book – and explicitly demonstrated in Levin's piece on investor behavior. Unfortunately, Polacheck's interpretation unduly narrows the terrain of feminist economics and permits him to misrepresent key feminist critiques of neoclassical theory[2].

Feminists' argument that the neoclassical picture of the economy is socially constructed challenges Polachek's position on the origin (and persistence) of earnings gaps across the sexes. While the notion of frictionless markets populated by anonymous, autonomous, rational actors is sometimes useful, the wise user does not confuse "blackboard economics" with real economies (McCloskey 1993). Let us examine Polachek's notion of how the world works. Families are, as he diagrams in Figure 4.1, influenced by "societal discrimination," which may work through family decisions in such a way as to cause men and women to make different investments in human capital, affecting their labor market outcomes. As an hypothesis, this has some initial plausibility[3]. But what about the demand side of the labor market? Here Polacheck falls back on Gary Becker's old argument that discrimination from the employer side cannot persist in competitive markets. Polachek's Figure 4.1 shows "corporate discrimination" as an exogenous box, disconnected from "societal discrimination," and linked to labor market outcomes only by dashed lines, indicating some doubt about its importance. Does Polachek mean to imply that firms are created via virgin birth? Does he believe that while families are social institutions, firms are not?

Polachek has, from a feminist (or even a common sense) viewpoint, taken blackboard microeconomics much too seriously. He has confused possession of a set of theories about how firms *might* work under restrictive assumptions with possession of knowledge about how firms *do* work as real institutions populated by real human beings. Polachek systematically downplays employer discrimination in his studies, not because careful observation and analysis have told him that employers do not discriminate much, but because large-scale employer discrimination is not consistent with his assumptions. "If the model and the world disagree," true believers in the neoclassical model seem to say, "then too bad for the world."

The feminist critique seeks to improve economics by removing such prejudices, which are often based, we believe, on gendered notions about the relative value of assumptions of autonomy vs. assumptions of situatedness; techniques of abstract analysis vs. techniques of concrete investigation, etc. In contrast to economists who take Polachek's view, feminist economists are more likely to recognize firms as social institutions, and see real world institutions as worthy of scholarly study[4].

Notburga Ott's chapter on marital bargaining models makes substantial contributions to the choice theoretic literature on household decisions. She expands on earlier formal marital bargaining models by discussing the effects of price changes on conflict outcomes, including problems of dynamic time allocation, and presenting a model of the effect that having children may have on relative power of spouses. She claims – justly, I believe – superiority for her models as contrasted to models of unitary marital utility functions. She also, commendably, seeks to compare her theoretical results, to some extent, with empirical evidence from household surveys. Such work by feminists from within the neoclassical mold plays a very important political role in getting feminist perspectives on marital behavior accepted as "serious" economics, by the current standards of the profession. But on this front too we can push further.

Economics, to be a discipline with anything worthwhile to say, should not just be about how economists talk to other economists, but should also reveal something about the subject of study. After reading Ott's contribution, do we have greater insight into the internal workings of families? Or have we primarily seen how *a priori* results can be made to fit a professionally acceptable mathematical frame? I tend (in agreement with Seiz 1991) to believe that while thinking about marital decision-making in a broad bargaining *framework* can be very helpful in gaining insights into behavior, formal bargaining *models* lend rather little extra to the analysis. The benefits of what little they add are often outweighed by the costs, as the requirements of formalism tend to determine what will be investigated and how. This has serious implications for the resulting analysis, as can be illustrated with examples from Ott's essay.

First, while the essay is billed as a study of "fertility and division of work within the family" only two actors – husband and wife – are considered. Children enter only in the last section, as goods in parental utility functions. This limitation is directed by the formal bargaining approach, since such modeling becomes radically more complicated for a number of agents greater than two. Such a redefinition of families as couples makes consideration of child welfare and child agency impossible[5].

Second, the focus on the cooperative Nash bargaining solution rules out other plausible bargaining solutions. The Nash solution is the unique solution *only* if we demand that the solution also satisfies a set of restrictive axioms. Consider, for example, an alternative game which violates the Nash axiom of symmetry of agents: person "m" can present person "f" with a take-it-or-leave-it offer. Instead of a solution at point C in Ott's Figure 5.1, the solution would be in an epsilon neighborhood of point A. While many mainstream economists seem to find the possible indeterminacy of many real-world bargaining problems unsettling, feminists and post-modernists (Mehta 1993) tend to see this as a problem with economists rather than a problem with the world.

Third and finally, Ott models welfare as defined over (variously) resources; goods; consumption and leisure; and some of the aforementioned plus the presence of children. Making all of the foregoing commensurate within a utility function distorts what I believe are qualitatively different aspects of welfare, all of which might be subject to marital bargaining. Consider, as an alternative, a way of thinking about marriage that includes agency, affiliation, and the standard of living as three distinct aspects of human welfare (Nelson 1994). Agency is the ability of each person to assert his or her will and make decisions. Differences in levels of agency are illustrated (though far from completely described) in the contrast between the Nash and take-it-or-leave-it bargaining solutions described above. Affiliation represents the need of human beings to belong and to be loved, as may be manifested in the desire to enter a marriage or rear children. The standard of living refers to the arguments of standard economics: the welfare one gets from goods and the use of one's time. A hackneyed example will serve to illustrate what is lost by the reductionist approach. Suppose person "m" buys person "f" a dozen roses after a fight. To an economist using standard resource-based models, only f's "consumption" of the roses is important: f has gained "utility" at m's expense. In the actual economy of the marriage, as perceived by the spouses, however, the standard of living effects of the roses (their sight, smell, etc.) are probably purely incidental in comparison to what the flowers are doing, or not doing, for the affiliative base of the marriage. Thus, while Ott makes a substantial contribution to a literature, it remains questionable how effective this literature can be in advancing our knowledge about how families function, given the restrictiveness of the assumptions that must be imposed to make the models tractable and the solutions unique.

Lee B. Levin's work on investment theory is an important example of how feminist theory can inform work on economic topics outside the range of "women's issues." Feminist theory, by undermining the hegemony of the notion of fully rational, fully autonomous, and entirely emotionless economic actors, creates the intellectual space for discussion of the social and emotional constitution of decision-making. Levin's synthesis of feminist, post-modernist, post-Keynesian, philosophical, and psychological insights is a *tour de force*. Levin is especially effective in showing how economists' theories of expectations can be enriched by borrowing, not just from the "hard" disciplines of math and statistics, but also from the "soft" disciplines of sociology and social psychology. The fact that many pieces of his analysis come from authors who are not explicitly feminist should not be surprising or disturbing. Many thoughtful scholars have hit on good explanations; the feminist methodological critique is not so much about creating new models and methods from scratch as it is about changing the standards we use to evaluate the quality of research.

I sense a degree of overkill, however, in Levin's assertion of the "baselessness" of knowledge and in his assertion that feminist theory is congruent with "radical subjectivism." Rejection of Cartesian radical objectivism need not require a turn towards the old dualistic opposite of "anything goes" and personal whim. As feminist philosopher Martha Nussbaum (1992) has put it, "When we get rid of the hope of a transcendent metaphysical grounding for our evaluative judgments . . . we are not left with the abyss. We have everything that we always had all along: the exchange of reasons and arguments by human beings within history" (213). Donald McCloskey (1993) has suggested that we call what we know together "conjective" knowledge. The recognition that investors' knowledge, like economists' knowledge, is socially and emotionally mediated need not preclude the recognition that people often also try to make their knowledge more reliable (to the extent possible) in systematic ways – including, for example, by poring over corporate balance sheets, by calculating mathematical expectations, or even by synthesizing post-Keynesian and feminist insights. Levin's work would point towards a fuller picture of investor behavior, as well as be less likely to alienate mainstream economist readers, if he modified his radical subjectivist rhetoric.

Much work remains to be done in developing feminist economic theory. While feminists certainly need to engage with standard neoclassical theory, formal game theory, and post-modernist theory, as illustrated here, I hope that continued engagement will be done in an open-minded way, with a common goal of the improvement of economic understanding.

## NOTES

1 In the present version of his essay, Polachek mostly speaks about "gender issues" instead of "women's issues." This, however, merely concerns a substitution of terms that has no consequences for the content of his analysis.
2 While there are some feminists who advocate abandoning neoclassical theory, I was rather surprised to see my own work (Nelson 1992) cited as evidence that feminists have "derided" the emphasis put on "logic, rigor, quantification, abstraction, precision and objectivity" in mainstream analysis. I always write about the enrichment of mainstream economics, rather than its demolition, and always argue that all of the above-named qualities should be recognized as among the "legitimate goals of economic practice" (Nelson 1992: 111).
3 Since this section is about economic theory, it is not the place for a point-by-point discussion of Polachek's empirical assertions. Let it suffice to say that the reader should not interpret an individual's review of work in which he has been closely involved as an objective overview of findings in the area.
4 Other economists recognize these points, too (Solow 1990).
5 For a discussion of how such an elision of children has seriously compromised one area of the economics literature, see Nelson (1993).

## REFERENCES

McCloskey, D.N. (1993) "Some Consequences of a Conjective Economics", in M.A. Ferber and J.A. Nelson (eds) *Beyond Economic Man: Feminist Theory and Economics*, 69–93, Chicago: University of Chicago Press.

Mehta, J. (1993) "Meaning in the Context of Bargaining Games: Narratives in Opposition", in W. Henderson, A. Dudley-Evans and R. Backhouse (eds) *Economics and Language*, 85–99, London: Routledge.

Nelson, J.A. (1992) "Gender, Metaphor, and the Definition of Economics", *Economics and Philosophy* 8, 1: 103–25.

——— (1993) "Household Equivalence Scales: Theory versus Policy?", *Journal of Labor Economics* 11, 3: 471–93.

—— (1994) "I, Thou, and Them: Capabilities, Altruism, and Norms in the Economics of Marriage", *American Economic Review* 84, 2: 126–31.

Nussbaum, M.C. (1992) "Human Functioning and Social Justice: In Defense of Aristotelian Essentialism", *Political Theory* 20, 2: 121–45.

Seiz, J. (1991) "The Bargaining Approach and Feminist Methodology", *Review of Radical Political Economics* 23, 1 and 2: 22–9.

Solow, R.M. (1990) *The Labor Market as a Social Institution*, Cambridge, MA: Basil Blackwell.

# Part III

# INTERPRETING ECONOMICS

*Editor Edith Kuiper*

It was absurd to blame any class or any sex, as a whole. Great bodies of people are never responsible for what they do. They are driven by instincts which are not within their control. They too, the patriarchs, the professors, had endless difficulties, terrible drawbacks to contend with. Their education had been in some ways as faulty as my own. It had bred in them defects as great. True, they had money and power, but only at the cost of harbouring in their breasts an eagle, a vulture, for ever tearing the liver out and plucking at the lungs – the instinct for possession, the rage for acquisition which drives them to desire other people's fields and goods perpetually; to make frontiers and flags; battleships and poison gas; to offer up their own lives and their children's lives. Walk through the Admiralty Arch (I had reached that monument), or any other avenue given up to trophies and cannon, and reflect upon the kind of glory celebrated there.

(Woolf [1928] (1957): 38)

# 8

# THE ECONOMIST AS STORYTELLER

## What the texts reveal

### *Diana Strassmann and Livia Polanyi*

In this chapter we argue that reconceptualizing economic practice as story-telling may further feminist efforts to transform economic knowledge and practice and help open the doors to potential economists currently under-represented in the profession[1]. Our argument builds upon the idea that all human knowledge is situated; any account of the world is inevitably shaped by the experiences and human lives of its producers. The concept that all knowledge is situated is not original with us but has been developed and extensively defended by feminist and other critical interpretive thinkers[2]. Of concern to us here is that economics accounts are in no sense exempt from this generalization, and are inextricably linked to the gender, social class, ethnic background and historical and personal circumstances of their producers.

Using insights drawn from the application of linguistic theory, we will show how the situated character of economic texts may be uncovered by careful examination of details in the language and content of the texts. Lying just below the surface of apparently simple illustrative examples of economics writing is a complex of interwoven assumptions about the world. When rigorously examined, these assumptions reveal a great deal about both the life positions of the narrators and the discourse in which they are participants. Further, the evidence of the situated character of economic knowledge contradicts the common claim that economic accounts can be constructed independently of the life circumstances of the dominant producers. We will argue that the rhetoric of the discipline's dominant practitioners plays an important role in the reproduction of the economics community and in silencing the voices of differently situated practitioners.

Making effective use of these insights, however, will require that economists overcome their modernist discomfort with acknowledging storytelling as an integral feature of economic practice. We therefore begin with discussing the implications of a narrative reconceptualization of economic theorizing.

## IF ECONOMICS IS STORYTELLING, WHERE IS THE SCIENCE?

In introducing economists to the narrative aspects of their craft, Donald McCloskey (1990) presents a prescriptive argument for understanding economic analyses as storytelling. He argues that if economists can learn to construct more interesting and compelling arguments, good ideas will have a better chance of winning out in the marketplace of ideas. While a number of economists have been persuaded by McCloskey's approach and have come to see economics as a kind of storytelling, many see little insight to be gained by a narrative reconceptualization of their practice. Feminist economists who contest perceived masculinist biases may also have difficulty accepting a characterization of economic practice as storytelling, fearing that envisioning economics (or any scientific practice) as storytelling will weaken feminist claims.

Economists, like other scientists, want a reliable mechanism for sorting out good theories from bad. Viewing economic analysis as storytelling might appear to make it impossible to separate good arguments from bad. If the methods of economic analysis do not lead reliably to "good" theory and do not provide a basis for asserting some claims over others, what, we may ask, are we left with as a science? Will all work in a discipline be given equal weight, reducing scientific practice to Anything Goes, Total Subjectivity, or Relativism? Surely not. But in order to understand why not, we must examine the epistemic basis of current scientific practice and contrast this view with the one we are taking that knowledge is situated in experience and interdependent with the language of expression.

Standard economic accounts assume that scientific knowledge is an immutable object separate from person or circumstance and independent of language or the mode in which it is made known. According to this view, the quality or value of any explanation is dependent either, as modernists believe, upon the methodology used to attain the explanation, or upon the value ascertained through a well-functioning marketplace of ideas – the view promulgated by McCloskey in his work on economic rhetoric. McCloskey has convinced some economists to abandon the search for an Archimedian lever with which to prove the superiority of one theory over another and to accept that ultimately only argument is available to demonstrate the adequacy of our assertions. With this rhetorical move, economic methodology as provider of truth can be supplanted by an allegiance to the authority of the conceptual marketplace, thereby allowing economists to acknowledge the social character of economics without reducing the discipline to a fearful Anything Goes. If we can have confidence in the opinions and well-reasoned decisions of the thousands of honest and intelligent economic scholars, the thousands of esteemed members of prestigious departments, the editors and referees of journals, the reviewers of grants, and all the other power brokers in the discipline, as McCloskey's (1983, 1985) argument goes, then we need not fear that acknowledging the social character of knowledge production in economics will put the discipline at risk.

This faith in the existing bulwarks of disciplinary control may be comforting at first glance. However, acknowledging the supremacy of argument in the social construction of knowledge inevitably invites a consideration of how some arguments come to be judged more persuasive than others. Specifically, we can ask how the evaluation of a particular argument is influenced by the identity and situated position of its evaluators. How do the human lives of members of an intellectual community influence and constrain the rhetoric of successful arguments? Do arguments need to be formulated in a particular way to be heard? Who chooses the topics of conversation, and who is allowed to change the topic? How does the rhetorical character and subject of disciplinary conversations influence how potential entrants evaluate their acceptability and success in the intellectual community? In short, what are the rules governing entry and participation in intellectual conversations? These questions suggest that the processes by which some ideas gain ascendancy over others is more complicated than generally believed by economists, and that the metaphor of the marketplace of ideas does not adequately capture the social construction of knowledge.

In particular, the metaphor of the intellectual marketplace gives no insight into why ideas and perspectives which reflect the experiences of women and others who differ from the discipline's most predominant practitioners are absent from standard economic accounts. This problem can be addressed much more satisfactorily by taking as a starting-point the alternative metaphor of situated knowledge. Situated knowledge specifically and persuasively acknowledges the contextual grounding of all accounts, and thereby allows a variety of accounts of the world. Unlike the marketplace of ideas, which implies that prevailing accounts are the best accounts, situated analyses of economic discourse show that the assumptions about the structure of situations and the norms of human behavior built into standard economic accounts resonate well with the experiences of those who have produced them; conversely, accounts more faithful to the experiences of others are less compelling to the predominant practitioners in the discipline. Less compelling to white, North American, heterosexual male economists does not, let us emphasize, necessarily mean less insightful or less scientifically valid.

Acknowledging that all arguments are situated in human experiences and that a plurality of reasonable accounts is possible is not equivalent to claiming that all accounts are equally valid. What such a position does

131

claim is that reasonable and honest scholars should acknowledge the positioned nature of accounts and arguments and consider such information in evaluating them – as economists and other scientists in fact already do. It is commonly accepted, for example, that a novel analysis of economic phenomena put forth by a prominent scholar from a leading economics department in a major American university will receive considerably more respectful attention than the identical analysis put forward by a less ratified member of the community[3]. Similarly, the political or intellectual orientation of economists is often taken into account as useful information in assessing the degree of credence to be accorded their work.

Accepting the situated nature of knowledge and a possible plurality of reasonable accounts does not, therefore, destroy the possibility of argument, but merely limits the authority with which any set of arguments may reasonably be presented. Many economists would like to believe in the existence of an authoritatively correct mechanism for "proving" that one account is superior to all others – a perfectly reliable mechanism for separating the "wheat from the chaff" (see Solow 1993: 157). However, accepting the impossibility of such an Archimedian lever does not lead to Anything Goes or Relativism. Making the positioned nature of argument more visible simply provides more information about arguments and accounts than normally revealed by practicing scientists, and thereby leads to a more reasonable and honest social process for the selection of favored perspectives and accounts – leading in short to better science.

## STORY OR MODEL: THE STAKES IN THE RHETORIC

Current accounts in mainstream economics are set forth as authoritative and dispassionate, uninfluenced by the lives and positions of their creators, and therefore pure and objective. Yet of all social scientists, economists are the most fervid believers in the motivating force of self-interest. So why do they claim a persona of detached disinterested objectivity for themselves? As both standard economic assumptions and the metaphor of situated knowledge direct us to consider, this claim is itself self-interested, and represents a defense against alternative accounts[4].

Feminist interests lead us in another direction. In seeking to promote economic accounts truer to the lives and experiences of women, we have a stake in uncovering the interests underlying established accounts and an epistemology which awards undue authority and universality to those accounts. If alternative accounts of economic phenomena are really to be given a fair shake in the intellectual marketplace of economics, then the situated character of economic argument needs to be uncovered; otherwise that marketplace will not be open equally to all[5]. While we may need to give up claims of absolute authority and universality in our alternative accounts, we will gain greater strength for those voices currently underrepresented in the profession and more honesty in the social construction of economics.

In the next section we present a methodology for revealing the situated character of economic texts.

## REVEALING THE SITUATED NATURE OF NARRATIVE ACCOUNTS

The sociolinguistic and ethnomethodological work of William Labov (1972), Erving Goffman (1981) and Harvey Sacks (1978) has shown how detailed textual analyses of ordinary and unremarkable accounts may be used to uncover much information about social and intellectual communities, including the positioning of community members in terms of race, ethnicity, gender, social status, historical epoch and geographical location. This research shows that communities of speakers have standard conventions of appropriate talk which typically vary according to the social situation. The rules and conventions of appropriate behavior and speech in a community are best revealed by examining the accounts regarded by a community's members as ordinary and unremarkable; the event which seems most "unremarkable" to an initiate reveals the most about the expectations and norms of the community. Competent members of a community know the conventions of speaking and are able to tailor their utterances to fit different social situations in their community.

Like speakers in any community, economists recognize and vary the way they communicate in different settings and to different kinds of people. Therefore, applying these insights to the language, speech, and accounts produced by economists requires that we examine very ordinary examples of economics writing. We will take our examples of economics accounts from a very conventional, indeed a hypernormal, source – a textbook. We use two simple and otherwise unremarkable passages from Ronald Ehrenberg and Robert Smith's (1994) *Modern Labor Economics: Theory and Public Policy,* one of the most popular labor economics textbooks in the United States.

Because textbooks belong to a specific academic genre aimed at introducing neophytes and outsiders to the received wisdom of a field, they differ in conventional form from journal articles, the genre for introducing new ideas to professional economists. Uncovering information about the basic norms, expectations, and situated character of economics requires that we use examples which professional practitioners will accept as unremarkable and appropriate, given their genre. In economics, such writing is easiest to find – and be sure that it counts as such – in popular and widely used textbooks. While the writing found in textbooks will differ in predictable ways from that commonly found in scholarly economics articles, the examples and writing in widely accepted textbooks must be perceived by disciplinary practitioners as appropriate vehicles for transmitting the received wisdom of the field to students. For a text to be a commercial success, such writing cannot include examples that instructors might view as idiosyncratic, or detracting from the theoretical or practical material under discussion. We can therefore learn a great deal about the commonly held assumptions of economics and its situated position by examining such hypernormal examples of economics writing.

In the following section of this chapter, we introduce some basic theoretical tools of linguistic analysis. As we will show, applying these tools to examples of ordinary economics texts affords much insight into the situated practices and perspectives of economics.

## The creation of a storyworld in narrative accounts

The first theoretical tool concerns the way language is used in all narrative accounts to create a "storyworld" in which the action takes place. The idea of a storyworld is similar to the notion of a model. While the term model is used to describe "abstractions" from the real world, where important material is represented in the model and unimportant material left out, the notion of a storyworld also presumes that only some information about the storyworld can be included in the narrative.

The assumption underlying storytelling in all world traditions is that the storyworld is very much like the world we live in every day. Since it is impossible to express in detail every aspect of the material, situation, or phenomena, language must be used parsimoniously. Much information about the storyworld is necessarily left out. In order to fill in the gaps, the reader is expected to make inferences or assumptions about the omitted material. Without specific reasons to assume otherwise, we imagine that the omitted material describes a world much like the one with which we are most familiar. The storyteller expects those to whom the story is directed to make specific "default" assumptions, these being the standard assumptions members of a community will make about omitted material.

While the idea underlying standard conceptions of models is that what is left out is extraneous detail, readers of all narrative accounts (including those explicitly presented as models) are in fact expected, and directed by the narrative content, to fill in the gaps of the text in specific ways. For example, if we learn in a narrative account that a young man and a young woman have gone for a picnic in a park, our imagination fills in two arms for each picnicker and a green colour for the grass. Unless we are given reason to suspend a default assumption about the world (e.g. the grass has died), we assume that all normal assumptions hold. Having default assumptions and using them in processing narrative accounts allows us to make inferences about the states and events described and to understand the action of the story without needing to be told every single detail.

All human beings, when asked to imagine a scene, will imagine a landscape of some sort in which gravity exists; those who live in a desert setting may well have an arid background against which action takes place, while those who live in a rain forest will imagine a lush, damp environment. Someone who has lived her whole life as a brown-skinned person surrounded by others with brown skin, when asked to imagine a person, will equip that person with brown skin. A person who has lived his life exclusively among white-skinned persons would probably not people his imaginary world with persons of other races. This, in itself, is not racism, although default assumptions and default inferences certainly play their roles in racist thinking. Rather, building a cognitive picture or model using default assumptions reflects the realities of cognitive processing. Without specific information to the contrary, one assumes the familiar. To do otherwise would be folly. One would need to invent the world anew at every turn, never learning from experience or using experience to structure expectations about a new situation.

Members of intellectual or social communities respond to the information included in texts by making similar default assumptions about the material left out. These assumptions are based on knowledge all humans have – for example that people normally do not have more than two legs – as well as cultural and socially specific beliefs, clichés and stereotypes. Members of cultures, members of communities of practice and members of other social organizations demonstrate their participation in a socially constructed collective in part in terms of the similar assumptions they make about *unspecified* portions of the storyworlds. While no two individuals (or one individual at two different times) will have identical default assumptions, the degree to which people are members of the same community (at a specific moment in time) will reflect the degree to which they respond similarly to specific textual information in making default assumptions about the nature of the world.

To exemplify this point, a standard default assumption in American economics until the 1960s was that husbands worked in the marketplace and wives stayed at home. The issue of "female labor supply" accordingly was scarcely an issue at the time, as economists assumed that married women did not "work." As increasing numbers of American women, including the wives of many economists, entered the marketplace, this assumption remained default increasingly less frequently (Brown 1989). The assumption that wives have the primary responsibility for childcare remains a default assumption in American economics primarily because that is indeed the current cultural norm in the United States.

## The role of "evaluation" in structuring meaning in narrative accounts

A second important linguistic concept concerns the way narrators use specific language to show how some information in an account is more important than other information. Linguists use the term "evaluation" to describe how narrators indicate the relative importance of various details in their accounts. "Evaluative devices," which we describe below, indicate to the listener how different pieces of information included in a story matter to the intended point of the story, and how they contribute to the story's being found appropriate in a particular conversation by the other conversational participants.

An important general process of evaluation occurs through redundancy and repetition. These function by impressing some information upon the story recipient by repeating that information more than once. The most redundantly encoded object sticks in the mind merely because it is mentioned most frequently. The related evaluative processes, evaluation through the unusual and evaluation by distinctive encoding, function by signalling the importance of a particular situation by treating it in an unusual or striking manner, giving a detailed account of one object when all other objects are mentioned briefly, or using metaphoric or colorful language to describe one object while all others are described in a more sober manner.

The presentation of a sophisticated graph, for example, is one way in which the authors of an economics article or text may indicate to the reader that the information encoded in the graph is to be viewed as more important than material or issues not developed and presented in such a way. For example, Ehrenberg and Smith (1994) mention in a few sentences (and without further analysis) that when both husbands and wives work outside the home, women still do most of the housework. Then they spend several pages developing and explaining a graph which shows how the model of comparative advantage provides insight into household decisions about which spouse should specialize in housework if only one works outside the home. Although the model does not explicitly apply to dual-earner households, readers are directed to infer that this conventional economic analysis provides the primary explanation for the chosen gender roles of all families.

Another evaluative method exploits the possible range of grammatical constructions which can be used to convey the same information. For example, the subject of a sentence carries out the action described by the verb. When a person is introduced into a text as a subject, one expects that individual to be an active participant in the immediate action, whereas when a person is introduced in relation to another person or a location, one expects that individual to be a less important participant.

The principles on which evaluation functions are essentially psychological: one remembers the redundantly encoded and the novelly encoded. The redundant and the striking emerge from a welter of detail, and are forefronted in relation to other materials which fall together to form the background.

We will now apply the concepts of default assumptions and evaluation to the two conventional economics passages from Ehrenberg and Smith (1994) which we are taking as our examples. By making use of the default assumptions evoked by the texts to us, both female, white, middle-class, healthy American academicians, socialized by our experiences and training to share certain default assumptions with other members of our culture and academic communities, we are able to show how the texts conjure an entire world into being.

## THE STORY OF THE ENJOYABLE FAMILY

Our first example is a discussion illustrating the application of utility theory to household production. The purpose of the discussion, analyzing a short text from Ehrenberg and Smith's (1994) *Modern Labor Economics: Theory and Public Policy* (reproduced in Appendix A), is to teach students how to conceptualize family decisions as optimization problems. The story is meaningful to economists because it is a variation on a standard narrative theme in the current conversation of the discipline, and also because it coheres with the fundamental way economists think about the world.

Linguistic details of this story and of another we will describe from the same text show that even more information is being provided to the reader than immediately apparent in the bare bones of the basic plot. By applying the concepts of default assumptions and evaluation, we can begin to uncover some of the markers of the situated character of this text. In analyzing these short texts, we leave unexamined both utility theory and the assumptions of neoclassical economics, focussing instead on the narrative details of the text, and considering the default assumptions they evoke to us as acculturated Americans.

### Default assumptions in the Enjoyable Family: living the enjoyable life

Upon reading this short passage from Ehrenberg and Smith, we find that we recognize in the textual details the stereotypic images of a fictional generic American family. The details tell us that "the family" – which must decide "what to consume and how to produce what it consumes" – has meals "from which family well-being is derived. A vacuum cleaner . . . an orderly home. Food, clothing, and supervision time . . . [to devote to] children, whom the parents hope to enjoy" and "a microwave oven to heat prepared foods" (1994: 213).

These details create images in our minds which fill in for details not included explicitly in the written account. The family's possession of a vacuum cleaner, microwave, food, clothing and time with which to "enjoy" and supervise children evokes a model world in which normal expectations include pleasant mealtimes, useful and expensive appliances, an orderly home, time to devote to supervision of the children, children whom the parents expect to find enjoyable.

These words evoke a complex of ideas conventionally accepted to be necessary for "mealtimes to be enjoyable" such as good food, enough food, abundant food, and a pleasant environment in which the food is eaten. "Mealtimes" also conjures up a kind of family – one which lives by the clock and where the comings and goings of family members are subject to a rigid schedule.

The vacuum cleaner, the microwave, the clean home, the well brought up children, the pleasant mealtime tell us a great deal more than merely these few facts: from these facts an entire world is brought into being. We know that this family is the conventional stereotype of an American family. Notice the social positioning of "the family." We are talking about defaults: mention "the family" in a textbook, on television, or in the popular press and do not modify the word with "poor," "African-American" (or "black" or "Negro"), "Hispanic," "single-parent," "immigrant," "Jewish" or "struggling", and the American default picture resembles the family in "Leave it to Beaver" (a popular American sitcom) with one of the kids a little girl.

## Evaluation in the Enjoyable Family

Evaluation – the emphasis given to different details in a story – functions in this small vignette of the text through all of the methods described above. We can easily see how certain features of the story are brought out through use of the unexpected in the details of lists of household appliances. The novelty of encountering an everyday, homey detail such as a "microwave oven" or a "vacuum cleaner" in a serious college-level textbook adds salience to the object, salience such an object would not have in a catalog from a kitchen appliance company. For a moment the complexity of the material falls away and one is surrounded by comfortable shiny appliances which stay in the mind after the details of the utility function, an ordinary object in the text, recedes into the background.

In this short piece of text, we also see evaluation through distinctive encoding, in this case through elaboration: picking some aspects of the storyworld circumstances and calling attention to them by elaborating on aspects of those details at length while leaving aside other potentially interesting material. The fact that the lives of family members are "enjoy-able" is underscored several times by the repeated use of the word "enjoy" in both adjective and verb form: "The family enjoys mealtimes with their enjoyable children" is a message which sticks with the reader – a message to which we will return and examine in some detail below.

We also find in this text another form of distinctive encoding: evaluation by extensive elaborate explanation of the family's optimization strategy, both mathematically and in "Figure 7.1," a compelling feature to students who know the economics genre convention "what's important is in the math." The extensive discussion and references to Figure 7.1 also show students that this material is important, further signified by the length and ponderous formal tone of the piece, different from the rest of this portion of the chapter so far (which has been somewhat less formal than the rest of the text). The heightened evaluation of this piece of the text signifies to students that the story of how families optimize is its important point.

### Tilling and weeding, canning and freezing: the story of the Other Family

We will now discuss a second story from Ehrenberg and Smith's text: the story of the Other Family (see Appendix B). As we will show, the discussion of this family's situation and optimization possibilities is totally unrealistic given the circumstances of most families for whom this analysis is purportedly designed to apply. In contrast to the coherent world familiar to all acculturated Americans invoked by the Enjoyable Family, close examination of the world described in the text of the Other Family reveals it to be an incoherent world: the story which is told about the Others does not make sense. This failure of the tellers to produce a compellingly ordinary story of the Others will lead us to speculate about the persons targeted as readers for this text.

We reproduce below the textual context in which the Other Family is introduced. (The complete text is reproduced in Appendix B.)

> The utility-maximizing mode of producing meals depends on the wage rate, nonwage income, and family preferences. In Figure 7.1 the budget constraint of a woman whose husband is disabled and cannot work, who has no nonwage income, and who has a relatively low wage is depicted by $XY$. The figure suggests that the utility-maximizing mode of meal preparation is to use homegrown food, for the simple reason that when one has a low wage, time-intensive activities are relatively inexpensive. Time spent weeding, tilling, canning, and freezing does not cost a lot, in terms of forgone earnings (goods), in this case. Thus, in the example shown, 9 hours a day would be spent at home, 7 hours performing work for pay, and meal production on isoquant $M_0$ represents the highest level of utility that can be attained.
>
> (Ehrenberg and Smith 1994: 214–15)

The first thing to notice about this text is that, unlike the Enjoyable Family, the reader does not meet "the woman" and "the disabled husband" in their own paragraph or even as active participants in their own sentence. Grammatically, "the man" is introduced into the discourse as the possessed object of "the woman." "The woman" herself, whose decision-making is the topic of the story, is also not honored by the syntax of the piece: she is the object of a prepositional phrase describing an attribute of the subject of the sentence "the budget constraint." Since the decision about consumption and production is the woman's problem – she copes without her husband – and taking into account the effects of having the "man of the family" (usually defined as coextensive with the family), introduced only as her dependent both in economic and linguistic terms, we surmise that the husband is really quite debilitated and that the weight of the household, psychologically as well as financially, is borne by her alone.

Unlike the Enjoyable Family, the reader does not learn very much about the details of the Other Family's circumstances. Yet we can still imagine this couple and their situation, our vision informed by conventional images and stereotypic plots. This family must live in circumstances where weeding, tilling, canning and freezing are feasible, as in the case of a comfortably situated farm family. As we will show, the story ultimately fails to provide a reasonable picture of the basic economic principle in operation. This incoherence signals not only the privileged social position of the text's authors, but also their expectation that readers will find their description of the Other Family as plausible as they do, an interpretation which would require a similar unfamiliarity with the actual circumstances presented in the story.

Where is a farm woman going to have a job outside the home during the "7 hours [she performs] work for pay" (in addition to the "9 hours a day . . . spent at home") (Ehrenberg and Smith 1994: 215)? How does she get to work? If she lives on a farm, transportation costs are relatively high since she must have a reliable car – buses, in small-town America, are few and far between. Or does she walk a few miles to the local truck stop, factory or convenience store where she works during the night? Who looks after her ailing husband and kids while she is away in the wee hours? She must work at night because tilling and weeding must be done during the day, unless we add an unlikely detail and install expensive floodlights to permit cultivation after dark. But where will she find a seven-hour night job in the country? One wonders, too, what the family eats from all of the "weeding, tilling, canning, and freezing." While the text confidently informs us that "store-bought food easily replaces homegrown food" (Ehrenberg and Smith 1994: 214), it is silent on the fact that the converse is not true. Homegrown foods do not easily substitute for store-bought foods. High-protein foods are notoriously difficult, time-consuming, expensive, and water- and land-intensive to produce.

And what if we place this family in a setting where she might more realistically be able to find a night job, that is, in a city or town? Where will she grow her food? Is growing soybeans – or even tomatoes – in a windowbox a viable possibility?

While we are criticizing this text, we do so with a serious purpose. We wish to point out how this story presents an unrealistic and basically patronizing picture of the Other Family, thereby revealing itself to be written from a perspective of privilege, one not intimately acquainted with the lives of the poor. An alternative account might suggest that this woman spend some of the nine hours a day she works producing food at home in the far more profitable activity of making the rounds of welfare offices, private charities, food banks, or other institutions charged with caring for the poor. In other words, instead of "weeding and tilling," obviously unfeasible agricultural activities for the impoverished city dweller, Figure 7.1 might suggest instead that the woman optimize by spending her time cultivating the system, filling her breadbasket through the skilful deployment of the resources her experience and environment have fostered. In glossing over pain, hardships, and deprivations, the authors present an idealized fantasy about the lives of the poor. Although not endowed with all the same choices as their more comfortably off fellow citizens, the Other Family lives a life which does not jar the reader into any disturbing thoughts.

The pastoral images evoked by the Story of the Other Family direct us to consider the hidden politics of this text, a politics which is to some extent independent of the basic notion of optimization contained in the story. The political agenda here dictates that poor people accept and work within the status quo, tilling and weeding, rather than taking on more activist forms of optimization. Further, the details of the Story of the Other Family direct the reader to see them as able to live a comfortable life – one where through accepting and working within the status quo, by tilling and weeding, they are able to live a pastoral life rather than a life displaying the less comfortable images of desperate poverty requiring social intervention. Readers are therefore able to feel satisfied with the basic analysis as providing a reasonably complete story of how even poor families are able to provide for themselves through rational choice.

In both of the textual examples, optimization through rational choice is indeed the governing principle of the economic outcome experienced by the families. While there exists a large and insightful economic literature on poverty, these textual illustrations make it quite clear that, for most economists, satisfaction obtained through optimization is the default outcome. Indeed, the story of how individuals attain higher degrees of satisfaction through rational optimization is part of the microfoundations of the discipline. As in other texts, students are not directed to consider the circumstances of families unable to make do and in which background constraints rather than "choices" dominate in determining the economic outcomes.

Consider an alternative possible account of the Other Family, an account presenting the family as unable to acquire adequate food given its "initial endowment" of skills and resources. Such an example could not be left without further analysis while the authors switched to the next topic, because a new issue would have emerged compelling immediate attention: how could economic analysis be used to provide insight into helping families who are not in a position to provide adequately for themselves? Yet an example of a family unable to make do presented in the theory part of a chapter, and not relegated to the section on poverty at the end of the book, would be highly unusual in a standard theory or labor text, although extreme cases or "corner solutions" are often presented for comparative purposes in texts in discussions of other topics, as in the case of firms forced to go out of business. By directing readers to make the assumption that families can make do, and by not including a picture of a life where "making choices" does not seem to be the governing principle of existence, these textual examples direct attention away from the need to theorize the constraints that guide and underlie choices as endogenous (and worthy of central attention), rather than continuing to treat them as exogenous (and the stuff of sociology and other disciplines)[6].

## DRAWING INFERENCES FROM ECONOMIC TEXTS

Is it possible to make general inferences about the conversational conventions of economics from the two short unremarkable passages we have just examined? If these two passages are indeed ordinary, not unusual or bizarre examples of economics writing, then they should provide us with information about the default assumptions of American economists. Using our abilities to draw inferences, we can conclude that the default assumptions evoked by the texts are also shared by active participants in economic conversations and that the way of viewing the sets of families described in the text will not raise many eyebrows among American economists.

Readers of accounts produced by economists feel resonance and communality with their stories to the degree that they themselves are situated as the imagined and expected recipients. Readers who experience no dissonance with the texts will largely remain unaware of how their easy acceptance of the assumptions and arguments made in those texts reveals them to be appropriate, expected conversational partners in the disciplinary discourse of the field. For those who do experience dissonance with the default assumptions and evaluative signifiers in a story, the situation is different. These people, often women or members of other underrepresented groups, will be jarred into the realization that they do not fit the terms of acceptability of the community. Readers of the story of the Other Family, for example, who have experienced urban poverty or poverty reenforced by handicap or illness, are likely to conclude that they are not among the expected recipients, as indeed they are not. Further, such readers are not likely to be compelled to try to enter a disciplinary conversation which complacently presents an offensive status quo as normal and acceptable.

Social exclusion is the lot of someone for whom a given story elicits a response "out of sync" with that of others who are full members of the group to whom it was told. Further, as conversational analytic research has shown, stories must be tailored to the audience and reflect in structure, content, style and detail the teller's judgment of the nature of the recipients: who they are, what they are interested in, what they believe to be common-place and thus worth mentioning only briefly, and what they believe to be unusual, demanding a detailed explanation. In addition, stories must seem to flow naturally out of the topics in general discussion. Therefore, in economics, stories which jar with the situated perspectives of established practitioners (such as those of feminists and those labeled heterodox), are deemed outside and irrelevant to the important conversations of the field. And because such ideas are not present in the syllabi of the prestigious training grounds of future economists, the narrow group of people for whom such texts resonate as reasonable are able to perpetuate their own situated way of thinking.

These phenomena therefore constitute a mechanism through which the community of practitioners reproduces itself. The default assumptions and patterns of evaluation which economists build into their narratives act to select their intended audience. The design of economic narratives and situated social restrictions on economic rhetoric thus effectively function as a social filter, screening out from the pool of prospective professionals those people whose experiences might lead them to produce alternative stories.

## CONCLUSION

While more general claims about the "situated" position of knowledge in economics will require further detailed textual examinations, our analysis shows how linguistic and narrative theory may be applied to economic texts to yield insights into the particular way current economic conversations are situated in the specific experiences and related world views of its predo-minant practitioners, white middle-class North American men.

We have argued that the stance of detached objectivity claimed by the predominant practitioners in the discipline systematically denies the posi-tioned nature of their own discourse as well as their own self-interest in keeping the doors closed against others with competing viewpoints. A rhetoric which labels the discourse of the dominant as "objective," "disinterested" and "scientific" while dismissing the rhetoric of others as "biased" or "unscientific" is inherently dishonest. By showing how eco-

143

nomic accounts are necessarily situated, with the positions of the tellers laid out clearly to any who take a look at the linguistic details of the text, our intent in this chapter has been to expose mechanisms of social control that for far too long have kept the gates closed to potential economists who might tell other stories, stories perhaps more resonant with the experiences of groups currently underrepresented in the ranks of the profession.

## NOTES

1 Both authors contributed equally to the work in this paper. In our work, we alternate the ordering of our names because academic administrative accounting practices do not necessarily consider that authorship conventions may differ among the various disciplines.
2 For an introduction to this perspective see Haraway (1988). Related readings include Marcus and Fischer (1986), Harding (1991), Polanyi (1989), and Traweek (1988, 1992). Some of these ideas have also been addressed by institutionalist economists. See Samuels (1992) for an introduction to this intellectual tradition in economics.
3 The position against double blind refereeing is that the identity of a paper's author helps referees make more efficient evaluations of submitted articles. Some economists have argued, however, that when referees know the gender of authors, they discount the likely value of the contributions by women, making it harder for their contributions to be accepted in prestigious economics journals. See Blank (1991) for a detailed examination of this issue.
4 We develop this position in detail in Strassmann and Polanyi (1992) and Strassmann (1993a, 1993b, 1994). Folbre and Hartmann (1988) discuss the relationship between economic rhetoric and the self-interest of economists in the history of economic thought.
5 Longino (1990) develops the argument that better (more objective) science requires that academic disciplines remain open to the potentially transformative criticisms which may be built upon alternative intellectual traditions and perspectives. Such openness requires, in her view, a sharing of intellectual authority.
6 See Strassmann (1993a) for an elaboration of this point.

## REFERENCES

Blank, R.M. (1991) "The Effects of Double-Blind versus Single-Blind Reviewing: Experimental Evidence from The American Economic Review", *The American Economic Review* 81, 5, December: 1041–67.
Brown, L.J. (1989) "Gender and Economic Analysis: A Feminist Perspective", paper presented at the American Economic Association Annual Meetings, Atlanta, December.
Ehrenberg, R.G. and Smith, R.S. (1994) *Modern Labor Economics: Theory and Public Policy* (5th edn), New York: Harper Collins.
Folbre, N. and Hartmann, H. (1988) "The Rhetoric of Self-Interest: Ideology and Gender in Economic Theory", in A. Klamer, D.N. McCloskey and R.M. Solow (eds) *The Consequences of Economic Rhetoric*: 184–203, New York: Cambridge University Press.
Goffman, E. (1981) *Forms of Talk*, Philadelphia, PA: University of Pennsylvania Press.

Haraway, D. (1988) "Situated Knowledges: The Science Question in Feminism and the Privilege of the Partial Perspective", *Feminist Studies* 14, 3: 575–99.

Harding, S. (1991) *Whose Science? Whose Knowledge?: Thinking from Women's Lives*, Ithaca, NY: Cornell University Press.

Labov, W. (1972) "The Transformation of Experience in Narrative Syntax", in *Language in the Inner City*, Philadelphia, PA: University of Pennsylvania Press.

Longino, H. (1990) *Science as Social Knowledge*, Princeton, NJ: Princeton University Press.

McCloskey, D. (1983) "The Rhetoric of Economics", *Journal of Economic Literature* 21, 2, June: 481–517.

—— (1985) *The Rhetoric of Economics*, Madison, WI: University of Wisconsin Press.

—— (1990) *If You're So Smart: The Narrative of Economic Expertise*, Chicago: University of Chicago Press.

Marcus, G.E. and Fischer, M.M.J. (1986) *Anthropology as Cultural Critique: An Experimental Moment in the Human Sciences*, Chicago: University of Chicago.

Polanyi, L. (1989) *Telling the American Story: A Structural and Cultural Analysis of Conversational Storytelling*, Cambridge, MA: The MIT Press.

Sacks, H. (1978) "Some Technical Considerations of a Dirty Joke", in J. Schenkein (ed.) *Studies in the Organization of Conversational Interaction*: 249–70, New York: Academic Press.

Samuels, W. (1992) "Institutional Economics", in D. Greenway, M. Bleaney and I. Stewart (eds) *Economics in Perspective*, London: Routledge.

Solow, R.M. (1993) "Feminist Theory, Women's Experience, and Economics", in M. Ferber and J. Nelson (eds) *Beyond Economic Man: Feminist Theory and Economics*, Chicago: University of Chicago Press.

Strassmann, D. (1993a) "Not a Free Market: The Rhetoric of Disciplinary Authority in Economics", in M. Ferber and J. Nelson (eds) *Beyond Economic Man: Feminist Theory and Economics*, Chicago: University of Chicago Press.

—— (1993b) "The Stories of Economics and the Power of the Storyteller", *History of Political Economy* 25, 1: 145–63.

—— (1994) "Feminist Thought and Economics; Or, What Do the Visigoths Know ?", *The American Economic Review* 84, 2, May: 153–8.

Strassmann, D. and Polanyi, L. (1992) "Shifting the Paradigm: Value in Feminist Critiques of Economics", paper presented at the First Annual Conference of the International Association for Feminist Economics, Washington, DC, 24–26 July.

Traweek, S. (1988) *Beamtimes and Lifetimes: The World of High Energy Physics*, Cambridge, MA: Harvard University Press.

—— (1992) "Border Crossings: Narrative Strategies in Science Studies Among Physicists at Tsukuba Science City, Japan", in A. Pickering (ed.) *Science as Practice and Culture*, Chicago: University of Chicago Press.

# Appendix A

# THE STORY OF THE ENJOYABLE FAMILY

*Quoted from Ehrenberg and Smith*
*(1994, Chapter 7: 212–14)*

## THE THEORY OF HOUSEHOLD PRODUCTION

Although many adults are unmarried at some points in their lives, most do marry and form family units. The family thus becomes a very basic decision-making entity in society, and many important decisions concerning both consumption patterns and labor supply are made in a family context. Our task in this chapter is to find out in what ways the implications of the individual labor supply theory in Chapter 6 are modified or expanded by consideration of the family.

We shall assume that many commodities the family consumes are produced, or can be produced, at home. Food and energy are combined with preparation time to produce the meals from which family well-being is derived. A vacuum cleaner and time are combined to contribute to an orderly home. Food, clothing, and supervision time all contribute to the growth of children, whom the parents hope to enjoy. Thus, a marriage partner who stays at home may be engaged more in the production of commodities from which the family derives utility than in the direct consumption of leisure.

## A MODEL OF HOUSEHOLD PRODUCTION

Household production models explicitly recognize that both consumption and production take place in the home. The family unit, then, must make two kinds of decisions: *what* to consume and *how to produce* what it consumes. Consider the second decision first by analyzing a family that does not have to worry about what to consume because it consumes only one commodity: meals. This family derives its utility only from the quantity and quality of food it eats. We shall drop the assumption about consuming just one commodity later, but the assumption permits us to make several basic points in an easily understood fashion.

Meals that yield equal utility can be produced in several ways. A family can buy prepared foods and simply warm them at home, in which case minimum time is spent in preparation and a maximum of market goods are consumed. The meal could be prepared at home with food bought from a market, or it could be prepared at home with food grown or made at home, which obviously represents a lot of preparation time. Since any combination of goods and household time can produce meals that are equally valuable (in terms of producing utility) to the family, we can draw a curve that represents all the time/goods combinations that can produce meals of equal utility. Such a curve can be called a utility isoquant, where iso means "equal" and quant means "quantity" (of utility). Two isoquants are depicted in Figure 7.1 as $M_0$ and $M_1$.

Several things should be noted about the isoquants in Figure 7.1. First, along $M_0$ the utility provided by family meals is constant. The utility produced by the time/goods combinations along $M_1$ is also constant, but it is greater than the utility represented by $M_0$ because meals produced by such combinations are of higher quality (involving more inputs of goods and time).

Second, the isoquants $M_0$ and $M_1$ are both negative in slope and convex (as viewed from below) in shape. The negative slope reflects an assumption that time and goods are substitutes in the production of meals. If house-

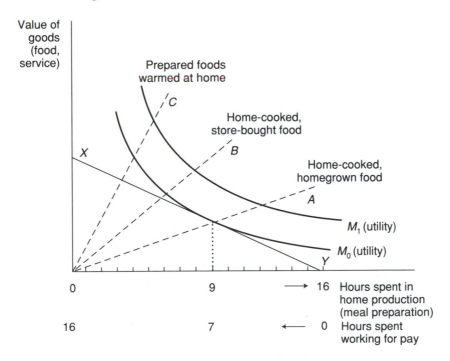

*Figure 7.1* The production of family meals

147

hold time is reduced, meal production can be held constant by increasing the purchase of goods. Thus, if a family decides not to grow its own food, it can buy food instead – or if it decides to spend less time cooking food, it could still maintain the same utility from meals by using a microwave oven to heat prepared foods.

The convexity of the isoquants reflects an assumption that as household meal preparation time continues to fall, it becomes more difficult to make up for it with goods. If the family spends a lot of time in meal preparation, it will be easy to replace some of that time with just a few goods (store-bought food easily replaces homegrown food, for example). However, when preparation time is very short to begin with, a further cut in such time may be very difficult to absorb and still keep utility constant. Thus, it will take many goods – a large increase in food quality, for example – to substitute for reduced cooking time.

Finally, along any one ray (A, B, or C) emanating from the origin of Figure 7.1, the ratio of goods to household preparation time in the production of meals is constant. When time and goods are combined in the ratio along ray A, time-intensive meals are produced using homegrown food. Meals produced with the time/goods ratio along B are home-cooked, using store-bought food, and the time/goods ratio along ray C represents the use of prepared foods.

# Appendix B

# THE STORY OF THE OTHER FAMILY

*Quoted from Ehrenberg and Smith (1994, Chapter 7: 214–16)*

The utility-maximizing mode of producing meals depends on the wage rate, nonwage income, and family preferences. In Figure 7.1 the budget constraint of a woman whose husband is disabled and cannot work, who has no nonwage income, and who has a relatively low wage is depicted by $XY$. The figure suggests that the utility-maximizing mode of meal preparation is to use homegrown food, for the simple reason that when one has a low wage, time-intensive activities are relatively inexpensive. Time spent weeding, tilling, canning, and freezing does not cost a lot, in terms of forgone earnings (goods), in this case. Thus, in the example shown, 9 hours a day would be spent at home, 7 hours performing work for pay, and meal production on isoquant $M_0$ represents the highest level of utility that can be attained.

Figure 7.2 shows what will happen if the budget constraint in Figure 7.1 shifts because of an increase in *nonwage* income. What happens to the wife's inclination to work outside the home if the family begins to receive governmental payments equal to $Y'$ for the husband's disability? This income grant does not change the wife's wage rate, so the new budget constraint facing the family has the same slope as constraint $X'Y'$ in Figure 7.1. However, the new constraint ($X'Y'$ in Figure 7.2) lies above the old one and reflects a pure *income effect*. Because it is wealthier, the family will want to enjoy higher-quality meals. It will have more money with which to buy goods, but it will also decide to have the wife spend more time at home to prepare the meals (remember, both goods and time are valuable in producing meals). She may change the time/goods ratio, as shown in Figure 7.2, by a movement from ray $A$ to ray $B$, depending on the shape of the isoquants.

Before discussing the changes that result from a change in the wife's wage, let us pause to make two points. First, the income effect in this household production model has exactly the same sign as the effect in the labor/leisure model discussed in Chapter 6. Second, the amount of work for pay and the mode of household production are jointly determined; that is, they are affected by the same constraint and are made as part of the same

149

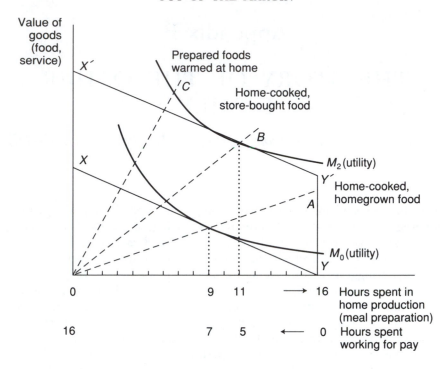

*Figure 7.2* Production of family meals: the income effect

decision. Emphasizing household production rather than leisure, therefore, does not change our conclusion about the effects of income on labor supply in this case. Emphasizing production rather than leisure, however, does highlight the interrelated nature of decisions concerning family "household production" and decisions about labor supply.

Let us continue for a moment with our example of a wife whose husband is disabled and unemployed. If he remains disabled but she obtains a wage increase, what will happen to her labor supply? Quite simply, there will be two opposing effects (as we found in the "leisure" model previously). The *income effect*, as above, will tend to drive her away from market work and toward more time at home, where she can spend more time in activities (meal preparation) that enhance family utility. However, the *substitution effect* will tend to push her out of the home and toward more work for pay. When her wages are increased, time spent at home preparing meals becomes more expensive than it was before. Thus, she will tend to move away from time-intensive modes of production to modes that rely more on goods, freeing her for more "market" work. The overall observed effect of her wage increase on her labor supply cannot be predicted based on theory alone.

# 9

# READING NEOCLASSICAL ECONOMICS

## Toward an erotic economy of sharing

*Susan F. Feiner*

## INTRODUCTION

Psychoanalytic theory urges us to examine that which we actively repudiate for the shadow of a loss we mourn.

(Bordo 1987: 105)

For the fully rational actors in the neoclassical drama all human interactions are an exchange. Every behavior is a giving up in order to receive. A psychoanalytic reading of such behavior uncovers some of the unconscious effects of this vision of economic relationships. This in turn sets the stage for a new, feminist understanding of economics which has the potential to recast the human activities of production, distribution and consumption as relations of sharing rather than as relations of exchange. For the ability, capacity, and will to share is a loss long mourned.

There are several cautions in order before we proceed. The reading of neoclassical economics offered here is only one among many; it is not the only accurate reading or even the best reading of mainstream economics[1]. Neither is this paper an analysis of the practitioners of economics. Nor is it an attempt to reduce economics to its essential core. Instead this work is part of a larger project which seeks to read the history of economic ideas through the psychoanalytic vision of human development formulated by the object relations school (Greenberg and Mitchell 1983). The object relations school considers the mother/child unit to be of primary concern since the qualities of this relationship play a profound role in the genesis of human capacities including of course the capacities to produce, distribute and consume[2].

That we are mothered by women, that in all societies women rather than men have primary parenting responsibilities, is an important social and cultural fact that still bears remarking and analyzing. In those individual and cultural cases where we have some insight into human emotions and psychodynamics, this fact also seems to have significant import for people's constructions of self and interpersonal relations, for their emotions, their fantasies, and their psychological apprehensions of gender.

(Chodorow 1989: 6)

Taking the mother/child unit as the entry point into psychoanalytic inquiry enables us to conceive of people as fully relational and semi-autonomous, since actions and behaviors are constituted by an individual's "overall orientation to reality, which conditions both the process and content of thought, the perception of reality and the quality of one's relationships" (Godwin 1993: 291). A vision of economic agents emerges in which agents are constituted by their contradictory, ambivalent, and emotionally charged connections to each other. In this way the psychoanalytic, object relations approach helps us to produce the "third term" needed to deconstruct key economic oppositions like individual and society, rational and irrational, choice and command[3].

Some have interpreted the radical individualism at the core of *homo-economicus* as a denial of social ties. Such a reading goes too far and misses the important point that even when individuals are seen solely as agents exchanging in markets, such exchanges do constitute relationships. The neoclassical representation of the system of exchange establishes this process as both fully conscious and non-contradictory. That is, each subject confronts every other subject fully aware of what they have and fully aware of what they want. None of the subjects, none of the exchanges and no aspect of the market process is contradictory: all is fused in a smoothly functioning, frictionless whole.

In contrast the psychoanalytic reading put forward here interprets the neoclassical vision from the premise that the key ontological concept of exchange along with the implied concepts of individualism, rationality, and scarcity, convey both conscious economic meanings and unconscious symbolic contents. At the level of the unconscious these concepts express "wishes," the desire to recreate relationships from the past. Illuminating these meanings opens more and more of the unconscious (repressed) to our scrutiny. On the basis of the insights which emerge we can attempt to conceive new forms of economic relations in which exchange and instrumentality are displaced by sharing and jouissance (pleasure) (Dallery 1989).

Many critical observations about neoclassical economics hold that this approach to political economy is an especially important part of bourgeois ideology. That is, neoclassical economics in both its scholarly and popular forms plays an important role in the reproduction of market-driven, male-dominated society. It is not adequate to end with the recognition that neoclassical economics legitimates, justifies or rationalizes inequalities of class, gender and race. Instead, we must press beyond this to understand how this system of ideas and symbols constructs and constitutes "a system

of hierarchical domination (in which) the regression to the original condition can only be approximated in so far as it is accompanied by a
phenomenon of scapegoating, or negative authority," or some other
defense mechanism (Hill 1984: 34).

Consider what we would accept as an interpretation of the role of the
Catholic Church in medieval Europe. Certainly most of us would
acknowledge that the Church was indispensable to the maintenance of
authority and the status quo. Yet who among us would settle for an
analysis which simply noted that "catholic ideology was powerful and it
was reproduced over time because it benefited the ruling class?" Instead,
we would insist that the analysis show how this was achieved, (i.e. we
would want to understand how church doctrines and institutions produced these effects).

> In the Catholic Church . . . decision-making (was) a virtual monopoly
> of the one on top . . . [and] in this situation Freud discovered not only
> the reward of grandiosity and omnipotence enjoyed by the leader but
> also the rewards of dependency and relief from responsibility enjoyed
> by the followers. Both, therefore, enjoy a kind of return to childhood as
> the child imagines it: a parent with unlimited powers who knows
> everything and takes care of the child and the child with unlimited
> freedom to feel safe and provided for. But while this constitutes the
> unconscious meaning of this structure, its effect on the world is utterly
> different.
>
> (Hill 1984: 32)

Following Freud's analysis of the Catholic Church as a vehicle for wish
fulfilment (the Church promulgated an ideology which permitted a regression), we can turn our attention to neoclassical economics and its unconscious effects[4].

This analysis focusses on the symbolic elements of neoclassical economics. The point is not that particular economists have consciously produced
the psychological aspects of economic theory which we identify[5]. The
point is rather that different individuals at different times and places have
found various pieces of the theory to be more or less compelling. We are
struck by the intensity with which many people, inside and outside the
circle of trained academic economists, defend one or more aspects of the
neoclassical approach, despite the startling incongruities between the
economy which neoclassicism describes and the economies of our lives.
Appeals to the virtues of exchange, side-by-side with neoclassical notions
of human nature, often support very regressive social policies. Consequently, it is of some significance to understand the symbolic inner life of
the theory.

## ECONOMICS AND PSYCHOANALYSIS: THE UNDREAMT CONNECTION

> Our experiences as men and women come from deep within, both within our pasts and, relatedly, within the deepest structures of unconscious meaning and the most emotionally moving relationships that help constitute our daily lives.
>
> (Chodorow 1989: 2)

We are all familiar with the literary search for symbolisms in texts as diverse as Shakespearean sonnets, rock videos, horror movies and presidential speeches. Only if economics texts are granted a privileged exemption from interpretation can we reject the hypothesis that the texts of neoclassical economics have a symbolic content independent of the conscious intentions of either their authors or consumers. An interpretation of the unconscious wishes and conflicts expressed in these texts goes beyond the rational, conscious surface of economics to reveal an aggressive, narcissistic posturing which functions as a defense against dependence, gratitude, and nurturing.

We note the discursive silence of the paradigm *vis-à-vis* gender/sexuality and community/class. The simultaneity of these repressions refer us to their cartographers: Freud and Marx[6]. Louis Althusser (1991) has written persuasively about the connection between these approaches. According to Althusser, Marx believed that:

> bourgeois ideology and its theoretical formulations are designed to dissimulate as they perpetuate the exploitation and domination of the bourgeois class. Marx was convinced that the adversary of the truth that he discovered was not accidental error or ignorance but the organic system of bourgeois ideology, an essential component of the struggle of the bourgeois class.
>
> (Althusser 1991: 20)

Consider next Freud's contribution as regards the unconscious "conceived as an 'apparatus' composed of 'different systems' irreducible to a single principle. . . . This apparatus is not a centered unity but a complex of instances constituted by the play of unconscious repression" (Althusser 1991: 28). What then are the unconscious instances at work within the organic science of bourgeois ideology?

Psychoanalysis recognizes that there are no fully conscious (or rational) processes through which individuals come to know themselves as contiguous with some social attributes and not others[7]. One of the remarkable characteristics of neoclassical economics is the intensity with which the discourse insists that race, gender, and class are irrelevant to the understanding of rational behavior – there is just choice, *sui generis*. The denial of these core elements of identity warrants examination.

These social categories (race, gender, class, ethnicity) are alternative (sometimes complementary, sometimes conflictual) ways of organizing difference. Following Winnicott (1988), Chodorow (1989) and others, we insist on the importance of the first experience of difference (i.e. the infant's perception of mother). Unconscious mental organizations of difference, and the social constructions of race, gender, class, and ethnicity, are thoroughly impregnated with representations of motherhood, femininity, and sexuality on the one hand, and the processes of meeting needs on the other. Original experiences of difference (separateness from mother) come to be represented by other differences which are commonly, but arbitrarily, associated with it[8]. The intimate connection between the social representation of difference and the individual experience of difference fuels the neoclassical repression of exploitation and oppression and replaces them with symbols (concepts) which are their opposites: freedom and choice. This repression and the anxiety associated with it dominate the symbolic gendered content of the theory.

## THE SYMBOLIC RESOLUTION OF WANTS

As we try to sever want from need, we find that sexual needs, the need for intimacy, and even the need to make meaning of life, take on an unwholesome or frivolous cast. In unavoidable consequence, life begins to make less and less sense. Life is meaningless without wanting, but there is no wanting without needing and therefore no desire without need. As need drains from desire, so does meaning bleed from life. To eliminate need is to kill desire and therefore any appetite for living.

(Dimen 1991: 46)

The Greek root "ecos" means home – and our intellectual as well as emotional homes are contradictory sites of physical, affective and mental production. One of the principal contributions of feminist work in the past two decades has been increased attention to and refinement of the notion that production does occur in the home. To date most of this work has focussed on "housework" as either the unpaid surplus labor of house spouses (Matthaei 1991) or as the non-market work of rational economic actors (Blau and Ferber 1986). In either case there remains a glaring absence: economists have yet to conceptualize adequately the meaning and impact of the emotional activity, conceived as productive work, done in households which so strongly influences psychological life.

This lacuna is a consequence of the fact that affective behavior contradicts the implicit *quid pro quo* which undergirds existing approaches to economics. Conceptualizing non-market activity as work, through either the opportunity cost notion of neoclassical economists or through the surplus labor notion of Marxist economists does no violence to the "give and take" framework. In this sense, both Marxian and neoclassical approaches depend on the *quid pro quo* of exchange, and in capitalism that exchange is understood as the exchange of equals. But emotional work cannot be made to fit this frame without completely violating its affective, passionate, spontaneous dimensions. Why does economic science defend the boundary between exchange and sharing?

One of the unique features of modern science is that it "consciously and explicitly proclaimed the 'masculinity' of science as inaugurating a new era" (Bordo 1987: 105). Following the work of Bordo (1987), Harding (1986), Merchant (1980) and Noble (1992) on the emergence of the scientific as masculine we note how this process equated the object of science with that which is external to the scientist. In some prehistoric fantasy world, man and nature (man and who?) were not separate. But the modern perspective erected nature as the external source of maternal supplies. Man demands the appropriation of nature to satisfy wants. Nature becomes female and nurturing becomes the province of women. Now in the economists' version of "the fall," boundless wanting counterposes a parsimonious nature in a drama redolent of frustration. Yet salvation is at hand: the site at which wants are met, "the sphere of exchange," that "very Eden wherein alone rule Freedom, Equality, Property and Bentham" (Marx 1977: 280) undoes man's frustration. The accidental play of language is revealing: as Eden is an anagram for need, the market is a gendered site at which needs are met.

In this material we see economic theory making the market a symbolic representation for the meeting of human needs. Moreover, in this symbolism we also find a very early orientation to the "not-I." For infants wants and needs are met through the actions of (m)other. In economic theory wants and needs are met through the actions of markets. The market as a symbol comes to represent motherhood: "patriarchal culture seeks to repress the primordial memory of fusion with and later separation from the maternal body; this fear of the mother is masked in male sexuality" (Dallery 1989: 57). The notion of the free market can be seen as an expression of a wish. In its theoretic and cultural elaboration, the market functions as a substitute for the perfect mother who is unfailing in her capacity (and willingness) to meet all needs and wants. Thus the idealized market (the home of *homoeconomicus*) of neoclassical economic theory mirrors the fantasy mother of the unconscious[9]. Mainstream economics means something very specific when it refers to the outcomes for human satisfaction derived from exchange in markets. In a system of perfect markets everyone is as satisfied as they possibly can be precisely because markets work best[10].

There is a sense then that neoclassical economics creates a particular community, the members of which participate in a shared group fantasy – the fantasy that a system of production, distribution and consumption based on the systematic exploitation of both people and the environment is a "fair" system in which rewards (high incomes) and punishments (low incomes and unemployment) are meted out on an "objective" basis. In so far as the internal constructs of neoclassical economics contain symbolic images which give life to this fantasy while dissolving contradictions and repressing conflicts, and to the extent that these fantasies resonate with unfulfilled wishes, then part of our struggle against exploitation and oppression must occur at the level of the symbolic.

Every economist learns early on that "economics is the study of the allocation of scarce resources to the infinity of human wants"[11]. This initial definition of the object of economic science has many effects, one of which is representational. It is obvious that this definition of economic science depicts the relationship of an infant to its primary caretaker – usually its mother. Newborns exist in a world formed by the immediacy of needs. Pressing infantile needs for food, warmth, and nurturing dominate the first months of experience. The utter dependency of an infant on its caretakers is remarkable. The deep affective, erotic bonds which give meaning to the infant/mother pair are built at least partially by the empathetic resonance between mother and infant. "Our ideal picture of a truly maternal woman is one of an omnipotent, all knowing mother who knows what to do with her infant by sheer intuition" (Kestenberg 1956: 260, quoted in Welldon 1988: 18).

> Infancy, (no matter how the social world is organized) is characterized by a state of dependence and powerlessness as well as intense wishes. The infant becomes aware of its dependence on others and its inability to satisfy its own needs. Frustration is projected onto whomever is present for the child, and when the person becomes an internal object, these frustrations, fears, desires, etc., are introjected along with the person. Therefore the mother is internalized along with the child's own powerful feelings about her. The boy, as he represses the mother, must repress all these feelings, too, since they are part of the experience of her. Given how powerful she is in infancy, the son must carefully guard against her power (since it is part of his self). Thus, repression must be as complete as possible so that this internal object can be kept as separate from the conscious self. Otherwise, it would threaten masculine identity and ego boundaries.
>
> (Flax 1983: 246–7)

Mothers, in affirming relationships with their children, try to recognize the child's needs and then set out to meet those needs. Notice the striking similarity between the mother/infant relation and the relation of adults to the market in capitalist society. How can we avoid the anthropological parallel: it is a commonplace of secular analysis to point out that people "create" GOD to help them cope with feelings of powerlessness in the face of a capricious, sometimes hostile NATURE. With the important caveat that the notion of nature as external to man is thoroughly modern, it remains the case that "modern man," lives a life in which the vicissitudes of the market are as capricious as nature. No single individual can possibly produce all that is desired or all that is needed for survival, and so we – strangers in the night – become inescapably dependent upon each other. Dependence as complete and total as this is frightening. Ambivalence and anxiety rear their heads: "Where there is anxiety, there will almost certainly be found a mechanism of defense against that anxiety" (Bordo 1987: 75).

We can be even more specific about the dependency relations in capitalism. For example, the classes of capitalists and workers can only be understood if some reference is made to markets. Whether one takes the traditional position that markets are the *sine qua non* of capitalism, or if one takes the position that markets are conditions of existence of capitalism, it must be acknowledged that with absent markets capitalists will not realize profits or surplus value and workers will not get paid. In short, both capitalists and workers are in fundamental ways as dependent upon markets for their survival as are infants upon their mothers. Everyone who lives in a capitalist society is dependent upon the market for their very existence.

The pervasiveness of this dependency is, however, denied by the privileging of exchange. From the point of view of the individual, separation is scarcity. Individuals are seen in neoclassical economics as separated from all others so there is no way to secure subsistence except through exchange. As an individual, everything is scarce and exchange is the only possible solution. The defenses at work here are complex. Representing exchange as ordered by wanting undoes the problem of scarcity while constructing the world as scarcity represses the realities of dependency. "The conversion of a nightmare into a positive vision is characteristic of Descartes" (Bordo 1987: 100). The representation of the market as its opposite reflects this Cartesian solution.

What do markets do? In neoclassical economics markets are the registry of desire backed by purchasing power. The perfectly empathic mother becomes the perfectly competitive market. In such markets, as with fantasy mothers, all wishes are fulfilled. Gratification is total, instant and infinitely repeating. These markets are sensitive; the intensity of one's desire is represented by the magnitude of purchasing power devoted to the satisfaction of particular wants. As the intensity of desires change demands shift. In perfect settings, the market responds to these desires just as instantly as we wish our mothers could. Prices rise, signalling a flow of resources.

The mother-baby unit is at a biological-psychological peak when the mother is ready with her breasts filled with milk just as her baby is being awakened by hunger. Both partners get together and a world of bliss is open to them. Of course, having accepted the reality principal we know that two individuals will never be able to realize these moments in the same way. However, some people have not yet come to accept the reality principle . . . they are still seeking a promised land of bliss.

(Welldon 1988: 12–13)

## EXCHANGE AND THE DENIAL OF SHARING

Although the dream of total union can persist throughout life, another contradictory project may be conceived, psychoanalytic thinkers have suggested, centered around the denial of any longing for the lost maternal union. Instead, the child seeks mastery over the frustrations of separation and lack of gratification through an assertion of self against the mother and all that she represents and rejection of all dependency on her. In this way the pain is assuaged, paradoxically, by an even more definitive separation – but one that is chosen this time and aggressively pursued. It is therefore experienced as autonomy rather than helplessness in the face of discontinuity between self and mother.

(Bordo 1987: 107)

The significance of the market-as-mother metaphor ramifies through the gendered body of neoclassical economics. We can understand this representation as a "reaction formation, a denial of the separation anxiety . . . which is facilitated by an aggressive intellectual flight from the female cosmos and 'feminine' orientation toward the world" (Bordo 1987: 100). Indeed, the gendering of economic concepts maintains these defenses.

We begin by noting that in this theory exchange is posed as the fundamental economic act and satisfaction occurs as exchanges take place. Exchanges in markets set loose the forces of supply and demand and, as if by divine providence, all desires are satisfied: there is never too much and there is never too little. Thus, the economists' market (quite unlike the market we all know) symbolizes the wish for the empathic mother who not only anticipates all needs, but meets them instantly. Marx was quite correct to see this as an Eden: a lost but longed for world of bliss. And so we can redo his famous circuits of capital in which the infinite sequence Commodities-Money-Commodities (C-M-C) stands alongside the infinite sequence Money-Commodities-Money (M-C-M). Simultaneous with the circulation of commodities in the market is the circulation of meanings: Child-Mother-Child (C-M-C) alongside Mother-Child-Mother (M-C-M).

But the repressed femininity which is the core of the neoclassical fantasy is also a source of anxiety. First consider Say's Law of Markets, the proposition which, in its popular form states that supply creates its own

159

demand, to see yet another of these most curious inversions[12]. One of the primary fears of infancy and early childhood is that demands will not create their own supplies[13]. To the extent that children experience mothers as withholding (after all, a child must first cry to let her needs be known) then food, love, security, and nurturing are not immediately available. Frustration, like other negative emotional states aroused deep within us by those whom we most love, may be internalized and experienced as guilt. The exaltation of market institutions by and within economic theory can be interpreted as a defense against anxieties provoked by the guilty feelings, associated with infantile rage at mothers/markets for not being perfect. In this material we clearly see a projection of the wished for fusion with the perfect mother.

This portrait of the market as a site at which desires are met so perfectly is conjoint with the notion of a general equilibrium: not just one market satisfies desires perfectly, but all markets taken as a whole satisfy desires. This satisfaction emerges simultaneously with the infinity of exchanges. We can see in this another element of the Cartesian response to the shattering of the feminine Cosmos. In medieval world views, the universe was not only limited, it was also centered, "with a core toward which all movement tended," but the discovery of infinity made the notion of such a core "unintelligible" and the universe now appeared as not only limitless but "decentered, perplexing and anarchic" (Bordo 1987: 71–2). The general equilibrium model inverts the experience of anxiety in the face of the limitless unknown by ordering the economic cosmos. General Equilibrium – that wondrous state in which Aggregate Demand = Aggregate Supply – becomes the new "core" of the universe. That toward which all markets tend returns us to our HOME (ECOS) again resolving anxieties of separation. The rule of the mother/market ensures the return to, or at least the movement toward, home. That which is "not home" is presented as an "imperfection," or "rigidity" and so can (in contrast to the perfection and fluidity of mother markets) be read as a masculine interference in the child's wish to merge with mother[14].

Note the doubly defensive role of the market fantasy. First, the market as represented precludes frustration. Yet the very mechanisms through which the market accomplishes the meeting of wants is impersonal, cold, and objective. This image is the antithesis of a caring mother and so denies the reality of warmth, emotional contact and passion as essential to human satisfactions. This "undoing" of infantile dependence on mother calls into being the auctioneer[15] whose *tâtonnement* or groping ("touch me, please!") guarantees a return to this womb-like home. Reaching the perfect state where all desires are met involves no emotional contact. The meeting of needs and the satisfaction of desire require nothing but exchange. Who says "You can't always get what you want?" *Homoeconomicus* always gets what he wants, but he gets it without affective connection. This fantasy eliminates the very possibility of frustrated needs since exchange makes all exchangers better off, all desires are met perfectly, and there is no trading outside equilibrium.

To satisfy desire individuals must go outside themselves and recognize the other, but the specific way that neoclassical economics poses this recognizing is "infantile." That is, the neoclassical vision of subjects as fully autonomous, all knowing, and in possession of true knowledge of the choices available constitutes a regression. The individual autonomy celebrated in neoclassical theory and the omnipotence which accompanies it are reaction formations: in contemporary society people are dependent on each other in ways that they neither choose nor control. Not only are these many dependencies hidden from general view, but the illusion of autonomy is maintained and reproduced through a general celebration of separation.

Separation of the "objective" from the "subjective," and separation of "reason" from "the senses," are an essential part of the play of unconscious repression which animates the neoclassical subject. Yet as Freud noted (Gray 1989: 387) "What, in the conscious, is found split into a pair of opposites often occurs in the unconscious, as a unity."[16] In and through the many dimensions of radical separateness, economic subjects come to a unique and privileged knowledge position: not only do economic subjects thoroughly know themselves as repositories of unlimited wants and desires, they also know the infinite array of scarce goods and services which are available to them. Although the representation of omnipotence is a blueprint for self-actualization through choice, this functions psychologically to infantilize subjects, since every action produces only what the subject wants. In the shared group fantasy of economics the exaltation of exchange reconstitutes the individual as autonomous and grandiose, thereby "undoing" the anxiety associated with the memory of infantile dependence on (m)other. In this way neoclassical economics constitutes and constructs a psychic defense – a denial in theory – against these anxieties.

## CONCLUSION

The elevation of exchange in modern economics displaces classical concerns for concrete, embodied activities like labor and production. These inescapably physical activities – some would even say womanly – vanish, replaced by autonomous, rational, choosing minds. This flight to objectivity is a retreat to pure (men)tation to "undo" the havoc now wreaked by the dynamics of a new mother, the market (which consequently appears as natural as the nature which markets constantly seek to subdue). This reading shows us how the intra-personal theory of value, and the idealized vision of market exchange which sustains it, functions to relieve separation anxieties. By exalting scarcity and the impossibility of satisfying all wants, neoclassical economics masters separation. What the theory claims as the inevitable state of humanity becomes a solution to itself: the competitive self-interest of rational individuals is the way to satisfaction. The metaphor is doubly revealing and doubly defensive. As human needs are always satisfied in markets choice is the necessary vehicle to fulfilment and at the same time the market/choice metaphor guarantees that choices are themselves fulfilling.

We note that grandiosity and omnipotence are associated with the pre-oedipal, and that in this position there will be a "failure of gratitude," an inability to recognize "just how contingent one's success has been upon the assistance of others. But contingency is incompatible with omnipotence and gratitude is an emotion that is firmly established in the depressive position" (Godwin 1993: 295–6)[17]. We understand that one of the appeals of the individualistic, competitive pursuit of desire through market exchange is that these concepts may block a transition to a state in which dependency is not a threat to individuality. The seductive power of neoclassical economics is not simply its formal mathematical elegance, nor is it the reality of its politically regressive policy stance. The seductive power of the paradigm also emanates from a symbolism that gives voice to the unresolved conflicts produced and reproduced in modern society.

The inner fantasies of the neoclassical paradigm are its teflon coating. This paradigm has survived critiques on virtually all fronts. Its assumptions, methodology, rhetoric, internal consistency, and naive dynamics have all been shown to be seriously, even mortally, flawed. And the beat goes on – economic theory as neoclassical stomp. How is it that this approach which counterposes an assumed scarcity of nature (mother) to the insatiability of *Homoeconomicus* (manchild), and then elevates this tension to the guiding principle of economic science, is able to continue to attract adherents while drowning out most voices of dissent? Through what symbolic appeals does this paradigm gather the strength to monopolize our economic vision? It seems safe to say that it is not the market which meets needs but it is rather the neoclassical representation of the market which meets needs.

## ACKNOWLEDGEMENTS

Very sincere thanks are owed to Sandra Morgen and others at the Center for the study of Women in Society, The University of Oregon, Eugene OR. Many friends and colleagues also provided advise, encouragement and assistance with this project; Jack Amariglio, Susan Bordo, Nancy Chodorow, Harriet Fraad, Rob Garnett, Sandra Harding, David Levine, Lee Levin, and Richard Lichtman read various versions of this paper and offered suggestions for improvement. I hope this version is true to their comments. Edith Kuiper deserves special thanks for the excellent work she has done to bring this whole project to fruition. Any problems remaining with this essay are entirely my responsibility.

## NOTES

1 Such a contention would violate the spirit of psychoanalytic inquiry since work in this tradition takes as a premise that all signs have multiple, overdetermined meanings.

2 While the object relation school derives from the psychoanalytic tradition associated with Freud, this school does not conceive of behavior in terms of the irreducible instincts or drive of classical Freudianism. Another key difference is that the father and oedipal conflicts are not the central interpretative themes.

3 This approach, through its insistence on the fully relational nature of human perception and action, provides a way out of the dualisms of traditional (neoclassical and Marxian) approaches to economics. For a discussion of the role of dualism in economics see Nelson (1993).

4 While neoclassical economics and its institutions undoubtedly play a role in maintaining social order, this role is probably not equivalent to that played by the Church in the Middle Ages. The point of this comparison is to suggest that economic ideas, like religious ones, carry unconscious meanings which are probably not part of the conscious awareness of the people who articulate them.

5 The emotional state of the economist is not the subject of this paper.

6 See Fraad (1981) for a discussion of this relationship.

7 The categories of race, gender, ethnicity and class are of course "social," since these categories could not be "thought" of were there only one person. A set of readings indispensible to this connection concern the use of Robinson Crusoe metaphors within neoclassical economics. See Steven Hymer (1971), Gillian Hewitson (1994) and Ulla Graphard (forthcoming). These essays demonstrate the symbolic contiguity of race and sex in economic exchange metaphors.

8 This is an example of metonomy and the reader will find the set of essays on the use of Robinson Crusoe metaphors in economic theory very helpful in illuminating these connections.

9 Consequently any in-the-real shift from *homoeconomicus* (to, perhaps, *heteroeconomicus*) could be likened to weaning. Just as the successfully weaned infant has learned the capacity to trust and through trust is able to deal with loss, communities which give up markets must be able to trust: "[the] infant who is just about ready to be 'weaned', [is] able to deal with loss without quite losing what is [in one sense only] lost" (Winnicot 1988: 35).

10 Of course there are disagreements about which circumstances are most favorable for markets, with conservatives arguing that if left alone markets work best, while liberals argue that proper intervention makes markets work better. But within the mainstream the ultimately benevolent nature of the market system is not open to question.

11 Lionel Robbins characterized economics as "the science which studies human behavior as a relationship between ends and scarce means which have alternative uses" (1952 [1935]). Contemporary textbooks recast this as the relationship between scarce means and infinite wants.

12 This is of course an aggregative concept: no-one ever meant that a bumper crop of wheat, for example, gives rise to more demand for wheat. The point is

instead that the market system considered as a whole can not experience a "glut" of commodities, the situation in which there is general overproduction.

13 I remember when in my first pregnancy I began to read the La Lèche League literature on breastfeeding. Their bulletins and newsletters frequently repeated the dictum that in breastfeeding "demand creates its own supply." I am not making this up! I was completely taken aback by what I thought then was yet another imperialism of economics – now though I know that it is Say's Law and not the La Lèche League which is expressing a wishful fantasy.

14 As Jane Flax (1983) so brilliantly argues in "Political Philosophy and the Patriarchal Unconscious: A Psychoanalytic Perspective on Epistemology and Metaphysics" another element of interference in the world of the perfect mother is "the state."

15 Has anyone in the history of economic thought/practice ever hypothisized the auctioneer as female?

16 Freud goes on to point out that for some men one of the "pre-conditions" for the choice of love object is that the "object" of affection must not be unattached. The woman becomes desired only if "another man can claim a right of possession" (Gay 1989: 387). The source of this type of object choice is derived from "infantile fixation of tender feelings on the mother," so that all love objects are stamped with maternal characteristics (quoted in Gay 1989:390). How close this is to the role of choice and desire in the fantasy of the omnipotent economic subject.

17 A person in the "depressive position" is not suffering from depression. Rather this psychoanalytic term distinguishes between narcissism which blocks gratitude and an orientation in which gratitude becomes possible.

## REFERENCES

Althusser, L. (1991) "Marx and Freud", *Rethinking Marxism* 4, 1.

Blan, F.D. and Ferber, M.A. (1986) *The Economics of Women, Men, and Work* (2nd edn), Englewood Cliffs, NJ: Prentice Hall.

Bordo, S. (1987) *The Flight to Objectivity: Essays on Cartesianism and Culture*, Albany, NY: State University of New York Press.

Chodorow, N. (1989) *Feminism and Psychoanalytic Theory*, New Haven, CT: Yale University Press.

Dallery, A. (1989) "The Politics of Writing the Body: Ecriture Feminine", in A. Jaggar and S. Bordo (eds) *Gender, Body, Knowledge*, Rutgers, NJ: Rutgers University Press.

England, P. (ed.) (1993) "Theory on Gender", *Feminism on Theory*, Hawthorne, NY: A. de Gruyter.

Ferber, M. and Nelson, J.A. (eds) (1993) *Beyond Economic Man: Feminist Theory and Economics*, Chicago, IL: University of Chicago Press.

Flax, Jane (1983) "Political Philosophy and the Patriarchal Unconsciousness: A Psychoanalytic Perspective on Epistemology and Metaphysics", in S. Harding and M.B. Hintikka (eds) *Discovering Reality, Feminist Perspectives on Epistemology, Metaphysics and Philosophy of Science*, Dordrecht: Reidee.

Fraad, H. (1981) "Marx and Freud: Brothers in Overdetermination", AESA discussion paper series, University of Massachusetts at Amherst.

Freud, S. (1918) "A Special Type of Choice of Object Made by Men (Contributions to the Psychology of Love)": in P. Gay (ed.) (1989) *The Freud Reader*, New York, NY: W.W. Norton.

Gallup, J. (1982) *Feminism and Psychoanalysis. The Daughter's Seduction*, Ithaca, NY: Cornell University Press.

Gay, P. (ed.) (1989) *The Freud Reader*, New York, NY: W.W. Norton.

Godwin, R. (1993) "On the Deep Structure of Conservative Ideology", *Journal of Psychohistory* 20, 3.

Goux, J. (1978) *Symbolic Economies: Marx after Freud*, Ithaca, NY: Cornell University Press.

Graphard, U. "Robinson Crusoe: Quintessential Economic Man", (forthcoming in *Feminist Economics*).

Greenberg, J. and Mitchell, S. (1983) *Object Relations in Psychoanalytic Theory*, Cambridge, MA: Harvard University Press.

Harding, S. (1986) *The Science Question in Feminism*, Ithaca, NY: Cornell University Press.

Hewitson, J. (1994) "Deconstructing Robinson Crusoe", *Australian Journal of Women's Studies*.

Hill, M. (1984) "The Law of the Father: Leadership and Symbolic Authority in Psychoanalysis", in B. Kellerman (ed.) *Leadership: Multidisciplinary Perspectives*, Englewood Cliffs, NJ: Prentice-Hall.

Hunt, L. *The Family Romance of the French Revolution*, Berkeley, CA: University of California Press.

Hymer, S. (1971) "Robinson Crusoe and the Secret of Primitive Accumulation", *Monthly Review Press*.

Jaggar, A. (1989) "Love and Knowledge: Emotion in Feminist Epistemology", in A. Jaggar and S. Bordo (eds) *Gender, Body, Knowledge*, Rutgers, NJ: Rutgers University Press.

Jaggar, A. and Bordo, S. (eds) (1989) *Gender, Body, Knowledge*, Rutgers, NJ: Rutgers University Press.

Kellerman, B. (1984) *Leadership: Multidisciplinary Perspectives*, Englewood Cliffs, NJ: Prentice-Hall.

Langer, M. (1992) *Motherhood and Sexuality*, New York, NY: Guilford Press.

Marx, K. (1977) *Capital, Vol. I*, New York, NY: Vintage Books.

Matthaei, J. (1991) "Marxist-Feminist Contributions to Radical Economics", in B. Roberts and S. Feiner (eds) *Radical Economics*, Norwell, MA: Kluwer Academic Press.

Merchant, C. (1980) *The Death of Nature*, San Francisco, CA: Harper & Row.

Nelson, J.A. (1993) "The Study of Choice or the Study of Provisioning? Gender and the Definition of Economics", in M.A. Ferber and J.A. Nelson (eds) *Beyond Economic Man: Feminist Theory and Economics*, Chicago, IL: University of Chicago Press.

Noble, D. (1992) *A World Without Women: the Christian Clerical Culture of Western Science*, Oxford, UK and New York, NY: Oxford University Press.

Robbins, L. (1952) (1935) "An Essay on the Nature and Significance of Economic Science", (2nd edn) London: Macmillan.

Roberts, B. and Feiner, S. (eds) (1991) *Radical Economics*, Norwell, MA: Kluwer Academic Press.

Rustin, M. (1991) *The Good Society and the Inner World: Psychoanalysis, Politics and Culture*, New York, NY: Verso.

Stern, D. (1977) *The First Relationship*, Cambridge, MA: Harvard University Press.

—————— (1985) *The Interpersonal World of the Infant*, New York, NY: Basic Books.

Strassman, D. (1993) "The Stories of Economics and the Power of the Storyteller", *History of Political Economy* 25, 1, Spring: 147–65.
Welldon, E. (1988) *Mother, Madonna, Whore: The Idealization and Denigration of Motherhood*, New York, NY: Guilford Press.
Winnicott, D. (1988) *Human Nature*, New York, NY: Schocken Books.

# 10

# FEMINIST INTERPRETATIVE ECONOMICS

## Comments on chapters by Strassmann and Polanyi, and Feiner

### *Arjo Klamer*

The preceding two contributors are two of a kind. Call them exercises in interpretation. Instead of taking knife and scissors to dissect their target and use the pieces to deduce reality – the analytical method – the authors have woven rich compositions around a complex reality which they have read as if it were a text. Theirs is the interpretative approach in the hermeneutical and rhetorical traditions.

Judgment of interpretative studies like these is hampered by a pernicious prejudice that is cherished inside neoclassical circles and tacitly entertained by many outside. This is the idea that interpretative work is easy and analytical work difficult. The reason for this prejudice may be that analytical studies tend to rely heavily on mathematics whereas interpretative studies use . . . well, mere words. How mistaken this is. Mathematics may be difficult for some, but that does not make it better, or more scientific, than a "verbal" approach. The math may even be a major distraction in case we want to make sense of the world around us. As Kenneth Boulding wrote (in a review of the mathematical *Foundations of Economic Analysis* by Paul Samuelson): "Conventions of generality and mathematical elegance may be just as much barriers to the attainment and diffusion of knowledge as may contentment with particularity and literary vagueness" (1948: 247). How prophetical a statement this has proven to be. The current playing field of economics resembles a wasteland littered with mathematical debris. One chance of the restoration of the moral science that once economics was is the recovery of the interpretative tradition in economics. It will not be easy. Those who have tried know how difficult it can be to compose rich texts that make sense of the reality explored.

Good interpretative work is so important because in the end we can know the world only interpretatively. In knowing other humans, for example, we can learn a lot from analytical investigations, such as psychological tests and laboratory tests of blood or hair. From these we learn their blood type, genetic code and psychological profile. Fine. But all the analytical knowledge of the world will not enable us to know these strangers intimately. No analytical knowledge can match the knowledge that we generate interpretatively, that is, by talking and observing. In our interpretative mode we compose pictures of strangers from the flood of signals that they communicate to us. We watch the eyes, the hands (John Maynard Keynes believed that he could derive someone's character from just looking at that person's hands), and listen, of course, to what they say and their response to what we say.

In each instance we have to draw on our background knowledge. This is where the difficulty comes in. It requires special interpretative skills to know what to make, for example, of people who are complaining about their spouses and mothers. How could Keynes determine that Franklin Roosevelt was a disagreeable fellow by just looking at his hands? What to do with people who like economics? And what about economists who seem obsessed with market equilibrium? What to do with market equilibrium? You see: interpretation is a practice that is altogether different from the solving of a system of equations. Different it is; easy it is not.

What applies to the making sense of people also applies to the making sense of economic phenomena. Accordingly, this most difficult of all challenges – the composition of a good and rich interpretation that makes sense – faces us when we try to understand the economy or, for that matter, economists.

Feiner, Strassmann and Polanyi, among many other contributors to this volume, have faced this challenge straight on. Amidst the mathematical form of navel staring that currently dominates economic practice, their studies are a delight and a relief. They are provocative as well, forcing us, the readers, to engage in an interpretative effort ourselves. But, after all, the question to ask is: do their readings make sense? Do they agree with what we already know? Do they force us to change our minds? Are we seduced? Or do we find them wanting – for being incomplete, one-sided or, worst of all, of no interest? Scissors will not help us. We can not expect to find solutions and other types of definite answers. As soon as we enter the realm of interpretation, we have to cope with ambiguity and are given the honor to grope for, and back up, our own opinions. Yours may be as valid as mine. The difference is that the editors have asked me to write down mine.

"If it is not erotic, it can't be interesting." The person who formulated this maxim has eluded my memory. The maxim is titillating even if it is an overstatement. Not having been much titillated by neoclassical texts, I was intrigued by Feiner's title. "An erotic economy of sharing?" In neoclassical economics? So how erotic is neoclassical economics?

Imagine being in the skin of a neoclassical economist and, if needed, read Feiner's text once again. You must agree with me that then her text does not titillate as much as generate a sense of embarrassment, if not shame or guilt. This is not, however, how the audience to which Feiner presented her paper "read" her text. The reaction during the conference session is better described as "*schadenfroh*" (German for humor at someone else's expense).

If we judge papers as performance pieces, Feiner's paper has to stand out. As the chair of the session I was able to watch the delighted reactions of the fifty-plus people that had gathered in the room. Her psychoanalytic reading was unheard of, it was also humorous and irreverent – a deadly combination. By zeroing in on the relationship with their mothers Feiner had caught neoclassical economists with their pants down – at least in the imagination of her audience. It was a remarkable performance that would have made any serious critic at that moment seem like a hopeless and humorless beach head. So when Sandra Harding, the assigned commentator, got up to predict that we had just heard a classic, she did justice to the mood of that moment. Feiner had struck a cord.

Various options are available to us, the readers. We could side with Harding and declare Feiner's contribution a classic. We could also go along with the audience at the conference and decide to enjoy her reading and laugh at or commiserate with the masculine neoclassical economists. Alternatively, we could decide that her psychoanalytic reading is too cavalier, too general, to make sense, as a therapist friend concluded to whom I presented the argument. Or her reading could incite us to follow her lead and probe further. You pick and choose.

If you care to know, I opt for all four possibilities. This paper has the potential for becoming a classic if only because of its originality and irreverent tone; it is surely entertaining, and although it does not convince me, Feiner has pointed me to the erotic dimension in neoclassical economics and thus changed my world view a little.

Feiner must be right: there must be a psychological dimension to what neoclassical economists do. Their fascination with "markets" as the construct that deals with all economic problems, must have an explanation over and beyond its analytical potential. But the reduction of that fascination to the simple fact that some of us have a penis and others do not is hard to take in the rebound. It is as if all neoclassical economists have been on Feiner's couch collectively to walk away with one single diagnosis. The seduction in that diagnosis is the mother because she makes virtually everyone vulnerable. And how can I negate the importance of the first experience of difference ("Hey, I am not my mother; I am even different from her!")? I don't remember it. Yet, it sounds plausible and recent psychoanalytic literature makes a great deal of it. I am persuaded by the hypothesis that our lives are dedicated to overcoming the sense of loss and separation that came with the realization of the self. I refuse to roll over, however, for the thesis that the "market" is the idea with which (masculine) economists overcome their sense of loss. It is too simple to be true.

In another reading, Goux (1978) singles out "money" as the outstanding symbol of the market. The fascination with the market then becomes a fascination with money, which resembles, at least in Goux's reading, the fascination with logos (the word) and, would you know it, the phallus. So whereas Feiner exposes neoclassical economists in their pursuit of reunion with their mother and fulfilment of unmet desires – the market-as-mother metaphor – Goux presents them in their thrust to exert themselves – the market-as-father metaphor. Again, you have a choice. Choose Goux and, presuming you do not identify with the neoclassical economists or share their fascination with the market, you beat up the big guys, symbolically that is. Choose Feiner, and you are able to think of the big guys in diapers. Choose both, and you have grasped the tension between the father and mother in us that in my mind takes us further towards an understanding of all human life, including that of the neoclassical economist.

Be a neoclassical economist, and I bet you are annoyed with either reading, as several neoclassical colleagues were when I tried to convey the diagnosis. And right they were, for these psychoanalytic interpretations are too hypothetical and too general to do justice to any particular individual case. If the personalization of her interpretation can be avoided, Feiner's article has added another dimension to the world of neoclassical economics. When that dimension becomes part of our collective consciousness, her article deserves the status of a classic.

Whereas Feiner highlights a metaphor in neoclassical economics – the market-as-mother metaphor – Strassmann and Polanyi read for the narrative in neoclassical texts. Like Feiner's, their interpretation is intended to pierce the scientific armor of neoclassical economics and expose the human flesh. Like Feiner they detect a gender bias. Only now that bias is in the story that neoclassical economists tell about the family and the gender division of labor. With their ingenious reading Strassmann and Polanyi imply that neoclassical economics is inaccessible to anyone who wants to tell a different, less masculine story about our lives.

On the important points I concur. After extensive explorations of the metaphors in economic discourse I have become convinced for myself that narrative is the key to understanding anything human. Get the story of *The Wealth of Nations*, a new acquaintance, a nation, an economist, or yourself, and you understand. In stories we enact our lives, construct our texts; through stories we make sense of ourselves and others. I would even go so far to claim that we cannot understand anything human, and possibly even anything natural, if we do not recognize a story. So I go along with Strassmann and Polanyi in their exploration of the narrative in neoclassical economics. I am also persuaded when they present in their labor textbook the story of the "Enjoyable Family." My only doubts concern the applicability of their interpretation to neoclassical economics in its academic form.

The limitation is due to the choice of text. A textbook constitutes a particular genre with the peculiar requirement that it communicates to the unitiated. It cannot do justice to the discourse that it intends to represent. Textbooks, more than academic texts, tell stories because of their pedagogical effectiveness. The choice of the textbook as a text, therefore, is the easy choice when it comes to finding stories. The textbook writer will bend over backwards to liven up an otherwise dry account by filling in details and throwing in examples that would be unheard of in academic situations. So this is more an interpretation of how the economics profession by means of a textbook tries to make sense of its academic exploits to the novice. The text reveals as much of what economists think of their non-economic audience as their own academic constructions of a world as that of the family.

Turn to the academic texts themselves and all the characters that enliven textbooks disappear to make way for the only character that allows identification. Academic texts in economics are about economists themselves; all other characters are subsidiary or simply left out altogether. An economic analysis poses invariably a problem that is a problem for economists, and works through a solution that can only please and satisfy economists themselves. Because the non-economist can not identify with the economist, the explanation of an academic text requires a transformation that includes the insertion of story elements that allow for a meaningful identification. In the labor economics text that apparently is the story of the Enjoyable Family.

The account of Strassmann and Polanyi is of particular interest because of its strategy. Aspiring interpretors take note of their use of default assumptions to situate the knowledge that a text produces. I furthermore learned from the application of "evaluative devices" a way to get into the text. If only for these applications, I found their contribution most useful. In addition, their interpretation makes good sense.

These two studies apply to the economics profession. The next step would be to take what we learn from these exercises and move on to the economy and the metaphors and stories that dictate economic processes. If we take that step, Boulding may finally be proven right. For after lamenting the rise of mathematical conventions in his 1948 review, he mused that "the lovely and literary borderland between economics and sociology will be the most fruitful building ground during years to come and that mathematical economics will remain too flawless in its perfection to be very fruitful" (1948: 247). Feminist economics, at least in the form that these three authors give it, may very well lead the way.

## REFERENCES

Boulding, K.E. (1948) "Samuelson's Foundations: the Role of Mathematics in Economics", *Journal of Political Economy* 56, June: 187–99.
Goux, J. (1978) *Symbolic Economies: Marx after Freud*, Ithaca, NY: Cornell University Press.

# Part IV

# ECONOMIC MEASUREMENT

## *Editor Zafiris Tzannatos*

But whatever effect discouragement and criticism had upon their writing – and I believe that they had a very great effect – that was unimportant compared with the other difficulty which faced them (I was still considering those early nineteenth-century novelists) when they came to set their thoughts on paper – that is that they had no tradition behind them, or one so short and partial that it was of little help. For we think back through our mothers if we are women. It is useless to go to the great men writers for help, however much one may go to them for pleasure. Lamb, Browne, Thackeray, Newman, Sterne, Dickens, De Quincey – whoever it may be – never helped a woman yet, though she may have learnt a few tricks of them and adapted them to her use.

(Woolf [1928] (1957): 76)

# 11

# THE EMPIRICAL CHALLENGES OF FEMINIST ECONOMICS

## The example of economic restructuring

*Martha MacDonald*

### INTRODUCTION

The feminist critique of neoclassical economic theory is by now well articulated, whether or not it has had an impact. While some feminist economists are grappling with producing ever more sophisticated critiques, others are trying to get on with the business of doing meaningful research on important economic issues. They find that the standards for empirical research and data collection in mainstream economics create difficulties in dealing with feminist concerns. Issues such as power relations in households and the subtle processes which create the glass ceiling in the work world are not easily investigated and measured. Just as neoclassical theory gives rise to certain data needs, so does feminist theory. Feminist economists are borrowing methods from the other social sciences, including survey research, case studies and participant observation. These are suspect endeavors, for which economists are neither trained nor rewarded.

Technical problems confront feminist economists in their day-to-day research as they try to collect new kinds of data and measure previously unmeasured economic phenomena. They realize that their graduate training instilled skills for analyzing data but not for collecting it. Research methodology courses are not part of the typical economics graduate program. Most econometric courses emphasize the theoretical derivations and proofs for the techniques, rather than providing hands-on practice with secondary data analysis. The challenges of creating primary data – even survey data which might be amenable to econometric techniques – are untouched[1].

This essay discusses the empirical challenges of developing a feminist economics, drawing on my own experience confronting the barriers imposed by traditional economics data and methods. My on-the-job training began in the late 1970s in my first research work with a team of sociologists studying labor market segmentation. While I was critical of

175

their more primitive statistical techniques, I found myself totally dependent on them on issues of questionnaire design and sampling. I spent a year collecting exciting data on a small sample of low-wage firms, conducting in-depth interviews with managers and employees as well as a survey. I naively hoped the data would meet the needs of a sociology-driven research agenda and also be usable for an economics dissertation. In the end, all of the qualitative case study insights were omitted from the dissertation. The only usable parts of my data were those which were amenable to econometric analysis, and of course the sample size limitations made it a rather inferior econometric study of wage determination.

I learned to appreciate how empirical approaches are deeply embedded in the underlying assumptions and theoretical framework of a discipline. Whereas economic methods were designed to test rather abstract models explaining economic behavior, the sociological methods reflected a desire to tease out of the data an understanding of relationships.

As I reflect on this now, I recognize the gender biases implicit in the methods for studying work sanctioned by both sociology and economics. While gender clearly emerged in my study as a key factor in wage-setting processes in firms, the methodology limited the analysis to the standard procedure of "adding gender as a variable." The framework motivating the research systematically undermined gender as a central analytical component.

Now, of course, feminists are much more sophisticated about the implicit male bias of so-called objective social science. This theme has been applied to neoclassical economics by many feminist economists who show that the economy analyzed is the visible, male-dominated, public, cash economy, rather than the full range of human economic endeavor (Cohen 1982; McCrate 1991; Nelson 1992, 1993; Pujol 1992; Strassmann 1993). The methodology sanctioned reflects the dominance of male values. The profoundly gendered nature of the economy is not accorded any analytical relevance and because it is conceptually unimportant, the data are not collected to support an alternative economic analysis. The data collected by statistical agencies and made available for economic analysis bear the direct imprint of the male bias of the discipline.

## THEORY/EPISTEMOLOGY/METHODOLOGY/METHODS

Feminist scholars have made major contributions to revealing this complex interweaving of theory, methods and data. A useful distinction is made in the feminist methodology literature between epistemology, methodology, and methods (Harding 1986, 1987; Stanley and Wise 1990). An epistemology is a "theory of knowledge." Who can be a knower? What tests must beliefs pass to be legitimized as knowledge (Harding 1986: 3)? The epistemology defines what are acceptable, relevant data. For instance, is there a value placed on objectivity, or are subjective perceptions admissible? The epistemology of neoclassical economics is scientific positivism.

Methodology means the way that questions of theoretical interest are translated into a plan of research – how would one go about collecting and analyzing data to best shed light on the questions? The theoretical paradigm dictates what questions are being asked and what information will be deemed relevant. In neoclassical economics the methodology is to use quantitative statistical analysis to test rigorous mathematical models of economic behavior. There are other possible methodologies which could be used to analyze economic relationships, such as detailed observation of economic processes at the level, say, of the firm or the household or the community. This methodology is not acceptable in the neoclassical paradigm. As I joked in the middle of a summer spent collecting data in small fishing villages, a good anthropological study is based on one year of field work, a good sociological study on one month of field work and a good economics study on no field work. This is a problem for economics in general. Economists lack a "feel" for many real world issues they address.

Empirical research involves a choice of methods also, once the methodology has been established. Harding defines a research method as "a technique for (or way of proceeding in) gathering evidence" (Harding 1986: 2–3). Methods include both data gathering techniques and data analysis techniques which turn the raw data into evidence. Econometrics and statistically rigorous data collection techniques make up the method of neoclassical economics. This results in a heavy reliance on secondary data sets, which provide the large samples suited to complex econometric analysis. In principle, one could collect primary survey data and analyze them using standard econometrics, though this is not common practice in economics. Econometrics provides a menu of techniques which may be used once one has developed a model and found a suitable data set. Qualitative methods are not part of the "hard" science of economics.

Each method has its own technical literature. With any data collection/ construction undertaking, there are numerous issues to be addressed. In survey research there are endless decisions to be made about sampling, questionnaire design, data collection, and coding. Similarly, in doing a case study, one must decide whom to interview, whether to use open ended questions, whether to tape interviews, and so on. These technical issues, and their implications for the interpretation of the data, remain largely invisible to the economist working with secondary data. Data limitations are an accepted fact of life in applied economics. The technical emphasis is on manipulating inadequate data and creating proxies for missing variables, rather than collecting data to fit the research question at hand.

Data are constructed, then, in the interplay of epistemology, methodology and methods. Feminist work has revealed the potential gender bias in each of these. What can economists learn about these issues from the interdisciplinary feminist methodology literature? This literature has developed over a fifteen- to twenty-year period, beginning with the early attempts to make women visible.

The early concern in the feminist methodology literature was to develop a critique of existing empirical approaches in the social sciences. The emphasis tended to be on research that focussed on women, carried out by women who were feminist, for other women. There was an acceptance that feminist research was political in the sense that it was aimed at redressing inequities (Stanley and Wise 1990: 21). There was also an emphasis on qualitative methods.

In recent years, the emphasis has shifted away from challenging male biases towards analyzing problems within feminist research, including deconstructing categories such as women and gender. The initial gain of legitimating the experience of women – beginning with women's experience as valid data – has led to lengthy struggles with issues such as whose experience is known and which researcher can know. Differences of race, class and sexual orientation challenge feminist methodology.

There is not, then, a hegemonic feminist methodology or epistemology. Harding (1987) distinguishes feminist empiricism, which tries to do "better" science by adding gender to existing research frameworks to remove male bias, from feminist standpoint epistemologies which are based on a different understanding of scientific knowledge. She further distinguishes this from post-modern feminism, with its profound skepticism of science. Harding (1986) argues that the distinctiveness of feminist research is at the level of epistemology or methodology, rather than at the level of method. Feminist scholars use a variety of familiar methods, adapting them to their own purposes.

Feminist economics is at a relatively early stage in addressing these issues and can learn from this literature. The focus in economics has mainly been on exposing and opposing the male bias in mainstream research. However, a little feminist empiricism goes a long way toward revealing the more fundamental problems with the frameworks being adapted. When we add women and stir, we often produce strange new brews. The feminist methodology literature helps us understand the dynamic process of theoretical and methodological change and the necessity of moving beyond feminist empiricism. For example, Nelson exposes the rhetoric of "detachment" in economics and argues that new approaches to economic theory will open up new empirical possibilities, such as admitting the relevance of more qualitative data (Nelson 1993). It is also true that new data and research feed back and necessitate a reconsideration of the theory, as has resulted from feminist research on wage differentials and on intra-household inequality. Feminists in other disciplines who study economic issues hope that the empirical work of feminist economists will help undermine the hegemony of neoclassical economics by revealing the fundamental problems with its assumptions.

Although Harding argues that there are not feminist methods *per se*, it is particularly likely in economics that the methods adopted will be outside of the traditional economist's toolkit. While there is nothing revolutionary in sociology about conducting a survey, it is still an underutilized method in economics. Methods such as in-depth interviews and participant observation are even further afield. Economists can learn from the experiences of feminists in other disciplines how to use these methods in unbiased ways.

There is also much to learn from feminist researchers in other fields on the issue of difference among women. The complexities of race, class, sexual orientation, North/South differences – so critical in feminist debates today – will become increasingly important in economic research. There are also some lessons to be learned from this literature regarding how not to proceed. For example, there has been a very negative tendency towards infighting, which threatens to destroy the feminist project.

While feminist economists can learn from the feminist methodology literature, they also have important contributions to make. The goal is not only to challenge and alter economics, but to be a voice within the broader feminist academic community. The literature on feminist methodology will be enriched by more economists joining the debates.

## FEMINIST RESEARCH ON ECONOMIC RESTRUCTURING

Research on economic restructuring provides one illustration of the different empirical approaches needed to address feminist concerns. My current research is on the gendered restructuring of work in Canada[2]. The objective of this research is to understand the changing conditions of women's waged and unwaged labor by examining it in the context of broader economic restructuring and debates about flexibility and the missing middle (Harrison and Bluestone 1988; Kuttner 1983; Economic Council of Canada 1991; Levy and Murnane 1992). It is crucial that the discourse on restructuring on both the right and the left be challenged for its gender blindness. Explanations of the apparent missing middle increasingly draw on the flexibility/post-Fordism literature, which has been criticized for its failure to deal with gender (MacDonald 1991; Pollert 1989a,b; Jenson 1989; Walby 1989). The insights of the feminist literature have generally not been incorporated into the analysis of the polarization of jobs and increased earnings inequality, even when findings are disaggregated by sex.

Other kinds of data are needed to understand the gender aspects of restructuring and get beyond the narrow confines of the missing middle debate. The research must be broadened from a narrow focus on the paid labor market to include all kinds of work. A unifying theme of feminist work is to challenge the distinctions made between the formal and informal economy, paid and unpaid work, market/non-market activities, productive and reproductive labor. Restructuring affects the totality of economic activities as the combined strategies of corporations, states and households shift economic effort across these dimensions. We are using secondary data, industry case studies and household interviews to reinvestigate the restructuring of work from a feminist perspective. This requires investigating gendered processes in the household and the labor market. It also involves an examination of the gendered impact of government policy. We are conducting research at the level of the individual and the household.

While my own research focusses on the North, pioneering work on many of these issues has been done in the South. Both the North and the South have experienced profound restructuring in the last decade, reflecting heightened international competition, shifts in the centers of economic power, and rapid technological change. There has been an increased emphasis on the market. National governments have deregulated and imposed fiscal restraint, while international institutions such as the IMF and World Bank have imposed the policies of structural adjustment.

While most of the literature on restructuring fails to include gender adequately, there is a growing body of feminist research on the topic. In the South, feminist concern with restructuring takes the form of analyzing the importance of gender in understanding structural adjustment and macropolicy (Cornia *et al.* 1987; Elson 1989; Moser 1989; Ward 1990; Haddad 1991; Palmer 1991; Bakker 1992; Mayatech 1991), as well as the role of women's labor in the successful industrialization of some countries. In the North it takes the form of engaging in debates about the missing middle, flexibility and the feminization of labor (Jenson *et al.* 1988; Rubery 1988; Wagman and Folbre 1988; MacDonald 1991; MacPhail 1993; Van Wagner 1993).

Three of the central theoretical and empirical concerns of feminist economics over the years converge in research on economic restructuring in the North and South. These are:

1 Measurement/valuation of women's unpaid work.
2 Intra-household distribution of income and resources, labor allocation, decision-making and power relations.
3 Gendered processes in the paid labor market.

These are essential components in a holistic analysis in which gender is a fundamental organizing principle of the economy. Each component is discussed, focussing on the empirical challenges and giving examples of efforts to collect new data. The discussion draws on research from the North and South.

## Measuring and valuing women's unpaid work

To understand the restructuring of the whole economy information is needed on subsistence production, informal paid work, domestic production and volunteer work (Beneria 1992). These measurement issues challenge us in our own primary data collection, and are important in terms of the data collected by national statistical bureaus on GNP and labor force activity. Work by Waring (1988) and others (Folbre 1991, 1993; Aslaksen 1992; Anderson 1992) shows that gender-biased statistical conventions for the definition and measurement of economic activity and output developed as a result of systematic sexist and patriarchal decisions.

Feminists have challenged these conventions for over two decades and significant progress is now being made in accounting for women's work by national statistical agencies (Beneria 1981, 1992). The ILO and INSTRAW have been instrumental in the initiative to revise national accounting to include unpaid work (Goldschmidt-Clermont 1982, 1987; Dixon-Mueller 1985; Dixon-Mueller and Anker 1988), and the momentum has increased since the *Forward-looking Strategies* (UN 1985) endorsed the issue. Interestingly, there are also many men pushing this agenda (Eisner 1988, 1989; Thoen 1993). Beneria argues that while the conceptual battle has largely been won, work is needed on four fronts: definitions used in data collection (work, primary activity, family); "how to" issues such as questionnaire design; cultural issues, to avoid imposing inappropriate cultural norms; and implementation issues such as interviewer training (Beneria 1992: 156).

While feminist economists support these efforts, there is also caution being expressed. First, there is concern that maintaining the integrity of the existing accounts is paramount in the eyes of most economists and statisticians involved. Unpaid work is being added on in satellite accounts, to be used for certain purposes but not for general economic analysis. Furthermore, the need to be consistent with existing accounting practices constrains discussions of how to measure and value unpaid work – the standard is still the market. No significance is accorded to the different social relations and institutional organization of non-market work.

Although a case is made that the best way to measure/value unpaid work is by outputs (Goldschmidt-Clermont 1993), the approach being taken by most statistical bureaus is to measure inputs, which means estimating the cost of performing the unpaid work in the market (replacement cost). This requires good time-use data and decisions about the market equivalent labor. Feminists are concerned that time-use surveys will measure only the menial tasks performed, and miss the more abstract management function. They are also concerned that the market wages used to value the work will be the undervalued wages of female-dominated occupations. Should the value of childcare services be calculated using the wages of daycare workers or child psychiatrists? Feminists fear that the valuing of unpaid work will reflect the undervaluing of women's paid work.

There are also theoretical concerns about the meaning of aggregating the unpaid and paid economies. The central interest of feminists is the interaction between the two; the unpaid economy is embedded in the measured market economy, not an adjunct to it. There is not a simple one-to-one tradeoff between the two.

Feminists are also concerned about the uses of the data. Assigning a value in the accounts does not alter the fact that the work is unpaid, and may convey a false message of recognition. While feminist researchers will certainly be able to use these data, they can also be used to support anti-feminist initiatives. There is suspicion about why measuring this unpaid output is suddenly popular. It may be part of the search for better numbers by nation states. GNP measures which used to show consistent growth for the North as the market expanded now show consistent stagnation, as work has shifted from the public sector to the volunteer and domestic sphere, and from the formal to the informal economy. This may be as much the cause of the interest in satellite accounts as two decades of pressure from both academics (Beneria 1981; Waring 1988; Goldschmidt-Clermont 1982, 1987; Dixon-Mueller 1985, 1988; Chadeau 1992; Eisner 1988, 1989) and the international women's movement (UN 1985). Revised GNP figures can paint a rosier picture. As one person said at a Statistics Canada International Conference on the Measurement and Valuation of Unpaid Work (Statistics Canada 1993), if you add together the household and market economies, as he called them, the business cycle practically disappears.

Another important initiative related to measuring the aggregate economy is the attempt to develop alternative indicators of economic and social well-being. Social indicators are being more widely used, such as the UNDP Human Development Index (1992) which combines indicators of national income, life expectancy and education. The UNDP also calculates a gender-sensitive HDI for thirty-three countries. While this initiative is laudable, the index is based on the gender-biased measures of GNP and labor force activity discussed above.

Despite their shortcomings, these initiatives at the national and international level represent major gains. However, ongoing feminist involvement in the technical issues is necessary to ensure their integrity and usefulness. This lesson has been learned in Canada in the case of pay equity legislation, where translating the principle of comparable worth into policy and practice has posed an ongoing challenge to feminists (Fudge and McDermott 1991). The technical details cannot be left to the men, once the principles have gained recognition.

Some feminist economists have attempted to revise historical statistics that rendered the work of women invisible. For example, Folbre and Wagman (1993) re-estimated nineteenth century growth rates for the US using imputed values for non-market household work. Jane Humphries (1990) re-evaluated the effects of the enclosures in Britain by considering the value of the commons to women. This involved creative estimation of the value of a cow, kindling and gleaning. Humphries' work also used the feminist standpoint approach of listening to what the historical actors had to say. While other economic historians discounted statements and actions from the time expressing serious concern with the loss of the commons, Humphries takes these as indicators that women did indeed know the value of the commons in their economic survival strategies.

I have used surveys and in-depth interviews in my research to capture the movement of economic activities in and out of the formal market. In our project on the fishery we tried to trace this over time as the industry changed (MacDonald and Connelly 1989). We wanted to measure unpaid fisheries-related work done by women as well as subsistence production and informal sector income-generating activities (taking boarders, babysitting). These are very hard to measure directly. Activities vary by season and by life cycle and they overlap. We tried listing types of activities and getting yes/no responses as well as measuring the relative importance of these activities. We also asked open-ended questions, such as "what did your mother do to contribute to the household economy." We ran into the standard problems faced by everyone, including the national statistical bureaus. The ideology that these activities are not real work is so prevalent that women themselves have trouble recognizing them as work. In one survey we prompted, "Did she keep chickens, cows or boarders," and of course we found that the most frequent subsistence or income-generating activities were chickens, cows and boarders! The inadequacies of one's own data are so obvious, compared to secondary data, where the problems are largely invisible to the researcher.

Measurement of unpaid work must also include dependent care and household chores. Survey methods range from detailed time diaries to lists of tasks (who usually does each task, or how much time do you spend on this task in a week). There are problems with all methods. In task lists, there can be bias in the choice of tasks, and omission of tasks. For example, care of the elderly is increasingly important, but is often not asked about. There can also be inappropriate assumptions made about who might be expected to share in certain work – immediate family members, neighbors, extended family? There is also the problem of overlapping tasks, which are difficult to measure. A Canadian colleague pointed out that Statistics Canada data showed that women with children under five spend an average of two hours on childcare per day. Does that reflect national child neglect, or measurement problems?

There is a wealth of experience in the women and development literature in using survey research to measure unpaid economic activity, and the ILO and INSTRAW have been active in publishing discussions of the methodological problems involved (Dixon-Mueller 1985; Dixon-Mueller and Anker 1988; Goldschmidt-Clermont 1982,1987; Anker *et al.* 1988). These are invaluable guides for people contemplating their own surveys. It is also important to appreciate the role of open-ended questions in this kind of research, given the lack of basic information about the structure and allocation of local non-market economic activity. Participant observation and other anthropological methods are of relevance to economists working on these issues.

The goal is not counting and measuring for its own sake, but gathering information that will enable us to understand how the unpaid/informal economy functions and integrates with the cash/market. Who does unpaid work for whom? What do they get in return? What obligations do people feel to family and non-family members? What networks of support exist in communities? How does cash support unpaid work and vice versa? Are paid and unpaid work substitutes or complements? How elastic is the provision of unpaid work? In all cases, of course, the gender dimensions of these arrangements are of utmost concern.

This information provides the basis for understanding how economic policies and changes in the market sector will alter patterns of work and impact on well-being. In our current project, for example, we expect that expenditure cutbacks in health and education services transfer work from the market to the home, threatening women's jobs in the public sector, and increasing their unpaid workload in the home. This does not eliminate the costs of these services but renders the cost invisible and imposes it on women.

Research on gender and structural adjustment examines similar impacts, including the intensification of labor on subsistence activities. While some researchers have emphasized the welfare and equity aspects of these policies, many have also raised "efficiency" concerns. The anticipated gains from the policies are often not realized due to unmeasured costs (Elson 1989; Palmer 1991). Policies will backfire if they are not based on an understanding of the gender division of labor and the social relations of unpaid work. Considerable work is being done on these issues in the South. The work of Appleton (1991), Sollis and Moser (1991), Haddad (1991) and Palmer (1991) provide useful guides to data possibilities and limitations. The issue of determining causation is particularly difficult, given the lack of historical data in most studies.

Researchers in the South are also trying to take account of the gendered impact of price changes resulting from structural adjustment policies. This requires detailed data on intra-household income and expenditure patterns, preferably disaggregated by gender. This is the second major empirical issue challenging feminist economists.

## Intra-household distribution of income and resources, household decision-making

Feminist work on restructuring emphasizes the importance of intra-household processes. Household strategies interact with employer and government strategies. This has been an important area of focus in feminist economics, responding first to the lack of attention to the household as an economic site, and then to the problematic analysis of the household in the "new home economics" (Hartmann 1981; Humphries and Rubery 1984; MacDonald 1984; Folbre 1986; Woolley 1993). For feminists, the minimum requirement is a model of the household that allows for conflict of interests and patriarchal power relations within and outside the family. Feminist economists have turned to game theory to develop bargaining models of the household (McElroy and Horney 1981). These models are in turn criticized for their inability to handle perceived interests and contributions (Sen 1990) and group as opposed to individual self-interest (Folbre 1986, 1993; Wilson 1991). Economists have yet to incorporate satisfactorily basic sociological concepts such as social norms, endogenous preferences and collective action into these models (Folbre 1994).

Empirical work on the household has demonstrated significant intra-household inequality in the distribution of income and other resources. The women and development literature has emphasized inequality in access to education, food, land, technology, and credit. There is evidence of differential mortality and health for male and female children (Blumberg 1988). Studies also show that it matters who spends the income in a household (Phipps and Burton 1992; Thomas 1990; Blumberg 1988). This evidence is inconsistent with Becker-style models.

Many researchers have commented on the lack of adequate data to analyze household decision-making and resource allocation. McElroy (1990: 571), for example, points out that the estimation of a Nash demand system requires more data than would the corresponding neoclassical equations. Specifically, data are needed on separate non-wage incomes for each family member and "extra-household environmental parameters" that shift the threat points – information not available in most secondary data sets. In a recent review of the literature on children and household economic behavior, Browning (1992) also emphasizes the lack of appropriate data such as life histories.

Wilson (1991) discusses some of the practical problems involved in using a cooperative conflict model to collect and interpret data on household finances. She discusses the problem of dominant ideology and the relationship between experience, private accounts and public accounts. Not only may the interviewer get a public account that differs from the person's private account, but it may also be the case that the person herself has no vocabulary to create a private account. For example, Wilson had difficulty getting information on the individual income shares of household members, because the ideology was that the shares were equal. There was an inability to look realistically at shares by both men and women interviewed. Similar ideological problems affect collecting data on the household task division of labor and decision-making (Woolley and Marshall 1992). One approach is to ask multiple questions on the same issue. Economists have much to learn from the sociological and anthropological literature on researching these issues (Pahl 1983; Sollis and Moser 1991).

Household decision-making, division of labor and allocation of resources are important in the feminist analysis of economic restructuring. In this literature the concern is not with testing economic models of the household but in seeing how the household articulates to the rest of the economy. How do households respond to external economic pressures, such as price changes for consumer goods, provision of government services, changes in labor market alternatives? How is labor allocated and reallocated? How do the workloads, status and well-being of family members change? The crucial questions have to do with the gendered division of labor in the home, household labor allocation (market and non-market) and the intra-household allocation of income and resources. For the most part, this means collecting primary data through survey or in-depth interview methods, though it is also necessary to challenge the data which are publicly collected. We need carefully designed national household surveys that are administered on a regular basis (Appleton 1991). Household data must be combined with data on other levels of the economy, preferably disaggregated by gender.

An excellent example of research that spans these levels is Beneria and Roldan's study of industrial homework in Mexico City (1987). While they begin at the level of the household, they carry the analysis up to the level of the strategies of multinational corporations in a changing international economy. They include household interviews in their methodology as well as employer interviews and secondary data. Because this sector is by definition unrecorded, they cannot use standard statistical sampling procedures and must use less rigorous snowball sampling. They analyze the joint work histories of the female homeworkers and their partners, showing not only the gender inequalities within the household but how these affect the external labor market processes and the relations between capital and labor. In the process of studying the illegal homework sector they clarify its articulation to other aspects of production, both through the labor of other household members and through other levels of the labor process in the firm.

Thus, while feminist research often starts at the level of the household, the analysis is by no means confined to the domestic sphere. I have used similar methods to understand the articulation of gender relations in the household with conditions in the market economy. In our research on restructuring in the fishery in Atlantic Canada we showed that a focus on gender and household dynamics facilitated a clearer understanding of changes in the labor process and the transformation of the industry (MacDonald and Connelly 1989). The household plays a crucial role in the interrelationships between the harvesting and processing sectors of the fishery. The bargaining power of a fisherman may depend on whether his wife works in the fish plant, and vice versa. Detailed family work histories are crucial for this analysis. We also demonstrated that state policy related to the fishery is based on implicit assumptions about gender relations in the household, and that supposedly gender-neutral policies, related to licenses and quotas, have very definite gender impacts (Connelly and MacDonald 1992) as they get filtered through the household. Failure to understand economic processes in the household resulted in unintended consequences of government and corporate policies.

Before leaving this discussion of the household, one final consideration must be raised. The term "household" has been used uncritically in the above discussion. However, even the definition of the household is problematic conceptually and empirically. The nuclear household is still the implicit, if not explicit norm in economics. The researcher must be on guard for how such assumptions get built into the data. For example, I once did a household survey that systematically omitted single parent households from the sample, and then fell into the trap of writing about "women" in a universal sense. There is more general awareness of the problems with the concept of household head, both in theory and data collection. There are many issues in how to define a household unit – those under one roof? those related? those who share resources? The conventions on this are often culturally biased, gender biased and out of touch with reality.

We must also question this emphasis on the household (however defined) as the unit of analysis. For example, if our interest is to understand non-market processes, then social relations much broader than the household are important. The proper unit of analysis to use should be an empirical question, not an assumption. "Intra-household decision-making/resource allocation" is thus for now only a shorthand for our interest in the personal, gendered, non-market relations that are a crucial part of our economy. Unfortunately, secondary data construction norms based on neoclassical economics typically leave us with only two choices for a unit of analysis – the individual, with little information on any of the social relations in which the person is embedded; or the household, with artificial limits set on what relations of pooling, sharing or exchange are recognized. This is an area that is particularly challenging even when collecting primary data.

## Gendered processes in the paid labor market

The final component in feminist research on restructuring is to examine changes in the paid labor market from a gender perspective. Feminist labor economists have done extensive empirical work in this area, therefore a brief summary of issues is sufficient for the purposes of this essay. Feminists have participated in the empirical literature on female labor force participation and gender wage differentials and have run into problems with both theory and data in trying to improve on the traditional work in these areas. I recently refereed an article on the gender wage gap which used the standard decomposition technique to derive the portion due to characteristics and that due to discrimination. My eyes glazed over and I thought that the world did not need another set of human capital wage equations, even if they were adjusted for sample selection bias! The list of variables is typically very limited; occupational categories are too broad; experience is poorly measured; demand measures are inadequate; and typically there is little information on the individual's family characteristics. Furthermore, the analysis is usually not informed by a knowledge of the feminist literature. Similar data problems are encountered when analyzing changes in the occupation and industry distribution of female employment (Jenson *et al.* 1988; Rubery 1988; Wagman and Folbre 1988; Standing 1989; Connelly and MacDonald 1990; Van Wagner 1993).

Secondary data available from national statistical agencies to study women in the labor market are inadequate in many ways:

- There is a preponderance of cross-sectional data, and very little panel data.
- The level of aggregation makes it impossible to study issues of segmentation within occupations.
- Labor force data are collected on the individual, with information on the family context either missing or inadequate.
- The use of categories such as "personal or family reasons" versus "economic reasons" in labor force surveys to code reasons for not looking for work or for working part-time imbed gender biases in the data.
- Skill measures used (SVP, GDP) have been shown to be gender biased (Boyd 1990).
- It is difficult to measure changes in the quality of jobs.

Considering these difficulties, many feminist economists have turned to primary data collection to understand further issues of skill, technological change, occupational segregation, non-standard work, internal labor markets, and the gendered institutional processes that help explain the differential returns to characteristics identified in the wage equations. While specialized survey data can address some of these issues, using either household or employee samples, case study methodology is also useful to analyze the labor process within firms. These case studies usually combine qualitative and quantitative data. Only rarely do the data lend themselves to sophisticated econometric analysis. Usually they involve key informant interviews with managers, union representatives and workers, as well as observation of day-to-day processes in the firms and access to company records if possible.

These case studies lie outside the traditional methodology of neoclassical economics and are criticized for being non-representative and subjective. Certainly one has to guard against making unwarranted generalizations from such studies. An interesting article by Linda Lim (1990) criticizes much of the feminist literature on Third World women's work in export factories, arguing that it often perpetuates negative stereotypes and fails to appreciate the differences by country, industry and time. She says there is a tendency to employ a static, a-historical approach and to generalize from observations in one particular location at one time (1990: 113). Poorly conducted case studies do not further feminist interests, and can never hope to achieve respectability in economics. However, until this methodology is recognized within economics, it will fail to develop sophistication. This is a vicious circle for feminist economists and other labor economists interested in the labor process and institutional issues[3].

Our approach to these dilemmas with both secondary and primary data is to use a mixture of methods. In our current project on restructuring we have two separate components: extensive analysis of standard Statistics Canada micro data tapes on employment characteristics, earnings and income, and industry case studies chosen to capture various dimensions of restructuring in the public and private sectors.

Our challenge with the secondary data analysis is to go beyond work already done using these data. Our view is that despite disaggregation by sex in most studies of the missing middle, the analysis has tended to focus on what is happening to men. There is a preoccupation with the loss of lucrative (male) manufacturing jobs. Many studies of the polarization of earnings have focussed on changes in the distribution of wages for full-time, full-year workers (i.e. "real" jobs). This biases the research to a focus on male jobs and does not give a full picture of the many dimensions on which restructuring is occurring. The focus is on changes in the distribution, which are more dramatic for men. Never mind that women have a more unequal earnings distribution in each year (MacPhail 1993) or that more women have been and continue to be in the low end of the wage distribution. The concern is not that some workers are low paid, but that some jobs that used to pay adequate wages have disappeared or been downgraded. There is also a tendency in the empirical literature to focus on one dimension at a time. For example, gender is discussed, and then age, missing the gendered nature of the youth labor market. Our challenge is to re-examine the available secondary data to understand more meaningfully the gender dimensions of the changes. For example we need to examine claims in the literature concerning the feminization of labor (Standing

1989). Related studies are being done in other countries by Rubery (1988), Cagatay and Berik (1991), Van Wagner (1993), and others.

In our industry case studies we want to understand the gender dimensions of the restructuring of the labor process. How have wages, skills, working conditions, hours, job security and promotion opportunities changed for women and men? In doing this research, we call into question male-biased measures of skill (Gaskell 1986; Jenson 1989; Boyd 1990). We also want to identify gendered flexibility strategies. For example, are women being used when numerical flexibility and pay flexibility are sought, while men benefit from functional flexibility strategies? In our research on the fishing industry we found women were hurt more than men by employer attempts to gain flexibility. In our case studies we are using open-ended key informant interviews with management, employees and union representatives as well as administering a survey questionnaire to a sample of employees. We would like to interview workers who have lost their jobs through restructuring, which poses a sampling challenge.

Finally, in both our secondary data analysis and our case studies we want to focus on the household, not just the individual worker. This presents problems in both cases. Secondary data sets usually do not have equal detail on the activities or incomes of all household members. One needs lengthy, expensive questionnaires to address these issues in primary surveys, and the choice of respondent is problematic. In-depth interviews are useful for getting proper detail, but then limit one to qualitative analysis. Despite these problems, a household focus is essential to understand things like the gender effects of changes in location of economic activity. What kind of migration is required? Are women able to take advantage of new opportunities? How do families respond to these changes? How are patterns of remittances among extended family members affected? Feminist work on structural adjustment in the South has also drawn attention to these issues, as mentioned earlier (Elson 1989; Bakker 1992).

## CONCLUSION

This essay has touched on some of the empirical issues faced by researchers interested in gender and restructuring. Feminist economists working on other topics would face related empirical issues. Feminist economics necessarily challenges the data and methods of economics. Data collected by national statistical agencies directly reflect the gender biases of neoclassical theory. GNP accounts measure market production; household income and expenditure surveys do not collect information on intra-household access to resources; labor force surveys reflect a notion of the "typical" (i.e. male) worker – the lone individual. It is no accident that we sometimes feel that the data and the methods conspire to limit our results when we try to use secondary data for our purposes. Feminists are challenged to work creatively with these data to tease out a gender analysis. They are also working to force changes in the data collected, for example through revised GNP accounts, and household panel data with more information on intra-household differences in resource access and workload.

Primary data collection is also an important component of feminist economics research. While specialized surveys may lend themselves to standard econometric techniques, other more qualitative methods necessarily place the researcher outside the economics mainstream. Most feminist economists experience the insecurity of working "on the margin." We face many challenges in perfecting alternative methodologies and constructing new data. This kind of empirical economics is not easier, contrary to popular belief in the profession. It is important that the on-the-job training of this generation be translated into research methodology texts and courses for the next generation of feminist economists.

Clearly economic theory and methodology both have to change if they are to serve feminist purposes, and the changes are interactive. This essay has emphasized empirical issues, but it will be clear that the theoretical approach of the research reported is outside the neoclassical mainstream. I think feminist economics integrates more easily with institutional and radical/political economy approaches, though these frameworks too must change. There is not unanimity amongst feminist economists at present on the issue of which economic framework to work from. No matter what approach is taken, it is important to pursue our common interests in the most collegial way, learning from each other and from feminist colleagues in other disciplines and in the women's movement, sharing our experiences across the North and the South, and maintaining the momentum in feminist economics. This new economics will not just better address feminist issues. It will be better economics.

## NOTES

1 In this paper primary data refers to data collected by the researcher while secondary data refers to "off-the-shelf" data sets, often collected by a government statistical bureau.

2 My partner in this research is Pat Connelly, a sociologist with whom I have collaborated for ten years. This project builds on earlier work on restructuring in the fishing industry, based on community case studies.

3 For now, journals such as the *Cambridge Journal of Economics, Work, Employment and Society* and the new journal of *Gender Work and Organization* provide outlets for case study research as do journals within the political economy tradition, such as *Studies in Political Economy.*

## REFERENCES

Anderson, M. (1992) "The History of Women and the History of Statistics", *Journal of Women's History* 4, 1, Spring.

Anker, R., Khan, M.E., and Gupta, R.B. (1988) *Women's Participation in the Labor Force: A Method Test in India for Improving Its Measurement*, Geneva: International Labor Office.

Appleton, S. (1991) "Gender Dimensions of Structural Adjustment: The Role of Economic Theory and Quantitative Analysis", *IDS Bulletin* 22, 1.

Aslaksen, J. (1992) "National Accounting and Unpaid Household Work: A Feminist View on the Concept of Value in Economics", paper presented at the Conference on Feminist Economics, July, Washington, DC: American University.

Bakker, I. (1992) *Engendering Macroeconomic Policy Reform in the Era of Adjustment and Restructuring: A Conceptual Overview*, Ottawa: North-South Institute.

Beneria, L. (1981) "Conceptualizing the Labor Force: The Underestimation of Women's Economic Activities", *Journal of Development Studies* 17, 3.

—— (1992) "Accounting For Women's Work: The Progress of Two Decades", *World Development* 20, 11, November.

Beneria, L. and Roldan, M. (1987) *The Crossroads of Class and Gender: Industrial Homework, Subcontracting and Household Dynamics in Mexico City*, Chicago: University of Chicago Press.

Blumberg, R. (1988) "Income Under Female Versus Male Control", *Journal of Family Issues* 9, 1, March.

Boyd, M. (1990) "Sex Differences in Occupational Skill: Canada, 1961–1986", *Canadian Review of Sociology and Anthropology* 27, 1.

Browning, M. (1992) "Children and Household Economic Behaviour", *Journal of Economic Literature* XXX, September.

Cagatay, N. and Berik, G. (1991) "Transition to Export-Led Growth in Turkey: Is there a Feminization of Employment", *Capital and Class* 43.

Chadeau, A. (1992) "What is Household's Non-Market Production Worth?", *OECD Economic Studies* 18, Spring.

Cohen, M. (1982) "The Problem of Studying Economic 'Man'", in A. Miles and G. Finn (eds) *Feminism in Canada: From Pressure to Politics*, Montreal: Black Rose Books.

Connelly, M.P. and MacDonald, M. (1983) "Women's Work: Domestic and Wage Labor in a Nova Scotia Community", *Studies in Political Economy* 10, Winter.

—— (1990) *Women and the Labor Force*, Ottawa: Supply and Services.

—— (1992) "State Policy, The Household and Women's Work in the Atlantic Fishery", *Journal of Canadian Studies* 26, 4.

Cornia, G.A., Jolly, R., and Stewart, F. (1987) *Adjustment With A Human Face: Protecting the Vulnerable and Promoting Growth*, Oxford: Clarendon Press.

Dixon-Mueller, R. (1985) "Women's Work in Third World Agriculture", 9, Geneva: ILO, Women Work and Development.

Dixon-Mueller, R. and Anker, R. (1988) *Assessing Women's Economic Contributions to Development*, Geneva: ILO, Training in Population, Human Resources and Development Planning.

Economic Council of Canada (1991) *Employment in the Service Economy*, Ottawa: Supply and Services Canada.

Eisner, R. (1988) "Extended Accounts for National Income and Product", *Journal of Economic Literature* XXVI, December.

—— (1989) *The Total Incomes System of Accounts*, Chicago: University of Chicago Press.

Elson, D. (1989) "How is Structural Adjustment Affecting Women ?", *Development* 1.

Folbre, N. (1986) "Hearts and Spades: Paradigms of Household Economics", *World Development* 14, 2.

———— (1986) "Cleaning House: New Perspectives on Households and Economic Development", *Journal of Development Economics* 22.

———— (1991) "The Unproductive Housewife: Her Evolution in Nineteenth Century Economic Thought", *Signs* 16.

———— (1993) "'Guys Don't Do That': Gender Groups and Social Norms", presented at the meetings of the AEA, Anaheim, California, January.

———— (1994) *Who Pays for the Kids*, New York: Routledge.

Folbre, N. and Wagman, B. (1993) "Counting Housework: New Estimates of Real Product in the United States, 1800–1860", *Journal of Economic History*, May.

Fudge, J. and McDermott, P. (eds) (1991) *Just Wages: A Feminist Assessment of Pay Equity*, Toronto: University of Toronto Press.

Gaskell, J. (1986) "Conceptions of Skill and the Work of Women: Some Historical and Political Issues", in R. Hamilton and M. Barrett (eds) *The Politics of Diversity*, Montreal: Book Centre.

Goldschmidt-Clermont, L. (1982) *Unpaid Work in the Household: A Review of Economic Evaluation Methods*, Geneva: International Labor Office.

———— (1987) *Economic Evaluations of Unpaid Household Work: Africa, Asia, Latin America and Oceania*, Geneva: International Labor Office.

———— (1993) "Monetary Valuation of Unpaid Work", presented at the Statistics Canada International Conference on the Measurement and Valuation of Unpaid Work, 28–30 April, Ottawa.

Haddad, L. (1991) "Gender and Adjustment: Theory and Evidence to Date", paper presented at the Workshop on the Effects of Policies and Programs on Women, December, Washington, DC: International Food Policy Research Institute.

Harding, S. (1986) *The Science Question in Feminism*, Ithaca: Cornell University Press.

———— (ed.) (1987) *Feminism and Methodology*, Bloomington: Indiana University Press.

Harrison, B. and Bluestone, B. (1988) *The Great U-Turn: Corporate Restructuring and The Polarizing of America*, New York: Basic Books.

Hartmann, H. (1981) "The Family as the Locus of Gender, Class and Political Struggle: The Example of Housework", *Signs*.

Humphries, J. (1990) "Enclosures, Common Rights and Women: The Proletarianization of Families in the Late Eighteenth and Early Nineteenth Centuries", *Journal of Economic History* 2, 1.

Humphries, J. and Rubery, J. (1984) "The Reconstitution of the Supply Side of the Labour Market", *Cambridge Journal of Economics* 8, March.

Jenson, J. (1989) "The Talents of Women, the Skills of Men: Flexible Specialization and Women", in S. Wood (ed.) *The Transformation of Work ?*, London: Unwin Hyman Limited.

Jenson, J., Hagen, E., and Reddy, C. (eds) (1988) *Feminization of the Labor Force*, New York: Oxford University Press.

Kuttner, R. (1983) "The Declining Middle", *The Atlantic Monthly*, July.

Levy, F. and Murnane, R. (1992) "U.S. Earnings Levels and Earnings Inequality: A Review of Recent Trends and Proposed Explanations", *Journal of Economic Literature* XXX, September.

Lim, L. (1990) "Women's Work in Export Factories: The Politics of a Cause", in I. Tinker (ed.) *Persistent Inequalities*, Oxford: Oxford University Press.

Livingstone, D. and Luxton, M. (1989) "Gender Consciousness at Work: Modification of the Male Breadwinner Norm Among Steelworkers and Their Spouses", *The Canadian Journal of Sociology and Anthropology*, 26 May.

McCrate, E. (1991) "Rationality, Gender and Domination", Working Paper, University of Vermont.

MacDonald, M. (1984) "Economics and Feminism: The Dismal Science?", *Studies in Political Economy* 15, Fall.

───── (1991) "Post-Fordism and the Flexibility Debate", *Studies in Political Economy* 36.

MacDonald, M. and Connelly, M.P. (1989) "Class and Gender in Fishing Communities in Nova Scotia", *Studies in Political Economy* 30, Autumn.

McElroy, M.J. and Horney, M.B. (1981) "Nash-Bargained Household Decision-making", *International Economic Review* 22.

McElroy, M. (1990) "The Empirical Content of Nash-Bargained Household Behaviour", *Journal of Human Resources* XXV, 4.

MacPhail, F. (1993) "Has the Great U-Turn Gone Full Circle?: Recent trends in Earnings Inequality in Canada, 1981–89", Working Paper No. 93-01, Dalhousie University, Halifax.

Mayatech Corporation (1991) *Gender and Adjustment*, Report Prepared for Office of Women in Development, Bureau for Program and Policy Coordination, U.S. Agency for International Development.

Moser, C. (1989a) "Gender Planning in the Third World: Meeting Practical and Strategic Gender Needs", *World Development* 17, 11.

───── (1989b) "The Impact of Recession and Structural Adjustment on Women: Ecuador", *Development* 1: 75–83.

Nelson, J. (1992) "Gender, Metaphor and the Definition of Economics", *Economics and Philosophy*.

───── (1993) "Value Free or Valueless ? Notes on the Pursuit of Detachment in Economics", *History of Political Economy* 25, 1.

Pahl, J. (1983) "The Allocation of Money and the Structuring of Inequality within Marriage", *Sociological Review* 13, 2.

Palmer, I. (1991) *Gender and Population in the Adjustment of African Economies: Planning for Change*, Geneva: ILO.

Phipps, S. and Burton, P. (1992) "'What's Mine is Yours?' The Influence of Male and Female Incomes on Patterns of Expenditure", Working Paper No. 92–12, November, Halifax: Dalhousie University.

Pollert, A. (1988a) "Dismantling Flexibility", *Capital and Class* 34, Spring.

───── (1988b) "The 'Flexible Firm': Fixation of Fact?", *Work, Employment and Society* 2, 3, September.

Pujol, M. (1992) *Feminism and Anti-feminism in Early Economic Thought*, Aldershot: Edward Elgar.

Rubery, J. (ed.) (1988) *Women and Recession*, London: Routledge and Kegan Paul.

Sen, A. (1990) "Gender and Cooperative Conflicts", in I. Tinker (ed.) *Persistent Inequalities: Rethinking Assumptions About Development and Women*, New York: Oxford University Press.

Sollis, P. and Moser, C. (1991) "A Methodological Framework for Analysing the Social Costs of Adjustment at the Micro-Level: The Case of Guayaquil, Ecuador", *IDS Bulletin* 22, 1.

Standing, G. (1989) "Global Feminization Through Flexible Labor", *World Development* 17, 7, July.

Stanley, L. and Wise, S. (1990) "Method, Methodology and Epistemology in Feminist Research Processes", in L. Stanley (ed.) *Feminist Praxis*, London: Routledge.

Statistics Canada, (1993) *Summary of Proceedings: International Conference on the Measurement and Valuation of Unpaid Work*, Ottawa: Supply and Services.

Strassmann, D. (1993) "Not a Free Market: The Rhetoric of Disciplinary Authority in Economics", in M. Ferber and J. Nelson (eds) *Beyond Economic Man: Feminist Theory and Economics*, Chicago: University of Chicago Press.

Thoen, M. (1993) "The Value of Household Production in Canada, 1981, 1986", Discussion Paper, Statistics Canada National Accounts and Environment Division, April.

Thomas, D. (1990) "Intra-Household Resource Allocation, An Inferential Approach", *Journal of Human Resources* XXV, 4.

UNDP (1992) *Human Development Report*, New York: United Nations.

United Nations (1985) *The Nairobi Forward-Looking Strategies for the Advancement of Women*, New York: UN Department of Public Information.

Van Wagner, M. (1993) "Are Men's Jobs Becoming Women's Jobs? Substitution and Segmentation in the U.S. Labor Force", *Review of Radical Political Economics* 25, 2: 75–84.

Wagman, B. and Folbre, N. (1988) "The Feminization of Inequality: Some New Patterns", *Challenge*, November–December.

Walby, S. (1989) "Flexibility and the Changing Sexual Division of Labor", in S. Wood (ed.) *The Transformation of Work ?*, London: Unwin Hyman Limited.

Ward, K. (ed.) (1990) *Women Workers and Global Restructuring*, Ithaca, NY: ILR Press.

Waring, M. (1988) *If Women Counted*, San Francisco: Harper-Collins.

Wilson, G. (1991) "Thoughts on the Cooperative Conflict Model of the Household in Relation to Economic Method", *IDS Bulletin* 22, 1.

Woolley, F. (1993) "The Feminist Challenge to Neoclassical Economics", *Cambridge Journal of Economics* 17, 4, December.

Woolley, F. and Marshall, J. (1992) "Measuring Inequality Within the Household", paper presented at the Canadian Economics Association Meeting, June, Charlottetown: PEI.

## FURTHER READING

Agarwal, B. (1985) "Women and Technological Change in Agriculture: The Asian and African Experience", in I. Ahmed (ed.) *Technology and Rural Women: Conceptual and Empirical Issues*, London: George Allen & Unwin.

Amott, T. and Matthaei, J. (1991) *Race, Gender and Work: A Multicultural Economic History of Women in the United States*, Boston: South End Press.

Amsden, A. (ed.) (1980) *The Economics of Women and Work*, London: Penguin Books.

Armstrong, P. and Armstrong, H. (1988) "Taking Women Into Account: Redefining and Intensifying Employment in Canada", in J. Jensen, E. Hagen, and C. Reddy (eds) *Feminization of the Labor Force*, Cambridge: Polity Press.

—— (1990) *Theorizing Women's Work*, Toronto: Garamond Press.

Arriagada, I. (1991) "Latin American Women and the Crisis: Impact in the Work Market", in N. Aquiar and T. Corral (eds) *Alternatives: The Food, Energy and Debt Crisis in Relation to Women*, Rio de Janeiro: Rosa dos Tempos.

Bergmann, B. (1986) *The Economic Emergence of Women*, New York: Basic Books.

Bettio, F. (1988) *The Sexual Division of Labor: The Italian Case*, Oxford: Clarendon.

Blau, F. and Ferber, M. (1986) *The Economics of Women, Men and Work*, Englewood Cliffs, NJ: Prentice-Hall.

Bordo, S. (1990) "Feminism, Post-modernism and Gender-Scepticism", in L. Nicholson (ed.) *Feminism/Post-modernism*, London: Routledge.

Brown, C. and Pechman, J. (eds) (1987) *Gender in the Workplace*, Washington, DC: Brookings.

Cassels, J. (1992) "Damages for Lost Earning Capacity: Women and Children Last", *The Canadian Bar Review,* September.

Cohen, M. (1988) *Free Trade and the Future of Women's Work,* Toronto: Garamond.

Commonwealth Secretariat Expert Group on Women and Structural Adjustment (1989) *Engendering Adjustment for the 1990s,* London: Commonwealth Secretariat.

Crompton, R. and Sanderson, K. (1990) *Gendered Jobs and Social Change,* London: Unwin Hyman.

Day, T. (1992) "Women's Economic Product: Unmeasured Contributions to Measured Output, or the Perils of Woman-Blindness", presented at the Canadian Economics Association Meetings, June, Charlottetown: PEI.

Economic Council of Canada (1990) *Good Jobs, Bad Jobs: Employment in the Service Economy,* Ottawa: Supply and Services Canada.

Elson, D. (1991a) "Gender Issues in Development Strategies", paper presented to the Seminar on Integration of Women in Development, Vienna.

———— (ed.) (1991b) *Male Bias in the Development Process,* Manchester: Manchester University Press.

Elson, D. and Pearson, R. (eds) (1989) *Women's Employment and Multinationals in Europe,* London: Macmillan.

Ferber, M. (1987) *Women and Work, Paid and Unpaid, A Selected, Annotated Bibliography,* New York: Garland Publishing.

Ferber, M. and Green, C. (1983) "Housework vs. Market Work: Some Evidence of How the Decision is Made", *Review of Income and Wealth* 29, 2, June.

Ferber, M. and Nelson, J. (eds) (1993) *Beyond Economic Man: Feminist Theory and Economics,* University of Chicago Press.

Goldin, C. (1990) *Understanding the Gender Gap,* Oxford University Press.

Goldschmidt-Clermont, L. (1990) "Economic Measurement of Non-market Household Activities: Is it Useful and Feasible?", *International Labor Review* 129, 3, July.

Harding, S. and O'Barr, J. (eds) (1987) *Sex and Scientific Inquiry,* Chicago: University of Chicago Press.

Hartmann, H. (1976) "Capitalism, Patriarchy and Segregation by Sex", *Signs* 1, 3, Spring.

Keller, E. Fox (1982) "Feminism and Science", *Signs* 7, 3, Spring.

McCloskey, D. (1985) *The Rhetoric of Economics,* Madison: University of Wisconsin Press.

———— (1993) "Some Consequences of a Conjective Economics", in M. Ferber and J. Nelson (eds) *Beyond Economic Man: Feminist Theory and Economics,* Chicago: University of Chicago Press.

Manser, M. and Brown, M. (1979) "Bargaining Analysis of Household Decisions", in Lloyd, Andrews, and Gilroy (eds) *Women in the Labor Market,* New York: Columbia University Press.

Marsden, L. (1981) "The Labor Force is an Ideological Structure: A Guiding Note to the Labor Economists", *Atlantis* 7, 2, Fall.

Michael, R., Hartmann, H., and O'Farrell, B. (eds) (1989) *Pay Equity: Empirical Inquiries,* Washington, DC: National Academy Press.

Robb-Edgecombe, R. (1991) "Gender and Economics: Some Issues", paper presented at the Canadian Economics Association Meetings, Kingston, Ontario, June.

Sen, G. (1991) "Macroeconomic Policies and the Informal Sector: A Gender Sensitive Approach", Working Paper No. 13, Vassar Department of Economics.

United Nations (1989a) "Improving Statistics and Indicators on Women Using

Household Surveys", *Studies in Methods* Series F, 48, New York: Statistical Office, INSTRAW.

———— (1989b) *World Survey on the Role of Women in Development,* New York: United Nations Publication.

———— (1991a) *The World's Women 1970–1990: Trends and Statistics,* New York: United Nations Publications.

———— (1991b) *Handbook on Compilation of Statistics on Women in the Informal Sector in Industry, Trade and Services in Africa,* New York: United Nations Statistical Office/INSTRAW.

Young, K. (1988) "Reflections on Meeting Women's Needs", in K. Young (ed.) *Women and Economic Development,* Oxford/Paris: Berg/Unesco.

# 12

# MEASURING EQUALITY IN OPPORTUNITY 2000

*Diane Perrons*

## INTRODUCTION

Equal opportunities policies are now becoming common place in organizations. However, the extent to which the existence of these policies gives rise to greater equal opportunities for women is more doubtful. One of the purposes of this paper is to identify an index of gender equality so that progress towards equality and the effectiveness of equal opportunities policies can be measured more adequately.

This paper is divided into four sections. The first deals with the concept of equality and the short and long agendas for equal opportunities. The second deals with Opportunity 2000, the initiative launched by Business in the Community in the UK in 1991. The third section focusses on the question of monitoring and measuring gender equality in employment. Existing practices are briefly reviewed and then the index developed by Harvey *et al.* (1990) is modified and applied to the UK economy for the period 1981 to 1992. In section four wider applications of the index are considered.

## EQUAL OPPORTUNITIES

Equal opportunities policies have been in existence for nearly twenty years and although there has been some improvement for women, in relation to relative hourly earnings (Zabalza and Tzannatos 1985) and to some degree in the extent of employment segregation (Watts and Rich 1993) women nevertheless remain in low-paid, often insecure jobs and are disproportionately concentrated at the bottom of any employment hierarchy.

There has been a renewed interest in equal opportunities issues in organizations recently. This interest may have been stimulated by the estimated reduction in the numbers of school leavers entering the labor market in the early 1990s, referred to as the demographic time bomb, and the identification by various non-feminist writers of a "business case" for greater equality (Opportunity 2000 1992: 5). The recession of the early

1990s has invalidated the labor market forecasts (Atkinson 1992: 77) and some of the enthusiasm for enhancing the role of women in organizations has correspondingly evaporated. Indeed, in an internal report of the Confederation of British Industry (CBI) it was stated that a business case for equal opportunities policies could no longer be made as the anticipated labor shortage had failed to materialize (Clement 1992: 28). In the absence of a business case then for the CBI and Opportunity 2000, there is no case at all for such policies. The CBI's change of perspective reveals the inherent limitations of voluntarist policies, for their success depends on there being a compatibility of interest between the initiators of action and the intended beneficiaries.

However the question arises as to what exactly is meant by equal opportunities. It is useful to use Cynthia Cockburn's distinction between the short and the long agenda (Cockburn 1991). For example, the objective of equal opportunities policies could be to promote high-flying women to key positions within the existing hierarchical structure of firms in order to capitalize upon the belatedly recognized skills and talents of women in the context of contemporary theories of effective management and in a possibly tightening labor market. This would be the short agenda for equal opportunities policies and its effectiveness might adequately be encapsulated in simple measures such as the proportion of women workers occupying different positions in the employment structure and hierarchy.

On the other hand equal opportunities policies could be designed to address equality more fundamentally. This would involve the replacement of traditional hierarchical employment structures, in which women disproportionately reside at the base, with flatter structures, where the skill profile of all workers could be raised by the use of human-centered technologies and work practices and where the contributions of all workers would be more appropriately rewarded – the long agenda. Indeed, from different perspectives and for different reasons both enlightened management and socialist theories recognize that more egalitarian employment structures, in which workers are encouraged to work cooperatively and to contribute their intelligence and skills to the labor process, obtain higher levels of productivity than those where labor is simply viewed as flexible variable capital to be utilized and dismissed in accordance with changing patterns of demand (i.e. where Taylorism prevails) (Cooley 1987; Zuboff 1988; Leborgne and Lipietz 1991).

The choice of agenda then is not only a question for individual organizations but also depends on the whole question of the relations between capital, labor and the state. The long agenda would require equal opportunities policies to be adopted or applied not only within particular companies but throughout the whole economy, if the terms and conditions of employment of the disproportionately female, temporary, part-time and flexible workers are to be adequately addressed. Indeed more general regularized employment protection has been found to be more significant than equal opportunities policies in enhancing the position of women in the labor market (Whitehouse 1992).

The choice of agenda also depends on philosophical questions about the nature of equality. Cockburn refers to liberal, socialist and radical feminism as each having rather different conceptions of equality and correspondingly different ideas about the scope of equal opportunities policies (Cockburn 1991). It is also possible to refer to distinctions between the equality, merit and welfare principles of equality which likewise have different implications for the extent of such policies. The equality principle, which implies that all social goods including property, power and prestige should be distributed equally and the welfare principle which implies that social goods should be allocated to the poorest and most powerless members according to relative need (Jaquette 1990: 56) are not likely to be adopted in the current political and economic context. However the merit principle, compatible with liberalism, has been used to justify much of the equal opportunities legislation.

In the liberal market perspective social goods should be distributed in proportion to productive contributions. However in neoclassical theory it is assumed that the market correctly values these contributions. These values are in turn assumed to be the outcome of exogenous resource endowments rather than also being endogenously determined through the structure and organization of work and through social relations more generally. Correspondingly the merit principle limits the scope of the equality strategy to one of removing transparently discriminatory obstacles to women. This principle does not address the systemic low valuation of women's skills and the specificity of women's contributions to the economy and society. Ideas from socialist and radical feminism address these issues more directly and would have to be incorporated if any serious attempt was to be made to improve the position of the majority of women if only in the workplace. "What we are seeking is not in fact equality, but equivalence, not sameness for individual women and men but parity for women as a sex or for groups of women in their specificity" (Cockburn 1991: 10–11).

At present it would seem that official equal opportunities polices and policies carried out within companies very much follow the short agenda, reflecting the ideas of liberal feminism and the "merit principle." This is certainly true of the Opportunity 2000 policy discussed below. Any movement made in this direction will be regarded as progress because a wider distribution of women throughout the employment hierarchy and the presence of women in high positions may bring progressive/feminist influences to bear on the course of events and may provide role models for others to follow (Coyle 1989). Nevertheless the limitations of these policies, or of the short agenda have to be recognized. The establishment of more effective measures of inequality, particularly a composite measure, may enable the limitations of the short agenda to be made more transparent.

## EQUAL OPPORTUNITIES POLICIES AND OPPORTUNITY 2000

In the mini economic boom of the late 1980s there was concern over the shortage of school leavers forecast for the mid-1990s. Firms began to think about ways of tapping hitherto underutilized forms of labor – ethnic minorities, the elderly and, what is of particular significance in this context, women. Managerial theories which emphasize what are taken to be more feminine or people-oriented skills, such as establishing consultative, collaborative and caring relations between people working in organizations were also becoming popular. It was probably this context rather than any liberal or feminist concern with equal opportunities that stimulated Opportunity 2000.

Opportunity 2000 was launched by Business in the Community, a voluntary body financed by participating firms in both the public and private sectors. In 1991 61 firms became members including 25 per cent of *The Times* Top 100 Companies. Within two years membership increased to 188 organizations covering over 25 per cent of the total workforce (Opportunity 2000 1993). It was given a high public profile by the explicit support of the UK government but is limited in scope owing to its voluntary nature and narrow conception of equality. What is useful and interesting, however, is the methodology used. Participating organizations are required to commit themselves to achieving "the campaign objective of increasing the quality and quantity of women's participation within their own workforces." To do so they must carry out an audit of the existing employment structure, set goals for the achievement of greater equality and specify an action plan through which these goals are to be attained (Opportunity 2000 1992: 2). Organizations are then required to monitor their performance and report on the extent to which their specified objectives have been achieved.

The scope of the objectives varies considerably between organizations. Some companies restrict these to carrying out surveys of employees' attitudes towards equal opportunities while others, now two thirds of the members, set numerical targets (Opportunity 2000 1993: 4). However, there is no possibility of disqualification if targets are not met or if organizations have women "unfriendly" policies which they retain.

Nevertheless in pursuing these limited goals certain "family friendly" policies are often introduced such as job shares, flexible patterns of working, maternity leave and leave for carers, which can be extended to less high-flying workers (Hogg and Harker 1992). However these changes are not always motivated by any desire, liberal or otherwise, for equality of opportunity. Flexible working patterns may serve to reinforce rather than counter the unequal domestic division of labor[1] (Cockburn 1991: 24; Moss 1992: 12–13) and moreover have many advantages for firms (Atkinson 1985).

Firstly, flexible working enables firms to cope with peaked patterns of demand and allows the working day to be extended. Second, use of part-time workers or job shares may create efficiency gains as some jobs are so repetitive that productivity falls sharply after four to six hours per day. Use of short-term shift working also enables employers to avoid paying for rest periods[2]. Further a business case for harmonizing conditions between full- and part-time workers in relation to pay, training, promotion, and pensions in order to obtain increased commitment to the company can also be made (Ward 1992). However attaining this equivalence between workers may occur through a reduction in the overall quality of employment conditions and even the very existence of full-time workers[3].

While some firms or organizations may be trend setters towards equal opportunities they alone can do little about the general employment situation with which women are confronted and which inevitably impinges upon their own employment policies and rates of pay. Thus it is essential to focus upon the situation of women in the economy as a whole as well as their position within particular companies.

To examine the question of equality of opportunity in the workforce overall it is necessary to look at the equality legislation together with legislation relating to general employment practices. Here the literature is unequivocal and the overall and consistent finding is that countries with more regulated employment conditions and with centralized forms of bargaining, including minimum pay legislation, are the ones where greater equality is found (Rubery 1992; Perrons 1994). Thus adopting and enforcing the Social Chapter of the Maastricht Treaty may be more effective than voluntarist equal opportunity policies. Resistance to the Social Chapter by the UK government seems to indicate a limited commitment to equal opportunities. There is little evidence that social protection costs jobs or long-term competitiveness, as the UK government claims, and growing evidence that the introduction of deregulation and flexible working practices leads to increasing wage polarization and an expansion in the numbers of working poor (Harrison and Bluestone 1990; Deakin and Wilkinson 1991; Michie and Wilkinson 1994).

The main contribution of Opportunity 2000 has been to provide a methodology for the evaluation of equal opportunity policies. However many participating firms have limited their equal opportunity objectives to the short agenda, for example, specifying that a proportion of managerial posts should be filled by women (Opportunity 2000 1992: 30). The development of a composite indicator of gender equality would enable more accurate, sophisticated and extensive monitoring of changes in both the quantity and quality of women's participation in the economy as a whole and within particular organizations.

## MEASURES OF INEQUALITY

In the remainder of the paper an attempt will be made to identify a composite indicator of gender equality in employment. A vast literature exists on the measurement of poverty and income inequalities (Cowell 1977), and in some instances these measures are combined (Sen 1976). However the question of gender inequality has been less explicitly considered though there are notable exceptions (Sugarman and Straus 1987).

There is a growing body of literature on measuring occupational segregation, which is seen to underlie other forms of gender inequality – especially income (Hakim 1981, 1992; Siltanen 1990; Tzannatos 1990; Barrientos 1992; Watts and Rich 1993). These measures have largely been adapted from measures of income and race inequality but again are not fully comprehensive.

However the work of Harvey et al. (1990) provides a method of obtaining a composite index of gender inequality. This index is adapted and applied to aggregate UK data but it could also be applied at the company level. To calculate the index a number of steps have to be taken. First, the variables to be included in the index are identified. These variables are then transformed, standardized and indexed leading to the calculation of the composite indicator of gender equality (Harvey et al. 1990).

### Identification of the variables – dimensions of labor market inequality.

Some dimensions of labor market inequality relating to earnings, employment structure and segregation are discussed and then the variables to be included in the model are specified.

#### Earnings inequalities

Earnings inequalities by gender exist in a variety of forms. In this paper three forms are considered: by manual and non-manual occupations; by occupational category; and by age. Data from the New Earnings Survey for full-time workers indicate that income inequalities by gender for full-time workers have been narrowing during the course of the 1980s, although there has also been a significant polarization of incomes between women and between men. For both manual and non-manual workers on the basis of either hourly or weekly earnings movement towards greater equality has been obtained, especially for the non-manual workers in the late 1980s boom. The size of the differentials remains high especially in the case of

203

weekly earnings and for manual workers and the extent of the narrowing quite small (see Figure 12.1).

Data by specific occupations are not available for the whole period, and the definition of occupations changes in 1990. However, taking four main occupational groups covering the employment spectrum from management to routine assembly work there is a similar drift towards greater gender equality in earnings but with some important variations see (Figure 12.2). In the case of nurses and clerks, where women are numerically dominant or over-represented[4], the ratio of female to male earnings is quite high and has improved during the course of the decade from 79 per cent of male earnings in 1990 to 93 per cent in 1990. For painting, repetitive assembling and related jobs, where women have become increasingly under-represented, the female-male earnings ratio is low and remained largely unchanged throughout the period, being 67 per cent in both 1981 and in 1990. However, given the association between male presence in an industrial or occupational group and higher earnings (Hakim 1992: 135–6) an improvement in the relative position of women to men in any particular sector is not necessarily associated with an absolute improvement in the position of women. It should also be noted that the figures relate to the weekly earnings of full-time workers on adult rates and so may overstate

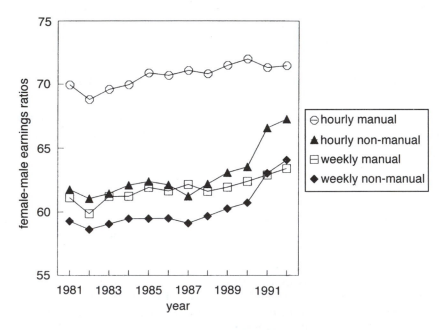

*Figure 12.1* Earnings ratios
*Note*: Full-time workers
*Source*: New Earnings Survey

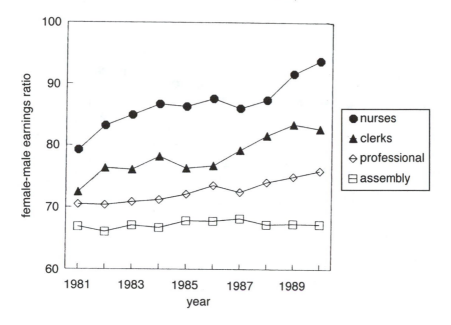

*Figure 12.2* Earnings by occupation
*Note*: Weekly earnings, full-time workers
*Source*: New Earnings Survey

the movement towards equality as female part-time workers often on lower rates of pay will not have been considered.

A striking feature of the earnings data however is the differential between women and men by age especially among older workers at their peak earnings. Here the differential is large and remains generally unchanged throughout the decade. For younger workers the extent of the differential is smaller and there has been a greater movement towards equality (see Figure 12.3).

There are a variety of possible explanations for this variation by age. It could reflect lower levels of occupational segregation among younger workers which would suggest that earnings differentials would continue to narrow as these workers progressed through their working lives and indeed that younger people are more accustomed to equal opportunities policies and thus demand equal treatment. Clearly this cannot be tested until lifetime earnings' profiles are obtained for this particular cohort of workers. Less optimistically, however, it could also indicate that vertical segregation by gender remains but only takes effect in the upper age groups. The extent of vertical segregation also varies across occupations with the jobs in which women predominate typically having flatter employment hierarchies and so the scope for women to obtain high earnings is more limited[5].

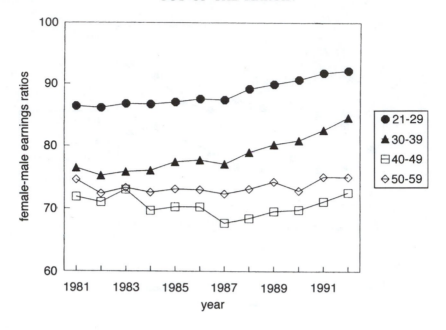

*Figure 12.3* Earnings by age
*Note*: Hourly earnings, full-time workers
*Source*: Central Statistical Office

## Employment structure

In the UK there has been a narrowing of the differential between the labor force participation rates of women and men (Humphries and Rubery 1992: 237). The activity rate for men of working age fell from 91 per cent in 1979 to 88 per cent in 1989 while that for women rose from 63 per cent to 71 per cent in the same period. However a high proportion of women work part time – 39 per cent in 1981 and 44 per cent in 1990 – and of these some work only a small number of hours (Hakim 1992: 135–40). Thus to use the labor force participation rate alone as a measure of employment structure would disguise a significant form of inequality which relates to the extent of participation in the labor force rather than just the act of participation itself.

In this paper two measures of labor force involvement are used. The first measure relates to the proportion of full-time jobs occupied by women. Hakim notes that the proportion of women working full time increased significantly in the latter part of the 1980s having previously remained largely static since the 1950s[6]. Moreover she attributes both the narrowing of earnings differentials and the narrowing of occupational segregation to this factor (Hakim 1992: 141).

The second measure relates to the overall proportion of jobs carried out by part-time male workers. This proportion, although very small, has also been increasing during the course of the decade. It is unclear whether this represents a choice by men or whether it is a response to the moves towards greater deregulation and flexibility in the UK labor market in the context of high unemployment and economic recession forcing men to accept terms and conditions of employment customarily associated with women (Mitchell 1986: 36). However, the increase in male part-time work gives rise to greater equality between women and men in terms of their experience of work, even if it has taken place in the context of deteriorating employment conditions for all. Additionally, if a wider cross-section of the labor force becomes involved in this kind of work there would be greater pressure for a convergence in the working conditions and rights of full- and part-time workers, something which is widely acknowledged would increase the welfare of working women who are disproportionately found among the part-time employed.

### Employment segregation

Both horizontal and vertical segregation are found to exist in the labor force. During the course of the 1980s there has been some lowering of the degrees of segregation in the sense that there has been an increase in the share of women in the majority of occupational groups, especially in managerial occupations, which may be attributed to the breaking down of traditional barriers to women's employment (Humphries and Rubery 1992: 241). Even so, the proportion of women in top management remains very low. For example, only 3.6 per cent of the members of the British Institute of Management are women (Atkinson 1992: 77). Women have increased their representation in some of the more prestigious occupations, for example, in law, general administration in national and local government, personnel and industrial relations managers and in other professional activities. They have decreased their over-representation in some of the lower level occupations such as personnel services, catering and hairdressing. While some occupations have become integrated in the sense that their gender composition roughly approximates that of the workforce overall, nevertheless segregation continues to exert a profound effect on women's earnings and opportunities (Hakim 1992: 136–9).

Employment segregation has proved difficult to measure and is highly susceptible to method of calculation used (Tzannatos 1990; Hakim 1992: 131). The main indices that are currently used are the Hakim index, and the Duncan index or the index of dissimilarity, although new indices have recently been devised (Watts and Rich 1993; Blackburn et al. 1993). Despite problems of measurement, it is important to include a degree of segregation in any index which tries to measure gender inequality. In the construction of the composite index the measure had to be one capable of being expressed in terms of a 0–1 range or between 0 and 100 per cent.

The Duncan index, which meets these criteria and thus provides "a measure of how far from complete segregation the actual distributions of the sexes are" was used (Tzannatos 1990: 107–8). The data for the Duncan Index were calculated by Barrientos using data from the Labour Force Survey (Barrientos 1992: 8–9).

*Other variables to be included in subsequent estimations of the index*

There are many other dimensions of labor market inequality that could be included in the model if data were available. In particular it would be desirable to include measures relating to training, pensions, promotion, fringe benefits, employment volatility, an adequate indicator of exclusion from work to overcome deficiencies with unemployment measures for women in the UK and so on. The index would in principle allow any of these measures to be included and it could be applied equally well to company data. However, in this paper only five variables relating to UK national data are used: two variables in relation to earnings – the female-male ratios for all full-time workers on an hourly and weekly basis; two variables which relate to employment structure: the proportion of total jobs filled by full-time women and the proportion of part-time jobs filled by men; and one variable which measures employment segregation.

## Data transformation

The variables used have to be expressed in such a way so as to ensure that they all run in the same direction (i.e. such that as the ratio of the measure increases it represents a step towards greater equality). In our case all the variables used have this property with the exception of the Duncan index of segregation. Consequently this index is inverted. The variables are all expressed as ratios or proportions, for example, the ratio of female to male earnings or the proportion of the total number of jobs occupied by full-time female workers. Following the method adopted by Harvey *et al.* the

*Table 12.1* Correlation Matrix

|       | V1    | V2    | V3    | V4    |
|-------|-------|-------|-------|-------|
| V2    | 0.832 |       |       |       |
| V3    | 0.775 | 0.767 |       |       |
| V4    | 0.780 | 0.919 | 0.843 |       |
| V5    | 0.768 | 0.944 | 0.819 | 0.988 |

*Note:* V1 = female full-time employment as a percentage of total employment.
V2 = male part-time employment as a percentage of total employment.
V3 = Duncan index of employment segregation.
V4 = female-male earnings ratio for hourly earnings for all full-time workers.
V5 = female-male earnings ratio for weekly earnings for all full-time workers.

variables are then transformed into natural logarithms in order to avoid any extreme values in the data from having undue significance (Harvey *et al.* 1990).

In their study Harvey *et al.* carried out a factor analysis in order to check that the variables they identified were indeed related to each other and hence to the main factor, the composite measure of gender inequality. Indeed in factor analysis or principal components analysis, factors or components are identified which are linear functions of all the observed variables. The first factor or first component would be the one on which all the observed variables correlated most highly. "The first principal component is the linear function which accounts for the greatest possible part of the total variance in the data, i.e correlates most highly with the observed variables" (Ehrenberg 1982: 207–8). The observed variables which score highly on the first component would be incorporated into the index of inequality and other variables would be excluded. However, factor analysis or principal components analysis should not be used as a substitute for thought. Indeed Ehrenberg argues that an examination of the correlation matrix should reveal which variables are related to each other, making a factor analysis or principal components analysis unnecessary (Ehrenberg 1982: 206). In this paper, a principal components analysis was carried out and the first component that accounted for more of the variation than any of the others was interpreted as the index of gender equality. All the variables scored highly on this component and are clearly related to each other as indicated by the correlation matrix (see Table 12.1).

## Data standardization

The variables are then standardized in order to compensate for the fact that the original variables are expressed in different units, for example, persons and pounds which might have different distributions over time and to ensure that they contribute equally to the final index (Harvey *et al.* 1990: 306). If a variable is considered to be more important than others then weights can be explicitly introduced to reflect this, but standardization ensures that differential significance of the variables does not occur simply because of the different units in which they have been expressed. Standardization takes place by calculating Z scores for the variables (i.e. each value is recalculated in relation to the mean and standard deviation of the series from which it comes). See Table 12.2. An examination of Table 12.2 indicates how the different values have changed over time. For example, full-time female employment has increased by 2.6 standard deviations while the proportion of jobs carried out by part-time male workers has increased by 3.6 standard deviations. Both weighted and unweighted versions of the composite index were calculated. In the weighted version the variable for male part-time employment was scaled by the proportion of male part-time

Table 12.2 Z scores

| | V1 | V2 | V3 | V4 | V5 |
|---|---|---|---|---|---|
| 1981 | −1.836 | −1.708 | −0.675 | −0.828 | −0.832 |
| 1982 | −1.771 | −1.297 | −0.819 | −1.270 | −1.334 |
| 1983 | −0.771 | −0.662 | −0.962 | −1.105 | −0.882 |
| 1984 | −0.410 | −0.500 | −1.022 | −0.584 | −0.581 |
| 1985 | −0.222 | −0.378 | −0.701 | −0.338 | −0.506 |
| 1986 | −0.088 | −0.089 | −1.022 | −0.226 | −0.293 |
| 1987 | 0.452 | 0.141 | −0.264 | −0.564 | −0.295 |
| 1988 | 0.958 | 0.271 | 1.128 | 0.116 | 0.048 |
| 1989 | 1.251 | 0.056 | 0.695 | 0.635 | 0.463 |
| 1990 | 0.826 | 0.796 | 1.455 | 0.890 | 0.718 |
| 1991 | 0.848 | 1.420 | 1.215 | 1.434 | 1.475 |
| 1992 | 0.763 | 1.952 | 0.974 | 1.841 | 2.018 |
| Difference over time | 2.599 | 3.661 | 1.650 | 2.669 | 2.851 |

*Note:* Z score is equal to ($V$-$V$ mean/St dev $V$)
Variables are defined as in Table 12.1

workers in the labor force so that the comparatively large rate of change in this variable did not have a disproportionate effect on the value of the index overall.

The Z scores are then converted in to index figures (with 1981 as the base year equal to 100) in order to trace changes over time. These index values for the different variables are then summed up for each year and divided by the number of variables to produce the composite index of gender equality (see equation 1)[7].

$$IGE = \left( \frac{\sum\limits_{i=1}^{n} Vi}{n} \right) \qquad (1)$$

where $IGE$ = index of gender equality

$Vi$ = indexed value for variable $i$

## INTERPRETATION OF THE RESULTS

The resulting index is displayed in Figure 12.4. This has been termed an index of gender equality as at least for the variables and data employed in this model it would seem that there has been an improvement in the position of women in full-time work during the course of the 1980s and early 1990s.

The results obtained are highly dependent on both the variables included and the way in which they have been measured. The estimation implies that gender inequality has decreased during the course of the 1980s and especially in the late 1980s mini boom. While this may be a surprising finding in relation to common-sense experience it is less surprising given that the data used have been for full-time workers and that from 1986 the number and proportion of women working full time has increased. Moreover, the finding is consistent with other analyses of the UK economy which suggest that there has been a lowering of employment segregation and some women have moved into jobs with higher pay and status (Bruegel 1994). However, it is important to recognize that the 1980s has also been a decade of polarization both within wage earners and between wage earners and those excluded from paid work. Indeed if some women have been moving into higher positions in the labor market in the context of no overall change in the hierarchical structure of employment then it is inevitable that there will be an increase in the polarization of earnings between women. However, the introduction of flexible working practices at the opposite end of the employment spectrum which has given rise to a reduction in the earnings of the lowest decile has also contributed to this polarization (Rowthorn 1989: 289; Hakim 1991; Humphries and Rubery 1992: 246–50; Michie and Wilkinson 1994).

If this improvement in gender equality is attributed largely to the increase in the proportion of women working full time then the conclusion is far from optimistic. First the situation whereby both members of a dual

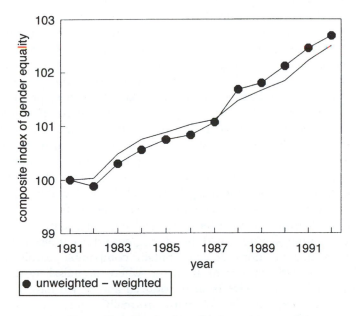

*Figure 12.4* Gender equality in employment
*Note*: The weighted index reflects the small proportion of male part-timers

211

income household are in full-time employment does not seem to be desired by many people who would prefer to be less fully engaged in paid work, especially where there are young children (Kiernan 1992: 495). Moreover much of this increase in full-time work has occurred without any corresponding social infrastructure to facilitate women's involvement in full-time work (Humphries and Rubery 1992). So again to the extent that progress has been made it may well be at considerable cost to the women involved in terms of both their total working hours including childcare and domestic work and in terms of paying for private childcare. Finally, a further contributory factor to the increase in equality could be the decline in relatively highly paid, full-time male manual employment in manufacturing and a deterioration in overall working conditions.

Thus, although a movement towards greater gender equality in employment has been found, it is not clear that it has been achieved in the most desirable way. Further, the way in which the index has been calculated means that the experiences of many women have been excluded.

## CONCLUSION AND FURTHER WORK

Emphasis has been placed on inequality in work as it is through work that most people obtain their means of survival and work contributes to the formation of personal identity. Although a composite single scalar measure of gender equality allows progress to be measured, its development is impeded by the absence of gendered data on many issues. For example, employment security, redundancy payments, pension entitlements, and inequalities by ethnic groups, as well as the existence of an accurate measure of unemployment or of the exclusion from paid work for many women.

However, it is maintained that the technique has validity and could in principle be useful at both company and national levels, provided the problems of data availability were overcome. Given that companies joining Opportunity 2000 profess a commitment to enhancing the role of women within their organizations, and may be gaining status from doing so, it is important to provide a measure which incorporates the multi-dimensional aspects of inequality and which therefore provides a means of assessing the validity of their equal opportunities policies and claims. Variables that could be included would be the gender ratio of part-time to full-time workers, and of managers or people at different tiers of authority, status and control. Further the earnings ratio could be disaggregated to indicate whether women in senior positions actually obtain comparable earnings. This would be particularly important in firms where appraisal systems and performance related pay have been introduced and which have been said to reintroduce inequality in otherwise formally equal pay structures (Humphries and Rubery 1992: 250). The measure proposed would enable aspects of the long rather than the short agenda for equal opportunities to be evaluated. At a national level the technique could be used to estimate the effectiveness of equal opportunities policies, different regulatory structures and macroeconomic policies on gender equality by correlating the gender index with other dimensions of economic change. The index could also be extended to encapsulate the general position of women in society by including a broader range of measures particularly relating to overall income inequalities, levels of political representation and status more generally.

## NOTES

1 As Cockburn argues "Such strategies for profit, accumulation and cost efficiency are quite transparently predicated on the continuation of the sexual contract. Young women anticipate, older women live out, the social relations of housewife, owing duties to husband, children and home, undertaking paid work (for an income that is an economic necessity to the household) only in ways that can be made to fit" (Cockburn 1991: 24).

2 For example a supermarket chain in the UK employs people for three-and-three-quarter-hour shifts. If the workers were employed for four hours then a rest period would have to be paid for. It is not uncommon for a single worker to work two such periods in one day (personal interview with a supermarket supervisor, 1994).

3 Recently in a clothing chainstore, Burtons, 1,000 full-time jobs have been converted into 3,000 part-time posts in the context of a general restructuring, including some losses of jobs together with a standardization of employment conditions including equal pay for women and men workers (Cowe 1993: 20).

4 Hakim defines an integrated workforce as one that falls within a 20 per cent band around the average of 40 per cent overall female share of the workforce. Where women comprise more than 50 per cent of an occupation they would be said to be over-represented. On this definition in 1979 only 9 per cent of the workforce were in integrated occupations while by 1990 12 per cent of the female workforce and 16 percent of the male workforce were. The integrated occupations include pharmacists, dentists, laboratory technicians, publicans, authors and journalists, general management and administration, bakers, fishmongers and officials of trade unions (Hakim 1992: 138–9).

5 The typical age earnings profile is one in which earnings rise quite steeply and steadily with age until the mid-age ranges where a plateau is reached before earnings fall towards the higher end of the age profile. However, the age earnings profile for women tends to be different in the sense that the height of the plateau is typically much lower. Explanations for this vary. Human capital theory emphasizes that for women rational choice leads them to invest in themselves to a lower extent than their male counterparts and therefore their productivity levels will be lower. Dual labor market and feminist theories emphasize the significance of structural constraints and exclusionary tactics employed by male workers and which limit career choice and progress for women.

6 Hakim points out that the "much trumpeted rise in women's employment in Britain consisted entirely of the substitution of part-time for full jobs". The number of full-time jobs for women actually fell between 1951 and 1983. The 1951 level only being exceeded in 1989. Moreover the percentage of women working full time remained at between 30–33 percent in those years. Only after

1986 does this proportion increase to reach 38 percent in 1990 (Hakim 1992: 139–40).

7 The values of the Z scores for the base year 1981 are set equal to 100 and the values of the other Z scores are transformed accordingly. Take the case of the variable fem-full. The value of the Z score in 1981 is $-1.8359$, or roughly 1.8 standard deviations below the mean of its series. This value is set equal to 100. The Z score for the following year 1982 is $-1.7712$ or 1.77 standard deviations below the mean. The transformed value is equal to the sum of 100 and the difference in standard deviation units between the base year and this year. Or $100 + (Z score_t - Z score_{tb})$, where t = any year and tb = the base year.

## REFERENCES

Atkinson, J. (1985) *Flexibility, Uncertainty and Manpower Management*, Sussex: IMS.

—— (1992) "Corporate Employment Policies: Women and 1992", in R. Lindley (ed.) *Women's Employment: Britain in the Single European Market 71–80*, London: HMSO.

Barrientos, A. (1992) "UK Trends in Gender Occupational Segregation", mimeo, Department of Economics, University of Hertfordshire.

Blackburn, R., Jarman, J., and Siltanen, J. (1993) "The Analysis of Occupational Gender Segregation Over Time and Place: Considerations of Measurement and Some New Evidence", *Work, Employment and Society* 7, 3: 335–62.

Bruegel, I. (1994) "Municipal Feminism: Relating Gender and Class to Hierarchies, Markets and Networks", paper presented to ESRC Women and Welfare Seminar.

Clement, B. (1992) "How to Make Opportunity Knock", *Independent* 28, 29 April.

Cockburn, C. (1991) *In the Way of Women – Men's Resistance to Sex Equality in Organisations*, London: Macmillan.

Cooley, M. (1987) *Architect or Bee? The Human Price of Technology*, London: Hogarth Press.

Cowe, R. (1993) "Burtons Cuts 2000 Jobs as Union Attacks Move to Part Time Work", *Guardian* 20, 8 January.

Cowell, F.A. (1977) *Measuring Inequality*, Oxford: Philip Allan.

Coyle, A. (1989) Women into Management: A Suitable Case for Treatment, *Feminist Review* 31: 117–25.

Deakin, S. and Wilkinson, F. (1991) "Labour Law, Social Security and Economic Inequality", *Cambridge Journal of Economics* 15: 125–48.

Ehrenberg, A. (1982) *A Primer in Data Reduction*, Chichester: John Wiley and Sons.

Hakim, C. (1981) "Job Segregation: Trends in the 1970s", *Employment Gazette*, December, 521–29.

—— (1992) "Explaining Trends in Occupational Segregation: The Measurement, Causes and Consequences of the Sexual Division of Labour", *European Sociological Review* 8, 2: 127–52.

Harrison, B. and Bluestone, B. (1990) "Wage Polarisation in the US and the Flexibility Debate", *Cambridge Journal of Economics* 14: 351–73.

Harvey, E., Blakely, J., and Tepperman, L. (1990) "Toward an Index of Gender Inequality", *Social Indicators Research* 22: 299–317.

Hogg, C. and Harker, L. (1992) *The Family Friendly Employer: Examples from Europe*, London: Day Care Trust.

Humphries, J. and Rubery, J. (1992) "The Legacy for Women's Employment: Integration, Differentiation and Polarisation", in J. Michie (ed.) *The Economic Legacy 1979–1992*: 236–55, London: Academic Press.

Jaquette, J. (1990) "Gender and Justice in Economic Development", in I. Tinker (ed.) *Persistent Inequalities: Women and World Development*, Oxford: Oxford University Press.

Kiernan, K. (1992) "The Roles of Men and Women in Tomorrow's Europe", *Employment Gazette*, October: 491–8.

Leborgne, D. and Lipietz, A. (1991) "Two Social Strategies in the Production of New Industrial Spaces", in G. Benko and M. Dunford (eds) *Industrial Change and Regional Development*, London: Belhaven.

Martin, J. and Roberts, C. (1984) *Women and Employment: A Lifetime Perspective*, London: HMSO.

Michie, J. and Wilkinson, F. (1994) "The Growth of the Unemployment in the 1980s", in J. Michie and J. Grieve-Smith (eds) *Unemployment in Europe*, London: Academic Press.

Mitchell, J. (1986) "Reflections on Twenty Years of Feminism", in A. Oakley and J. Mitchell (eds) *What is Feminism*, Oxford: Blackwell.

Moss, P. (1992) "EC Perspectives", in C. Hogg and L. Harker (eds) *The Family Friendly Employer: Examples From Europe*: 11–26, London: Day Care Trust.

Opportunity 2000 (1992) *First Year Report*, London: Opportunity 2000.

—— (1993) *Second Year Report*, London: Opportunity 2000.

Perrons, D. (1994) "Measuring Equal Opportunities in European Employment", *Environment and Planning A* 26, 8: 1195–1221.

Rowthorn, B. (1989) "The Thatcher Revolution", in F. Green (ed.) *The Restructuring of the UK Economy*: 281–96, London: Harvester Wheatsheaf.

Rubery, J. (1992) "Pay, Gender and the Social Dimension to Europe", *British Journal of Industrial Relations*, 30, 4: 605–21.

Sen, A. (1976) "Poverty: An Ordinal Approach to Measurement", *Econometrica*, 44, 2: 219–31.

Siltanen, J. (1990) "Social Change and the Measurement of Occupational Segregation by Sex: An Assessment of the Sex Ratio Index", *Work Employment and Society* 4, 1: 1–29.

Sugarman, D. and Straus, M. (1988) "Indicators of Gender Equality for American States and Regions", *Social Indicators Research* 20: 229–70.

Tzannatos, Z. (1990) "Employment Segregation: Can We Measure It and What Does the Measurement Mean", *British Journal of Industrial Relations*: 105–11.

Ward, T. (1992) "Equal Opportunities: Policy into Practice", contribution made by the Director of Human Resources, Kingfisher Group, to the Equal to the Task Conference, Birmingham.

Watts, M. and Rich, J. (1993) "Occupational Sex Segregation in Britain, 1979–1989: The Persistence of Sexual Stereotyping", *Cambridge Journal of Economics* 17: 159–77.

Whitehouse, G. (1992) "Legislation and Labor Market Gender Inequality: An Analysis of OECD Countries", *Work, Employment and Society* 6, 1: 65–86.

Zabalza, A. and Tzannatos, Z. (1985) "The Effect of Britain's Anti-Discriminatory Legislation on Relative Pay and Employment", *Economic Journal* 95: 679–99.

Zuboff, S. (1988) *In The Age of The Smart Machine*, London: Heineman.

# 13

# TOWARD A FEMINIST ECONOMETRICS

## *Esther Redmount*

Economists and econometricians have always given primacy of place to prices and incomes in explaining agents' behaviors. When economists acknowledge gender in analysis, they do so by using simple, binary indicator functions, so-called dummy variables, to alter intercept and/or slope coefficients in regression. Such dummies are often significant explanatory variables and are, no doubt, methodologically preferable to ignoring gender phenomena altogether, though they are poor analytical substitutes for more complete models of the role gender plays in market and non-market transactions.

Feminist scholarship points out that gender is neither a simple nor a binary construct, but the result of a complex process of socialization and transaction through which all children (of both sexes) pass. All those "arrangements of work, sexuality, parental responsibilities, psychological life, assigned social traits and internalized emotions" which constitute a "gender system" (Stansell 1990: xii) should, at least, be modeled as an agent's endowment. Even if we accept that such endowments are, within the framework of analysis, exogenously determined, the market is presumably responding to the more complex aggregate that is gender.

The principal goal of this paper is to go beyond the model of gender as a fixed factor of production and implement a methodology to evaluate how gender influences labor supply and investment in human capital, what Blau and Ferber have called the negative feedback from discrimination to women's return on their human capital (Blau and Ferber 1986). Feminist theorists certainly reject the stability and inevitability of gender distinctions, pointing out that gender attributes are not fixed or stable across time:

> If we write the history of women's work by gathering data that describe the activities, needs, interest and culture of "women workers", we leave in place the naturalized contrast and reify a fixed categorical difference between men and women. We start the story . . . too late, by uncritically

accepting a gendered category ("the woman worker") that itself needs investigation, because its meaning is relative to its history.

(Scott 1988: 175)

Because markets appear to be sensitive to gender, parents, schools and the individuals themselves socialize and are socialized in a way that is determined by the expected gain to some set of characteristics deemed apposite to the various sexes. Maleness and femaleness are learned at home, in school and at work. Gender patterns may then be reenforced by "regulatory agencies" with vested (literally and figuratively) interests in the current gender-related distribution of resources and wealth.

Explaining why work is so highly gendered is of less interest here than acknowledging the existence of patriarchy and modeling the returns (positive or negative) to being gendered. Most economic stories about how gender came to be established begin in household production models with technologies favoring division of labor (hierarchical or not) by gender or are variants of E.O. Wilson's story about women's comparative advantage in child-rearing and nurturing. The speculation is that gender roles arose as an innovation that coped with some indivisibility in the archaic environment, a world in which infant mortality was high (Lerner 1986). High infant mortality would loom as an important problem not amenable to marginal changes in behavior until large-scale public health measures and a revolution in medical science reduced early childhood deaths to any significant degree. Once public health measures became effective, gender relations pertaining (and appearing to be "natural") to child-rearing become technologically redundant. Their persistence becomes a matter of personal choices and regulatory constraint.

In this paper I consider not the genesis of gender systems, but the economic choices which reinforce or are influential in sustaining them. Assume that a household's members choose among competing activities and invest in human capital until the marginal benefit from investments and reallocations equal their marginal costs. Marginal benefits are derived from a money metric utility function and are measured as the utility of the gains in the value of household, market and leisure-time activities,

$$MB_i = w_{it} (gH_t + \Theta M_t + \rho L_t)/(1+r)^t \qquad (1)$$

The individual's expected wage at time t is $w_{it}$; $g$, $\Theta$, and $\rho$ are the gains in productivity associated with household production, market activity and recreation, respectively; H, M and L refer to time spent in household production, in the market and at leisure.

Underlying this equilibrium condition is a household that maximizes utility as a function of three goods: consumption items purchased for cash in the market, $C_t$; those goods (services) produced in the household, $G_t$; and leisure or recreational goods, $R_t$. If we further imagine that

217

these three sets of goods are produced according to some production functions,

$$C_t = \Theta(M_{it}, M_{jt}; X_{ct-1}) \tag{2}$$
$$G_t = g(H_{it}, H_{jt}; X_{ht-1})$$
$$R_t = \rho(L_{it}, L_{jt}; X_{Rt-1})$$

where $M_i$, $M_j$ represent hours allocated to market activity by the ith and jth members of the household; the Hs are hours allocated to household activity by the ith and jth members and the Ls, time allocated to recreation, R, by individual i and individual j. The Xs are the fixed factors of production in these functions and may be thought of as the capital stock associated with the various activities. In household production, G, the Xs are perhaps appliances. In recreational production they may be sailboats, bowling balls and the like. Both $X_{ht-1}$ and $X_{Rt-1}$ are subsets of $C_{t-1}$ and were purchased in the market in the previous period.

The ambiguous reference to the ith and jth individuals is deliberate, an attempt to move away from the gender-specific production coefficients that lead analysts to assume (impose) a comparative advantage in household production for women. Assume that each individual has access to the same technology, but consider the possibility that the production coefficients, g, described in $G_i = H_i'g_i + e_i$ ($e_i$ distributed $N(0,\sigma_e)$), are themselves a function and vary among individuals in ways having as much to do with taste, past investments and whimsy, as with sex.

$$g_i = \Gamma Z_i + u_i \tag{3}$$

Z is a vector of exogenous or predetermined variables that describe the attitudes and abilities of the individual and $\Gamma$ is a matrix describing how the attributes of the individual translate into labor productivity in household (or market or recreational) production. The $u_i$ are also normally distributed $N(0,\sigma_u)$.

$$G_i = H_i'\Gamma Z_i + \gamma_i \tag{4}$$
$$\gamma_i = H_i'u_i + e_i$$

The advantage of this specification is twofold. It gives some insight into how individuals i and j can become gendered in production and we see how errors in inference regarding gender might be made. Consider the first point. Let $G_i = H_i\Gamma + \gamma_i$, where

$$H_i = Z_i \otimes H_i$$
$$\otimes \tag{5}$$

refers to the Kronecker product of the Hs and the Zs. $\Gamma$ is the unobservable, underlying structure of production based on aptitudes and abilities. What may be more readily observable are the gs which are productivities closely identified, even confounded, with gender

$$g = [g_f, g_m]$$ (6)

where subscripts f and m refer to female and male respectively. This notion that there is some underlying self which may be sexed, but not gendered will not be universally popular, but provides, I think, a more readily testable model than other tropes. The philosophical and psychological underpinnings of this construct of gender lie beyond the scope of this paper, but are at the heart of feminist discourse.

Second, because the error term, $\gamma_i$, is heteroscedastic, we see how errors in inference about the importance of gender in allocation and investment (even using enriched variables, $H_i$) might arise. Estimates of the variances of explanatory variables will be biased and will alter the outcomes of the hypothesis tests.

In the remainder of this chapter, I explore one possible estimation strategy for a model of endogenous gender. The discussion is intended to stimulate thought on the subject and is not in any sense a final product. I close with a very brief discussion of the data requirements of estimating such a model.

## GENDER AS THE BINARY INDICATOR OF SOME LATENT VARIABLE

Consider that an individual i chooses or is chosen to be and acquiesces in being gendered female. For women who do not wish to be so identified the options for rebellion and resistance are perhaps restricted and costly, but are not now and probably were not over the period and regions of this study non-existent. For the sake of discussion let us assume that the individual can be said to be maximizing expected utility over a gender choice set which is really a choice defined over ways of life.

$$U_{if}* = \max_z (U_{i1}, U_{i2}, \ldots , U_{ig})$$ (7)

where $U_{if}*$ is the unobservable, indirect utility associated with being in one of the g gender categories (I am unprepared to stipulate that there are always only two), category $g_f$.

Unobservable utility $U_{if}*$ has an "observable" systematic component, $U_{if}$, and an "unobservable" stochastic component which captures errors in optimization and errors in observation, regarding gender roles,

$$U_{if}* = U_{if} + v_i$$ (8)

The "observable" portion of utility is assumed to depend on real wage offers and hours supplied to market, household and leisure and may be thought of as a conventional economic money metric that describes the economic agent – *mulier economicus*. There is an observable dummy variable,

D=1, if $U_{if}^* > 0$, the individual is female and D=0, otherwise. The residual $v_i$ is normally distributed with zero mean vector and variance $\sigma_v$. Any estimation would of course be complicated by some individuals' specialization to market or household or leisure activities (a censoring problem).

Let the reservation wage equation for individual i be,

$$W_R = a_0 + a_1 X_1 + a_2 M + a_3 H + \eta_1. \tag{9}$$

Heckman (1974: 691) assumed the coefficient on market activity M would be positive. Given diminishing marginal returns to in-house activity, the coefficient on H will be negative.

The vector $X_1$ is comprised of predetermined or exogenous variables characteristic of the individual.

Labor supply to household production is given by,

$$H = b_0 + b_1 W_R + b_2 X_2 + b_3 U_f^* + \eta_2. \tag{10}$$

The coefficient on the reservation wage is assumed to be negative. $X_2$ may be thought of as the attributes of household work that affect the individual i's productivity – possibly the size of the house, the number of its dependents, the presence of "labor-saving" appliances. The coefficient $b_3$ measures the importance of being female to household production and is assumed to be positive. The less satisfaction one gets from practising the womanly arts, the less time one presumably spends in home production.

If $H > 0$ (i.e. $b_0 + b_1 W_R + b_2 X_2 + b_3 U_f^* > \eta_2$), the reservation wage becomes a function of $X_1$ and $X_2$, the level of one's market commitment, M, and of the general level of satisfaction with one's traditional gender role, $U_f^*$. The sign of the reduced form coefficient on $U_f^*$ is ambiguous in this model, depending on whether $a_3 b_3 / (1 - a_3 b_1) > 0$.

If $H > 0$ and $M > 0$, then hours worked in the market have adjusted to the point where the reservation wage equals a market wage described as follows:

$$W = c_0 + c_1 X_m + \eta_3. \tag{11}$$

This is a most kindly view of the labor market. Wages depend only on a vector of education and experiential data and on job characteristics. There is no discrimination here, though the equation could be amended to include it. Hours worked, $M > 0$, become,

$$M = d_0 + d_1 X + d_2 U_f^* + \eta, \tag{12}$$

where $X = [X_1 \; X_2 \; X_m]$. The probability that $M = 0$ ($W_R > W$) is the probability that $\eta < d_0 d_1 X - d_2 U_f^* = \Phi((-d_0 - d_1 X - d_2 U_f)^* / (Var(\eta)^{1/2}))$ and appears in the likelihood function when estimating the joint density of wages and hours worked (Heckman 1974). The likelihood function would need to be similarly adjusted for the probabilities that $M > 0$, $H = 0$ or $H > 0$, $M = 0$ (Kiker and Oliveira 1992).

Where this model differs from that of Heckman is in the presence of the latent variable, $U_{if}*$. That variable will undoubtedly appear in all of the odds functions (reduced form probabilities) that consistent estimation of the structural equations requires. In most estimation, $U*$ is confined to the error term because it is unmeasurable and, analysts piously hope, uncorrelated with the included variables. Alternatively, it is modeled as an exogenously determined dummy variable, since its manifestation is assumed to be binary and stable. Finally, some authors seek to bypass the issue by apologetically confining their analyses to men or to women exclusively. But $U*$ is itself a reduced form with determinants of its own and should be modeled explicitly. The object of this exercise has been to explore the payoffs to a richer specification for gender even in the context of otherwise censored regression. There is however an additional consideration worth exploring. In considering what variables affect $U*$, we turn our attention to the question of whether gender might be endogenously determined.

Consider equation (8) again, $U_{if}* = U_{if} + v_i$. If the residuals are independently and identically distributed, the probability that individual i "chooses" gender f equals $\exp U_{if}/\Sigma_g \exp U_{ig}$. The deterministic portion $U_{if}$ can be specified as a function of personal, experiential and social and economic characteristics relevant to personal development,

$$U_{if} = \Gamma Z_i + \gamma_i \tag{13}$$

To the extent that gender is the outcome of a process of socialization, the Zs might be specified as a vector of times spent in gender-specific activities with same sex companions. Females (and males) "apprenticed" by their families as children to household production and who have through extensive practice learned the arts, may derive greater joy from the practice thereof. The human household capital thus acquired may alter reservation wages and economic behavior. As a trivial example, consider the movie *Kramer v. Kramer*, in which the husband's labor market activity is drastically affected as he re-genders to become the primary care-giver to a small child. The shock of the movie comes in part from the fact that he is male experiencing the kind of discrimination practised against women, but I have argued all along that the correlation between sex and gender is imperfect.

## DATA REQUIREMENTS

All this argues for a melding of economic and sociological/psychological data sets. We need to know how individuals spent time in their formative years and with whom they spent time. Collecting the data over time in a way that might allow us to see evolution is essential.

The common view of gender is rather like the common view of health. One was either sick or well. Not until analysts had identified the benefits we can confer on ourselves by investing in nutrition, athletic activity and disease prevention did health become a continuous and endogenous variable in individual choice models. I wish to argue by analogy that gender is like health. Moreover, what is now gender may be vastly different than what is sex. Once, function may have followed form with near perfect correlation, but technology appears to have changed all that. Feminists have certainly been considering the possibility of endogenous gender for a long time. It is time economists did likewise.

## REFERENCES

Blau, F.D. and Ferber, M.A. (1986) *The Economics of Women, Men and Work*, Englewood Cliffs, NJ: Prentice-Hall.

Heckman, J. (1974) "Shadow Prices, Wages and Labor Supply", *Econometrica* 42, 4: 679–94.

Kiker, B.F. and Mendes de Oliveira, M. (1992) "Optimal Allocation of Time and Estimation of Market Wage Functions", *Journal of Human Resources*, 27, 3, Summer: 445–71.

Lerner, G. (1986) *The Creation of Patriarchy*, New York: Oxford University Press.

Scott, J. (1988) *Gender and the Politics of History*, New York: Columbia University Press.

Stansell, C. (1990) *City of Women: Sex and Class in New York, 1789–1860*, Urbana, IL: University of Illinois Press.

# 14

# ECONOMIC MEASUREMENT

## Comments on chapters by MacDonald, Perrons and Redmount

### Siv S. Gustafsson

Martha MacDonald proposes ways of gathering data other than those currently analyzed by economists. Diane Perrons proposes a way of constructing a single scalar index of gender equality that will allow measurement of the movement towards or away from gender equality in the labor market. Esther Redmount proposes an econometric model where gender is a choice variable produced by the rewards (negative or positive) that an individual receives from traditional "womanly" or "manly" arts. All three papers are inspiring, eye-opening and provoke independent and challenging thinking. The papers are in the spirit of improving economics, not substituting for economics. They are addressing scientific problems with an intended audience of scientifically trained economists. I comment on them in turn.

## ECONOMISTS' DATA NEEDS

MacDonald describes in her paper the fruitfulness of her long-term joint research with a sociologist. One of the advantages with this cooperation is the different attitude to data collection that a sociologist has in comparison with an economist. Sociologists are more open to data collection through own survey research, case studies and participant observation. Secondary data are seen by sociologists as inferior to collecting data that are tailored to their specific research question.

In contrast, economists rarely collect their own data and more often analyze large survey data sets collected for multiple purposes. There may be a 100 different dissertations based on a data set like the Michigan Panel which has data for about 6,000 American households collected each year from 1967 onwards. Many of these large data sets are internationally comparable and are continuously improved and made more consistent over time. Similar data sets exist in countries like Germany, Sweden, England, Denmark, Ireland, Luxembourg and Belgium and would be better described as multipurpose data sets, not secondary data sets as MacDonald calls them.

The difference between an economist's interest in multipurpose data sets and the sociologists' interest in primary data lies in the different scientific approaches employed by the two disciplines. The strength of economics is that it analyzes trade-offs, secondary – often unintended – effects on other sectors, and aggregate probabilistic rates rather than specific individual behavior. It is for these reasons that economics in Scandinavia is called national economics (*national-ekonomi* in Swedish, *sosialøkonomi* in Norwegian) to distinguish it from "company" economics ( *företagsekonomi* in Swedish, *bedrijfseconomie* in Dutch).

I therefore disagree with MacDonald when she pleads that economists should more often use data collection methods as case studies, in depth interviews or participating observations. These methods do not fit the questions that we ask as economists and should continue to ask because our training gives us a comparative advantage over other social sciences. It is evident that when you collect your own data you can more easily incorporate feminist ideas than when you have to negotiate improvements into a multipurpose data set with uninterested male colleagues who pursue their interests against the limited budgets for data collection. However, this is still what feminist economists will have to do.

## EXAMPLES OF MISSING DATA

With reference to missing data, the charge is made that what is not measured is often considered by economists not to exist. MacDonald gives the example of trying to get answers to the question, "What did your mother do to increase household income?" By reformulating the question to "Did she keep chickens, cows or boarders?" the respondents were alerted to the fact that their mothers performed one or all three of the aforementioned economic activities, but still did not spin off into thinking of other economic activities performed by their mothers.

Time use studies are an improvement in measuring the economic value of unpaid work but there are still difficulties in measuring and classifying joint activities such as cooking while looking after a child or watching a children's TV program with a child. Also the time use data can easily miss more abstract home management tasks such as remembering and organizing a child's visit to the doctor, having clean clothing ready when the child needs it for sports, knowing when the child's friends give a birthday party and organizing for the child to get there in time and be picked up on time, or other organizational tasks such as getting the child to visit the grandparents at frequent intervals and so on. Time use studies do not measure management tasks.

Another topic that MacDonald questions is how one can get data on intrahousehold allocation of resources. The ideology and the legislation rest on the assumption that there is equal sharing within the household.

However Ott (1992 and in chapter 5) reports data on intrahousehold differences in power and finds that these differences are determined by the respective command of resources in terms of own income, spouse's income, home work load and whether or not the family house is owned. It is strange that economists generally assume that there is equal sharing in the family because economic theory generally tells us that in a production process you get what you contribute valued at the marginal value of that contribution, that is, the competitive distribution. If women are exploited in the home sector, so that the marginal revenue of their labor is small and they also have low outside option or threat point, there is no reason to believe that they get equal shares out of marriage (Cigno 1991: chapter 4; Ott 1992).

## A SINGLE SCALAR INDEX OF EQUAL EMPLOYMENT

If one had a reliable and generally known index of equal employment that was as well known as the gross national product (GNP) it would be easy to demand that equal employment be a macroeconomic policy goal together with full employment, economic growth and price stability. Such an index could then be calculated by industrial branch level, regional levels, and even at company levels. Diane Perrons computes such an index for Britain annually from 1981 through 1992.

Ideally, the variables that should enter such an index are earnings inequality between men and women within and between occupations, employment structure measured by labor force participation rates of men and women, working full time or part time, occupational sex segregation, unemployment differentials and the volatility of employment. Perrons ends up with an index based on five variables:

1 The proportion of total jobs filled by full-time working women.
2 The proportion of part-time jobs filled by men.
3 An index of sex segregation by occupation.
4 Female to male hourly earnings ratio for all full-time workers.
5 Female to male weekly earnings ratio for all full-time workers.

The computed index shows an increase from 1981 (=100) to 1992 (=102.69). The conclusion is that there has been an improvement in women's situation in Great Britain in the 1980s. Perrons does not find her index ideal. It fails to capture unemployment, and the fact that many women are not in the labor force. This produces a polarization between women with jobs and women without jobs, which has not been reflected in the index. Unemployment was not included in the index because British unemployment figures do not give a just picture of male/female differentials. The reason is that unemployment data cover registered unemployment and people register as unemployed only if they are eligible for unemployment benefits. Since unemployment benefit is means tested against spouse's income, married women have no reason to register and female unemployment is therefore underestimated.

I think that Perrons attempt to construct an equal employment index is interesting and worth further development. I agree with her that it is necessary to integrate exclusion from the labor market into it. Perrons did not expect the result that the index would show an improvement of equality during the 1980s, but ascribes this to the fact that some variables that ought to be in it are not included. The remark that it is difficult to get the right measures is no argument against attempts to create an equality index. It is not easy to measure gross national product either. I think that the feminist claims would be more clear if we had such an index, and its development is therefore a task for feminist economics.

## AN ECONOMETRIC MODEL OF PRODUCED GENDER

Esther Redmount proposes an econometric model where gender is produced and not given exogenously. The common view of gender is like the common view of health: one was either sick or well and not until analysts had identified the benefits we can confer on ourselves by investing in nutrition, athletic activity and disease prevention did health become an endogenous variable in individual choice models! There is an imperfect correlation between sex and gender. A man that takes primary responsibility for a small child "re-genderizes" into the female gender and his value on the labor market is likely to devalue, as many mothers of small children experience if they cannot rely on child minders.

I fully agree with Redmount that gender is produced. The question now is how gender is produced and how we can estimate it. Redmount proposes an estimation technique which is inspired by Heckman's (1974) model of labor force participation where the reservation wage is unobserved but possible to estimate from known information on the characteristics of the individual. In the same way we can estimate femaleness on the basis of an observable systematic component and an unobservable stochastic component. If the individual is female there is an observable dummy variable like in Heckman's model where we can observe if someone is a labor force participant. The deterministic part of a person's utility of femaleness is specified as a function of personal, experiential social and economic characteristics. Redmount proposes that those variables might be specified as a vector of time spent in "gender specific activities with same sex companions." The paper rounds off with a hope that a melding of economic with sociological/ psychological data sets might give us data to estimate the produced gender model.

The theoretical results from this model are bound to show that being a womanly woman is negative for your labor market productivity. Redmount analyzes three categories of time use. The third category is recreation. In equation (10) the produced variable gender enters as a determinant of labor supply to household production with a negative expected coefficient. In equation (12) it enters with a probably positive coefficient upon labor supply to market work although Redmount does not say so. A corresponding equation for recreation is missing. Does gender not enter recreation?

If femaleness and maleness are produced by time spent in same sex groups during childhood, we have a possible way of measuring it. Women who went to girls' schools as children would then be more likely to derive a high utility from femaleness and therefore become housewives. Then it would be possible to estimate the model and we would know, for example, how much femaleness can explain (as opposed to sex) in analyzing the male/female wage differential.

I think that Redmount's work is important. As economists we need to aspire to increase the domain of measured variables. One task of science is to make the unmeasurable measurable. This is a step in that direction. But what if one developed survey instruments to measure other aspects of femaleness such as how important is it to wear a nice dress, to have your hair done regularly, to wear make-up, to spend an hour with your child each evening, to call your adult children once a week, to see your grandchildren at frequent intervals and so on? Would we then find that these aspects of femaleness were negative for your labor market productivity? Is it then negative to be a womanly woman?

## REFERENCES

Cigno, A. (1991) *Economics of the Family*, Oxford: Clarendon Press.
Heckman, J. (1974) "Shadow Prices, Market Wages and Labor Supply", *Econometrica* 42: 679–94.
Ott, N. (1992) *Intrafamily Bargaining and Household Decisions*, Berlin: Springer-Verlag.

# Part V

# EMPOWERMENT OF WOMEN

## Editor Notburga Ott

"Indeed, if woman had no existence save in the fiction written by men, one would imagine her a person of the utmost importance; very various; heroic and mean; splendid and sordid; infinitely beautiful and hideous in the extreme; as great as a man, some think even greater. But this is woman in fiction. In fact, as Professor Trevelyan points out, she was locked up, beaten and flung about the room.

A very queer, composite being thus emerges. Imaginatively she is of the highest importance; practically she is completely insignificant. She pervades poetry from cover to cover; she is all but absent from history. She dominates the lives of kings and conquerors in fiction; in fact she was the slave of any boy whose parents forced a ring upon her finger. Some of the most inspired words, some of the most profound thoughts in literature fall from her lips; in real life she could hardly read, could scarcely spell, and was the property of her husband."

(Woolf [1928] (1957): 43, 44)

# 15

# THE USE AND ABUSE OF NEOCLASSICAL THEORY IN THE POLITICAL ARENA

## The example of family and medical leave in the United States

*Eileen Trzcinski*

## INTRODUCTION

This chapter examines the role played by economic paradigms in shaping the terms of the family and medical leave debate in the USA. It describes the use of neoclassical theory by the different coalitions advocating and opposing leave. It also describes the role and nature of empirical research used in the family and medical leave debate. Finally, it examines the philosophical and practical significance of the use of neoclassical theory to block legislation aimed at improving labor market access for employees with caregiving responsibilities.

Until the enactment of the Family and Medical Leave Act on 5 February 1993, opponents of the legislation were successful in blocking its passage, relying in large part on standard neoclassical analyses to form the corner-stone of ideological and theoretical opposition to mandated job-guaranteed family and medical leave. When President Bush vetoed the Family and Medical Leave Act on 23 September 1992, he stated that he opposed mandates in general and claimed that such policies cannot meet the needs of US families. He also contended that mandating family and medical leave would impose an undue burden on employers and ultimately cost jobs. These arguments were also strongly advanced by the business community.

As a political strategy, proponents of mandated family and medical leave have not rejected the neoclassical paradigm. Instead they have argued that the effects of family and medical leave must be examined based on (a) empirical evidence measuring the actual costs to business of leave compared with other alternatives; (b) analyses examining traditional market failures that could be present in the market for leave. Research that used the externality argument played a large role in the passage of the Family and

Medical Leave Act in both the House and the Senate of the US Congress. In addition, a research base was developed that investigated the actual costs of leave to business based on the experiences of businesses with and without leave policies.

This chapter is organized as follows. First, it describes the current status of family and medical leave in the US at the federal and at the state level and includes a brief description of the history of the US Family and Medical Leave Act. It then turns to a description of how the free market argument was used as the basis for opposition to mandated leave. It describes both the public policy arguments and the theoretical basis for these arguments, including a description of how family and medical leave is analyzed in the labor economics textbooks that dominate the US market. The following sections demonstrate the parallels between the political and the textbook analyses and show how the political and economic arguments against leave were challenged with empirical research.

## FAMILY AND MEDICAL LEAVE LEGISLATION IN THE UNITED STATES

On 5 February 1993, President Clinton signed the Family and Medical Leave Act (US Public Law 103–3). Family and medical leave legislation had been debated in Congress from the mid-1980s to the early 1990s and had passed both the House and the Senate in two sessions, but by an insufficient margin to override a veto by President Bush. In the 1992 presidential campaign, President Bush's September veto of the Family and Medical Leave Act became a pivotal issue, highlighting the differences between Bush's policies towards women and families and the policies advocated by Bill Clinton. With the election of Bill Clinton as President, the Family and Medical Leave Act quickly moved to the forefront of the federal legislative agenda and became the first act signed into law by the new President. Under this act, which became effective on 5 August 1993, employees who work for employers who employ at least 50 employees are eligible for unpaid job-guaranteed leave of 12 weeks per year for family and medical emergencies. The Act also requires that the employer continue to pay the group health insurance premium for the employee. Since health insurance coverage is not mandated by law in the USA, this provision only applies to employers that provide health insurance.

The Act has a number of conditions that must be met before an employee is eligible to take leave. First, the employee must work at a worksite at which the employer employs 50 or more employees. Second, the employee must have worked for at least 12 months with the specific employer from whom leave is requested and must also have worked for at least 1,250 hours during the previous 12 months. Third, the Act contains certain allowable exclusions for highly paid employees, where the employee is a salaried employee who is among the highest paid 10 per cent of the employees employed by the employer within 75 miles of the facility at which the employee is employed.

The US Family and Medical Leave Act covers three separate types of need for leave. The first need for leave deals with leave because of the birth of a son or daughter or because of the placement of a son or a daughter with the employee for adoption or foster care. The second need for leave is in order to care for the spouse, a son, daughter, or parent of the employee, if such spouse, son, daughter, or parent has a serious health condition. In this case, the act only entitles an employee to leave to care for their own parent; a spouse is not entitled to leave to care for the parent of his or her spouse. The third need for leave stems from a serious health condition that makes the employee unable to perform the functions of the position of such employee.

Prior to the enactment of the Federal Family and Medical Leave Act, the only protection for employees was obtained through state statutes. In general, most US workers had no legal protection against termination on account of illness or disability, unless the employer chose voluntarily to offer job-guaranteed leave. If an employer offered job-guaranteed medical leave, then US law did mandate that this leave be available to women who needed it for maternity-related disabilities. Under the conditions of the Pregnancy Discrimination Act, an amendment to Title VII of the 1964 Civil Rights Act, employers must treat disabilities that result from pregnancy or childbirth on terms as favorable as other disabilities. If a firm provides sick leave or temporary disability leave, it must allow employees to use this leave for pregnancy or childbirth-related disabilities.

Family leave was also provided primarily at the discretion of the employer. Even in firms that provided family policies, these were almost universally subject to qualifying clauses such as "subject to supervisory discretion." The incidence of family and medical leave prior to the enactment of the Federal Family and Medical Leave Act is described below.

By 1992 the District of Columbia and 25 states had enacted some version of job-guaranteed maternity, parental or broader family leave legislation (see Women's Legal Defense Fund 1990; Finn-Stevenson and Trzcinski 1991; Freeman 1991). In the US, state statutes apply where the state law has more extensive provisions than the federal law. The federal statute applies in all other cases.

At the state level statutes range in coverage from leave that is limited to maternity-related disability to comprehensive family and medical leave. In general, the more narrow the specification of leave, the lower the firm size exemption. All enacted legislative statutes that cover parental or family leave have minimum firm size exemptions of at least 50 employees. The firm size exemptions tend to be far less stringent when the mandated leave is restricted to maternity-related disabilities. For this type of leave the exemption is usually set beneath 25 employees.

State legislation usually provides a number of key employer protections including notice of leave requirement, certification of illness, eligibility requirements, and limitations on leave taken within a one- or two year period. Employee protections often include protection against termination and retaliation and employer penalties for violation of law. (See Finn-Stevenson and Trzcinski 1991 for an extensive discussion of how these provisions vary across the states.)

## THE FREE MARKET ARGUMENT AND THE FAMILY AND MEDICAL LEAVE ACT

The free market argument, together with its corollary that government intervention must introduce inefficiency through regulation of markets, forms the cornerstone behind opposition to mandated leave legislation in the US. The primary opponents to mandated leave at both federal and state level are small businesses and the organizations that represent them, such as the US Chamber of Commerce, National Federation of Independent Business, Small Business Legislative Council, and the US Small Business Administration. These organizations unilaterally reject any type of mandated benefits.

Specific arguments raised by the different groups (e.g. National Federation of Independent Business 1989; US Small Business Administration 1989; US Chamber of Commerce 1987) in their testimony and position papers against leave include:

1 Required long-term leave poses a problem for small business, which can least afford to expand coverage.
2 The legislation would discourage small businesses from hiring younger or part-time workers.
3 Mandated benefits reduce other preferred benefits.
4 In those countries with generous maternity leaves, women are remaining, for the most part, in menial low-skilled jobs or are unemployed.
5 The US free market approach to business has encouraged job creation, economic growth, and entrepreneurial activity – the likes of which are virtually nonexistent in countries where business is over-regulated by government-mandated benefits.
6 Existing law is fair and effective.

The overall argument ties these pieces together as follows. These organizations contend that the US labor market already provides an adequate level of leave and that where leave is unavailable businesses are finding other flexible ways to meet their employees' need. Government intervention would therefore force employers to offer benefits that their employees prefer less, thus reducing flexibility and increasing costs. Both of these factors would inhibit the ability of firms to create new jobs and to spur economic growth. The impact would be particularly severe on growth and productivity because the primary source of job creation in the US is the small firm sector. Furthermore, these organizations contend that mandated leave would lower US competitiveness in the international economy. They argue that US competitors now suffer a disadvantage because their governments dictate how firms must meet certain employee needs regarding leave and other benefits. Opponents of mandated leave conclude that governments in other countries end up hurting women by increasing their rates of unemployment and by restricting their job opportunities. Were leave policies to be mandated in the US, these organizations argue that American women would suffer the same fate. These arguments formed the basis for President Bush's veto of the Family and Medical Leave Act.

Economists who use the dominant paradigm in microeconomics, the neoclassical model, contend that the competitive model produces an allocation of goods and services in which no one can be made better off without making someone else worse off. They label this condition a "Pareto-efficient allocation of goods." Labor economics have extended this theory to deal with wage determination in competitive markets. This model provides a theoretical framework for the premise that a market-determined wage-fringe mix is efficient. In this application, the optimal mix occurs when employees can select among a menu of benefits – where the menu is provided either by a single employer via a cafeteria plan or by a range of employers, each providing a different mix of wages and fringe benefits. In this analysis each firm allocates its total costs for labor across a vector of characteristics such as wages, health insurance coverage, vacation leave, life insurance, and other fringe benefits and across other characteristics of the job, such as how safe or pleasant the work environment is. The particular mix offered by a given employer depends in part on how much the different components cost relative to one another – a factor that can be affected by type of product and available technologies. Employees choose a particular employer based on their individual preferences regarding these characteristics. If the market is producing an optimal mix of wages and leaves, then a government mandate that forces employees to have more leave than they are currently taking would necessarily reduce labor market hours and increase non-market time.

## Treatment of family and medical leave in labor economics textbooks

Three labor economics textbooks dominate the US academic market: Kaufman (1989) *The Economics of Labor Markets and Labor Relations*; Ehrenberg and Smith (1991) *Modern Labor Economics*; Hamermesh and Rees (1993) *The Economics of Work and Pay*. Kaufman's treatment is the most extensive. He includes maternity leave within the body of the text itself. His exposition includes the application of the above analyses of fringe benefits to maternity leave benefits. A standard indifference curve analysis is included, where Kaufman analyzes the implications of a quote from a spokesperson for the Merchants and Manufacturers Association. He concludes this section with the following statement:

> Just as the spokesperson for Merchants and Manufacturers Association claimed, therefore, competitive pressures would eventually induce those firms without maternity leave benefits to add them, both to keep their work forces and because not doing so puts them at a profit disadvantage relative to firms that do.
>
> (Kaufmann 1989: 380)

Kaufman then argues that his analysis rests on the assumptions that the labor market is competitive and that workers are both well informed and mobile. He also contends that under the optimal solution women have to be willing to work for a lower wage. He claims that men do not benefit from maternity leave plans and would therefore desire to work at firms that offer fewer fringe benefits but higher wages. To obtain this optimal solution, he argues that firms must be able to offer one wage/fringe combination to men and another to women. According to Kaufman, however, this alternative is not possible because of government interference: "As it is," he writes, "the *Pregnancy Discrimination Act of 1978*, as well as various equal pay laws, require that men and women be treated equally with respect to wage rates and types of fringe benefits." Hence well-intentioned laws have their unintended consequences.

Ehrenberg and Smith make no mention of family or parental leave within their chapter on the economics of employee benefits. They do, however, discuss parental leave in their chapter on the demand for labor with a side subsection entitled "Mandating Employee Benefit," which provides their application of fringe benefit analyses to parental leave. Hamermesh and Rees have no references to maternity leave, parental leave, or family and medical leave.

## ASSUMPTIONS IN THEORY AND IN THE POLICY DEBATE

### The incidence of leave in the US and its implications

Even if an analyst accepts the basic premises of neoclassical theory, it is always an empirical question of whether a particular social change brings the market closer to or further away from the neoclassical economist's presumed ideal state. In his treatment of maternity leave, Kaufman at least indicates that his results depend on the assumption that the labor market must be competitive. Structurally, however, his argument implies that this caveat is unimportant. It is included only as a qualification and contains no quote to counter the quote from the representative of business interests. Kaufman did include accurate statistics concerning the low incidence of maternity leave in large firms and the near non-existence of maternity leave in small ones, but he made no attempt to suggest that the lack of leave could be attributed to discriminatory practices. In the presence of high labor force participation rates for women, very low incidences of maternity and family leave undermine the contention that the labor market is working as neoclassical economists contend it operates. Although Kaufman left it to his readers to deduce this contradiction and Ehrenberg and Smith conveniently excluded any mention of these statistics, the business lobby found the empirical evidence too embarrassing for its arguments and grossly misrepresented the incidence of leave.

The business lobby routinely contended that 90 to 95 per cent of medium and large business provided family leave and frequently referred to a US Small Business Administration study (Trzcinski and Alpert 1990) as a basis for this number. The study showed that most businesses provided medical leave for their employees. However, a substantial percentage of these businesses provided neither a job guarantee nor health benefit continuation. Most businesses did not provide family leave. Furthermore, most firms did not permit employees to use medical leave to care for the needs of family members. In most firms the only leave available for family needs was vacation leave. This low incidence of family leave is substantiated by other surveys, such as the surveys of the US Department of Labor Bureau of Labor Statistics (1991) and the Connecticut survey (Trzcinski and Finn-Stevenson 1991).

The Family and Medical Leave Coalition accurately represented these statistics in their press releases and in their interviews with the media. Politicians who supported the legislation were also careful to distinguish between medical leave and family leave and between leave with job guarantees and without job guarantees. In addition, the supporters of the legislation relied heavily on case studies of individuals who lost their jobs because of lack of job-guaranteed leave (see Trzcinski 1994).

## Flexibility or transfer of power: leave as a rigid, inflexible mandate

The analyses used in the labor economics texts do not accurately model the legislation that was proposed and enacted in the US. This inaccuracy also appears in the political arguments. The labor texts refer to maternity and/or parental leave as a mandate that forces employees to choose maternity/parental leave, whether or not they want this benefit. Unlike a long-term insurance program or health insurance coverage, which involves costs

237

premiums regardless of whether the employee draws benefits from the policies, unpaid family and medical leave generates no costs unless an employee takes it. The bills in the US did not mandate that an employee take leave, that is, a biological mother is not required to be absent from the labor force. Nor were there any other requirements that an employee take leave for caregiving or for medical reasons. Under the bills the employee always maintained the right to choose whether and how much leave to take, within the rigid constraints provided by the legislation. The bill increased the flexibility available to employees by changing the power dynamics in the leave negotiation. Now it is the employee and not the employer who is vested with the ultimate decision-making power of whether a leave is necessary. This characteristic of the legislation is central to any economic model of its labor market effects. A standard textbook example of the wage/fringe benefit trade-off misses the essence of the legislation and cannot be defended as a simplifying assumption. This misrepresentation of the legislation pervaded the political attacks against mandated leave. Typical examples of this description of the Family and Medical Leave Act include:

> Opponents were just as adamant about what they termed a "one-size fits-all" family leave plan that would impose additional government requirements on businesses without consideration of the cost or of their employees' wishes. "Sometimes a single issue illuminates an entire (election) campaign," said House Minority Leader Robert H. Michel (R.-Ill.), arguing that family leave was a good practice but was a matter to be worked out between each business and its employees.
>
> (*Los Angeles Times*, 1 October 1992)

> "This bill is an example of good intention leading to unintended consequences," said Minority Leader Robert H. Michel (R-Ill.), who made the administration's case during yesterday's floor debate. Mandating leave, Michel said, could induce employers to drop other, perhaps more desirable, benefits. "It's rigid and simplistic, and it's a big government dinosaur out of the past."
>
> (*The Washington Post*, 14 November 1991)

> If these policies are to meet the diverse needs of our nation, they must be carefully, flexibly, and sensitively crafted at the workplace by employers and employees, and not in Washington, D.C., through government mandates. Bush said in his veto message.
>
> (*The Washington Post*, 23 September 1992)

## Harmony or conflict of interests and the role of power in the employer/employee relationship

In his scathing 1930 attack on classical and neoclassical economics, *The Political Element in the Development of Economic Theory*, Gunnar Myrdal (1990 edition) pointed out that neoclassical theory is premised on a harmony of interests. In addition, he stated that standard neoclassical economics ignores the element of power. The treatment of family and medical leave in the US public policy debate and in the economic texts demonstrates that these criticisms still hold sixty years later. Neither Kaufman nor Ehrenberg and Smith suggest that the interests of workers with caregiving responsibilities may run counter to the interests of the businesses that employ them. In the economic models and in the arguments of leave opponents, mandated family and medical leave represents an interference in the workings of a labor market that would inadvertently hurt the interests of those it is intended to help. Presumably it is only the business community that understands the working of a capitalist society, having been well trained in labor economic courses throughout the country. The organizations that joined the National Family and Medical Leave Coalition (over 125) were apparently misguided in understanding how their own interests are played out in an economy guided by market forces of supply and demand.

Although neoclassical economists and business frame the debate over family and medical leave as a debate over government involvement, past US law concerning terminations on account of family and medical reasons provided employers with the legal right to determine whether leave is granted. This status quo denied flexibility to the employee by explicitly protecting the right of the employer. A family and medical leave act with job guarantee transfers the right from the employer to the employee. The analyses in the labor economic texts give no indication that the mandate vests the decision-making authority over leave-taking for family and medical purposes in the employee, not in the government. The level of government interference or involvement is unchanged; the legislation simply transfers legal protection from one party to the other. Neoclassical economists veer their comments away from the language of rights and entitlements, but the mandate is first and foremost a transfer of rights. Employees gain more flexibility; they obtain the power to exercise a right that they were previously denied. The mis-characterization of the bill appears in the following citation:

> Rep. Dick Armey (R.-Tex.) supported the veto, saying the bill "would reduce the freedom of working people to exercise their rights" by imposing a benefit that they might not want and thus prevent them from obtaining other benefits they might prefer, such as life insurance or additional paid time off.
>
> (*Los Angeles Times*, 1 October 1992)

In general, however, the misrepresentation was more implied than explicit as the following quotes indicate:

> "We're not voting on whether family leave is a good idea – we all support family leave," Senate Minority Leader Bob Dole (R-Kan.) told the chamber. "We're voting on whether the government should mandate it."
>
> (*Los Angeles Times*, 25 September 1992)

> In his veto message, Mr. Bush said, "I want to strongly reiterate that I have always supported employer policies to give time off for a child's birth or adoption or for family illness and believe it is important that employers offer these benefits. I object, however, to the Federal Government mandating leave policies for America's employers and work force."
>
> (*The New York Times*, 23 September 1992)

## Negative effects of legislation

Pervasive in labor economic analyses is the assumption that government legislation interferes with the market and hurts those it intends to help. This assertion can be implied, as it is in Kaufman's concluding statement that the Pregnancy Discrimination Act prevents businesses from offering the optimal point on the indifference curve. Oftentimes the assertion is made explicitly, as Ehrenberg and Smith demonstrate with their remarks that:

> While the benefit to employees of each proposal for mandated benefits *seems* clear, each also imposes a cost on employers that, *unfortunately,* might ultimately fall on these same employees. . . . As with payroll taxes, these costs on employers may be partially or fully passed on to workers in the form of lower wages. However, if they are not fully passed on . . . *inevitably employers will* respond to these cost increases by cutting back employment – especially among those groups of workers (primarily low-wage) for whom the cost increases are greatest.
>
> (Ehrenberg and Smith 1991: 93; emphasis added)

Notice that Ehrenberg and Smith use the language "inevitably employers will," indicating linguistically that we have at issue here a proven, natural law, not a theoretical analysis based on a series of questionable hypotheses about human behavior. The theme that mandated leave would lead to discrimination against women was pervasive in the arguments of its opponents. The argument that leave would hurt low-income workers also appeared with regularity in news stories and editorials. President Bush again provides us with his own interpretation of neoclassical theory:

> But Mr. Bush maintained that laws that mandate sexual equality or confer social benefits, like family leave in emergencies, were in fact counter-

productive because they cost businesses money, forced layoffs and slowed the economy. Better, he said, to help the economy create more jobs and to give women more opportunities to advance in those jobs.

(*The New York Times*, 19 September 1992)

Proponents of comprehensive family and medical leave have developed extensive legal and economic analyses that address the issue of potential discrimination. (See in particular Trzcinski 1991; Lenhoff and Becker 1989.)

## EMPIRICAL RESEARCH AND THEORETICAL ARGUMENTS USED BY PROPONENTS OF MANDATED LEAVE

### Empirical verification and the issue of costs

The labor economics texts (Hamermesh and Rees are the one exception) begin with the usual discussions of the distinction between positive and normative economics. Although a discussion of the effects of family and medical leave depends crucially on an investigation of a number of empirical questions, none of the authors followed their own dictates in maintaining a positive/normative split in addressing this particular issue. In this case, theory needs no empirical verification.

The labor economic analyses and the opposition to mandated leave centered on the costs of leave to business. In Ehrenberg and Smith and in the opponents' arguments, the standard line was that family leave:

> imposes a cost on employers that, unfortunately, might ultimately fall on these same employees. . . . In the case of parental leave, employers' costs would include any loss of output suffered when workers are on leave and the costs of hiring and training temporary replacement.
>
> (Ehrenberg and Smith 1991: 93)

Similar quotes heard throughout the debate from politicians opposing leave include:

> In a written statement issued about 9 p.m. Tuesday near the end of 15 hours of campaigning, Mr. Bush said he supported the concept of family leave but rejected the legislation because the financial burden it would impose on business would further dampen the growth of the economy and new jobs.
>
> (*The New York Times*, 24 September 1992)

> "It's easy for government to mandate without paying for it," said House Republican Whip Newt Gingrich (R-Ga.). "The workers will pay for it with layoffs."
>
> (*Chicago Tribune*, 1 October 1992)

241

The U.S. Business and Industrial Assn. said yesterday that supporters of the family leave "are killing off small business in the middle of a recession."

(*The Boston Globe*, 25 September 1992)

The question of costs is, of course, an empirical one that will be affected (a) by the level of managerial efficiency in covering for the leave-taker's work and (b) by the likelihood that a worker who is denied leave will permanently terminate employment. The opponents of leave had little research to support their contention that family and medical leave was a costly benefit. The one exception was an early study by the US Chamber of Commerce that made a number of assumptions about how businesses deal with leave-taking (US Chamber of Commerce 1987). The Chamber assumed that firms always hire outside replacements from temporary agencies. Every study that looked at actual business practices found that the use of outside temporary replacements was the option used least frequently (See US General Accounting Office 1988; Families and Work Institute 1991; Trzcinski and Alpert 1991; Trzcinski and Finn-Stevenson 1991).

The proponents of leave addressed the issue of the cost of leave as an empirical question. Two of the studies that were useful in the debate included the 1990 and 1992 Trzcinski and Alpert studies. Other studies that dealt specifically with burdens to business included two Families and Work Institute studies (Bond *et al.* 1991; Marra and Lindner 1992), although only the later study contained actual cost data. This study was also a case study of one large firm, as opposed to the Trzcinski and Alpert studies, which were based on a national sample of businesses.

The Trzcinski and Alpert studies received extensive coverage in the media and in the congressional debates, including such high profile exposure as front-page coverage in the *Wall Street Journal* and numerous citations in *The New York Times, Washington Post,* and *Los Angeles Times.* The business community responded to these studies with rancor, although they never challenged the studies on methodological grounds. It is amusing to observe that lobbyists for the business community, which rested its arguments on the contention that employees did not know their own best interests, were quick to sneer at the suggestion that the harmony of interests lay in the other direction. Hence the Small Business Administration attempted to suppress the 1990 report and refused to distribute it, although it was eager to distribute its own research summary, which bore only passing resemblance to the actual findings in the report. (See Taylor 1991, 15 April, *The Washington Post,* "Family-Leave Report Creates Commotion".) A lobbyist for the business community had this response to the 1992 study:

The study also concluded that businesses wasted $500 million on hiring and training new workers instead of holding the jobs of sick workers

242

until they could return. But Tracy Wurzel, a lobbyist for the National Federation of Independent Business, ridiculed that finding. . . . "It's lunacy," she said.

(*Los Angeles Times*, 15 September 1992)

A number of other explanations, neoclassical as well as non-neoclassical, do exist that could account for why firms do not provide job-guaranteed leave, although they could cut costs by doing so. Even from a neoclassical standpoint, family and medical leave can be viewed as a technological innovation. For example, some firms adopt cost-saving innovations quickly; other firms learn more slowly and can continue to operate in the short-run using less efficient and outmoded managerial and technological practices.

## Public goods: theory and research

Economics texts in general and labor economics texts in particular do not treat children as public goods. In the early stages of the family and medical leave debate, however, the public goods argument received considerable attention. The research base calling for a national mandate was developed in large part by child psychologists and child development experts (see Zigler and Frank 1988). In the US, the ideology of individuality and the ideology that a woman's place is in the home are so strong that interest groups, such as the US Chamber of Commerce, and private citizens can sometimes block legislation on the grounds that children are the individual and exclusive responsibility of parents. Employer organizations in the USA reject the public goods argument surrounding children, at least when they are asked to share part of the societal costs for the investment. Typical of US sentiment is the following statement by the US Chamber of Commerce (1987: 3): "Ultimately, family responsibility is individual responsibility. Balancing a family and career is a challenge each of us confronts at the most personal level."

The National Federation of Independent Business has also consistently argued that business should not be legally required to take responsibility for personal choices of employees (*The New York Times*, 15 June 1990). These same values are implicit in Kaufman's neoclassical analyses when he states that economic optimality rests on the premise that to obtain maternity leave benefits, women *have to be willing to work for a lower wage* (1989: 381, emphasis added). To restate this contention more strongly, neoclassical theory as it is presented in the US holds that women alone must pay for any potential costs associated with leave and they must pay this cost through reductions in their wage.

Although the public goods argument forms the backbone for many of the family policies that countries have implemented in Europe and in other parts of the world, these arguments tend to be unsuccessful in the US, particularly when the legislation imposes clearly defined costs on the business community or other identifiable groups. In analyzing the evolution of the Family and Medical Leave Act, Radigan (1988) and Spalter-Roth and Hartmann (1989) contend that the US Chamber of Commerce and other business organizations were successful in discrediting the public goods argument and in changing the debate on family and medical leave from the benefits to family and society as a whole to the costs to business. Unable to shift the argument back to concern for children and the future of society, the coalition supporting the Family and Medical Leave Act nevertheless sought to regain control in the costs and benefits debate. Spalter-Roth and Hartmann report that: "Donna Lenhoff, one of the coalition leaders, lamented that the only data available to the supporters of the Family and Medical Leave Act was on child-parent bonding. Surely, she suggested, there must be costs to women and their families of not having leave" (1989: 106). This argument represents an externality argument.

### Externalities: theory and research

Economists have defined externalities as a potential source of market failure. In the US, social externalities, particularly externalities generated by employer choices of organization and employee policy, remain largely unexplored in economic theory. Labor economics texts do not address the issue of family and medical leave within the context of social externalities. Despite the lack of attention by academic labor economics to the existence of market failures, proponents of family and medical leave legislation have relied on the externality argument as (a) a grounds to justify why this legislation is socially desirable; (b) as a means to counter the arguments that family and medical leave should not be enacted because it generates costs to business. The externality argument played a large role in the passage of the Family and Medical Leave Act in both the House and the Senate.

The initial political stages of the Family and Medical Leave Act met with little opposition (Radigan 1989). Not until the US Chamber of Commerce and other business organizations realized that the Family and Medical Leave Act had become a serious contender for enactment did they mount an oppositional campaign. Part of this campaign entailed discrediting the notion that children are public goods as noted in the previous section. More central to the Chamber's attack, however, was a cost analysis in which it produced a $13 billion price tag for the legislation. Though the Chamber later scaled down the magnitude of these projected costs, it nevertheless managed to change the terms of the debate from benefits to families to costs to businesses.

Proponents of the legislation reacted to this tactic with their own assessment of the costs, but this position entailed looking at the costs of the status quo – the unnecessary losses suffered by individuals, families, and taxpayers, that is, they used the externality argument. Lenhoff and Becker describe the short-term costs and their implications as follows:

> Society's failure to respond to the overwhelming proportion of families that lack a full-time caregiver at home inflicts devastating costs on these families, especially in the stress associated with two fulltime wage earners maintaining a family. Families in which medical or other emergencies exacerbate the day-to-day pressures of domestic life suffer still more serious losses. In such cases, the lack of societal supports may have immediate economic consequences if one of the wage earners is forced to quit her or his job to take care of the family's needs.
>
> (Lenhoff and Becker 1989: 405)

In this argument, employers are directly responsible for these costs because their production process, which includes organization of the workplace and related personnel policies, ignores the consequences to individuals and families of not having the flexibility to deal with medical emergencies and nurturing responsibilities. These costs are quantifiable using the same analytical techniques of cost/benefit analysis used by economists to deal with environmental externalities.

Such an analysis was undertaken by the Institute for Women's Policy Research (Spalter-Roth and Hartmann 1990). The results of this research report, entitled *Unnecessary Losses*, became an important part of the public policy debate concerning the benefits and costs of mandated family and medical leave. *Unnecessary Losses* estimated the current economic costs of the lack of a national family and medical leave policy to working women and men, and to taxpayers, in terms of added earnings losses and public income assistance. The report concluded that the costs to workers and taxpayers of the current lack of national policy were $100 billion. This research study predated the survey-based studies on costs to businesses of providing leave. Together the two sets of research became powerful tools in the struggle to obtain passage of the Family and Medical Leave Act.

## CONCLUDING REMARKS

When the historical record is examined, President George Bush is not a politician who will be heralded as a champion of women's rights. Nor will his record demonstrate concern for the needs of employees who must balance work and family needs. His opposition to legislation on gender equity and on family policy was ideological, but in the US ideology must appear to be based on a theoretical, objective base. In the case of family and medical leave, which represents a typical example not an aberration,

245

President Bush echoed the theories that are presented to economics students in universities and colleges across the country. Neoclassical economics, as it is applied and taught in the US, more often serves conservative than progressive agenda. It is also disturbing that the theoretical precepts can be presented so easily as facts, without reference to empirical verification.

In the US family and medical leave debate, proponents of leave were able to demonstrate the net benefits of leave policies without abandoning the neoclassical model in its entirety. The major research studies used in the debate were in fact economic analyses that relied on traditional methods of addressing economic issues. Most proponents and even opponents of leave (who found these studies so grating) would probably assess these works as important elements in the debate, suggesting that neoclassical economics need not be antithetical to developing progressive policies.

Despite the role of these studies, however, a dependence on neoclassical theory, with its bias towards maintaining and justifying the status quo, tends to place advocates for gender equity at a disadvantage. Hence I believe a dual strategy is needed. In the US (and probably in other countries as well), economists who are advocates for women need to understand thoroughly neoclassical theory, so that they can confront its inconsistencies, logical flaws, and political biases with both logic and empirical evidence. But we also need continuously to plant and cultivate the seeds for theoretical analyses of society, gender, and employment where a conflict of interests can be openly acknowledged and addressed, with each person having a voice in shaping the conditions under which we work and care for each other and ourselves.

## REFERENCES

*Note*: All citations for newspaper quotations are noted in the text.

Bond, J.T., Galinsky, E., Lord, M., Staines, G.L. and Brown, K.R. (1991) *Beyond the Parental Leave Debate: The Impact of Laws in Four States*, New York: Families and Work Institute.

Ehrenberg, R.G. and Smith, R.S. (1991) *Modern Labor Economics: Theory and Public Policy* (4th edn), Glenview, IL: Scott, Foresman and Company.

Finn-Stevenson, M. and Trzcinski, E. (1991) "Mandated Leave: An Analysis of Federal and State Legislation", *American Journal of Orthopsychiatry* 61, 4: 567–75.

Freeman, J. (1991) "Controversial Family Rights Law Allows Four-month Leaves of Absence to Care for Family Members", *California Employment Law Reporter* 11: 337–42.

Hamermesh, D. and Rees, A. (1993) *The Economics of Work and Pay* (5th edn), New York: Harper Collins College Publishers.

Kaufman, B. (1989) *The Economics of Labor Markets and Labor Relations* (2nd edn), Chicago: The Dryden Press.

Lenhoff, D.R. and Becker, S.M. (1989) "Family and Medical Leave Legislation in the States: Toward a Comprehensive Approach", *Harvard Journal on Legislation* 26, 2: 404–63.

Marra, R. and Lindner (1992) "The True Cost of Parental Leave: The Parental Leave Cost Model", in D. Friedman, E. Galinsky and V. Plowden (eds) *Parental Leave and Productivity*, New York: Families and Work Institute: 55.

Myrdal, G. (1990) *The Political Element in the Development of Economic Theory*, New Brunswick: Transaction Publishers.

National Federation of Independent Business (1989) *Statement of John Motley for the National Federation of Independent Business on H.R. 770, The Family and Medical Leave Act of 1989 before the Subcommittee on Labor-Management Relations of the Committee on Education and Labor*, House of Representatives, 101st Congress, Hearing held on 7 February 1989, Washington, D.C.: U.S. Government Printing Office.

Radigan, A. (1988) *Concept and Compromise: The Evolution of Family Legislation in the U.S. Congress*, Washington, D.C.: Women's Research and Education Institute.

Spalter-Roth, R. M. and Hartmann, H.I. (1989) "Science and Politics: The 'Dual Vision' of Feminist Policy Research – The Example of Family and Medical Leave", in *Proceedings of the First Annual Women's Policy Research Conference*: 105–16, Washington, D.C.: Institute for Women's Policy Research.

—— (1990) *Unnecessary Losses: Costs to Americans of the Lack of Family and Medical Leave*, Washington, D.C.: Institute for Women's Policy Research.

Trzcinski, E. (1991) "Separate versus Equal Treatment Approaches to Parental Leave: Theoretical Issues and Empirical Evidence", *Law and Policy* 13, 1: 1–33.

—— (1994) "Family and Medical Leave, Contingent Employment, and Flexibility: A Feminist Critique of the U.S. Approach to Work and Family Policy", *Journal of Applied Social Sciences* 18, 1: 71–88.

Trzcinski, E. and Alpert, W.T. (1990) *Leave Policies in Small Business: Findings from the U.S. Small Business Administration Employee Leave Survey*, Washington, D.C.: Final Report, United States Small Business Administration, Office of Advocacy.

—— (1991) "Handling Work During Leaves: Strategies and Costs", *Journal of Managerial Issues* 3, 4: 403–26.

—— (1992) "Job Guaranteed Medical Leave: Reducing Termination Costs to Business", Cornell Cooperative Extension Fact Sheet, Ithaca, New York: Cornell University, Consumer Economics and Housing.

Trzcinski, E. and Finn-Stevenson, M. (1991) "A Response to Arguments Against Parental Leave: Findings from the Connecticut Survey of Parental Leave Policies", *Journal of Marriage and the Family* 52, 3: 445–60.

U.S. Chamber of Commerce (1987) *Statement of the Chamber of Commerce of the United States on S.249, The 'Parental and Medical Leave Act of 1987' to the Subcommittee on Children, Family, Drugs, and Alcoholism of the Senate Committee on Labor and Human Resources*, Washington, D.C.: U.S. Government Printing Office.

U.S. Department of Labor Bureau of Labor Statistics (1991) *BLS Reports on Its First Survey of Employee Benefits in Small Private Establishments*, News. Washington, D.C.: Bulletin Released 10 June.

U.S. General Accounting Office (1988) *Parental Leave: Estimated Cost of Revised Parental and Medical Leave Act Proposal*, GAO/HRD–88–132, Washington, D.C.: U.S. General Accounting Office.

U.S. Small Business Administration (1989) *Family and Medical Leave: The Impact on Small Business, In Focus on the Future: Small Business in the 1990s*, Proceedings of the 10th National Legislative Conference on Small Business Issues, Washington, D.C.: U.S. Small Business Administration.

Women's Legal Defense Fund (1990) *State Laws and Regulations Guaranteeing Employees Their Jobs After Family and Medical Leaves*, Washington, D.C.: Women's Legal Defense Fund.

Zigler, E. and Frank, M. (1988) *The Parental Leave Crisis: Toward a National Policy*, New Haven: Yale University Press.

# 16

# WOMEN AND CHILDREN LAST

## A feminist redefinition of privatization and economic reform

### *Barbara E. Hopkins*

One of the most difficult problems currently in Czechoslovakia is that old neglect of women's issues risks being combined with a potentially even greater neglect due to the current economic changes towards a market economy. . . . To merely . . . take over western social arrangements will mean that women's positions here may change but they will not improve!

(Alena Valterova, founder of Political Party of Women and Mothers, (quoted in Castle-Kanerová 1991))

We are against society hypocritically using its failure to establish family values as a reason for forcing women out of the sphere of paid and visible labor into unpaid invisible labor.
Independent Women's Democratic Initiative (NEZHDI, Russia 1991)

Privatization generally refers to the resurgence of private property in Eastern Europe. It also describes pushing women out of public life into the household. When enterprises are sold to private citizens, managers and workers become autonomous actors in a public sphere, but women become dependent actors in a private sphere. Women are the first workers laid off when factories attempt to improve efficiency. Women receive less support for combining children with paid labor, forcing them to depend on their husbands for financial support and their mothers for childcare.

Socialism did not liberate women from a patriarchal order. But, the promotion of market ideology pushes women's concerns farther from public consideration. Marketization is transferring the socialist state's responsibility for children to women. Reformers are closing childcare centers in the name of efficiency. When children are consumption goods, as in mainstream economic theory, childcare is an accessory. Parents choose between buying a new washer/dryer, a vacation on the Black Sea, or sending little Misha to childcare. Misha's welfare is not considered except as a component of his parents utility function. The market addresses childcare only as part of Misha's parent's utility.

Children are people with their own welfare. Nevertheless, although frequently self-interested, children are not yet the autonomous actors of mainstream economics. They are dependent on someone to care for them. A complete picture of economics must acknowledge that the institutions created by societies to care for children are economic institutions. In both socialism and capitalism this institution has been the family and in particular the labor of women.

Economic analysis of the distribution of wealth has neglected the allocation of responsibility for dependents. Yet we all know that a couple with a household income of $50,000 a year does not have the same standard of living as a couple with a household income of $50,000 a year and two daughters in college. We also know that a man with a salary of $30,000 a year married to a woman who bears all responsibility for a son does not have the same standard of living as she does even if she also earns $30,000 a year.

The allocation of responsibility within the family and the allocation of responsibility between the family and the state or the workplace affect the distribution of welfare. When a society allocates responsibility based on gender, the state can alter the relative burden by taking on some of the responsibility. When a woman's ability to fulfil her responsibility is dependent on others, the state can increase her autonomy by lifting some of the burden. Understanding the complex allocation of responsibility to women, men, and the state is necessary for a feminist evaluation of economic reform. I begin with an explanation of the ideologies of capitalism and socialism.

## HOMOECONOMICUS AND THE THEORETICAL FOUNDATIONS OF CAPITALISM

At the center of mainstream theory of capitalism is the individual. *Homoeconomicus* is self-interested and autonomous. He enters into contracts and exchanges goods freely. He is not dependent on any other individual for his survival. *Homoeconomicus* is free from the tyranny imposed by a central government that chooses where he should sell his labor and what he should consume. He registers his preferences on the free market and the market supplies him with all he can afford. The logical extension of this assumption is that there is no need for government intervention except to promote the free market by enforcing the contracts that *homoeconomicus* has entered into freely.

However, *homoeconomicus* cannot come to us fully grown. He must first be born and raised. Young *homoeconomicus* cannot sell his labor or express his preferences. Someone must sell their labor to feed and clothe him. Someone must prepare his food and change and wash his clothing. Someone must watch after him in case his preferences unknowingly lead him into danger or he will never grow old enough to sell his labor or express his preferences through consumption.

Alfred Marshall suggested that young *homoeconomicus* could be ensured of survival if adult *androeconomicus* were given a family wage to support his wife and child and if *gynoeconomicus* were excluded from the labor market, focussing her attention on young *homoeconomicus* (Pujol 1992). Most contemporary theory simply neglects the problems of young *homoeconomicus* and assumes that Marshall's nuclear family is the norm[1]. Consumer theory considers only an adult head of household (*androeconomicus*) whose preferences we assume include the needs of young *homoeconomicus* and his mother. *Androeconomicus* is self-interested in his behavior towards the outside world and completely altruistic towards his family.

Young *homoeconomicus* becomes a consumption good for his father[2] and not a human being in his own right. Childcare, schools, childhood vaccinations, adequate nutrition are all consumer goods for the father of *homoeconomicus* as if he were playing with other kids, learning geography, taking care of his health, and enjoying a good meal.

*Gynoeconomicus* becomes an investment good. Marriage is a semi-permanent labor contract, whereby women exchange household labor for room and board. She looses her autonomy as a person. All choices that may determine her income were made as part of the original marriage contract. She becomes as financially dependent on *androeconomicus* as young *homoeconomicus*. However, she is also responsible for using the financial resources she receives as part of the marriage contract to satisfy all the needs of young *homoeconomicus*. She is responsible for him but does not have the autonomy to control his material well-being.

She is hampered in the labor market by social attitudes that assign her responsibility for young *homoeconomicus* as well as any aging relatives who can no longer care for themselves and many of the needs of *androeconomicus* that are not available on the market. Her responsibility is then reinforced by her limited access to jobs offering better remuneration. Even women without children have limited opportunities, because employers expect them to drop out of the labor market.

When we acknowledge dependency, the failure to maintain *gynoeconomicus'* autonomy reduces the appeal of capitalism. Autonomy and free choice are the virtues of capitalist ideology. Capitalism is about creating a world where *homoeconomicus* can act and think for himself.

## *HOMOCOLLECTIVUS* AND THE THEORETICAL FOUNDATIONS OF SOCIALISM

In the Marxist tradition autonomy is valued[3], but individualism is not assumed. *Homocollectivus* is an interdependent being. He is dependent on the labor of others for his survival. When the industrial revolution took from him the means of production, he could no longer provide for his own survival within his family. His labor became a commodity. He was not guaranteed the opportunity to exchange his labor for the goods produced by others. If he is unable to find a buyer for his labor he is unable to buy bread. If he does find a buyer the interests of the capitalist to buy (labor) low and sell (products) high leads to the exploitation of *homocollectivus* under capitalism. *Homocollectivus* does not receive all the fruits of his labor. In order for *homocollectivus* to have autonomy he must have control over the means of production through social production.

In Marxist thought, women's oppression and exploitation under capitalism are derived from their dependence on men. The worker (male) is dependent on the capitalist who owns the means of production and the wife is dependent on her husband who owns everything else. In order for women to be emancipated they must participate in the labor force outside the home (Buckley 1981). In the constitutional traditions of communist countries women are equal. As the Hungarian New Family Law of 1952 states, "Women's equality within marriage is . . . primarily ensured by . . . participation in productive labor, economically independent of her husband" (Lampland 1989: 306).

The writers of the Hungarian Family Law quoted above seem to have retained the capitalist bias for what constitutes "productive." Labor not exchanged on the market is not productive. Planning priorities indicate that the production of labor-saving devices such as refrigerators, washing machines and dryers, and microwave ovens was also viewed as a waste of resources.

However, when women rush off into the labor force, what will become of young *homocollectivus*? The dream of socialized housework was never achieved and never really attempted. When societies recognize that women's labor in the household is necessary alternative institutions are needed to provide these services.

The possibility that men would absorb some responsibility for providing the labor necessary to care for young *homocollectivus* is not part of the Eastern European Marxist tradition. Barbara Einhorn (1989) and Lynn Duggan (1993) point out that the policies of East Germany (GDR) served to reinforce the responsibility of women for household labor. Not until 1987 did the possibility of men taking responsibility for household labor become a public issue in the Soviet Union (Buckley 1989).

When men are not expected to perform more household labor, a commitment to women's labor force participation requires that alternative institutions bear some responsibility. An East German report to the central committee congratulated itself on the successful creation of the "necessary precondition to enable women to better harmonize employment, social commitment, and maternal duties, which generally benefits family life"

(Einhorn 1989). Through generous maternity leave benefits[4], household days, shorter hours, childcare, and health coverage, women who work in paid employment can meet their household responsibilities without giving up their jobs.

Thus, socialism differs from capitalism because the state takes on some responsibility for young *homocollectivus*. State provided social services replaced the patriarchal nuclear family.

## REAL WOMEN IN CAPITALISM

In the real economies of Western Europe and North America families are more complex and varied than a theory that treats the household as an extension of the "head" suggests. The extension of the father's utility function to incorporate his entire family is an oversimplification of actual relationships within households of the traditional family type. Furthermore, the traditional nuclear family of "father knows best" has always been a minority. Increasing numbers of women work out of desire or necessity. And they continue to have children.

Women are not completely powerless in the traditional family. In the USA women who oppose sexual equality work against it precisely because they do not want to see their power in the family eroded. Surveys of attitudes on sex roles indicate that a majority of women do not support men's participation in childcare because they "fear losing not only their traditional power and domination in the home . . . but their exclusive importance to children" (Segal 1990: 48). However, women's attitudes must be seen in the context of women's poor prospects to achieve authority and power in the "public" sphere.

Although advertisers target women as the decision-makers, the choice between powdered or liquid laundry detergent does not constitute the same level of autonomy as the choice of where the family will live and work. It is a common misconception that wives have as much say in how to spend the family income as husbands who are the primary breadwinners. The distribution of household income tends to follow a pattern where income is divided between the male householder's personal expenses and the household expenses. Thus when the cost of food goes up or the children need new clothes for school the money is more likely to come out of the discretionary budget of mothers and not fathers[5].

Many women in capitalist economies work. A market for childcare exists. In some western countries the state takes some of the responsibility and subsidizes childcare, but in most countries women must pay for the privilege to work. When children are sick women must take time off, encouraging the stereotype that women are unreliable workers. This can be a rational economic calculation, because women usually earn less than men. Thus, a woman is caught in a vicious cycle where her responsibilities to children lower her opportunities in the labor market, which in turn lower her opportunity costs relative to the father's opportunity costs of taking responsibility for children. Women who do not earn enough to pay someone to perform necessary household tasks must do a full-time job for wages and another full-time job at home.

As more and more women work, women have begun to take over more of men's traditional financial responsibility for dependents. Liberal divorce laws have made it easier for men to relinquish financial responsibility for children. In poor inner city communities with high male unemployment, high male homicide rates, and high incarceration rates, women's responsibility for children is all encompassing.

When responsibility for dependents is assigned to women, all women suffer from the view that women are or will become mothers and therefore unreliable workers. Meanwhile, only men who chose paternity leave will be perceived as unreliable workers. Thus only men who have authority over the organization of work can take paternity leave without damaging their career. Women with weak job opportunities married to men with high paying jobs that are vulnerable to layoffs or risk being overlooked for promotion will end up taking responsibility for household labor.

Many capitalist countries have made progress in freeing women from financial dependence on men. However, the result of women's economic "independence" has been to ease men's financial responsibility for children, and increase women's financial responsibility. Thus women in modern capitalism are becoming both financially and materially responsible for children. Meanwhile only a few men are becoming more responsible for material needs.

## REAL WOMEN IN SOCIALISM

For real women in Eastern Europe and the Soviet Union emancipation was more complicated than entering the workforce. Women had equality in name, but were not likely to be in positions of authority – factory managers, politburo members. Work is not so liberating when it is low status and low paid and when the services provided to help with household chores are still inadequate. Sexual discrimination, sexual harassment, and the powerlessness felt by workers at the bottom continued to be part of women's work experience under socialism. Furthermore, work experience for many women included the additional guilt and frustration of leaving her children in inadequate childcare facilities while wasting time at a job where she felt redundant.

The Bolshevik revolution granted legal autonomy, but the fledgling state was in no position to provide the necessary economic resources that would allow women actually to assert their independence. The USSR had abolished the inferior legal status of women, allowing them to own property and establishing liberal divorce laws. However, the state's attitudes on the liberation of women became superficial by the 1930s. Wendy Goldman presents a persuasive argument that material conditions prevented the progress of the "socialist" agenda for women (Goldman 1989). It is impossible to tell if the communist party, having established its authority, would have broken its promises if these conditions had not interfered.

By the time Eastern Europe had adopted Soviet-style communism, the commitment to women's emancipation was largely rhetorical[6]. Women were encouraged to enter the labor force. However, many observers attribute this encouragement of women's entry into the labor market to the labor shortage that followed World War II (USSR – Buckley 1981; Hungary – Lampland 1989). Women entered the labor force not to find emancipation, but to pay for necessities.

Once in the labor force, women found themselves at the bottom and in poorly paid industries. These jobs did little to alleviate economic dependence on men. In the USSR the percentage of women industrial workers in unskilled jobs was 74 per cent in 1970 (Buckley 1981). Although Eastern European women were able to acquire greater skills and education than their western counterparts, women are underrepresented in higher paying jobs than their education level would predict (USSR – Buckley 1981; GDR – Rudolph 1992). Not only were educated women concentrated in fields that received lower wages, they had little opportunity for advancement. In the Soviet Union, women were 40 per cent of engineers, but only 9 per cent of factory managers (Buckley 1981). Furthermore, advancement in socialist economies was often tied to party membership which demanded an additional burden. Housing shortages in Eastern European cities posed additional barriers to independence for both sexes (Bollobás 1988).

Although, the state socialist governments of Eastern Europe absorbed some responsibility for dependents, women were still considered primarily responsible for children. Government policies make it easier for women to fulfil household responsibilities while holding jobs by demanding less at work. These policies reinforced women's role as mother. In the GDR the "baby year" (maternity leave), and the "household days" (days off to catch up on the housework), and shorter work week were not available to men (Einhorn 1991; Duggan 1994). In Hungary where parental leave was open to men, few men took it. Paternity benefits were fixed. Because men's wages were generally higher than women's, the loss in family income was greater when fathers stayed home (Lampland 1989).

Although women did not risk losing their jobs in state-owned enterprises when they took time off work to care for sick children or a newborn, they were still seen as less reliable workers. Managers were aware of government affirmative action policies, but were rewarded for fulfilling the plan. Workers who must leave work to care for sick children or who take a year off to care for a newborn, and workers who cannot work late because they must

255

pick up their children at childcare are less able to contribute to completing the plan. They are less likely to be promoted.

Although the services provided by Eastern European states such as childcare may have absorbed some of the responsibilities for children, the low priority placed on consumer goods increased the amount of time women had to spend on household chores. Shortages meant long queues that lengthened the time women spent shopping. The lack of consumer goods was particularly severe in the Soviet Union. Lack of refrigerators meant that many women had to shop more often. In 1976 only 67 per cent of families had refrigerators in the Soviet Union. The average soviet woman spent six hours per week shopping. Lack of washing machines meant women had to spend more time washing clothes and dishes. The average soviet woman spent another six hours per week on laundry. Lack of prepared foods and restaurants meant more time cooking – 10 to 12 hours per week (Buckley 1981). Poor transportation meant more time commuting.

Nevertheless, although women retained primary responsibility for household tasks, some men in socialist economies, like some in capitalist economies, took on more responsibility. Men in the GDR performed a higher share of household work – 39 per cent – than men in the Federal Republic of Germany (FRG) – 30 per cent. However, the share of total work was almost the same at 45 per cent and 44 per cent respectively. The difference was much smaller – 39 per cent and 41 per cent – for men whose wives worked full time. Furthermore, the total amount of work in the GDR was larger for both men and women than in the FRG (Duggan 1993).

Nevertheless, the provision of childcare in the GDR did make a difference in women's lives. The gap between the work done by women with children and women without is much larger in West Germany than East Germany (Duggan 1993)[7]. Women were able to combine work and children more easily. The provision of childcare must also have increased women's autonomy. A larger number of women chose not to marry or to exit their relationships with men in the GDR (Duggan 1993). Although the childcare provision in the GDR was the best in Eastern Europe and the experiences of East German women were not universal, these statistics illustrate the changes that can come from childcare provision.

## THE TRANSITION FROM SOCIALISM TO CAPITALISM

When Eastern European countries dismantled the subsidies and support services of the socialist system, Eastern European women were not thrust into the environment inhabited by Western European women. New consumer goods are expensive and unemployment is high.

Governments adopted an ideological separation between public and private to prevent the influence of family life on work life. Privatizing the responsibility for dependents, the state gave up responsibility for children. To transform the socialist economy, reformers and their western advisors adopted a nineteenth-century ideal of entrepreneurial capitalism. The ideology of selfishness needed to be instilled in the population. Representative of the ideology imported to build capitalism, Anatoly Sobchak writes, "a market economy, in order to function requires . . . responsibility. Every person must be responsible and solve his or her own problems" (Sobchak 1991). Private enterprises, unlike state enterprises, do not concern themselves with women workers' responsibilities at home. "There is one and only one social responsibility of business – to use its resources to engage in activities designed to increase its profits" (Friedman 1962).

Economic reforms do not ask what is the best way to care for children. The IMF and the World Bank devised adjustment policies to encourage reduction of state-funded services such as healthcare, childcare, education, and housing, which allow women to combine productive and reproductive work. "Such expenditures are conceptualized as unproductive, and the assumption is made that reproduction is compatible with market-oriented productive work without requiring expenditure and investment from the state" (Pearson 1991). In World Bank publications social services are a last resort for the poor. Social services are described as a safety net rather than necessary services that allow women to combine paid employment with household responsibilities (van de Walle *et al.* 1994).

Privatizing state wealth leads to a change in the distribution of wealth. Some people inevitably end up with more than others. Women bear a heavier burden of unemployment. Privatization also leads to a redistribution of responsibility. As the state gives up responsibility for dependents, women more than men are expected to pick up the slack. As I stated above, the causation is circular: women are more likely to be unemployed because they are responsible for the care of dependents which in turn makes it easier for women to spend more time caring for children.

Shrinking labor markets are sending more women home than men. In East Germany women are 60 per cent of the unemployed and under-represented in retraining programs (Rudolph 1992). Women are 50 to 75 per cent of the unemployed in Russia. Before restructuring women were concentrated in non-competitive industries, unskilled jobs, and administrative positions which are the most vulnerable (GDR – Rudolph 1992; USSR – Buckley 1981; Pearson 1991; Hungary – Lampland 1989; Szalai 1991). In Poland, where women are only slightly more than half the unemployed, restructuring in a highly segregated labor market means that fewer jobs are opening up for women. Matching job vacancies to unemployed in 1990, women are less likely to find a new job than men (Tarasiewicz 1991). The expansion of the service sector will provide women only with poorly paid low-skill jobs (Einhorn 1991). In Hungary, the chances for promotion have decreased more for women than for men (Szalai 1991).

Predictably, inequality among women has increased. In a study of urban households in Poland, although the average wage for women moved closer to the average wage for men, the gap between men's and women's median wage grew (Leven 1991). In other words, not all women shared in the narrowing gap between men and women. At the beginning of the study the median wage for women was the same as that for men. By the end of the study the median women's wage was only two-thirds of the median men's wage. The wage gap among men and among women also grew during the year (Leven 1991). Julia Szalai's study of Hungarian women points to a similar division between the women who were able to move into the second economy and women who stayed dependent on employment in state enterprises that is low status and low paid. These relatively well-off women represent 32 per cent of the owners, managers, and members of small enterprises (Szalai 1991). However, if this figure represents women's participation in a new capitalist economy it implies sending many women home. If women represent half the population, women have been more than 40 per cent of the state sector labor force[8].

Attitudes about women's labor market participation have changed with shrinking labor markets. As Barbara Einhorn points out, "the trend in high female unemployment is accompanied by an explicit rebirth of the ideology of women's primary role as mother" (Einhorn 1991). In Poland, "With the growth of unemployment there are government plans to send women home from their jobs in order to improve the situation on the labor market" (Tarasiewicz 1991: 183). It is easier to maintain political legitimacy with high female unemployment. "The neo-classical type of economic restructuring will create massive unemployment, and it is easier and more comfortable to get rid of the female work force, which is considered unreliable anyway. . . . It is also an ideological message. The new conservative right-of-centre government puts the emphasis on the family . . . and women are expected to be the pillars" (Kiss 1991). "It is generally accepted in Poland that a man needs a job more than a woman" (Tarasiewicz 1991).

Governments assign responsibility to women without children along with women who already have children. Women are seen as potential mothers and responsible for giving birth to the next generation. While women's responsibility for children is implied in the changing priorities associated with the privatization of state-owned enterprises, it has been explicit in the rhetoric of the new governments. Milica Antic describes the attitude of the Slovene government toward women. "Women are mentioned only as mothers. [In the new draft constitution] motherhood represents a special highly appreciated value. A mother's place is, of course, with the children in the family, and here I'd like to point out that the proposal for a constitution privileges the family above any alternative patterns of living" (Antic 1991:

152). Legislation in Poland restricting abortion further emphasizes women's role as mothers. According to the introduction to the draft act of "legal protection of the conceived child," procreation is "the supreme mission of women" even when it entails risks to her health or her life (quoted in Fuszara 1991: 125).

The responsibility for children disadvantages women in the new competitive labor markets. Besides restructuring industry, privatization means that childcare centers are raising costs or being labelled an inefficient burden on newly "freed" enterprises. Women must give up income either in the form of higher payments for childcare or lower income if they stay home. Because both socialist and capitalist systems place responsibility for maintaining families on women, women will pay the costs of privatizing responsibility for dependents. Einhorn points out that the first subsidy to be removed in many East Central European countries was that on children's clothes. Because women are responsible for feeding and clothing the family, they are the ones most affected by the removal of subsidies (Einhorn 1991). One study estimated that childcare costs in Poland amounted to 81 per cent of the average salary for urban women (Leven 1991)[9]. For 50 per cent of the women surveyed childcare for one child would cost them 92 per cent or more of their salary. If we consider that the women who were able to retain jobs with rising salaries or obtain better positions are more likely to be women without small children the effect of allocating responsibility for children becomes apparent.

Women are not simply more likely to lose their jobs they are more likely to be forced to leave them because they cannot afford childcare. This may seem desirable after many years of the double burden. However, men are not seeing a rise in real wages to make up for the loss of their wives' incomes. Women still feel the need to work to provide basic necessities. Furthermore, feminists have been pointing out the risks of relying on men's wages for support since Mary Wollstonecraft wrote her treatise in the eighteenth century. Men can leave. In Poland, for example, 16 per cent of households with children were headed by women in 1984[10]. Furthermore, most women do not want to stay home. A survey in East Germany indicated that only 3 per cent of women wished to restrict themselves to household labor (Rudolph 1992).

As the state-owned enterprises are sold off and workers lose guaranteed employment, both women and men are less secure in their jobs. This hinders women and men attempting to combine paid work with parenting. The threat of unemployment prevents parents from demanding time to care for a sick child or refusing to work late so they can be with their children. Fewer women and men are taking sick leave in Poland, presumably because they are aware of rising job insecurity (Leven 1991). Also a smaller number of women are applying for the three-year maternity leave in Hungary because it would increase their job insecurity (Szalai 1991).

While the costs of childcare can price women out of the market, the increased job insecurity reduces workers' power when bargaining for a work structure that facilitates combining work and home responsibilities. Under full employment policies women were in a better position to demand that work accommodate household responsibilities. Women in Eastern Europe may have had fewer job opportunities than men in Eastern Europe, but they were more likely to have an opportunity. In the new labor market allowing household responsibilities to interfere with work could increase the probability of being laid off. Unlike in West Germany, being single or childless in East Germany was not linked to labor market participation (Rudolph 1992). A woman is caught between the inability to improve her job prospects because she has full responsibility for her children and the inability to get her husband to share more responsibility for household tasks because it will lower his job prospects.

With the insecurity of markets, women's power to bargain for a new distribution of household labor declines. In the West, women's household bargaining power is linked both to her own job opportunities and her husband's (Segal 1990). When her job opportunities are reduced her credibility is weakened should she threaten to leave the relationship and support herself. When his job opportunities are reduced claims that household responsibilities may threaten his employment become more credible.

## PRIVATIZATION, EFFICIENCY, RESPONSIBILITY, AND WELFARE

Privatization is not just a part of the transition from socialism to capitalism. Privatization of state-owned enterprises and social services have been popular in Western Europe and other capitalist economies long before Solidarnosc took the reins in Poland. Privatization has been advocated as a way of improving efficiency. However, if efficiency does not include a concept of responsibility, we cannot determine what is truly more efficient and what is not.

We should make a distinction between improving efficiency and paying women (or men) less to do more. An improvement in efficiency should be reserved for situations where the same resources – raw materials, hours of skilled labor, and machines – can be used to produce more. If privatization simply lowers workers' bargaining power and, therefore, lowers their wages, an improvement in efficiency has not occurred. A redistribution of income has occurred. Prices are supposed to provide information about scarcity. If no reallocation of resources occurs, there cannot be an improvement in efficiency.

The transfer of responsibility for children to women does not necessarily improve efficiency. It lowers the costs of labor to the factory where the women work. It increases women's workload. If women do not leave work, there is no reallocation of resources: no efficiency gain. When childcare costs are so high that women must drop out of the labor force to care for their children it reduces their autonomy. It increases their financial dependence on their husbands. With fewer autonomous actors, we can no longer take for granted the ability of the market to register preferences and allocate goods. If women are unable to care for themselves and their children at even the lowest standard of living, they cannot make the most basic choice: to be married or not.

Recognizing that responsibility affects the well-being of economic agents it is easy to see how women's position in Eastern Europe could go from bad to worse. Before privatization women held segregated jobs that did not reflect their education and faced a double burden. After privatization many women with children were or will be pushed out of paid employment. They are unable to pay rising costs of luxuries and are more dependent on their husbands for basic survival. Many women with children who keep their jobs will increase their burden by taking less money home after paying for childcare. They will have to work more hours because their employers will tolerate fewer absences to care for sick children or catch up on the housework. Many women without children will be forced to bear unwanted children when reproductive health services are reduced. They will face fewer job opportunities from employers who expect them to drop out of the job market to have children.

When responsibility for children is assigned to women and not men, markets are like a game of monopoly where women start the game with less cash, and therefore, buy fewer properties and receive less income. When the state gives up responsibility to private families the disparity between men's and women's welfare increases. Because women are responsible for children, the trade-off between work and childcare or staying home is made based on women's income not men's. Childcare costs come out of women's paychecks and when the cost of childcare goes up, a woman's share of household income goes down. Her ability to support herself and her child alone is eliminated and her bargaining power within the family falls.

The point is not that socialism and public ownership are inherently better for women than capitalism. Nevertheless, responsibility for those who cannot care for themselves is a necessary component of the evaluation of different institutional structures. Institutions should be able to value both women's autonomy and the value of caring for those who cannot care for themselves.

## ACKNOWLEDGEMENTS

I gratefully acknowledge the comments and criticisms of Hana Havelkova, Perry Paterson, Kate Lingley, Lynn Duggan, and the participants of the

"Out of the Margin" conference, Amsterdam, June 1993. All remaining errors are, of course, mine.

## NOTES

1 See Nelson (1991) for a review of neoclassical economic theory of families.
2 See Gary Becker (1976).
3 Many scholars might argue that socialism condemns autonomy, but I interpret the emphasis on workers controlling the means of production as a desire for autonomy.
4 In Hungary how generous leave benefits were depended upon the government's emphasis on pro-natalist and labor shortage policies (Lampland 1989).
5 See Michelle Barrett and Mary McIntosh (1982) – UK; Dwyer and Bruce (1988) – developing nations; Barbara Einhorn (1990) – East Central Europe.
6 We should not discount completely the value of rhetoric. An explicit government position and legal structure that defines women's status as equal is not the same as an institutional structure that supports women's equality. However, simply saying that women's status is equal and telling entire generations of women that they are equal to men all their lives makes a difference.
7 The data in Duggan was compiled from German socio-economic panel data. The household work includes overlapping tasks.
8 Based on men's and women's labor force participation by age listed in Szalai (1991). In most age groups employment share was closer to 45 per cent.
9 Average monthly daycare costs rose from 130,000 zlotys in July 1989 – 58 per cent of the average woman's salary – to 550,000 zlotys in July 1990 – 81 per cent of the average woman's salary (Leven 1991).
10 Calculated from data in *Rocznik Statystyczny* [statistical yearbook] (1988; Warsaw: Glowny Urzad Statystyczny.

## REFERENCES

Antic, M.G. (1991) "Democracy Between Tyranny and Liberty: Women in Post-'Socialist' Slovenia", *Feminist Review* 39, Autumn.
Barrett, M. and McIntosh, M. (1982) *The Anti-Social Family*, London: Verso.
Becker, G. (1976) *The Economic Approach to Human Behavior*, Chicago: University of Chicago Press.
Bollobás, E. (1988) "On the Situation of Women in Hungary", mimeo of paper presented at the meeting of Hungarian Democratic Forum.
Buckley, M. (1981) "Women in the Soviet Union", *Feminist Review* 8, Summer.
——— (1989) "The 'Woman Question' in the Contemporary Soviet Union", in S. Kruks, R. Rapp and M. Young (eds) *Promissory Notes: Women in the Translation to Socialism*, New York: Monthly Review Press.
Castle-Kanerová, M. (1991) "Interview with Alena Valterova, Founder of the Political Party of Women and Mothers", *Feminist Review* 39, Winter.
Duggan, L. (1994) "The Effect of Family Policy on the Household Division of Labour: A comparison of East and West Germany", *Vierteljahrshefte zür Wirtschaftsforschung* 1–2, Deutsches Institut für Wirtschaftsforschung: 104–111.
Dwyer, D. and Bruce, J. (eds) (1988) *"A Home Divided: Women and Income in the Third World"*, Stanford: Stanford University Press.
Einhorn, B. (1989) "Socialist Emancipation: The Women's Movement in the

GDR", in S. Kruks, R. Rapp, and M. Young (eds) *Promissory Notes: Women in the Translation to Socialism*, New York: Monthly Review Press.

—— (1991) "Where Have All the Women Gone ?: Women and the Women's Movement in East Central Europe", *Feminist Review* 39, Autumn.

Friedman, M. (1962) *Capitalism and Freedom*, Chicago: Chicago University Press.

Fuszara, M. (1991) "Legal Regulation of Abortion in Poland", *Signs*, Autumn.

Goldman, W.Z. (1989) "Women, the Family, and the New Revolutionary Order in the Soviet Union", in S. Kruks, R. Rapp, and M. Young (eds) *Promissory Notes: Women in the Translation to Socialism*, New York: Monthly Review Press.

Independent Women's Democratic Initiative (NEZHDI) (1991) "Democracy Without Women Is No Democracy", *Feminist Review* 39, Winter.

Kiss, Y. (1991) "The Second 'No': Women in Hungary", *Feminist Review* 39, Winter.

Lampland, M. (1989) "Biographies of Liberation: Testimonials of Labor in Socialist Hungary", in S. Kruks, R. Rapp, and M. Young (eds) *Promissory Notes: Women in the Translation to Socialism*, New York: Monthly Review Press.

Leven, B. (1991) "The Welfare Effects on Women of Poland's Economic Reforms", *Journal of Economic Issues* 25, 2 June.

Nelson, J. (1991) "Towards a Feminist Theory of the Family", mimeo, University of California, Davis.

Pearson, R. (1991) "Questioning Perestroika: A Socialist-Feminist Interrogation", *Feminist Review* 39, Winter.

Pujol, M. (1992) *Feminism and Anti-Feminism in Early Economic Thought*, Aldershot, United Kingdom: Edward Elgar.

Rosenberg, D.J. (1991) "Shock Therapy: GDR Women in Transition from a Socialist Welfare State to a Social Market Economy", *Signs*, Autumn.

Rudolph, H. (1992) "The Status of Women in a Changing Economy: East Germany", mimeo.

Segal, L. (1990) *Slow Motion: Changing Masculinities, Changing Men*, New Brunswick, NJ: Rutgers University Press.

Sobchak, A. (1991) "Transition to a Market Economy", *The CATO Journal* 11, 3, Fall.

Szalai, J. (1991) "Some Aspects of the Changing Situation of Women in Hungary", *Signs*, Autumn.

Tarasiewicz, M. (1991) "Women in Poland: Choices To Be Made", *Feminist Review* 39, Winter.

263

# 17

# GENDER, PROPERTY, AND LAND RIGHTS

## Bridging a critical gap in economic analysis and policy[1]

*Bina Agarwal*

Please go and ask the *sarkar* [government] why when it distributes land we don't get a title. Are we not peasants? If my husband throws me out, what is my security?

(Message conveyed by poor peasant women to the West Bengal government in 1979 through their women representatives on the village council)[2]

Economic analyses and policies concerning women have long been pre-occupied with employment, to the neglect of a crucial determinant of women's situation, namely the gender gap in command over property. This is especially (but not only) true in analyses relating to South Asia. It is argued here that the gender gap in the ownership and control of property is the single most critical contributor to the gender gap in economic well-being, social status and empowerment. In primarily rural economies such as those of South Asia the most important form of property is arable land. A struggle for gender equality in command over landed property will there-fore need to occupy center stage in South Asian women's struggle for egalitarian gender relations.

The discussion below is divided into five sections. Section one examines the conceptual links between gender, property, and land rights. Section two elaborates upon why it is important for rural women to have independent rights in land, especially for women's empowerment. Section three looks at gender relations historically in those South Asian communities in which women traditionally enjoyed rights in land. Section four identifies the obstacles women face in realizing effective land rights in most parts of South Asia today, and illustrates how women's command over economic resources is crucially mediated by non-economic factors. Finally, section five highlights some aspects of the interventions needed for change.

264

# GENDER, PROPERTY AND LAND: SOME CONCEPTUAL LINKS

In examining the relationship between gender and property, five interrelated issues need particular focus: gender relations and a household's property status; gender relations and women's property status; the distinction between ownership and control of property; the distinctiveness of land as property; and what is meant by rights in land. The first three issues are discussed in the subsection below, and the last two in separate subsections.

## Household property and women's property

The links between gender subordination and property need to be sought in not only the distribution of property between households but also in its distribution between men and women, in not only who owns the property but also who controls it, and in relation not only to private property but also to communal property. Further, gender equality in legal rights to own property does not guarantee gender equality in actual ownership, nor does ownership guarantee control. The distinctions between law and practice and between ownership and control are especially critical in relation to women.

This formulation departs significantly from standard Marxist analysis, particularly from that of Engels' ([1884] 1972) still-influential though much criticized exposition, where intra-family gender relations are seen as structured primarily by two overlapping economic factors: the property status of the households to which the women belong, and women's participation in wage labor. Engels argued that in capitalist societies, gender relations would be hierarchical among the property-owning families of the bourgeoisie where women did not go out to work and were economically dependent on men, and egalitarian in propertyless proletarian families where women were in the labor force. The ultimate restoration of women to their rightful status, in his view, required the total abolition of private property (i.e. a move to socialism), the socialization of housework and childcare, and the full participation of women in the labor force[3].

In this analysis, therefore, the presumed equality of gender relations in a working-class family rested on both husband and wife being propertyless and in the labor force, and the inequality in the bourgeois family rested on men being propertied and women being both propertyless and outside the labor force. This underlying emphasis on the relational aspect of gender is clearly important. So is the emphasis on women's economic dependency as a critical constituent of the material basis of gender oppression. However, by advocating the abolition of all private property as the solution, Engels by-passed the issue of women's property rights altogether, and left open the question: what would be the impact on gender relations in propertied

265

households if women too were propertied as individuals? Entry into the labor force is not the only way to reduce economic dependence; independent rights in property would be another, and possibly the more effective way.

Engels' emphasis on women's entry into the labor force as a necessary condition for their emancipation has been enormously influential in shaping the thinking of left-wing political parties and non-party groups, including left-wing women's groups in South Asia[4]. They too give centrality to women's employment, but the necessary accompaniments emphasized by Engels, namely the abolition of private property in male hands and the socialization of housework and childcare, have largely been neglected, as has the question of women's property rights.

A critical additional point (missed in Engels' analysis and associated discussions) is that of property control. Property advantage stems not only from ownership, but also from effective control over it. In societies which underwent socialist revolutions, while private property ownership was legally abolished, control over wealth-generating property remained mainly with men; any positive effects on gender relations that could have stemmed from the change in ownership, if accompanied by gender-egalitarian mechanisms of control, thus went unrealized[5]. Indeed in most societies today it is men as a gender (even if not all men as individuals) who largely control wealth-generating property, whether or not it is privately owned, including as managers in large corporations. Even property that is under State, community, or clan ownership remains effectively under the managerial control of selected men through their dominance in both traditional and modern institutions: caste or clan councils, village-elected bodies, State bureaucracies at all levels[6], and so on. Also in most countries, men as a gender exercise dominance over the instruments through which their existing advantages of property ownership and control get perpetuated, such as the institutions that enact and implement laws[7], the mechanisms of recruitment into bodies which exercise control over (private or public) property, the institutions which play an important role in shaping gender ideology, and so on.

A second issue concerning the relationship between gender and property is: how do we define a woman's class? Marxist analysis, for instance, implicitly assumes that women belong to the class of their husbands or fathers. Hence women of propertied "bourgeois" households are part of the bourgeoisie and those of proletarian households are counted as proletarian. However, there are at least two well-recognized problems with this characterization:

- A woman's class position defined through that of a man is more open to change than that of a man: a well-placed marriage can raise it, divorce or widowhood can lower it.

- To the extent that women, even of propertied households, do not own property themselves, it is difficult to characterize their class position; some have even argued that women constitute a class in themselves[8].

In fact, neither deriving women's class from the property status of men nor deriving it from their own propertyless status appears adequate, although both positions reflect dimensions of reality. Women of rich households do gain economically and socially from their parents' or husbands' class positions. But women also share common concerns which cut across derived class privilege (or deprivation), such as vulnerability to domestic violence; responsibility for housework and childcare (even if not all women perform such labor themselves – the more affluent ones can hire helpers); gender inequalities in legal rights; and the risk of poverty if (parental or marital) family support ceases. This ambiguity in women's class position impinges with critical force on the possibilities of collective action among women. On the one hand, class differences among women, derived through men, can be divisive. On the other hand, the noted commonalities between women's situations and the relatively vicarious character of their class privilege make class distinctions between them less sharp than those between men, and could provide the basis for collective action on several counts[9].

A third aspect of the relationship between gender and property concerns the links between gender ideology and property. For instance:

- Gender ideologies can obstruct women from getting property rights. Assumptions about women's needs, roles, and capabilities impinge on the framing and implementation of public policies and property laws. Again, ideas about gender underlie practices such as female seclusion, which restrict women's ability both to exercise their existing property claims and to successfully challenge persisting gender inequalities in law, policy, and practice in relation to such claims. Hence ideological struggles are integrally linked to women's struggles over property rights.
- Those who own and/or control wealth-generating property can directly or indirectly control the principal institutions that shape ideology, such as educational and religious establishments and the media (including newspapers, TV, radio, film, theater, as well as literature and the arts). These can shape views in either gender-progressive or gender-retrogressive directions.
- The impact of gender ideologies can vary by a household's property status. For instance, both propertied and propertyless households may espouse the ideology of female seclusion, but the former group would be in a better economic position to enforce its practice, and in so doing reinforce its emulation by unpropertied households as a mark of social status. At the same time, gender ideologies and associated practices are

not derived from property differences alone, nor can they be seen in purely economic-functional terms. Rather they would tend to shift and change in interaction with economic shifts.

A fourth issue that arises in relation to women and property is the possible links of women's property rights with control over women's sexuality, marriage practices, and kinship structures. For instance, would women with independent property rights be subject to greater or lesser familial control over their sexual freedom than those without them? It would also be important to examine whether societies which historically recognized women's inheritance rights in immovable property, in order to keep the property intact and within their purview, tended to control women's choice of marriage partners and post-marital residence (as discussed later).

## The significance of land as property

Thus far we have discussed property in general, but not all forms of property are equally significant in all contexts, nor equally coveted. In the agrarian economies of South Asia, arable land is the most valued form of property, for its economic, political and symbolic significance. It is a productive, wealth-creating, and livelihood-sustaining asset. Traditionally it has been the basis of political power and social status. For many, it provides a sense of identity and rootedness within the village; and often in people's minds land has a durability and permanence which no other asset possesses. Although other types of property such as cash, jewellery, cattle, and even domestic goods (the usual content of, say, dowry in rural India and Nepal) could in principle be converted into land, in practice rural land markets are often constrained, and land is not always readily available for sale (Rosenzweig and Wolpin 1985). In any case, ancestral land often has a symbolic meaning (Selvaduri 1976) or ritual importance (Krause 1982) which purchased land does not. Hence in land disputes people may end up spending more to retain a disputed ancestral plot than its market value would justify. In other words, both the form that property takes and its origin are important in defining its significance and the associated possibility of conflict over it.

## What do we mean by rights in land?

Rights are defined here as claims that are legally and socially recognized and enforceable by an external legitimized authority, be it a village-level institution or some higher level judicial or executive body of the State. Rights in land can be in the form of ownership or of usufruct (that is rights of use), associated with differing degrees of freedom to lease out, mortgage, bequeath, or sell. Land rights can stem from inheritance, community membership, transfers by the State, or tenancy arrangements, purchase, and so on. Rights in land also have a temporal and sometimes locational dimension: they may be hereditary, or accrue only for a person's lifetime, or for a lesser period; and they may be conditional on the person residing where the land is located.

As distinct from rights in land, a woman may, in theory, also have "access" to land in other ways, including through informal concessions granted by kin or friends. For instance, a man may allow his sister the use of a plot of his land out of goodwill. But she cannot claim it as a right and call for its enforcement. Having "rights" thus provides a measure of security that other forms of access typically do not.

Four additional distinctions are relevant here. First is the need to distinguish between the legal recognition of a claim and its social recognition, and between recognition and enforcement. A woman may have the legal right to inherit property, but this may remain merely a right on paper if the law is not enforced, or if the claim is not socially recognized as legitimate and family members exert pressure on her to forfeit her share in favor, say, of her brothers. Second is the earlier noted distinction between the ownership of land and its effective control. (Control itself can have multiple meanings, such as the ability to decide how the land is used, how its produce is disposed of, whether it can be leased out, mortgaged, bequeathed, sold, and so on.) It is sometimes assumed incorrectly that legal ownership carries with it the right of control in all these senses. In fact legal ownership may be accompanied by legal restrictions on disposal: for instance, among the Jaffna Tamils in Sri Lanka, under the *Thesawalami* legal code a married woman needs her husband's consent to alienate land which she legally owns. Third, it is important to distinguish between ownership and use rights vested in individuals and those vested in a group. Fourth, one might distinguish between rights conferred via inheritance and those conferred by State transfers of land.

Given the different forms (ownership and usufruct, as vested in individuals or in groups) that land rights can take, and the varying organization of production and distribution that can accompany them, it is not always possible to specify *a priori* what would be the most desirable form for women's land rights to take. But a broad specification can be attempted. When speaking of women having rights in land I mean effective rights, that is rights not just in law but in practice. By "independent" rights I mean rights independent of male ownership or control (that is excluding joint titles with men). Independent rights would be preferable to joint titles with husbands for several reasons: one, with joint titles it could prove difficult for women to gain control over their share in case of marital breakup. Two, women would also be less in a position to escape from marital violence: as some Bihari village women said to me, "for retaining the land we would be tied to the man, even if he beat us." Three, wives may have different land use priorities from husbands which they would be in a better position to act upon with independent land rights. Four, women with independent rights would be better placed to control the produce. Five, with joint titles the question of how the land would be inherited could prove a contentious one. This is not to deny that joint titles with husbands would be better than having no titles at all; but many of the advantages of possessing land would not accrue to women by joint titles alone.

Here the distinctions mentioned earlier between rights vested in individuals and those vested in groups, and between privatized land transfers via inheritance and land transfers by the State, need elaboration. In relation to privatized inheritable landed property, effective land rights would mean inheritance as individuals linked with full rights of control over land use and its produce. In State transfers of land to women, effective rights could either mean individual titles conferring ownership and control rights exactly as with private land; or they could mean rights in land held by a group of women through joint ownership or long lease, and allowing full control over land use and its produce but excluding the right to sell or bequeath it. While individually owned land could be advantageous in distress circumstances in that it can be mortgaged or sold, group rights could protect the land from moneylenders or scheming relatives and enable its more productive use through group investment (as elaborated later).

## Some South Asian specificities

With the decline in communal land in South Asia, access to privatized land acquires a critical importance today which it did not have even a century ago. In India, for instance, by a rough estimate, about 85.6 per cent of arable land is likely to be in private hands[10]. Hence the importance of women's land rights spelt out in the next section, while couched in general terms, is especially focussed on rights in privatized land, with two caveats: one, given the importance of communal land (e.g. village commons) to the rural poor, and especially to poor women (who depend on it for firewood, fodder, and other items basic for survival: Agarwal 1992), there is a strong case for protecting the communal nature of any land which still exists in that form. Two, it is necessary to explore the possibilities of new institutional arrangements for jointly owned/controlled land holdings by groups of women, rather than by groups of households (as is the usual focus).

In legal terms women's property rights in South Asia are governed by "personal laws" which vary a good deal by religion and region, forming a complex mosaic. Most of these legal systems give women considerable inheritance rights, and in traditionally patrilineal groups much greater rights than they enjoyed by custom, as a result of legal reform, especially after 1950 (as detailed in Agarwal 1994). But in virtually all the legal systems, some gender inequalities remain. For instance, some systems prescribe lower shares for women (Islamic law, for example, prescribes a daughter's share as half that of a son). Some others restrict the conditions under which women can inherit and retain that inheritance (e.g. the *Maluki Ain* in Nepal only allows unmarried daughters over the age of thirty-five to inherit, and they forfeit their claims on subsequent marriage). Yet other legal systems restrict women's freedom to dispose of their inherited land (as noted for the Jaffna Tamils in Sri Lanka).

Inequalities also stem from gender discriminatory tenurial enactments which affect women's rights specifically in agricultural land. For instance, in India, agricultural land under tenancy is exempt from the scope of the Hindu Succession Act (HSA) of 1956 (which gave Hindu women considerable inheritance rights across India): such land is governed instead by the rules of devolution specified in state-level enactments[11]. In a number of states, mostly in northwest India, these enactments specify succession rules prevailing before the HSA was passed, and which give priority to male agnatic heirs. Again in the fixation of ceilings under land reform laws, many states allow the cultivating household to retain additional land on account of adult sons but not adult daughters. Also, in most states, the holdings of both spouses are aggregated in assessing "family" land, and there is considerable arbitrariness in deciding whose portion will be declared surplus and forfeited. As a result, in several cases the wife's land (and not many women have some) has been declared surplus and taken over by the government, while the husband's land has remained intact (Saradamoni 1983).

Even more critical than the persisting legal inequities is the gap between women's legal rights in land and actual ownership, and between ownership and effective control. Although economic surveys typically do not collect gender-disaggregated data, village studies (especially anthropological accounts) indicate that in most parts of South Asia women do not own land and even fewer are able to exercise effective control over it[12]. These gaps are especially apparent in communities which customarily practised patrilineal inheritance[13]. Communities traditionally practising matrilineal or bilateral inheritance were few and limited to northeast India, parts of south India, and to Sri Lanka. Before examining the nature of gender relations in the latter communities, consider below why having independent rights in land is important for women's well-being and overall empowerment.

## WHY WOMEN NEED INDEPENDENT RIGHTS IN LAND

The importance of South Asian rural women having independent rights in arable land rests on several interconnected arguments which can be grouped into four broad categories: welfare, efficiency, equality, and empowerment[14].

271

## The welfare argument

Especially among poor rural households, rights in land could reduce women's own and, more generally, the household's risk of poverty and destitution. This is due partly to the general positive effect of giving women access to economic resources independently of men; and partly to the specific advantages of possessing land.

Consider first the general case. In large parts of South Asia a systematic bias is noted against women and female children in intra-household access to resources for basic necessities such as health care, and in some degree also food. This is revealed in gender differences in one or more of the following indicators (detailed in Agarwal 1986, 1994): malnourishment, morbidity, mortality, hospital admissions, health expenditures, and female-adverse sex ratios (females per 1,000 males), although the evidence on food allocation *per se* is less conclusive (Harriss 1990). The extent of this anti-female bias varies regionally, but it exists in some degree almost everywhere, particularly as revealed by the sex ratios which are female-adverse across all of South Asia, except Kerala in southwest India. The bias is strongest in northwest India, Pakistan and Bangladesh, and much less stark in south India and Sri Lanka, where the sex ratios, although still female-adverse, are closer to parity.

Further, notable differences have been found in how men and women of poor rural households spend the incomes under their control: women typically spend almost all their incomes on the family's basic needs; men usually spend a significant part on their personal needs (tobacco, liquor, etc.) (Per-Lee 1981; Mencher 1988; Blumberg 1991). Research findings also suggest that children's nutritional status tends to be much more positively linked to the mother's earnings than the father's (Kumar 1978).

In other words, women's and children's risk of poverty and physical well-being could depend significantly on whether or not women have direct access to income and productive assets such as land, and not just access mediated through husbands or other male family members. For female-headed households without adult male support, this link between direct access to economic resources and physical well-being needs no emphasis. Such households constitute an estimated 19–20 per cent of all households in India and Bangladesh[15].

Moreover, as noted earlier, without independent resources even women from rich parental or marital homes can be economically vulnerable, in case of marital breakup or widowhood. In parts of western and northwestern India, not uncommonly, women – divorced, deserted or widowed – can be found working as agricultural laborers on the farms of their well-off brothers or brothers-in-law (Omvedt 1981, and personal observation). Similarly, in east India and Bangladesh, there are many cases of women, married into prosperous households, being left destitute after widowhood

(Cain *et al.* 1979; Vina Mazumdar, personal communication). "This fact," as Omvedt (1981:21) observes, "perhaps . . . more than any other, shows the essential propertylessness of women *as women.*"

Within this general argument for women's independent access to economic resources, the case for effective rights in land is especially strong. Consider, for a start, the relationship between land access and poverty at the household level. In India, in 1982, an estimated 89 per cent of rural households owned some land (Government of India 1987:9), and an estimated 74 per cent operated some (Government of India 1986:12)[16]. In Bangladesh, in 1978, the percentage of rural households owning some land (arable or homestead) was 89, and those owning arable land was 67 (Jannuzi and Peach 1980:101). In Sri Lanka, in 1982, 89 per cent of agricultural operators owned some land (including home gardens) (Government of Sri Lanka 1984:17). Although, due to high land concentration, the majority of these households across South Asia only have marginal plots, they face a significantly lower risk of absolute poverty than landless households: several studies note a negative relationship between the incidence of absolute poverty and land access (owned or operated) (Ali *et al.* 1981; Gaiha and Kazmi 1981; Sundaram and Tendulkar 1983). The direct advantages of possessing land (unless the land is of very poor quality) stem from the various production possibilities it provides, such as for growing crops, fodder or trees, keeping a vegetable garden or livestock, practising sericulture, and so on. In addition, land provides indirect benefits, such as increasing access to credit, helping agricultural labor maintain its reserve price and even push up the aggregate real wage rate (Raj and Tharakan 1983) and, where the land is owned, serving as a mortgageable or saleable asset during a crisis. Moreover, for widows and the elderly, ownership of land and other wealth strengthens the support they receive from relatives by increasing their bargaining power within the household. As an old man put it: "without property, children do not look after their parents well" (Caldwell *et al.* 1988:191).

However, given the noted biases in the intra-family distribution of benefits from household resources, exclusively male rights in land, which would render the household less susceptible to poverty by some average measure, will not automatically benefit all its members. And on grounds of both women's and children's welfare, there is a strong case for supporting women's effective rights in private or public land, independently of men. Although such rights are especially important as a poverty alleviation measure for women in poor rural households, they are also relevant, as noted, for women of better-off households, given the risk of poverty that all rural women face without independent resources.

It needs emphasis here that the welfare case for women's land rights stands even if the plot is too small to be economically viable on its own. Indeed those opposing female inheritance in land often emphasize that women might end up inheriting economically non-viable holdings. In my view, this could be a problem where cultivation is seen as the sole basis of subsistence, but not where land-based production is one element (although a critical one) in a diversified livelihood system. For instance, a plot of land which does not produce enough grain for family subsistence could still support trees or provide fodder. Moreover, although forced collective farming is likely to be inefficient, cases of people voluntarily cooperating to undertake land-based joint production and/or investment activities also exist (as elaborated later).

Of course, as the industrial and service sectors of South Asian economies expand, arable land would become a less significant source of livelihood and form of property. But today the majority of South Asia's population still depends on agriculture as a primary or an important supplementary source of sustenance. And, most villagers, even those deriving their income from non-farm activities, depend on village common land and forests for fuel and other basic necessities. Moreover, in none of the South Asian countries do projections predict a rapid absorption of labor (especially female labor) into urban industry in the foreseeable future. Also, since it is predominantly male workers who migrate from rural to urban areas (Bardhan 1977), women's dependence on the rural/agricultural sector remains greater than men's. Although the rural non-farm sector holds potential, its record in providing viable livelihoods has been regionally mixed, with some regions providing high returns/high wages (such as the Indian Punjab), but many others being characterized by low returns and low wages (Islam 1986; Basant and Kumar 1989; Hazell and Haggblade 1990). In particular, women's non-farm earnings appear characteristically low and uncertain (Islam 1987; Singh and Kelles-Vitanen 1987). Hence, although women's earning opportunities in the non-farm sector clearly need strengthening, for most women non-farm livelihoods can at best supplement not substitute for land-based livelihoods. Notably also, those who do well in the rural non-farm sector through self-employment are usually those with land (Islam 1986; Chadha 1992). Effectively, therefore, land will continue to occupy a place of primacy in South Asian livelihoods in general and female livelihood systems in particular, for quite some time to come.

Also, with sectoral shifts, although the importance of land as property may decline, income-generating property *per se* would remain a significant mediator of social relations and an important determinant of social status and political power. Who owns and/or controls property would therefore still be a relevant consideration; and many of the arguments for gender equality in command over landed property would apply to other types of property as well.

## The efficiency argument

In several contexts, titling women with land could increase output. There are many women operating as household heads with the primary and sometimes sole responsibility for organizing cultivation and ensuring family subsistence, but without titles to the land they are cultivating. For instance, due to long-term male outmigration many women are serving as *de facto* household heads, especially but not only in the hill regions of the subcontinent. Or widows are cultivating plots given to them from joint family estates (as part of their inheritance claims to their deceased husbands' lands), but the plots are still in their in-laws' names. Again, tribal women cultivating communal land rarely get titles to their fields when the land is privatized, since the State typically gives the titles only to male farmers. Titling women in these circumstances and providing them with infrastructural support could increase output by increasing their access to credit[17], and to technology and information on productivity-increasing agricultural practices and inputs (in the dissemination of which both a class and a gender bias prevails)[18].

A more general issue, however, is the likely efficiency effect of women inheriting land. Female inheritance is often opposed in South Asia on the grounds that it will further reduce farm size and increase land fragmentation, and thus reduce output and also marketed surplus. Is this fear valid? Existing evidence indicates otherwise. Small-sized farms typically have a higher value of annual output per unit cultivated area than large-sized ones: this inverse size-productivity relationship which was strong in the 1950s and 1960s (the pre-green revolution period) has sustained in the post-green revolution period, even if somewhat weakened, as studies for India, Bangladesh and Pakistan bear out (Berry and Cline 1979; Agarwal 1983; Boyce 1987). Small farmers have adopted the new technology in most areas where large farmers have done so, although after a time lag (Lipton and Longhurst 1989). The evidence on marketed surplus also does not support the skeptics' claim that this will decline because small farmers will retain a larger percentage for self-consumption[19]. In any case, an improvement in the consumption of the poor in the farm sector cannot, in itself, be seen as an inefficient outcome. Indeed, a dietary improvement may add to labor productivity (Strauss 1986; Deolalikar 1988).

The existing evidence thus gives no reason to expect that land distribution in favor of women would reduce output on account of the size effect. And the problem of land fragmentation can arise equally with male inheritance: in both cases it calls for land consolidation. There could of course be a negative output effect of female inheritance through what I term the "gender-transfer effect" (viz. some of the land which would have gone only to men would now go to women), insofar as women usually face some gender-specific disadvantages as managers of farms, when operating in factor and product markets. But again the answer lies in easing these constraints by institutional support to women farmers, rather than in disinheriting them.

Indeed the experience of non-governmental credit institutions such as the Grameen bank in Bangladesh suggests that women are often better credit risks than men (Hossain 1988). Also, supporting women as farm managers would enlarge the talent and information pool; and in very poor households allocating resources to women could increase their productivity by improving their nutrition.

The provision of land to women could have other indirect benefits as well, such as (a) reducing migration to cities, both by women themselves and by family members dependent on them; and (b) increasing farm incomes in women's hands, which in turn could generate a higher demand for non-farm goods that are produced locally and labor intensively, thus creating more rural jobs[20].

## The equality and empowerment arguments

Equality and empowerment concerns, unlike welfare and efficiency considerations, stem less from the implications of land access or deprivation in absolute terms, and more from the implications of men's and women's relative access to land. And they affect particularly women's ability to challenge male dominance within the home and in society.

The equality argument for land rights rests especially on two concerns. One is the larger issue of gender equality as a measure of a just society, in which equality of rights over productive resources would be an important part. The other relates to the specific link between gender equality in land rights and women's empowerment.

Empowerment is defined here as: *a process that enhances the ability of disadvantaged ("powerless") individuals or groups to challenge and change (in their favor) existing power relationships that place them in subordinate economic, social and political positions.* Empowerment can manifest itself in acts of individual resistance as well as in group mobilization. Entitling women with land could empower them economically, as well as strengthen their ability to challenge social and political gender inequities.

A telling illustration is provided by the Bodhgaya movement in Bihar (eastern India) in the late 1970s, in which women and men of landless households participated in an extended struggle for ownership rights in the land they cultivated, held illegally by a *Math* (a temple-monastery complex). During the struggle women demanded independent land rights, not only for reasons of economic security but also because this impinged on marital relations. They feared that if land titles went only to husbands, wives would be rendered relatively even more powerless, and vulnerable to domestic violence. Their fears proved correct. Where only men got titles there was

276

an increase in drunkenness, wife-beating and threats: "Get out of the house, the land is mine now" (Manimala 1983: 15). Where women received titles they could now assert: "We had tongues but could not speak, we had feet but could not walk. Now that we have the land, we have the strength to speak and walk" (Alaka and Chetna 1987: 26). Similar responses were noted in China, when the Chinese Communist Party promulgated the Agrarian Reform law in 1947, which entitled women to hold separate land deeds for the first time (Hinton 1972).

Land rights can also improve the treatment a woman receives from other family members, by strengthening her bargaining power (Dreze 1990, and personal observation in northwest India). Although employment and other means of earning could help in similar ways, in the rural context land usually offers greater security than other income sources – at the very least, a space of one's own. In the Bodhgaya case, for instance, the women being wage laborers were not economically dependent, but their husbands could still threaten them with eviction. Notably too the Bodhgaya women saw intra-household gender relations being affected not just by their own propertyless state, but by their remaining propertyless while their husbands became propertied. In other words, land titles were important to women not only for improving their economic well-being in absolute terms (the welfare argument), but also for improving their relative bargaining position *vis-à-vis* their husbands: their sense of empowerment within the home was linked to economic equality.

Outside the household as well, land ownership can empower women by improving the social treatment they receive from fellow villagers (Mies *et al.* 1986), and by enabling them to bargain with employers from a stronger fall-back position. Land ownership is also widely linked to rural political power (Solaiman and Alam 1977; R. Singh 1988). Although there can be social barriers to women's participation in public decision-making bodies, even for women endowed with land, land rights could facilitate such participation. The support of local women's groups would also help.

Indeed in a limited sense, group action may itself empower women by enhancing their self-confidence and ability to challenge oppression, although in a larger sense it is a means to empowerment, wherein empowerment lies not only in the process of challenging gender inequity but in eliminating it. Collective action is likely to prove a critical means for effecting change toward gender equality in land rights (as elaborated later).

While each of the above arguments for women's independent rights in land is important, it is notable that the welfare and efficiency arguments resonate more with State planners. Why? Part of the answer certainly lies in the fact that these arguments (especially those concerning welfare) focus especially on poor women, and can be subsumed within the poverty alleviation component of planning, with special targeting towards "the most vulnerable" groups, identified as women and female children. But part of the answer must also lie in deep-rooted notions of appropriate gender relations shared by many men who make and implement policy, for whom empowering women to transform those relations into more equal ones would appear inappropriate and even threatening to existing family and kinship structures. Hence it is easier to push for changes where the goal appears to be to give poor women a slightly better deal, than where the goal is to challenge basic inequities in gender relations across classes. It is also the case that programs for health and nutrition are more readily perceived in welfare terms than programs which call for gender-redistributive land reform. It is not a coincidence that land rights have yet to become a necessary component even of women-directed poverty alleviation schemes.

Consider now what can be learnt about the association between land rights and gender relations from traditionally matrilineal and bilateral communities.

## GENDER RELATIONS IN TRADITIONALLY MATRILINEAL AND BILATERAL COMMUNITIES

Historically, in some South Asian communities, women enjoyed significant rights in land, and even today do so there more than elsewhere. These are communities traditionally practising matrilineal or bilateral inheritance and concentrated in parts of northeast and south India, and Sri Lanka, as follows:

- Northeast India: the home of three matrilineal tribal communities, the Garos, Khasis, and Lalungs.
- South India: here the Nangudi Vellalars of Tamil Nadu practised bilateral inheritance, and several other groups in and around Kerala practised matrilineal inheritance, including the Nayars of north and central Kerala, the Tiyyars and Mappilas of north Kerala, and the Bants of Karnataka.
- Sri Lanka: here all major communities practised bilateral or matrilineal inheritance – the Sinhalese and Jaffna Tamils were bilateral, and the Muslim "Moors" were matrilineal[21].

Historical and ethnographic evidence (examined in Agarwal 1994) suggests that in regions other than these, inheritance practices were essentially patrilineal.

Women's land rights in the above communities fell broadly into three categories:

- In communities such as the Garos land was a clan's communal property and could not be inherited either by individuals or by joint family units. All clan members resident in the village had use rights to this land as individuals. Responsibility for land management vested with the

278

husband who took up residence with his wife, but a woman's contribution to field labor was substantial and critical, and she controlled the produce.

• In communities such as the Khasis, Nayars, Tiyyars and Mappilas, land, although inherited in the female line, was held as joint family property, and there were no individual rights of alienation. Responsibility for land management vested principally with older men (usually brothers or maternal uncles). However, in decisions concerning the partition or transfer of landed property, women's concurrence was necessary.

• In communities such as the Sinhalese, Jaffna Tamils, and Moors, women had individual inheritance rights in land, and among the former two groups men too held such rights.

The picture we get of gender relations among these groups is a mixed one. On the positive side, women enjoyed considerable social independence and relative equality in marital relations. Indeed, in all the groups, a daughter's rights in land, and the fact that she either remained in her natal home after marriage or had inviolable rights to return to it if she so chose, provided her with a strong fall-back position within marriage. Women could choose their husbands (although heiresses faced some constraints) and initiate divorce. Where uxorilocality or matrilocality was the norm, as it was in many of these groups, marital breakdown led to the husband departing, sometimes (as among the Garos) with only the clothes on his back[22]. (In contrast, in patrilineal, patrilocal contexts, it was women – especially if they violated sexual norms – who faced the very real risk of being evicted and being left destitute.) Norms of sexual behavior outside marriage ranged from relatively gender egalitarian (as among the Sinhalese and the matrilineal tribes of northeast India), to restricted for women (as among the Jaffna Tamils). But in comparison with Hindu and Muslim women of patrilineal groups, especially those shackled by seclusion practices in northwestern South Asia, women among all the matrilineal and bilateral groups enjoyed greater sexual freedom.

They also had considerable freedom of movement and of public interaction. Even among the (Muslim) Moors, Munck (1985:8, 108) remarks: "Women move freely about the village without veils covering their faces. . . . Interaction between men and women is frequent and casual and often sexual comments are exchanged publicly." This is strikingly different from women's situation among most patrilineal Muslims of the subcontinent. Daughters were also specially desired among groups such as the Nayars[23], in marked contrast to the strong son preference among patrilineal communities in northern South Asia.

However, these favorable features were counterbalanced by less favorable ones. First, women's property rights did not alter the overall gender division of labor: domestic work and childcare were still a woman's

279

responsibilities. Second, the range of sexual mores found among these communities indicates that rights in land did not guarantee women the same sexual freedom as men. Third, formal managerial authority over land in a number of matrilineal groups lay with men (as husbands, brothers and maternal uncles). In practice, this would have worked in various ways depending on the role women played in the household's economy, the form (individual or joint) in which property was held, and the size of the estates involved. Where women's role in production and market activities was important (as among the northeastern tribal groups), and/or where women held individual rather than joint property rights (as among Sri Lanka's bilateral groups), they exercised greater control over the land. But where women played little role in farm production, and property was held in large joint family estates collectively owned by several generations of a woman's matrilineal descendants, as among the Nayars of central Kerala and the wealthy Mappilas of north Kerala, men's managerial control over property and their overall authority in intra-household and public dealings appears to have been especially strong. (This also highlights an important difference between matrilineal and patrilineal inheritance systems: in the former there is often a gender divergence between property ownership and its control, while in the latter there is convergence: men (as a gender) own as well as control the property.)

Fourth, most importantly, in all the groups, customary institutions with jural power (such as tribal and caste councils) were monopolized by men and typically excluded women. Among matrilineally inheriting communities, this meant that despite men's restricted access to property ownership, their rights (as a gender) of control over that property on the one hand, and their access to public bodies on the other (with links between the two domains), often enabled them to consolidate social prestige and political power. The Nayar *karanavans*[24] of wealthy households and the Khasi chiefs commanded local influence in ways that the women heiresses of these communities appear not to have done as a rule. Also, among all groups, men's control of the public decision-making domain gave them critical influence over the modification of legal and social rules when external conditions began to change in significant ways, especially under British colonial rule.

In short, ownership rights in landed property clearly conferred important benefits on women, but their virtual exclusion from property management (in some groups) and from jural and overall public authority (in all groups) circumscribed the power they could derive from those rights. This holds lessons for women's struggle for land rights today, namely that women cannot derive the full advantages of land ownership if they continue to be excluded from managerial control and jural authority. And the arenas of contestation over effective land rights for women will therefore need to extend much beyond the courtyards of the household to encompass the complex institutions of community and State – the arenas where legal, social, and political rules are made and unmade. This is further illustrated below.

## OBSTACLES TO ACHIEVING EFFECTIVE LAND RIGHTS

Today, most arable land in South Asia (as noted) is in private hands, access to which is mainly through inheritance. Women enjoy considerable property rights in law, but gender inequalities and anomalies in land-related laws remain. Moreover, there is a vast gender gap between law and practice. As noted, most women do not own land; even fewer exercise full control over it. A range of factors – social, administrative and ideological – severely restrict the effective implementation of inheritance laws. These obstacles, (detailed in Agarwal 1994), are summarized below.

First, in most traditionally patrilineal communities, there is a strong male resistance to endowing women, especially daughters, with land. Apart from the reluctance to admit more contenders to the most valuable form of rural property, an important factor underlying such resistance is a structural mismatch between contemporary inheritance laws and traditional marriage practices. Among the matrilineal and bilateral communities discussed earlier, historically families sought to keep the land within the purview of the extended kin either by strict rules against land alienation by individuals, or, where such alienation was possible (as among the bilateral communities), by other means, such as post-marital residence in the village, and often an emphasis on marriage with close kin, especially cross cousins. In fact proximity of the post-marital residence to the natal home appears to have been virtually a necessary condition for recognizing a daughter's share in landed property.

Contemporary laws as framed by the modern State give inheritance rights to daughters as individuals among most communities, including in traditionally patrilineal, patrilocal ones. Marriage customs, however, are still under the purview of the local kin group and, on the relevant counts, have remained largely unchanged. In India this mismatch between inheritance laws and marriage practices is greatest among upper-caste Hindus of the northwest who forbid marriages with close kin and practise village exogamy, preferring marriage alliances in distant villages. Many such communities, moreover, have social taboos against parents drawing on the economic support of married daughters, even during crises. Hence, in the northern states (and especially the northwestern ones) endowing daughters is seen by Hindu parents as bringing no reciprocal economic benefit, while increasing the risk of the land passing out of the hands of the extended family. Resistance to entitling daughters tends to be greatest here. Resistance is less in south and northeast India where marriages within the village and with close kin are allowed and sought, and seeking the help of married daughters during economic crises is also possible.

Second, women in many parts of South Asia tend to forego their shares in parental land for the sake of potential economic and social support from brothers. A visit by a brother is often the only regular link a woman has with her natal home where she is married into a distant village, and especially where social taboos bar parents from accepting a married daughter's hospitality. After the parents' deaths the brother's home often offers the only possibility of refuge in case of marital failure or widowhood. A woman's dependence on this support is directly related to her economic and social vulnerability. Economically, low access to personal property (especially productive assets), illiteracy, limited income-earning skills and earning opportunities, and low wages for available work, can all constrain women's potential for independent economic survival. Socially, women's vulnerability is associated partly with the strength of female seclusion practices and partly with the extent of social stigma attaching to widow-hood or divorce. Both economic and social factors vary in strength by community, region, and circumstance, but typically, in anticipation of such support women give up their claims in parental land. Cultural constructions of gender, including the definition of how a "good" sister should behave, the widespread feeling that it is "shameful" for a sister to claim her share, also discourage women from asserting their rights (Hershman 1981). In practice, ethnographies give examples both of brothers helping a sister in need, and of their neglect and duplicity.

Third, dependence on brothers is part of a larger social context in which many aspects of rural women's relationship with the world outside the family is typically mediated through male relatives: fathers, brothers, hus-bands, and extended male kin. Such mediation is necessitated by a variety of factors, but particularly by the physical and social restrictions on women's mobility and behavior. In many South Asian communities these restrictions are explicit in the norms and ideology of purdah or female seclusion; in many others, they are implicit and subtle, but nevertheless effectively confine women. These restrictions are manifest not just in the veiling of women, but more commonly in the gender segregation of space and the gendered specification of behavior. In fact, strict veiling is limited to some communities and regions – being stronger among Muslims in northern South Asia and among upper-caste Hindus in northwest India, than else-where; and even here it varies in extent by the woman's caste, class, and age. More pervasive are the behavioral strictures imposed upon and internalized by women from late childhood, which define where women can go, whom they can speak to and in what manner, how they should dress, and so on. Although such gendering of space and behavior is strongest in commu-nities which explicitly endorse purdah, its more subtle manifestations constitute an implicit code of expected female behavior in large parts of the subcontinent, even where (as in South India and Nepal) purdah is not endorsed. This circumscribes rural women's interaction with men and institutions, their physical and social mobility, their domain of activity and knowledge, and their access to education and to economic (markets, banks, etc.), judicial and administrative institutions. All this severely limits women's ability to claim and control land.

Fourth, male relatives often take pre-emptive steps to prevent women from getting their inheritance. Fathers have been found to leave wills favoring sons and disinheriting daughters; and brothers have been known to forge wills or manipulate statements before the revenue authorities to make it appear that the woman has relinquished her right (Mayer 1960; Alavi 1972; Parry 1979; Jansen 1983). Natal kin are especially hostile to the idea of daughters and sisters inheriting land, since the property can pass outside the patrilineal descent group. A widow's claims to her husband's land are viewed with less antagonism, since there is a greater chance of the land remaining with agnates: she can be persuaded to adopt the son of the deceased husband's brother if she is sonless, or to enter into a leviratic union with the husband's (usually younger) brother, or made to forfeit the property if she remarries outside the family.

Where pre-emptive methods fail, intimidation is attempted. A common tactic is to initiate expensive litigation which few women can financially afford (Kishwar 1987). Some women drop their claims, others press on with the risk of having to mortgage the land to pay legal fees, thus possibly losing the land altogether. Land disputes involving women were rising in parts of the subcontinent even in the late 1950s (Mayer 1960). Today direct violence is also increasingly used to deter women from filing claims, or from exercising their customary rights: beatings are common and murder not unknown. Indeed in eastern and central India, the murder of women who have some land, through accusations of witchcraft, is on the rise (Chaudhuri 1987; Kishwar 1987).

Fifth, the logistics of dealing with legal, economic and bureaucratic institutions are often formidable and work against women staking their claims; and they may only decide to do so if they have male relatives who can mediate. Village women's typically low level of education, and the noted restrictions on their interaction with the extra-domestic sphere and with institutions constituted principally of men, the complicated procedures and red tape involved in dealing with judicial and administrative bodies, and so on, all work to women's disadvantage, as does their relative lack of financial resources. The problem is especially acute in communities with high female seclusion, but it is not absent even where seclusion is not prescribed.

Sixth, local-level (largely male) government functionaries, responsible for overseeing the recording of inheritance shares, often obstruct the implementation of laws in women's favor. Social and official prejudice tends to be particularly acute against inheritance by daughters; widows' claims (as noted) are somewhat better accepted in principle, although often violated in practice.

The gap between legal ownership rights and actual ownership is only one part of the story. The other part relates to the gap between ownership and effective control, especially managerial control, attributable to a mix of factors. Patrilocal marriages in distant villages make it difficult for women to directly supervise or cultivate land they may inherit in the natal village. But problems of directly managing land inherited even in the marital village (say as a widow) are compounded in many areas by factors such as the practice of purdah or the more general (implicit or explicit) gender segregation of public space and social interaction; high rates of female illiteracy; and high fertility (which increases women's childbearing and childcare responsibilities). Moreover, male control over agricultural technology, especially the plough (there are cultural taboos against women ploughing), and the noted male bias in the dissemination of information and technological inputs, disadvantage women farmers and increase their dependence on male mediation. Often added to this is the threat and practice of violence by male relatives and others interested in acquiring women's land. Pressure on women to sharecrop their land to relatives (at below market rates) is usually high, as are the difficulties of ensuring that they get their fair share of the harvest. Some of these factors, such as gender bias in access to production inputs and information, constrain women farmers even in traditionally bilateral and matrilineal contexts.

However, the strength of these constraints on women claiming and managing land varies considerably by region. There are geographic differences in the social acceptance of women's land claims (stemming in part from differences in traditional inheritance rights): in prevailing marriage practices; in the emphasis on female seclusion and control over female sexuality; in women's freedom of movement and labor force participation; in women's literacy and fertility rates; and in the extent of land scarcity. Obstacles stemming from these factors are greatest in northwest India, Bangladesh and Pakistan, and least in south India and Sri Lanka. In fact four geographic zones can broadly be demarcated, ordered in terms of the strength of resistance women are likely to face in exercising their legal rights: Pakistan, northwest India and Bangladesh fall at the high resistance end of the spectrum, and south India and Sri Lanka at the low resistance end; while western, central and eastern India, and Nepal and northeast India, come in between[25].

Over time, gender conflict over private land is likely to increase with its growing scarcity and skewness in distribution. On the one hand male family members will be increasingly reluctant to part with the land. On the other hand, the importance for women of asserting their inheritance rights will grow for several reasons, including the limited expansion of economic opportunities for non-land-related earnings, and the erosion of kin-support systems, as brothers and other relatives become less able or less willing economically to support female kin. In Bangladesh gender conflict over land is already on the rise, with an increasing number of women asserting or planning to assert their claims[26]; and we can expect this also to be the case in other acutely land-scarce parts of South Asia.

In the case of public land, that is land which is under government or community jurisdiction, the obstacles are of a somewhat different nature. Here women's struggle is more directly against the consistent male bias in the distribution of land under land reform programs, resettlement schemes, and various land development projects, and only indirectly against individual family members who may be rival potential beneficiaries. Government officials typically resist the allotment of public land to women on the grounds that allotments can only be made to household heads, whom they assume are men (Lal 1986). This bias is found even when land titles are distributed in traditionally matrilineal and bilateral communities (Schrijvers 1988; Agarwal 1994). And, it is found in the policies and programs of all the political regimes in the subcontinent, including communist ones.

## INTERVENTIONS FOR CHANGE: SOME CONSIDERATIONS

The discussion above indicates that today for women to gain effective rights in land will require contestation and struggle in many arenas – the household, the market, the community, and the State – and on diverse aspects: legal, administrative, social, and ideological. Apart from the struggle to establish legal equality, to enhance women's ability to claim and keep control over their rightful inheritance shares will need: establishing the social legitimacy of their claims; reducing gender bias in village land registration practices and village council rulings; increasing women's legal knowledge and literacy; improving women's fall-back position so that they are better able to deal with any associated intra-family conflict, including through external support structures that would reduce women's dependence on brothers and close kin; and so on. Similarly, male bias in government distribution of public land and in infrastructural support for farmers will need contestation.

The ideological struggle to establish women's claims is likely to be especially complex. It is part of an overall struggle for changing perceptions about women's needs, roles, and abilities, in which women's movements, both local and national, even when not focussing on the specific question of land rights, have a critical role to play. This contestation over meanings could take diverse forms, including countering popular arguments against giving women land, such as those relating to land size and fragmentation, questioning the validity of female seclusion and restrictions on women's economic and social participation outside the home, and promoting women's educational programs with an empowerment perspective.

In all this, the role of collective action is likely to be primary. For instance, the local bureaucracy is more likely to accurately register individual women's claims in family land if there were collective pressure on them from say gender progressive groups, especially women's organizations. Such organizations can also play a vital supportive role in providing women with legal information on laws and contacts with lawyers, should legal action be necessary; and in improving effective (not just nominal) female presence in village decision-making bodies. Women elected to all-women panels in village councils in parts of India (especially where supported by local women's organizations), and field-level development administrators in Bangladesh, are found to be more sensitive to women's concerns, and to give priority to local women's needs, in ways that male village council members and bureaucrats typically do not (Goetz 1990; Gandhi and Shah 1991). The presence of women in decision-making roles and positions of authority also has a wider ideological impact; and village women are more likely to take their grievances to female representatives than to all-male bodies.

Local gender progressive organizations could similarly strengthen women's fall-back position in intra-family conflicts over women's land claims, through economic and social support networks and programs which reduce women's dependence on male relatives, especially their brothers in whose favor women usually forfeit their claims. As a woman member of the Bangladesh Rural Advancement Committee (BRAC, a Bangladeshi development NGO which provides credit and technical support to poor village women and men, organized separately into small groups) tellingly asserted: "Well the Samity [organization] is my brother" (Hunt 1983: 38). After joining BRAC women have also been able to challenge purdah practices: "We do not listen to the *mullahs* [Muslim clergy] anymore. They did not give us even a quarter kilo of rice" (Chen 1983: 176). "They said . . . [w]e are ruining the prestige of the village and breaking *purdah*. . . . Now nobody talks ill of us. They say: 'They have formed a group and now they earn money. It is good'" (*ibid.*).

More generally, group support can take at least two forms: through separately constituted groups which provide specialized legal and other services to village women, and through organizations comprised of village women themselves. Initiatives of both kinds would be important not only for women from landed households seeking their inheritance claims, but also for landless women seeking rights in public land by challenging male bias in government land allocations.

In this context, it is worth considering the advantages of land ownership and/or management by groups of women, rather than by women individually. Although individual ownership can allow women the freedom to bequeath, mortgage, or sell the land as they wish, it also carries the risk of the land being appropriated by rapacious moneylenders or male relatives. An alternative arrangement to individual titles in the transfer of State land, or of land acquired by a peasant organization through a land struggle, could be titles held by poor peasant women as a group – each participating woman having use rights in the land but not the right to individually dispose of it. Daughters-in-law and daughters resident in the village could share these usufructuary rights; daughters leaving the village on marriage would lose them, but could reestablish their rights should they need to return to their parental homes on marital failure or widowhood. In other words, land access could be linked formally to residence, as was the case among some tribal communities (such as the Garos), the difference being that here the land would belong not to a clan but to a group of poor women.

Group ownership of land need not, however, imply joint management, just as individual ownership need not preclude joint management. Women holding joint ownership rights could either cultivate separate plots allocated on a household basis, or cultivate collectively as a group with each woman contributing labor time and sharing the returns. Or there could be some combination of individual and group management, such as family-based female cultivation along with joint investment in capital equipment and cooperation in terms of labor sharing and product marketing. Group investment through resource pooling could be advantageous even when women own land individually by reducing the resource crunch they may face at the individual level. In fact, some cases of joint land management and investment by small groups of women already exist in South Asia (see Chen 1983; Lal 1986; N. Singh 1988).

In such initiatives, and more generally to enhance women's ability to function as independent farmers, infrastructural support for women is critical, in the form of access to credit, production inputs, information on new agricultural practices, marketing, and so on. Again, the promotion of women's cooperatives for the provisioning of such services could prove important.

In this context it needs emphasis that it is not just an increase in women's command over economic resources, but also the process by which that increase occurs that has a critical bearing on gender relations. Land rights are not "given" and will not be "provided" to most South Asian women without contestation. As noted, acquiring these rights will require simultaneous struggles on both the economic and non-economic fronts and in several different arenas.

Indeed the theoretical premise of this paper is that gender relations and women's economic, social and political positions are the outcome of processes of contestation and bargaining between the genders (for elaboration, see Agarwal 1994). These processes may not always be explicit but are nonetheless revealed in final outcomes. They involve elements of both cooperation and conflict and take place in various arenas: the household, the market, the community, and the State – arenas which are interlinked in that change in one impinges on the others. For instance, a strengthening of women's bargaining power in the community, say through the formation of a women's organization, has also been found to enhance women's bargaining power within the household.

While it is clear that various forms of collective action will be necessary for empowering women to establish effective rights in land, bringing about collective action is not always easy. A number of complexities (detailed in Agarwal 1994) will need to be addressed, including those posed by class- (and caste-) associated conflict of interests among women, and the fact that even to organize collectively often requires challenging existing social norms, such as breaking the traditional bounds of female seclusion in some communities, for attending group meetings.

Indeed, the issue of gender equality in land rights – not only in law but in practice – calls for a much more multi-pronged and sustained effort than has been attempted so far on any gender-related issue in South Asia. While undoubtedly the noted obstacles appear formidable, their very complexity and range also make land rights a critical entry point for challenging unequal gender relations and power structures at many levels, and gives the struggle to overcome the obstacles a transformative potential.

For this and the other reasons noted, land (and more generally property) has a strategic importance that other gender concerns such as employment do not share in equal measure.

## NOTES

1 This paper draws substantially on the author's book, Agarwal (1994). A longer version of it appeared in *World Development* 22 (1), 1994.
2 Personal communication, Vina Mazumdar, Center for Women's Development Studies, New Delhi.
3 This is not meant as a summary of Engels' complex thesis, but merely of one part of it. Critiques of his analysis abound: see especially, Sacks (1975), Delmar (1976), Molyneux (1981) and Sayers *et al.* (1987). In particular, Engels' assumption that gender relations within propertyless groups, such as the industrial proletariat, and under socialism would necessarily be egalitarian has been widely criticized.
4 In socialist countries (including those which were socialist until recently), the influence of Engels' analysis led to a similar preoccupation with women's employment as the major means of eliminating gender oppression (Molyneux 1981).
5 Women's representation in top political and economic decision-making bodies in such countries remained minimal. For instance, in the late 1970s, in the USSR, Czechoslovakia, Poland, and Yugoslavia under 5 per cent of government posts were filled by women (Molyneux 1981).
6 In India, for instance, male dominance is apparent in the judiciary (in 1985

women constituted only 3.6 per cent of the state bar council advocates, and 2.8 percent of High Court and Supreme Court judges), the government administration (in 1987 only 7.4 per cent of the Indian Administrative Service Officers were women), and the legislature (in 1984 only 8 per cent of elected candidates in the Lok Sabha (lower house of parliament) were women). All figures are taken from GOI (1988:119, 126–7, 173).

7  Scandinavian countries have a relatively better record on this: in Norway and Finland, women constituted 34 and 32 per cent of all elected and appointed members of national legislative bodies in 1985–7, in sharp contrast to the 9–10 per cent in India, Bangladesh and Pakistan, and 5–6 per cent in the US and UK (United Nations 1990).

8  Firestone (1970), Millet (1970), and Delphy (1977) all deny the significance of class divisions between women, but from different standpoints.

9  Of course aspects of a person's identity other than class can also be divisive or adhesive, such as caste, ethnicity, and religion.

10  This was calculated from India's land use statistics for 1987–88 (Government of India 1992).

11  In India the term "state" relates to administrative divisions within the country and is not to be confused with "State" used throughout the paper in the political economy sense of the word. In Pakistan and Sri Lanka these administrative divisions are termed provinces.

12  None of the countries in the region, except Sri Lanka, collects gender-disaggregated land ownership and use data in its agricultural and centennial censuses or other large-scale rural surveys. Even in Sri Lanka, such data, collected in the 1981 agricultural census, covered only agricultural operators (that is, cultivators as well as purely livestock and poultry operators) and not all rural households. Also the published data do not give a genderwise breakdown of land ownership even among agricultural operators. Again, most studies of village agrarian structures by economists have confined themselves to the household unit. Hence to gain an idea of where women have been given or have claimed their shares in landed property and under what circumstances, I have drawn on anthropological, historical, and legal sources, supplemented by my fieldwork observations.

13  Ancestral property passes through the male line under patrilineal inheritance, through the female line under matrilineal inheritance, and to and through both sons and daughters under bilateral inheritance.

14  The discussion here concerns land linked to rural livelihoods, especially arable land, but excludes homesites, even though the available data on land ownership do not always separate land under homesites from the rest.

15  See Buvinic and Youssef (1978) for India, and Safilios-Rothchild and Mahmud (1989) for Bangladesh. According to the Indian census some 10 per cent of households are female headed, but this is a significant underestimate (see Agarwal 1985, on reasons for the undercounting).

16  In these estimates, the figure for land ownership covers all land owned by the household, whether or not cultivated, including that used for non-agricultural purposes.

17  There is considerable evidence from Asia that titling can critically enhance farmers' access to credit (in terms of sources, amounts and terms) by enabling them to use land as collateral (see e.g. Binswanger and Rosenzweig 1986; Feder 1989). Also see Saito and Weidenmann (1990) on the problems women farmers face in getting credit in the absence of titles.

18 For class bias in agricultural extension see Dasgupta (1977) and on gender bias see Kilkelly (1986).

19 For non-food crops the marketed surplus is often very high on farms of all size groups (Lipton 1992) and for food crops the higher productivity on small farms could outweigh their higher propensity-to-consume effect, as found, for instance, in Kenya (Lipton 1992).

20 This is partly because women's lesser mobility would confine them more than men to local markets; and it is partly derivative of the more general observation that villages with greater equality in land (and farm income) distribution in South Asia tend to generate more demand for local non-farm products, especially through consumption linkages (Islam 1986).

21 Although the nomenclature "Moor" (given to the Sri Lankan Muslims under Portuguese rule) has today largely been subsumed under the general category "Muslim," I have retained the term to distinguish the group both from partilineal Sri Lankan Muslims and from matrilineal Indian Muslims (such as the Mappilas) whose inheritance practices were different.

22 Uxorilocality implies that the husband takes up residence with the wife and (with or near) her parental family. Where this is a regular practice dictated by a preferred custom, this results in institutionalized matrilocal residence, where the normal residence of most husbands is with or near the matrilineal kin of the wives. Patrilocal implies that the wife takes up residence with the husband and (with or near) his patrilineal kin.

23 Personal communication, Joan Mencher, New York, 1992.

24 The *karanavan* was the head of the *taravad* and manager of the joint family estate; he was usually the seniormost male member of the *taravad*. *Taravad*: the matrilineal joint family, holding property in common and often sharing a common residence.

25 For maps showing these cross-regional patterns, see Agarwal (1994).

26 See, for example, Abdullah and Zeidenstein (1982); Jansen (1983); Nath (1984).

# REFERENCES

Abdullah, T. and Zeidenstein, S.A. (1982) *Village Women of Bangladesh: Prospects for Change*, Oxford: Pergamon Press.

Agarwal, B. (1983) *Mechanization in Indian Agriculture: An Analytical Study of the Indian Punjab*, Delhi: Allied Publishers (repr. 1986).

—— (1985) "Work Participation of Rural Women in the Third World: Some Data and Conceptual Biases", *Economic and Political Weekly* 21 December,: A155–A164.

—— (1986) "Women, Poverty and Agricultural Growth in India", *The Journal of Peasant Studies* July: 165–220.

—— (1992) "The Gender and Environment Debate: Lessons from India", *Feminist Studies* 18, 1: 119–58.

—— (1994) *A Field of One's Own: Gender and Land Rights in South Asia*, Cambridge: Cambridge University Press.

Alaka and Chetna (1987) "When Women Get Land – A Report from Bodhgaya", *Manushi* 40: 25–6.

Alavi, H. (1972) "Kinship in West Punjab Villages", *Contributions to Indian Sociology, New Series* 6, December: 1–27.

Ali, I., Desai, B.M., Radhakrishna, R. and Vyas, V.S. (1981) "Indian Agriculture at

2000: Strategies for Equality", *Economic and Political Weekly* 16, 10–12, March: 409–24.

Bardhan, K. (1977) "Rural Employment, Wages and Labor Markets in India: A Survey of Research", *Economic and Political Weekly* 12, 26–8.

Basant, R. and Kumar, B.L. (1989) "Rural Agricultural Activities in India: A Review of Available Evidence", *Social Scientist* 17, 1–2, January–February: 13–17.

Berry, R.A. and Cline, W.R. (1979) *Agrarian Structure and Productivity in Developing Countries*, Baltimore and London: Johns Hopkins University Press.

Binswanger, H.P. and Rosenzweig, M. (1986) "Credit Markets, Wealth and Endowments in Rural South India", paper presented at the Eighth World Congress of the International Economic Association, New Delhi, 1–5 December.

Blumberg, R.L. (1991) "Income Under Female vs. Male Control: Hypotheses from a Theory of Gender Stratification and Data from the Third World", in R.L. Blumberg (ed.) *Gender, Family and Economy: The Triple Overlap*: 97–127, Newbury Park: Sage Publications.

Boyce, J. (1987) *Agrarian Impasse in Bengal: Institutional Constraints to Technological Change*, Oxford: Oxford University Press.

Buvinic, M. and Youssef, N.H. (1978) "Women-headed Households: The Ignored Factor in Development Planning", Report submitted to AID/WID, International Center for Research on Women, Washington DC, March.

Cain, M.T., Khanam, S.R. and Nahar, S. (1979) "Class, Patriarchy and the Structure of Women's Work in Rural Bangladesh", Working Paper No. 43, New York: Center for Population Studies, The Population Council.

Caldwell, J.C., Reddy, P.H. and Caldwell, P. (1988) *The Causes of Demographic Change: Experimental Research in South India*, Wisconsin: The University of Wisconsin Press.

Chadha, G.K. (1992) "Non-farm Sector in India's Rural Economy: Policy, Performance and Growth Prospects", mimeo, Delhi: Center for Regional Development, Jawaharlal Nehru University.

Chaudhuri, A.B. (1987) *The Santals: Religion and Rituals*, New Delhi: Ashish Publishing House.

Chen, M.A. (1983) *A Quiet Revolution: Women in Transition in Rural Bangladesh*, Cambridge: Schenkman Publishing Co, Inc.

Dasgupta, B. (1977) "Agrarian Change and the New Technology in India", Report No.77.2, Geneva: United Nations Research Institute for Social Development.

Delmar, R. (1976) "Looking Again at Engels's Origin of the Family, Private Property and the State", in J. Mitchell and A. Oakley (eds). *The Rights and Wrongs of Women*, Harmondsworth: Penguin Books.

Delphy, C. (1977) *The Main Enemy: A Materialist Analysis of Women's Oppression*, London: Women's Research and Resources Center.

Deolalikar, A.B. (1988) "Nutrition and Labor Productivity in Agriculture: Econometric Estimates for Rural South Asia", *Review of Economics and Statistics* 70, 4, August: 406–13.

Dreze, J. (1990) "Widows in India", Discussion paper no. DEP 46, London: The Development Economics Research Programme, London School of Economics.

Engels, F.A. [1884] (1972) *The Origin of the Family, Private Property and the State*, Harmondsworth: Penguin Books.

Feder, G. (1989) "The Economics of Land Titling in Thailand", mimeo, Washington, DC: World Bank, April.

Firestone, S. (1970) *The Dialectic of Sex: The Case for Feminist Revolution*, New York: Bantam Books.

291

Gaiha, R. and Kazmi, N.A. (1981) "Aspects of Rural Poverty in India", *Economics of Planning* 17, 2–3: 74–112.

Gandhi, N. and Shah, N. (1991) *The Issues at Stake: Theory and Practice in the Contemporary Women's Movement in India*, Delhi: Kali for Women.

Goetz, A.M. (1990) "Local Heroes, Local Despots: Exploring Fieldworker Discretion in Implementing Gender-Redistributive Development Policy", paper presented at the Development Studies Association Conference, Glasgow.

Government of India (GOI) (1986) *Thirty-seventh Round Report on Land Holdings – 2: Some Aspects of Operational Holdings*, Report No. 331, Delhi: National Sample Survey Organisation, Dept. of Statistics.

———— (1987) "A Note on Some Aspects of Household Ownership Holding: NSS 37th Round (January–December 1982)" and "Results on Some Aspects of Household Ownership Holding: NSS 37th Round (January–December 1982)", *Sarvekshana* 11, 2, 33, October: 1–18, S1–S175, Dept. of Statistics, Ministry of Planning.

———— (1988) *Women in India: A Statistical Profile – 1988*, New Delhi: Ministry of Human Resource Development.

———— (1992) "Land Use Statistics, 1987–88", mimeo, Delhi: Directorate of Economics and Statistics, Ministry of Agriculture.

Government of Sri Lanka (1984) *Sri Lanka Census of Agriculture 1982*, Colombo: Dept. of Census and Statistics, Ministry of Plan Implementation.

Harriss, B (1990) "The Intrafamily Distribution of Hunger in South Asia", in J. Dreze, and A.K. Sen (eds) *The Political Economy of Hunger*: 351–424, Oxford: Clarendon Press.

Hazell, P.B. and Haggblade, S. (1990) "Rural-Urban Growth Linkages in India", Working Paper WPS 430, Washington, DC: Agriculture and Rural Development Department, World Bank.

Hershman, P. (1981) *Punjabi Kinship and Marriage*, Delhi: Hindustan Publishing Corporation.

Hinton, W. (1972) *Fanshen: A Documentary of Revolution in a Chinese Village*, Harmondsworth: Penguin Books.

Hossain, M. (1988) "Credit for Women: A Review of Special Credit Programmes in Bangladesh", draft paper, Dhaka: Bangladesh Institute for Development Studies.

Hunt, H.I. (1983) "Intervention and Change in the Lives of Rural Poor Women in Bangladesh: A Discussion Paper", Dhaka: Bangladesh Rural Action Committee, December.

Islam, R. (1986) "Non-farm Employment in Rural Asia: Issues and Evidence", in R.T. Shand (ed.) *Off-Farm Employment in the Development of Rural Asia*: 153–73, Canberra: Australian National University.

———— (1987) "Rural Industrialisation and Employment in Asia: Issues and Evidence", in *Rural Industrialisation and Employment in Asia*: 1–18, New Delhi: International Labor Organisation, Asian Employment Programme.

Jannuzi, F.T. and Peach, J.T. (1980) *The Agrarian Structure of Bangladesh: An Impediment to Development*, Delhi: Sangam Books.

Jansen, E. G. (1983) *Rural Bangladesh: Competition for Scarce Resources*, Oslo: Norwegian University Press.

Kilkelly, K. (1986) "Women's Roles in Irrigated Agricultural Production Systems during the 1985 Yala Season: Parakrama Samudra Scheme and Giritale Scheme, Polonnaruma District", Report, Colombo: United States Agency for International Development (USAID).

Kishwar, M. (1987) "Toiling Without Rights: Ho Women of Singhbhum", *Economic and Political Weekly* 22, 3–5.

Krause, I-B.(1982) "Kinship and Economics in North-West Nepal", unpublished PhD dissertation in Social Anthropology, London: London School of Economics, University of London.

Kumar, S. K. (1978) "Role of the Household Economy in Child Nutrition at Low Incomes", Occasional Paper No. 95, Cornell: Dept. of Agricultural Economics, Cornell University.

Lal, I. (1986) "Goats and Tigers", a video film by Ian Lal, Delhi: International Labor Organisation.

Lipton, M. (1992) "Land Reform as Commenced Business: The Evidence Against Stopping", draft paper, Sussex: Institute of Development Studies.

Lipton, M. and Longhurst, R. (1989) New Seeds and Poor People, London: Unwin Hyman.

Manimala (1983) "Zameen Kenkar? Jote Onkar: Women's Participation in the Bodhgaya Land Struggle", Manushi 14, January–February: 2–16.

Mayer, A.C. (1960) Caste and Kinship in Central India – A Village and Its Region, London: Routledge & Kegan Paul.

Mencher, J. (1988) "Women's Work and Poverty: Contribution to Household Maintenance in Two Regions of South India", in D. Dwyer and J. Bruce (eds) A Home Divided: Women and Income in the Third World, Stanford: Stanford University Press.

Mies, M., Lalita, K. and Kumari, K. (1986) Indian Women in Subsistence and Agricultural Labor, Geneva: International Labor Organisation.

Millet, K. (1970) Sexual Politics, New York: Doubleday.

Molyneux, M. (1981) "Socialist Societies Old and New: Progress Towards Women's Emancipation", Feminist Review 8, Summer: 1–34.

Munck, V.C. de (1985) "Cross-currents of Conflict and Cooperation in Kotabowa", unpublished PhD dissertation, Riverside: Dept. of Anthropology, University of California at Riverside.

Nath, J.N. (1984) "Dynamics of Socio-economic Change and the Role and Status of Women in Natunpur: Case Study of a Bangladesh Village", unpublished PhD dissertation, Dhaka: Dept. of Sociology, University of Dhaka.

Omvedt, G. (1981) "Effects of Agricultural Development on the Status of Women", paper prepared for the International Labor Office, Tripartite Asian Regional Seminar on Rural Development and Women, Mahabaleshwar, India.

Parry, J.P. (1979) Caste and Kinship in Kangra, Delhi: Vikas Publishing House.

Per-Lee, D.A. (1981) "Employment, Ingenuity and Family Life: Rajasthani Women in Delhi, India", unpublished PhD dissertation in anthropology, American University.

Raj, K.N. and Tharakan, M. (1983) "Agrarian Reform in Kerala and its Impact on the Rural Economy – a Preliminary Assessment", in A. Ghose (ed.) Agrarian Reform in Contemporary Developing Countries: 31–90, London: Croom Helm.

Rosenzweig, M.R. and Wolpin, K.I. (1985) "Specific Experience, Household Structure, and Intergenerational Transfers: Farm Family Land and Labor Arrangements in Developing Countries, Quarterly Journal of Economics 100, supplement: 961–87.

Sacks, K. (1975) "Engels Revisited: Women: The Organization of Production, and Private Property", in R.R. Reiter (ed.) Toward an Anthropology of Women: 211–34, New York: Monthly Review Press.

Safilios-Rothschild, C. and Mahmud, S. (1989) "Women's Roles in Agriculture: Present Trends and Potential for Growth", paper produced for the Bangladesh Agricultural Sector Review, UNDP/UNIFEM, Dhaka.

Saito, K.A. and Weidenmann, C.J. (1990) "Agricultural Extension and Women

Farmers in Africa", World Bank Working Paper WPS 398, Washington, DC: Population and Human Resource Department, World Bank.

Saradamoni, K. (1983) "Changing Land Relations and Women: A Case Study of Palghat District, Kerala", in V. Mazumdar (ed.) *Women and Rural Transformation*: 35–171, Delhi: Concept Publications.

Sayers, J., Evans, M. and Redclift, N. (eds) (1987) *Engels Revisited: New Feminist Essays*, London: Tavistock Publications.

Schrijvers, J. (1988) "Blueprint for Undernourishment: The Mahaveli River Development Scheme in Sri Lanka" in B. Agarwal (ed.) *Structures of Patriarchy: State, Community and Household in Modernising Asia*: 29–51, London: Zed Books; New Delhi: Kali for Women.

Selvaduri, A. J. (1976) "Land, Personhood and Sorcery in a Sinhalese Village", in L. Smith (ed.) *Religion and Social Conflict in South Asia*: 82–96, Leiden: E.J.Brill Publishers.

Singh, N. (1988) *The Bankura Story: Rural Women Organise for Change*, New Delhi: ILO.

Singh, R. (1988) *Land, Power and People: Rural Elite in Transition, 1801–1970*, Delhi: Sage Publications.

Singh, A.M. and Kelles-Vitannen, A. (eds.) (1987) *Invisible Hands: Women in Home-based Production*, Delhi: Sage Publications.

Solaiman, M. and Alam, M. (1977) "Characteristics of Candidates for Election in Three Union Parishads in Comilla Kotwali Thana", Comilla: Bangladesh Agency for Rural Development.

Strauss, J. (1986) "Does Better Nutrition Raise Farm Productivity?", *Journal of Political Economy* 94, 2, April: 297–320.

Sundaram, K. and Tendulkar, S. (1983) "Towards an Explanation of Inter-regional Variation in Poverty and Unemployment in Rural India", Working Paper No. 237, Delhi: Delhi School of Economics.

United Nations (1990) *The Situation of Women: Selected Indicators 1990*, Vienna: Dept. of International Economics and Social Affairs, Statistical Office.

# 18

# THE EMPOWERMENT OF WOMEN

## Comments on chapters by Trzcinski, Hopkins and Agarwal

*Diane Elson*

What do we mean by "empowerment?" The term is widely used by a variety of individuals and institutions across the whole range of the political and ideological spectrum. More or less everyone is in favor of "the empowerment of the people," but we have different views about what exactly that means and how to bring it about. In the 1980s and early 1990s the dominant view in many parts of the world saw markets as the instruments of empowerment of individuals and states as the instruments of their disempowerment. The three papers in this section show how limited that view is when we are considering the empowerment of women. Agarwal's chapter offers a formal definition of empowerment, as follows:

> a process that enhances the ability of disadvantaged ("powerless") individuals or groups to challenge and change (in their favor) existing power relationships that place them in subordinate economic, social and political positions.

Women's empowerment is distinguished by Agarwal from women's welfare (which is discussed in terms of poverty alleviation), and this seems appropriate, for women's welfare can be improved in ways that do not change the existing power relations and leave women still in positions of dependency. Agarwal also distinguishes empowerment, as a process, from gender equality, as an outcome, and discusses the kinds of activities, including individual resistance as well as group mobilization, which might constitute this process. Implicit in her definition is the idea that empowerment of women is about changing the parameters within which individual women live their lives.

It is, I think, important to stress this idea of changing the parameters. Empowerment for women is fundamentally about changing social institutions and practices; about changing rules, norms and rights; and about changing the balance between women's obligations and responsibilities and their command over the resources needed to discharge these obligations and responsibilities. As the chapters by Trzcinski and Hopkins show, participation in paid employment may be an important ingredient in the process of empowerment, but it is far from being sufficient, and may indeed entail forms of disempowerment as well as of empowerment.

All the chapters are agreed on the importance of women's economic rights. The structure of economic rights is one of the key parameters that has to be changed; and it is often a focal point around which public action can be mobilized, and individuals can make claims. But the real worth of rights depends on ongoing processes of decision-making through which rights are used, contested and adjudicated. These too must be changed.

The chapter by Agarwal focusses on land rights for women in the context of South Asia, a region in which arable land is crucial to the livelihood of the majority of the population. Agarwal points out that much of the literature on development speaks rather loosely of "access" to land. This is unsatisfactory because there are several ways in which women can get access to land. As well as access through rights of ownership and use, access can be granted through goodwill of husbands, brothers and fathers. However, this kind of access is vulnerable to the withdrawal of goodwill or the death of the male relative through whom access is mediated, and is therefore less secure than property rights in land. Agarwal is careful to differentiate between formal and substantive rights, and the role of social institutions in giving substance to rights:

> Rights are defined here as claims that are legally and socially recognized and enforceable by an external legitimized authority, be it a village-level institution or some higher level judicial or executive body of the State.

Moreover the power that women can derive from possession of land rights depends on the processes through which those rights are used and upheld. If women are excluded from the management of the property they own, and from the exercise of the authority that adjudicates land rights in cases of dispute, then their empowerment by way of land rights will be limited.

Trzcinski and Hopkins both focus on employment rights rather than land rights, in the context of US and Eastern Europe, respectively; and they focus on those rights pertaining to the articulation of the processes of getting a living and raising children. These rights are particularly crucial to women, given the way in which the responsibility for caring for children is typically socially assigned to women. Indeed the key structural factor that underpins male bias in the way economies work is the lack of independent economic entitlements for children and those who have responsibility for taking care of them (Elson 1991: 13). This puts most women and children in a dependent position in relation to men, which is perpetuated if the institutions through which women are employed do not recognize the social value of women's work as carers. As Hopkins notes:

> a woman is caught in a vicious circle where her responsibilities to children lower her opportunities in the labor market, which in turn lower her opportunity costs relative to the father's opportunity costs of taking responsibility for children.

To remove this trap, employment rights must be structured so as to share the obligations of parenting between employees (both men and women) and employers, through provision of childcare facilities and rights to parental leave.

Hopkins discusses how post-communist processes of marketization and economic reform are in fact reducing the social sharing of parenting, leading to the privatization of responsibilities for children as well as the privatization of industrial enterprises. The result is that while such enterprises gain in autonomy, women's dependence upon men is increased. Trzcinski discusses an attempt to increase the socialization of childcare responsibilities in the US through the introduction of the Family and Medical Leave Act. She makes the important point that while this Act was widely depicted by its opponents as involving an increase in the level of government intervention in labor markets, in fact it entails not an increase in government control but a transfer of rights from employers to employees. Its effect is to:

> [change] the power dynamics in the leave negotiation. Now it is the employee and not the employer who is vested with the ultimate decision-making power of whether a leave is necessary.

However, the estimation of the economic costs and benefits to an enterprise of an employee who does take parental leave still rests largely with men, who remain in control of decision-making in enterprise management in all economies. Influencing perceptions of these costs and benefits was a critical factor in the struggle for the Family and Medical Leave Act and, as Trzcinski shows, neoclassical economic theory was of major significance in this context. Those against the Act appealed to the standard theory of competitive labor markets to argue that it would be against the interests of workers, as it would raise labor costs and diminish employment – an argument that is deployed against a whole range of employment rights, such as minimum wages, protection against unfair dismissal, and severance pay. In reply, those campaigning for the Act pointed to the standard theory of externalities, and argued that childcare was in some respect analogous to the production of public goods, and that there were social costs involved if providers of childcare were not given more support in combining this task with paid employment. This case neatly illustrates the role that economic theory plays in the empowerment of women through the way in which it structures ideas about the consequences of particular social and economic policies; and also about the social legitimacy of particular claims to particular economic rights.

Agarwal and Hopkins also refer to this aspect of economic theory. For instance, the empowerment of women may be argued to lead to inefficiency. Agarwal points to ideas about the adverse impact of female inheritance on agricultural output, through increased land fragmentation, as a barrier to women obtaining land titles. But the weight of empirical evidence "gives no reason to expect that land distribution in favor of women would reduce output on account of the size effect." Another argument is that the empowerment of women is unnecessary because dependency brings many economic benefits. Indeed, it is the case that women often forego rights in exchange for economic and social support from men. But this points rather to the impoverishment of women's circumstances and the restrictions on the range of choices open to them. Hopkins discusses the way in which the standard neoclassical theory of the family assumes that women's dependency on men is unproblematic, through its invocation of the altruistic household head, the "benevolent despot" who makes decisions on their behalf in the best interests of all family members. In counter argument, it would be possible to draw on theories of asymmetric information, though doubtless a determined defender of the status quo could argue that the "benevolent despot" economizes on transactions costs.

Indeed, neoclassical economic theory will always be able to produce coherent arguments in defense of the status quo ("whatever exists is optimal, otherwise it would already have been changed"), which will be persuasive to those who accept the premise that the individual is prior to the social in the hierarchy of causation. Though it may often be a useful tactic to invoke some of the more interesting and complex neoclassical concepts to criticize the status quo, a more comprehensive and enduring strategy would be better served by theories which allow for a more dialectic relation between the individual and the social. Moreover, if the empowerment of women is a process involving challenge and change to existing male-biased structures of power, then it will be more adequately conceptualized through theories that emphasize process, rather than equilibrium; and that value the exercise of capacities for decision-making and are not simply concerned with the utility attached to the outcomes of decision-making. This is likely to mean a different style of theory, which will be regarded as disablingly incomplete by economists whose touchstone of success is the ability to prove a theorem in a closed circle of logic; but which will be understood as appropriately open by economists who feel that the point is not just to produce an interpretation of the world, but to change the world through practical actions.

Let the last word be with the Indian women in the State of Bihar who succeeded in getting land titles in struggles in the late 1970s: "We had tongues but could not speak, we had feet but could not walk. Now we have the land, we have the strength to speak and walk." That is what the empowerment of women is fundamentally about.We have to develop an economic theory through which women can speak and mobilize for change.

## REFERENCE

Elson, D. (ed.) (1991) *Male Bias in the Development Process*, Manchester: Manchester University Press.

# INDEX